To: Joshua Steuben
ALIAS: "Inquisitive Kid"
From: Aunt Sharon and Erika

CHRISTMAS - 1989

THE
MACMILLAN BOOK
OF
FASCINATING FACTS

AN ALMANAC FOR KIDS

ANN ELWOOD
AND
CAROL ORSAG MADIGAN

MACMILLAN PUBLISHING COMPANY
NEW YORK

To my friends, family, and Puppy
with thanks for their encouragement

—A.E.

To Betty, John, Brook, Johnny, and Linda
with love and gratitude

—C.O.M.

Macmillan Publishing Company
866 Third Avenue, New York, NY 10022
Collier Macmillan Canada, Inc.

First Edition
Printed in the United States of America

10 9 8 7 6 5 4 3 2 1

The text of this book is set in 11-point Palatino. The illustrations are black-and-white photographs and drawings in pen-and-ink.

Library of Congress Cataloging-in-Publication Data

Elwood, Ann.
  The Macmillan book of fascinating facts : an almanac for kids / Ann Elwood and Carol Orsag Madigan.
     p.   cm.
  Includes index.
  Summary: Presents a collection of articles, interviews, lists, and odd facts on a variety of subjects.
   ISBN 0–02–733461–9   ISBN 0-689-71363-0 (pbk.)
   1. Almanacs, Children's. [1. Almanacs.] I. Madigan, Carol Orsag. II. Title.
AY81.J8E44 1989 051—dc19 88–22844 CIP AC

STAFF

ASSOCIATE EDITOR: John Orsag, Jr.

CONTRIBUTORS: Carol Dunlap
Jim Natal

STAFF PHOTOGRAPHERS: Ronald Brook Madigan
John Wanchik
John P. Edwards

BOOK DESIGN: The Chestnut House Group, Inc.

COVER DESIGN: Constance Ftera

PEN-AND-INK DRAWINGS: Dick Martin

ACKNOWLEDGMENTS

First of all, we want to thank our families, friends, and colleagues who provided information and inspiration: Laurie Brannen, Steven Bryant, Ming Chen, Carol Dunlap, John and Sandra Edwards, Bill Gaupsas, Kathleen Gurney, Micheline Karas, Ronald Brook Madigan, Arlene Mattioli, Karie Miller, Jim Natal, John and Linda Orsag, Betty and John Orsag, Frank Phillips, Dylan and Mavis and Sigmund Porter, John Raht, Pamela Rogow, John Wanchik, Sylvia Zebrowski.

We are indebted to Judith Whipple, Cecilia Yung, and Charles Levine, who skillfully and diligently guided this project from start to finish. Thanks to Miles Zimmerman, Frank Okumura, and the staff at The Chestnut House Group, who masterfully combined text and illustration; and to Constance Ftera at Macmillan, for her lively cover design. Thanks also to Lottie Gooding at Macmillan for ably managing the production.

From the kids who participated, we gleaned perspective and humor, and we especially want to acknowledge Debbie Benchoff, Dana Delmonte, Jonah Edwards, Jamie Evans, Eric Kouvolo, Marissa Mach, Jazz-minh Moore, Bernadette and Connie Rittelmann, Lionel and Leon Rodriguez, Eric and Jon and Justin and Nikki Wanchik, Stacey Vezina. Also, we wish to extend our gratitude to the students at the Elizabeth Freese Elementary School of San Diego who contributed their creative voices, and to their teacher, James Brescia, who encouraged them to do so.

Finally, we wish to express our warmest appreciation to our editor, Maggie Rugg, whose professional skills, patience, and enthusiasm have truly been invaluable. Her considerable talents are evident on every page of this book.

TEXT CREDITS

We would like to acknowledge and thank the following for permission to reprint the written or published material listed below. The pages in *The Macmillan Book of Fascinating Facts* on which the material appears are given in parentheses.

Children's Express, a project of The Children's Express Foundation, Inc., for excerpts from *Listen to Us!*

(21–28). Field Publications for material from *Weekly Reader* surveys (30–31), copyright © 1986, by permission of the publisher. The Gallup Organization, Inc., for material from The Gallup Youth Survey (28–29), copyright © 1985, 1987. KABC Talkradio, Los Angeles, for winning entries in the "Save the Books" contest and campaign to help rebuild the Los Angeles Public Library (7–8). *L.A. West*™ magazine (formerly *Previews*) for excerpts from the Annual Junior Journalist Contest, copyright © January 1986, 1987 (3–6). National Restaurant Association for list of "The Top 15 Kinds of Restaurants" (91). Clarkson N. Potter, Inc., for excerpts from *Remarkable Names of Real People* by John Train (102–103), copyright © 1977 by John Train and for excerpts from *Poplollies and Bellibones* by Susan Kelz Sperling (164–165), copyright © 1977 by Susan Kelz Sperling, used by permission of the publisher. *San Diego Reader* for entries in "An Embarrassing Moment" writing contest (12–13). Simon and Schuster, Inc., for excerpts from *Miracles* by Richard Lewis (13–15), copyright © 1966 and for excerpts from *Journeys* by Richard Lewis (18–20), copyright © 1969, by permission of the publisher. Times Books, a division of Random House, Inc., for material adapted from *Durations: The Encyclopedia of How Long Things Take* by Stuart A. Sandow with Chrissie Bamber and J. William Rioux (198), copyright © 1977 by Stuart A. Sandow, Chrissie Bamber, and J. William Rioux, by permission of the publisher.

PHOTO CREDITS

We are grateful to the following for permission to reproduce the photographs used as illustration in this book. The pages in *The Macmillan Book of Fascinating Facts* on which the photographs appear are given in parentheses.

A & C Archives (20, 98, 101, 181, 236). The Adler Planetarium (296). The Alamo, The Daughters of the Republic of Texas (331). Courtesy of the All-American Soap Box Derby (139, 140). American Museum of Science and Energy (329). The American Numismatic Association (131). American Philatelic Society (132 bottom). American Red Cross (420, 421). Photograph by Ron Schramm for Ameripex (132 top). Courtesy of Apple Computer, Inc. (256, 258, 265, 267). Courtesy of Arkansas State Parks (188). Art Matrix/Cornell National Supercomputer Facility (266). Courtesy of AT&T Archives (240). Courtesy of the Atari Corporation (254, 270, 271). Australian Overseas Information Service (183). Baylor College of Medicine (242, 243). Mary Bloom (391, 426). Boy Scouts of America (87 bottom, 150, 151, 152, 154). "Mirror Maze," Buhl Science Center, a component of The Carnegie, Pittsburgh, PA (322 top). Busch Entertainment Corporation (292, 335). Courtesy of the California State Library (51). The Carter Center (32). Ming Chen (91, 390). Cherokee National Historical Society (320). © 1985 Chicago Zoological Society (213, 214 bottom, 360). Courtesy of The Children's Museum of Indianapolis (297). Courtesy of the Circus World Museum, Baraboo, WI (338). COCA-COLA, the Dynamic Ribbon device, and the Arden Square device are trademarks of The Coca-Cola Company and are used by permission (167). The Collegiate Schools (238 top). Photo by René Paulsen, courtesy Concordia Language Villages (39). Photo by Neil Larsen, courtesy Concordia Language Villages (68). Cottonwood Gulch Foundation (238 bottom, 239). Cumbres & Toltec Scenic Railroad (311). Courtesy of Dunlop Tire Corporation (227). Photo courtesy Ann Dwyer's California Rivers (138). Courtesy of the Edison National Historic Site (178). John P. Edwards (120, 218, 219, 221, 222, 344, 365, 367). Steve Delaney/EPA (225, 349). Estes Industries (106, 135, 136). Fairfax County Council of the Arts (358). Peter MacDonald, The *Forbes* Magazine Collection, New York (174). Nick Gatto (134). GE Research and Development Center (241). Girl Scouts of the U.S.A. (88, 147, 148). Photo by David Greer, WE4K (141). Art Grossman © 1981 (306). Theodore Roosevelt Collection, Harvard College Library (192). Courtesy of The Heard Museum (282). Courtesy Hearst San Simeon State Historical Monument (285). George Heinrich (359). Courtesy of Henry Ford Museum & Greenfield Village, Dearborn, MI (304). Courtesy of Hersheypark (322 bottom). The Hoover Company, North Canton, OH (228 right). IBM/Odyssey of the Mind (231, 232). International Museum of Photography at George Eastman House (44, 66). Courtesy of International Professional Rodeo Association (108, 198). Kentucky Department of Travel Development, Frankfort, KY (299). Courtesy of Kings Island (318). Courtesy of Knott's Berry Farm® (286 top). Photo I. C. Vanly, courtesy The Kurdish Program (70). Courtesy of the Library of Congress (43, 47, 56, 61, 189, 191, 193, 194, 199, 228 left). © 1988 Lionel Trains, Inc. Used with permission (117). Little League Baseball Museum (324 bottom). R. Brook Madigan (13, 19, 81, 87 top, 90, 102, 103, 109, 112, 169, 176, 197, 210, 211). Mattel, Inc. (116). McCall's Patterns (381). Courtesy of Memphis Convention and Visitors Bureau (330). By permission. By Merriam-Webster, Inc., publisher of the Merriam-Webster® dictionaries (163). Photography by Egyptian Expedition, The Metropolitan Museum of Art. All rights reserved (233). Gift of Julia A. Berwind, 1953 (53.61.5), The Metropolitan Museum of Art. All rights reserved (395). Karie Miller (52). Milwaukee County Historical Society photo (38). Minnesota Historical Society (46, 62). © 1987 Monterey Bay Aquarium (286 bottom). From the Muscular Dystrophy Association, Inc. (414, 415). Photo by Robert H. Martin, courtesy Museum of New Mexico, No. 4984 (50). Photograph by Byron, The Byron Collection, Museum of the City of New York (35). The Clarence Davies

Collection, Museum of the City of New York (42). Photograph by Jessie Tarbox Beals, Jacob A. Riis Collection, Museum of the City of New York (48). Museum of the City of New York (58, 65). NASA (34, 208, 246, 247, 248, 249, 251, 252). National Archives GC–297, 210–GC–423, 306–PS–49–15722, 47–G–7F–7795, 47–G–7F–2703 (53, 54, 373, 384 left and right). National Association of Police Athletic Leagues (142, 408). Courtesy of National Baseball Hall of Fame, Cooperstown, NY (315). Photograph and advocacy provided by the National Easter Seal Society (413). Wayne Brill, National Music Camp, Interlochen, Michigan (363, 364 top). National Park Service, photo by Richard Frear (281). National Park Service, Statue of Liberty National Monument (64). National Park Service (185, 186, 278, 327, 339). Courtesy of New York Power Authority (314). Print Collection, Miriam and Ira D. Wallach Division of Art Prints and Photographs, The New York Public Library; Astor, Lenox, and Tilden Foundations (36). Billy Rose Theatre Collection, The New York Public Library at Lincoln Center; Astor, Lenox, and Tilden Foundations (159). Olympus Corporation, Consumer Products Group (350, 354). © 1935, 1985 Parker Brothers, Division of Kenner Parker Toys Inc. (93 top). Pennsylvania Dutch Convention & Visitors Bureau (324 top). Courtesy of Plimoth Plantation (302). Polynesian Cultural Center (295). Preservation Society of Newport County (325 top). Pro Football Hall of Fame (319). C–2774 Public Archives of Canada (49). Courtesy of Radio Shack, a division of Tandy Corporation (262). River Way Ranch Camp, Sawyer, CA (122, 123). FDR Library (195). St. Augustine Alligator Farm © 1988 (293). St. Louis Zoological Park (93 bottom, 110). The Salvation Army (125). The Salvation Army Archives and Research Center (389). San Diego Wild Animal Park (105). San Diego Zoo photo by Ron Garrison (84). Scholastic Inc.

Art Awards (346, 409). Alisa Schulman (216, 217). Einars J. Mengis, Shelburne Museum, Shelburne, VT (333). Courtesy of Six Flags Great Adventure® (310). Greg Smith (99). National Air and Space Museum, Smithsonian Institution (245, 340). National Portrait Gallery, Smithsonian Institution (45, 59, 94, 104, 160, 187, 204). Transfer from the National Museum of American Art; gift of Mrs. E. H. Harriman to the United States National Museum, 1920; National Portrait Gallery, Smithsonian Institution (60). Wade Spees (325 bottom). Staten Island Historical Society (419). The Ukrainian Museum, New York, NY (79). UNICEF International Children's Art Collection, Information Center on Children's Cultures (347, 400, 405). Photo courtesy U.S. Chess Federation (129). USDA photo (396, 397). United States Patent Office (115). © 1986 Universal City Studios, Inc. (289). Flora Wallechinsky (182). John Wanchik (2, 71, 86, 95, 97, 113, 143, 144, 145, 156, 164, 352, 375, 378, 382). Harold Warp Pioneer Village (307). West Virginia Department of Commerce (337). Wham-O (118). Michael Evans, The White House (40). Winkler/Daniel Productions (379). Sylvia Zebrowski (100, 201, 411). Zoological Society of Philadelphia (214 top).

DRAWINGS CREDITS

Dick Martin's pen-and-ink drawings appear in *The Macmillan Book of Fascinating Facts* on the following pages: 4, 5, 22, 23, 27, 29, 30, 31, 76, 77, 96, 114, 119, 146, 166, 171, 203, 357, 361, 362, 364 bottom, 372.

CONTENTS

INTRODUCTION

Your world is fascinating and rich with things to know and do. It is also complicated, and getting the most out of it isn't always easy. This book—for kids, written partly by kids—is meant to act as a guide for you. It doesn't pretend to tell you *everything*. But in it you may find just what you need—an address, a fact, a method, or an idea—to get you started pursuing an interest or doing something exciting. You might want to look up a subject that interests you, in the table of contents or in the index. Or you might just leaf through the book until something catches your fancy.

Chapter 1, "Kids Speak Out," puts you in touch with other kids. What do they think about teachers, divorce, popularity, sex, and heaven? What have they written about their feelings and their lives? What great inventions have other kids dreamed up? Color braces, a magic slide, an elevator to the moon, a learning pill. While they didn't quite figure out how to make these inventions real, maybe you can.

You are part of a long line of people. Knowing about them can make your life richer. Chapter 2, "The United States and the Old Country," will help you answer questions about your ancestors and those of other Americans. You'll learn some fascinating facts. For instance, who were the Celestials? Hint: They were not a rock group. You can also learn how to make worry beads, play Seven Stones, eat with chopsticks, dance the waltz, make tacos, and do the Golden Rooster.

Amaze your friends with facts gleaned from "Lists," Chapter 3. The lists there may give you new ways of looking at things, of putting facts together. Do you know what's on the shopping list for a zoo? What Jack the Ripper, Paul McCartney, and Don Rickles have in common? Madonna's whole name? How fast a lion can run?

Chapter 4, "Sports, Games, Toys, Camp, and Clubs," tells you how to join a club for your special interest—or how to start one yourself! It gives you leads on entering contests—frog jumping to jump rope. And do you know the life story of Barbie or of the hero who started the Boy Scouts? Or what 11-year-old won the cowgirls' barrel racing event in 1975?

Bellibone and *poplolly* are lost words. Chapter 5, "Words and Language," contains fascinating facts, including words like these and their meanings. It's also where you can dig up a riddle to fool your friends or a tongue twister to drive them crazy.

You could make up a trivia quiz from Chapter 6, "Odd Facts." For instance, what was the world's longest kiss? What president liked to go skinny dipping? How did a pony get inside the White House?

Chapter 7, "Science," gives you information on everything from keeping your goldfish from going belly up to Odyssey of the Mind. How was the vacuum cleaner invented? What places let kids work on archaeological digs? How do astronauts take showers?

What's the difference between bytes, bits, and bugs? The dictionary in Chapter 8, "Computers," defines such fascinating jargon. It also tells you how to get into a computer network or an electronic bulletin board for fun, and how to use your computer to do homework for school. This chapter answers other questions, too, like what was Pac-Man's original name, and where did he come from?

You'll want to look through Chapter 9, "Kids' Trip Guide to the United States," for places of special interest to kids. It tells you where to find a space camp, children's museums, and theme parks. You might end up searching for diamonds or panning for gold, going eye to eye with an octopus or watching a glass blower.

Chapter 10, "The Arts," features art by kids. It also can get you started on making a home video, taking nature pictures, or organizing your own band.

All kids have problems, and you may find help with some of yours in Chapter 11, "Problems." For example, what can you do if your pet is lost? How can you handle family or school problems? What groups can you join if you're worried about your weight or want to fight drugs and alcohol? How do you write a résumé? What are some ways to volunteer to help others with problems?

After you have dipped in and out of *The Macmillan Book of Fascinating Facts,* *you* may have some ideas about what should be in our next book like this. Why don't you write and tell us?

THE
MACMILLAN BOOK
OF
FASCINATING FACTS

AN ALMANAC FOR KIDS

1
KIDS SPEAK OUT

JUNIOR JOURNALIST CONTEST

Every year a magazine called *L.A. West* sponsors a contest for students who go to school on the west side of Los Angeles. Kids are asked to predict what might happen in the future. They write stories about their predictions, and the stories are published in the magazine. Here are some of the best stories on the future that have been printed in *L.A. West* magazine.

BOY MAKES PAINT THAT COMES TO LIFE
by Josh Bush, age 9
The Mirman School

In Los Angeles, California, Alex Raven, age seven, mixed some chemicals and fiddled around with them. He then saw the mixture's thickness and tried to paint with it (he loved painting), and suddenly his picture of a meadow scene came to life!

He got in trouble with his mom when she discovered a live cow in his room, but when he explained everything, he got applauded for his terrific invention.

The president wanted the paint for military uses, but Alex would not sell his invention at any cost. The president said, "Think of all the possibilities we could have if we could use your invention. We could have an army appear out of nowhere, or even make another laser system from nothing!" Alex replied with, "I don't want my invention used for warfare. I'll only consider letting it be used for peaceful purposes."

NEW COLORFUL BRACES
by Jennifer Sadlier, grade 6
Marymount Junior School

Can you imagine colorful braces to match your new Esprit outfit? A new discovery in the orthodontic field was announced last week by the National

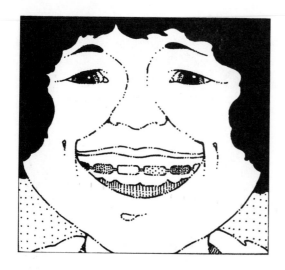

Dental Board Organization. The old, traditional silver braces, worn by many millions of people throughout the country to gain that "perfect smile," will have a new, clever device to allow the wearer to use some creativity.

A click-on appliance will be constructed in many different colors such as magenta, blue, red, purple, yellow, and many more so the orthodontic patients may match their many different colors of apparel. This clever invention will give the patient "a trendy, new look" while wearing braces and being "in" at the same time. The new brace look may be worn plain or with your favorite click-on color, depending on your outfit or mood for the day.

ELECTRIC SOCCER
by Courtney Stanton, grade 6
St. Matthews School

The compu-workers have invented a new sport called electric soccer. This new game promises to be a very fantastic invention.

The ball will move automatically without anyone having to touch or control the ball. This invention will help children learn to play soccer without having to make mistakes. The children will have a lot of fun trying to kick the ball when it is traveling their way.

The compu-workers have designed this game to eliminate kids getting hurt. No more bruised shins or skinned elbows! There is no more need for a goalie since there is a machine that automatically blocks the ball.

Every soccer field has an electric scoreboard on top of the goalpost. Another advantage of electric soccer is that the players don't get so tired running around the field. The ball automatically comes to them so they don't get out of their positions. The game is played indoors so that it can't be canceled because of rain.

If your child learns to play soccer by the electric soccer method, he will become a great soccer player!

FANTASTIC SLIDE
by Carrie Skvarla, grade 5
Carlthorp School

A new invention has just been designed. A genius named Scott Robinson just discovered a slide totally out of this world.

This is a slide that is for children age 14 and under. It connects a child's room with anyplace they want to go. The slide can bring the children to

Magic Mountain or the beach, depending on which button they push.

Mr. Robinson says what's really useful is the built-in alarm clock. The alarm clock is used for waking you up in the morning, so you can slide to school on time.

He says that the slide is really fine on a rainy day. You stay dry and see everything around you because the slide is made of see-through material.

When the slide is put on the market, it will sell for about $1,000.

THE LEARNING PILL
by Tenaya Rodewald, grade 6
Franklin School

The what? Yes, I know, it sounds weird; but it is here. A pill that automatically makes you smart. It was developed by The Witchy Medicine Company. They would not tell me how it works, because they stand to make millions off it. They did tell me, though, that each pill is a mass of memory cells that have been stamped with certain facts to be learned. For instance, if you took a Spelling Words pill, you would know all the words in the English language, plus how to spell them and their full definitions. This might change the world. However, it is up to the people whether they would like to have automatically smart children that may act like robots.

ELEVATOR TO THE MOON
by Oliver Hudson, grade 5
Carlthorp School

Scientists are going to make an elevator from the space station to the moon. This elevator will hold up to 500 people per trip. It will take 8 hours. People are seated, and drinks and food are served. This elevator operates in a tube.

When you arrive on the moon, you will get into a moon touring car. There will be a guide with you in your car to show you what the moon is like.

Elevator trips to the moon are expected to start by the year 2000.

HELP HAS FINALLY COME
by Whitney Stensrud, grade 6
Carlthorp School

Los Angeles—Dr. Sherman Rossly has just made world news. He has invented a new portable walking system. Why? He invented it because he was tired of seeing the handicapped being teased and humiliated. He knows about it because he *is* a handicapped person, and he is sick and tired of it. His invention is quite simple, to him at least.

Dr. Rossly explains, "Well, there is a little control switch that you hold. It has a button for every which way you want to go. The switch is hooked up to metal braces that you slip on your legs. The good thing about it is that no one can even tell you are really handicapped." The amazing thing about the whole device is that it is only controlled by a computer that sends out radio waves to the device.

Dr. Rossly is becoming a hero throughout the world. His invention has just been put on the market, and it is making the handicapped amazed at his miracle.

CHILD'S DREAM COMES TRUE
by Laurel Swigert, grade 2
Pacific Palisades Elementary School

Kids don't like to clean their rooms. So I have invented an automatic cleaner-upper. It has a walkie-talkie in it. You can talk to it from far away and it can hear you. It has arms so it can pick up things like books. It looks like a vacuum cleaner that can talk and has arms. It has a head too. It looks very funny when you first get it. But it works very well. Kids will like it, and if they are nice, they will let their parents use it.

WHAT A LIBRARY MEANS TO ME

Radio station KABC in Los Angeles held a contest, asking people in Los Angeles to write an essay that told how important the library was in their lives. More than 20,000 people entered the contest. Nineteen winners were chosen. Each winner got two round-trip airplane tickets—and six days of free hotel rooms—to either New York City, U.S.A.; London, England; or Frankfurt, Germany—cities where some of the world's greatest libraries are located. Of the 19 winners, six were from junior high schools in Los Angeles. Here are three of those wonderful essays about the library. These three happen to be in verse.

WHAT A LIBRARY MEANS TO ME
by Abigail Derecho, grade 9
Dodson Junior High School

A room
  of dimension, just a few meters wide
  yet containing an abundance, ages inside
A space
  holding words telling stories of strife
  which enrich, and enlighten, and fill human life
A window
  of print, through which worlds can be seen
  worlds of hate and of laughter, illusions and dreams
A lantern
  of darkness, a bringer of light
  which secludes and erases all troubles from sight
A page
  out of history, a complex diary
  which is known by one word, by one name: Library

WHAT A LIBRARY MEANS TO ME
by Adam Wilson, grade 8
Daniel Webster Junior High School

When I go to a library
My imagination runs free.
I see faces and places
That made history.
I look to my left.
And whom do I see?
It's General Washington
Leading troops to victory.
I turn the corner.
And guess who's there?
It's the Wright brothers
Soaring through the air.
I look to my right.
And where do I go?
On top of Mount Fuji
With the whole world below.
I look behind me.
And where do I stand?
Aboard the Titanic
Hoping to spot land.
You can visit these places too,
Because these books are here for you.

WHAT A LIBRARY MEANS TO ME
by Joshua Leach, grade 9
Nobel Junior High School

What does a library mean to me?
That's one tough question, but let's see.
The library is my sanctuary, my dream house, my world.
It holds books of time, people, life with each page unfurled.
The library is my link to the future and the past.
It connects all the todays and makes them last.
It contains man's dreams from theories to facts.
It holds historic records of treaties and pacts.
The library holds music and films and art.
It holds all remedies for the mind and the heart.
You ask what the library means to me?
It means I can learn, enjoy, and be free.

POEMS AND STORIES BY KIDS

Kids write about all sorts of things. Some of their poems and stories are funny. Others are sad. Some seem like dreams, while others are all too real.

These writings were taken from a book called *I Will Always Stay Me*. The authors are migrant children who follow the crops with their parents.

IF
by Damien Lopez, grade 6
Carrizo Springs, Texas

If I was a ring,
I would go around and
around in a circle and
I would be in the circle.

If I was a ring,
I would be the loop
of the world.

I AM AND WHAT I WANT TO BE
by Pam Hudson, grade 5
Dilley, Texas

I am four foot eight inches and have blond hair.
I wear jeans and T-shirts.
I fight with my brother and sister a lot.
I have three best friends.
I play the clarinet.

I wish I was five foot eight inches and had brown hair.
I wish I wore slacks and satin shirts.
I wish I could be kind with my brother and sister.
I wish I had four best friends.
I wish I played the saxophone.

WORK
by Ruben Gauna, grade 4
Dilley, Texas

When school ends, I go with my family to Indiana. We go in the back of a big black truck that is covered with a green tarpaulin. It takes us three days and two nights to get to Indiana.

In Indiana, we live in a little green house on the farm. At seven o'clock in the morning, we get up and go to work in the tomato fields. We are nine in our family, and we all work picking tomatoes. In the mornings, we take a big bag of lunch to the fields. We eat tacos of beans, potatoes, and steak pieces on tortillas and bread.

We work in the tomato fields until four o'clock. We pick 1,000 hampers of tomatoes a day. We get paid 25¢ per hamper. Then we get home and take a bath and eat supper. We watch the movies on the little TV we bring from Dilley, Texas.

THE PREHISTORIC STONE
by Ruben Escamilla, grade 7
Crystal City, Texas

About 70 million years ago, when dinosaurs roamed the earth, there were a lot of tall palm trees. They were about 70 feet tall. As the years passed, a little tree started to grow. It grew and it grew, until it was like the other trees. Then there was a big earthquake, and volcanoes began to roar and rumble. The trees crashed to the ground, and dinosaurs sank into the open ground.

Then the tree fell. It cracked into pieces that scattered, and a little piece fell into the mud. As the years passed, the piece of wood became a stone.

It was sitting in a pond close to an abandoned grammar school. It was sitting there under the mud, and then I picked it up and said, "I will use it as the paperweight I have always looked for. I will paint it blue."

But then I said to myself, "It looks like a tree. It has lines on it like a tree." I decided to leave it as it was, but I took it home anyway, to show to my father and my mother.

Then my mother said, "Ruben, it is a stone from long, long ago. It was once a giant tree, but as the time changed, the tree cracked and became stone. That's why it has the black lines on it."

I decided to take it back where I had found it. I hid it. I dug a hole and put the rock in the hole. I never saw the rock again. And now I wonder about it.

FAKE SNAKE
by Duane Wolf, grade 4
Pearsall, Texas

> *I saw a snake.*
> *He's down by the lake.*
> *It looks like a fake snake*
> *But I wouldn't get any closer.*

THE REASON FOR THE PELICAN
by Richard Duenes, grade 7
San Antonio, Texas

> *The reason for the pelican is difficult to see.*
> *His beak is larger than there's any need to be.*
> *It's not to bail a boat 'cause he doesn't own a boat,*
> *Yet everywhere he takes himself he has that beak to tote.*
> *It's not to keep his wife in, his wife has got one too.*
> *It's really not quite for anything*
> *And yet you realize,*
> *It's quite a splendid beak*
> *In quite a splendid size.*

I WILL ALWAYS STAY ME
by Carolina Garcia, grade 6
Carrizo Springs, Texas

> *A snail and a caterpillar went walking slowly (because of the*
> *snail) in the evening sun.*
> *Then the caterpillar halted and said, "I have to go now."*
> *"Why?" asked the snail.*
> *"I have to go change into a beautiful butterfly."*
> *So he walked away.*
> *Then the snail muttered to himself,*
> *"I will always stay me."*

LOVE
by Magdalena Guajardo, grade 6
Carrizo Springs, Texas

I was looking for love.
It's hard to live in a hard world without love.
You came to me like a hard wind.
Love is not a game to play around with.
When two people love each other
It is not a kiss.
Love is a force and belief in each other
And helping in any way.
Love is the nicest thing in the world
Someone can give you.

These stories of an embarrassing moment got honorable mention in a contest in a San Diego paper called the *Reader*. Have you had such moments?

AN EMBARRASSING MOMENT
by Ryan Wenger, age 9
San Diego, California

When I was four I loved a girl named Courtney Smith. One day I took her to church with me and said, "This is my friend, Courtney Smith. I am going to marry her."

My mom and her mom were good friends. They would shop together at University Towne Center, and Courtney and I would come along. We would go by a shop with dresses. In the window there was always an ugly wedding dress. Courtney would always say, "That's the dress I'm going to wear when I marry Ryan."

I was in a swimming class with her. Whenever the coach would tell us to jump into the pool I would not cooperate. Courtney would put her hands on her hips and yell, "Ryan, get in the pool!!" And I would do it because I was going to marry her.

I was not embarrassed then because I didn't realize anything. But now she is in my fourth grade class and I'm embarrassed. I hope no one in my class ever finds out that I loved Courtney Smith.

AN EMBARRASSING MOMENT
by Jan Peterson, age 10
Fallbrook, California

Whoever said kids have rights? Ever since I was a baby, grown-ups have been running my life. They said when I ate, what I ate, what I wore, and where I went. And I'll tell you, it was embarrassing. But the most embarrassing moment was when my grandma took a picture of me in my bare nothings. She ambushed me on the way to the bathtub. And just my luck, the picture turned out. And what's worse, she gave a copy to my mother. I'm sure they are saving that picture for blackmail purposes. They are going to spring it on me when I least expect it. Oh, brother. I have a feeling my most embarrassing moment isn't over yet.

The next writings were collected by Richard Lewis, *Miracles: Poems by children of the English-speaking world* (New York: Simon and Schuster, 1966). The kids who wrote them came from Australia, England, the United States, and other places where people speak English.

THE MAGIC FLOWER
by Danny Marcus, age 8
United States

Once there was a magic flower.
He lived out in the cold;
He lived in the dark and cold.
So he spun and spun

Until he grew very hot.
The whole world grew hot.
Then,
Out came the magic flower!

It was spun out,
Just as I am telling you.

La Fleur Magique (The Magic Flower)
by Aloysha Bryant, age 5, Paris, France
(R. Brook Madigan)

THE MINE
by Bronwyn Mason, age 12
New Zealand

Here are we; in the darkness.
Close to the very heart of Mother Earth,
Where her blood flows in seams of shining coal,
And our picks beat a rhythm to her heart,
Where her warm brown flesh encloses us
And her rocky bones trap us.

UNTITLED
by Susan Morrison, age 11
Australia

A dawn wind blows
breath on my bed.
A red haze fills the empty sky.

THE WITCH
by Patricia Thornton, age 7
England

A witch went into the forest
Down
Down
Down
Into the deep deep forest.
Picking lots of mushrooms in the
Deep
Deep
Deep
Forest.
And the wood stood very still
And the witch flew into the forest
To make many spells.

Now she's making them
Nasty wicked spells
Making all the people
Turn
To lots of pigs.
In the
Deep
Deep
Forest.
Now she goes home
To make quite sure
They have
Worked.

TIME
by Reg Cowie, age 8
New Zealand

The car stands still
As if it had never been driven.
People walk with their prams,
A dog runs down with a grin on his face.
The cross on the church reminds you of happy days
While sea gulls stick their tummies out like heroes.

DEATH
by John Erwin, age 11
Australia

Who set that endless silence
Of her breath?
Death is but death.
Death is like the growing of people.
It cannot be stopped.

UNTITLED
by Linda, age 8
Australia

It was midnight
The sky was dark black
The stars were threepenny bits
The sea was making a sound
Like a silk dress.

These thoughts about nature and color were written by children in grades 3 through 6 at Elizabeth Freese Elementary School in San Diego, California.

THOUGHTS ABOUT NATURE AND COLOR

Nature is a breath of life. It changes summer to winter.
It changes on its own.

—Tonya Brantley

The grass is as spiky as a bundle of nails.
It makes me feel like I have itching powder on me.

—James Alberto

When you see a bare tree, it looks like a skeleton hanging
from a doorway.

—Julien Zhivago

Nature is a soft bunny cuddled in your lap.
Nature is a hard rock sitting on the sand.
Nature is a dry leaf that falls from a tree.
Nature is me enjoying myself.

—Jenny Victa

Nature is a part of our life. Nature makes me feel like
I'm in a land that grows all the time. I'm thankful that we have
nature.

—Maria Pantig

Nature is a happy thing that shines brighter than a diamond ring. It blows like the wind, and splashes like the sea, and comes in various colors for me.

—Tarik Bennett

The sea is a blue blanket over the sand. Sea animals lying under it.

—Ellynne Alegre

Black is the night sky with flashing light bulbs in it. Black is a creepy dark cave with an animal with fangs. Black is my room when my lights are off.

—James Alberto

Black makes me think of sad and happy at the same time. Black is the color of silence. Black is a color that creeps up on daylight.

—Jaimee Siron

The color gray means a lot to me, because it describes how I feel, like clouds that change their shape. I can change how I feel too.

—Jennifer Baker

The next writings were also collected by Richard Lewis, *Journeys: Prose by children of the English-speaking world* (New York: Simon and Schuster, 1979).

UNTITLED
by Richard R. Crook, age 13
England

He settled himself down between two rocks, scrabbled with his feet idly in the sand, and surveyed the village. A dog limped behind the man and his white cow as they stumbled through the hot shade at the bottom of the hill, under the trees by the cracking houses. He could see the flies dodging on the cow's back through the heat. The village became further and further away as he stared at it; the trees shimmered in the heat; dust rose in small clouds as the cows kicked their way across the stones.

He was looking down, like a god, from above the trees. He could see the women congregating under one of the trees, with the pitchers; a cow nodded at the edge of the shade, swaying its thick, mottled head. The tufts of grass were running with sweat in the sun. The tufts of grass. He watched a caterpillar scurrying across the sand under one of the clumps. Into the cool, stony unknown. He moved his knee slowly away from the tuft of grass and sat up. His hair clung to his forehead; he pushed it back, glanced down at the village to see that no one was watching, and crouched by the tuft. A cow came wandering around the outcrop of rock, nosing the sand; it stopped and watched him. The flies settled on its eyelids.

He squatted down and tossed a stone at the grass. Nothing stirred. He smiled benevolently at the cow; it shook its head; the flies rose and settled again. The grass was sweating in the sun.

CHESS KING'S DIARY:
OCTOBER 27, 1952
by Danny Freedman, age 10
United States

I am tired as I look on my checkered battlefield. My Right Rook has come to me with news. He says that this bloody war is being fought by the Gods who called this war a game—a game which Gods call chess. I was about to banish him for this, but instead black Bishop roared in and took his life away. Then I saw a big thing that looked like a crane with little spears, and at the end I saw some blades—five of them, to be exact. And they picked up Rook and took him away.

But what was that! Bishop and my two gallant Knights have surrounded the enemy King. Slowly and softly a voice in the sky says, "Checkmate." The war is won on the field and the victory is ours. The day is glorious.

But what is this—we are being swept into . . . what! It's a monstrous box! Us and the enemy alike! It is not fair—we

If chess pieces could talk . . . (R. Brook Madigan)

deserve to live. We should stay—it is not fair!!

THE CAT AND THE DOG
by Michael Delany, age 10
England

Once upon a time there lived a brown cat and a black dog and one day the cat asked the dog to chase him around the kennel until he was puffed out and then their owner gave them a meat pie.

They loved chasing rats and mice and the cat was always stepping in the milk and making white stars on the floor so that he couldn't get lost in the house.

GRANDPOP PICKING FLOWERS
by Queenie Davies, age 10
New Zealand

Grandpop bends to pick some flowers; he is like a sea gull with a broken wing. When he goes to get in the car he slowly puts one foot in then the other

and now he has to put his head in. I look sadly at him, and as I look at him I know that he will have a tear coming down his face.

PLAYING SOCCER
by Tommy Waldie, age 10
New Zealand

When I was playing soccer I got shoved. I twirled and twisted as I lost my balance. I buckled and bent and folded up like an umbrella. I rolled along the ground. Colors blurred in my eyes, and they mixed into patterns of funny-shaped people and peculiar-colored houses.

Before the game starts, everything is calm. But when it begins . . . (A & C Archives)

UNTITLED
by George Semper, age 10
United States

There are two worlds one with eyeballs facing out and one facing in. My eyes are in, and the world I live in looks pretty good. There are long skinny red and blue tubes that's my water supply. It is always dark I'm scared.

This short piece was in *Great Writers Caper,* put out by Calverton Lower School in Maryland.

UNTITLED
by Christopher Connelly, age 7
Huntingtown, Maryland

I hear the bells ringing. I taste the sweat dripping down my face. When the water splashes in my face, it feels frosty. I smell the popcorn that the people are passing out. I am proud to be a boxer.

LISTEN TO US!

Listen To Us! is a book by Children's Express, a news service staffed by children 13 and under who work with teen assistant editors, 14 to 18. The kids at Children's Express have put together thousands of articles that have appeared in newspapers all over the United States—and overseas. Children's Express has eight bureaus (offices): New York, Harlem, and East Harlem, New York; Newark, New Jersey; Salem, Massachusetts; San Francisco, California; Melbourne, Australia; Wellington, New Zealand.

Children's Express has won a lot of awards because the children have done such a great job reporting on subjects that are important to kids. Stories about Children's Express and its reporters have been in magazines and on TV. Teams of Children's Express reporters have traveled to refugee camps on the Thailand-Cambodia border, to Hiroshima and Tokyo in Japan, and to the Soviet Union.

Listen To Us! is a book that describes the feelings, beliefs, and problems of kids from all parts of the United States. More than 2,000 children talked to reporters from Children's Express. They talked about parents, teachers, brothers and sisters, drugs, drinking, divorce, friendship, money, TV, adoption, dating, and many other subjects. If you want to find out if other kids think and feel the way you do, this is the book for you. You can order it from Children's Express. Here is the address.

Children's Express
245 Seventh Avenue
New York, NY 10001-7302

After you have read it, give it to your parents to read. They might learn some important things that you have had a hard time talking about with them or getting them to understand.

Here are some of the children's thoughts as reported in *Listen To Us!*

WHAT EMBARRASSES ME MOST ABOUT MY PARENTS

DEL, 12: The thing that embarrasses me most about my mother is that every time I invite somebody to my house, my mother says, "Hello, I am Del's mother." She must know everybody I bring home—she asks their life story.

My mother says, "Hello, there, little boy. What's your name?" She calls my friends "little friends." This one guy is 16, 6 feet tall, and she calls him "little." My sister brought her boyfriend to the house and she got the same thing. My mother called him a ''little boy''—he's bigger than she is! And whenever she comes in, she says, ''This is my only son, Del.'' They could care less if I'm her only son! That's what gets to me.

STEFAN, 11:   My mother is a fanatic about plants and birds. She talks to the plants; she talks to her birds. She asks questions, and then she says, ''Oh, really?'' as if they answered. And my friends are like, ''Wow! I mean, is your mother a Bellevue escapee, or what?'' I remember when one of our plants

was dying. This one episode embarrassed me most in my whole life, because I had to go with my mother. She took a plant, and its leaves were turning brown, it was dying, and she put it in a carrying pot and took it to the hospital! She walked into the emergency ward and she said, ''Treat it.'' One of the nurses came up and said, ''Is that your mother?'' I said, ''Well, yeah, I guess so.'' I swear, I was hysterical. I couldn't decide whether to cry or to crack up, so I did both. Ever since then, she hasn't done anything quite that crazy, but she's done pretty weird things.

ALISON, 12:   It embarrasses me when I have friends over and my father comes home and starts screaming at my mother for a bill or something and you hear the screaming two flights up. Usually I try to get my friends out of there so that they don't have to hear it. I take him or her by the hand and I move them out of the room. And I close the door. I don't think my parents realize. I tell them and they say, ''I'm sorry.''

GERRI, 12:   My mother always likes me to hold her hand when we're going shopping. So once I saw my friends, and I tried to jerk away because I didn't want them to see that I was holding hands with my mother. (WEIRD!) So I took my hand away and she started making this big thing, ''What's the matter? What's the matter?'' It was right in front of these kids and I was really embarrassed, so I just said, ''Nothing!''

TEACHERS

JILL, 12:   If I was a teacher, at the beginning of the year I'd be pretty strict. Then if my class really paid attention, I'd just get nice. I think it's good to incorporate fun with learning. Instead of learning French by just studying verbs or nouns, you can play French Scrabble or French hangman—it's more challenging and fun and you really learn a lot more. I hate it when teachers never admit their mistakes. Teachers should be careful about giving their opinions about a subject, because kids are going to think teachers are *always* right.

CAROLINE, 13:   I hate it when a teacher teases a student for something that's not their fault. Our English teacher teases one boy about the way he dresses. Most of us think it's because his parents don't really care about him. It hurts him when the teacher teases him.

JOHN, 13:   Teachers in general seem to think you're in the military. You speak when you raise your hand, and you go to the bathroom when you're allowed to. You have to ask to do everything. The teachers have all the control. They treat you like you're a piece of—like you're nothing at all.

KATHLEEN, 12:   A good teacher is someone who takes the time to teach you something when you don't understand it, and who'll keep on teaching you till you understand it.

ROBIN, 13:   It's amazing how much teachers gossip or talk about you. When you get there, the teachers already have a set opinion about you. They'll say, "Listen, I heard this and that about you." I haven't only had this just this year, it's been going on since I entered first grade. If there is a personality conflict, believe me, it is going to show, and if you do one thing wrong, it is going to go from teacher to teacher to teacher. They get this thing about you and it can really ruin you. The ideal system would be that every year the teacher doesn't look at your last grade's record until after they had you an entire year and then see what the other teachers might think, just to see the difference. They shouldn't be relying on the past achievement.

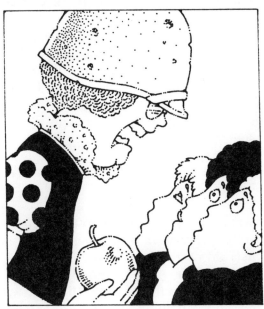

POPULARITY

LAURA, 10: I guess the worst thing about being popular is having people talk about you behind your back, the people who envy you. They say anything—true or untrue. A lot of popular people are so tangled up in not losing their popularity that they don't become themselves anymore. If I were unpopular, I would just try to find out why, and if it was something that was kind of hard to change or if I didn't want to change it, then I guess I would just have to accept it. If it were something that could be changed, then I would change it.

DIVORCE

DIANE, 10: If I were the only one, it would be worse, because it's hard to adjust to the fact that your parents are divorced and everyone else is happily married. But in places where a lot of people are divorced, it's not as embarrassing. A lot of famous people are divorced, and it's not like it's your fault, and it really isn't anything to be embarrassed about. I used to be embarrassed about it, but now when I think about it, it's really nothing wrong. It's just that two people could not get along as good as they thought they could. If they're going to be divorced, I guess that's the way I'm going to have to face life. But it's really hard.

PATTY, 13: At first I couldn't believe it. I ran to my room and I was crying. I just didn't think it could be true. I wrote a letter and I pinned it to my door. It was in the form of, "If you love me, how can you do this to me?" Then my brother came in, and I was terribly upset. He talked to me and helped me to realize that for me and my brother to be happy, they have to be happy too.

CINDY, 11: A friend of mine told me once that she was in a way glad that her parents were divorced because she said it was an "experience." I don't really know what she meant by an experience, but somehow I don't think it's any kind of experience for me.

KIMBERLY, 13: I've never seen my father. I asked my mother about it, and she said that they got married when they were very young. My mother dropped out of college, and they moved, and they just weren't happy. So they decided they were better off not married. I don't really think it was any of their faults—I think they were bright enough to realize that it wasn't working. I've learned to live with it. I think it's easier for me because if they had gotten divorced when I was old enough to understand what was going on, it would have been very traumatic for me. I would have hurt a lot worse. But it also hurts that my father doesn't want to see me. I asked my mother—

I said, "How come all my other friends whose parents are divorced, like, the father gets the kids on weekends?" And she said, "Well, your father just never wanted to see you. And I don't know why."

SEX

GLORIA, 12: I wish that my parents would talk to me about sex. I know it already, but I could act like I didn't. They're waiting too long, they're waiting too long. And that's why most kids, when they have sex, the parents go, "What? You don't know about sex." And the kids go, "Yes, I do." And they say, "How can you? I haven't told you." Parents think that if they don't tell you, you don't know. You can see when your child is grown up enough to understand it. You can see that. And I don't think that my father or my mother sees that I'm grown up enough. Parents go, "Oh, you're still a little baby. I can't tell you now. It would just break your heart to know." And you *know*. I just wish I hadn't found out with books. I wish I could have found out by my parents.

TIM, 12: When I was little, I was thinking, "A stork can't be bringing all those babies at one time! Suppose a lady has triplets—that stork has to have one strong beak. And besides, he's flying in 90-degree weather, you think he's

going to fry up there." Finally I got to kindergarten and the teacher let us read this book where it tells you how the mother and father have sexual intercourse and the baby is born.

OMAR, 11: My parents say it's interesting to learn sex, but they don't really tell me about it. They avoid me by saying, "Go to bed," or "Go out of the living room—family problems," or whatever. But I find out one way or another.

JESSIE, 12: I guess it's your natural instinct to want to know about certain things like that because everyone's always trying to keep it very hushed up. When it's hushed up, you want to find out—why are they keeping all this stuff quiet? I thought babies were adopted. It's not like you went shopping for a baby, but I thought there were people who would make babies, and they'd put them in display windows, and people would come around—like in the hospital.

JASON, 10:   I don't talk about sex with my friends because they always take it the dirty way. I don't talk about it with them that way, because sex is really nice. On the streets I'm always hearing bad things about it—like cursing. I just get nervous, and sometimes I get confused. Now I'm used to it, but because of my young age, I'm kind of a little shaky about it. That's why I get nervous when I talk about sex.

MONEY

JAN, 12:   I think money is a great thing to have, it helps a lot. But to be *born* rich, you'll be used to getting your way and that isn't how life is. I think it's much better if you are born *poor*, go to college, get a good job, and *then* become wealthy. It will change you some, but you are not going to become some stuck-up snob. If you just think about material value, you are really out of it!

KIRSTEN, 12:   Say there are two boys and one is rich and one is poor—they *still* like to play baseball. And two girls the same age—if one is rich and one poor, they *still* like to talk about clothes and giggle and things. I mean, you can't be *too* much different.

FRANKLIN, 12:   Grown-ups won't give us a chance. We can do the same things, but they won't give us a chance. Like, you have to be 15 years old to apply for a job. I think a ten-year-old kid can do just as good a job as a 15-year-old kid can do. Probably better if he sticks to it. Work gives you good experience. You know what responsibility is. You can always tell your friends, "Well, I have a job now. I don't have to take money from my parents every single solitary day. I can have my own money, I can start my own savings account." It gives you a feeling of importance.

BILLY, 12:   The job market is a fight and the strongest are going to win, but everybody is qualified for something or other. Kids are important on the job market. I think kids are open to education, and kids are more willing to work than adults. If you want to make money, you get out there and you work. Seriously, name all the rich people in the world. They *all* worked early. Howard Hughes started when he was eight!

HEAVEN

SUSANNAH, 12: I would really make heaven comfortable and have a lot of cushions. I would have no air pollution, and I would have all natural food, and everyone would kind of stay together. If there were people who like being alone, I would let them alone. I would let people move to wherever they wanted to move and I would not have houses. There would also be a place where you could go when you really wanted to be ridiculous. It would be sort of imaginary, like maybe a candy land. Or food land, where people could gorge themselves, and you could do all the fantasies that you have had in your real life, but of course you never got to do. I would also have some sort of formula where you could not get cavities.

DANIEL, 10: I'd like it to be swords and sorcerers and pinball machines. Every time you were rewarded for a feat of strength or a feat of magic, you'd get a pinball machine. I'd like to have a mansion and be real rich and have all these pinball machines. The clouds would be pinball machines and people would be the pinballs inside, and God would play the pinball machines.

NOAH, 11: If you go to heaven, or heaven happens, you're not really dead, because dying just might be something physical, something that happens when your heart stops. Your spiritual being keeps going, and you can watch over what's happening.

SARAH, 10: Heaven is what a person wants it to be. If the person wants it to be sunny and colorful, then it will be sunny and colorful, and if a person wants it misty, then it will be misty. It's what the person wants to have happen.

PATRICK, 9: I *hope* there's a heaven, because I don't just want to stay dead for the rest of my life. Or the rest of my deadness.

CHILDREN ARE PEOPLE TOO

ELIZABETH, 10:   It has been proven that children are treated as if they didn't have minds. I, myself, have been through many times when people treated me as if I weren't there. People think children can't understand anything and have no feelings. For example, the other day I went to a restaurant. I told the lady I wanted two pieces of fish. She said, "Where's your mother or father?"

I said, "My mother is working."

Then she asked, "Do you have any money? Can you pay for the fish?"

"Yes," I replied.

"Oh, so you do have money?" she said, and finally brought the fish.

This is just one of the many times that people think children can't think.

Another day I was trying to call Mom, but the switchboard was closed for the night. I thought something was wrong with the phone because it made funny noises, so I quickly called the operator and told him. He said, "The phone made a funny noise because *you* are playing with it. If you don't quit it, I'll call the police."

I don't understand why people figure children don't know what's going on in the world. I understand much of the world's problems like pollution and overpopulation. I want to hurry and grow up so I can help the world.

TEENAGE OPINIONS

A group called the Gallup Youth Survey talks to teenagers on a regular basis and asks them questions about many different topics. The questions are asked over the telephone. After all the answers are compared and added up, the people at Gallup write articles that appear in newspapers around the United States. Here is what teenagers thought about two questions that the Gallup Youth Survey asked. Answers are ranked from most to least frequently given. If two answers have the same number, it means they tied for that place.

WHAT THINGS WOULD YOU LIKE TO TALK ABOUT MORE OFTEN WITH YOUR PARENTS?

1. Family finances (money)
2. Drugs
3. Drinking
4. School
5. Politics
6. Sex
7. Religion

WHAT IS THE BIGGEST PROBLEM FACING TEENAGERS?

1. Drug abuse
2. Unemployment
3. Alcohol abuse
4. Peer pressures
5. Getting along with parents
5. School problems
7. Fear of war
8. Career doubts and uncertainty
9. Economic problems
10. Financing college
10. Growing up/finding a purpose in life
10. School dropouts

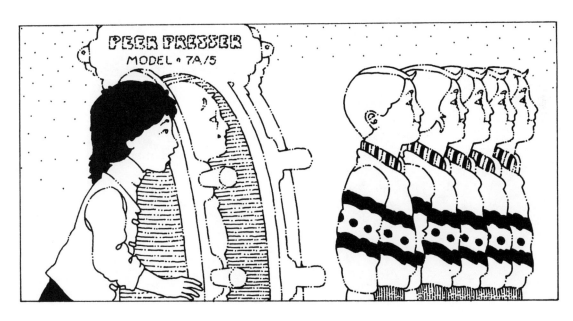

THE UNITED STATES IN THE FUTURE

What things would you most like to see happen in the United States in the future? *Weekly Reader*—the school newspaper for kids—did a survey on that question. More than 600,000 students answered. *Weekly Reader* gave the students ten things to choose from and asked them to rank them in order of importance—first, second, third—and so on. Here is the way the students ranked the ten things they would like to see happen in the United States in the future.

1. Women and men will be treated equally in all ways.
2. There will have been a woman president of the United States.
3. Most people will be better off than people are now.
4. People will be more physically fit than ever.
5. Most people will have the chance to travel in space.
6. People will work shorter hours and have more time to do other things.
7. More people will do their work at home using computers, rather than go out to work.
8. Children will learn at home more and at school less.
9. People will be watching more TV than ever.
10. Most children will grow up in families that do *not* have both a father and a mother living with them.

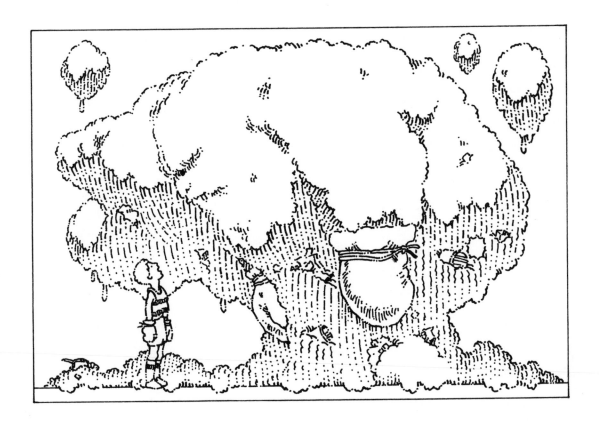

PROBLEMS IN THE UNITED STATES

Adults are always asked what they think are the most important problems that the government should work on. But what do kids think? *Weekly Reader* decided to find out. The school newspaper put together a list of problems and asked students from across the country to put them in the order in which they should be solved. Here is the order the kids chose. If two things have the same number, it means they tied for that place.

1. Keeping us out of war
2. Providing work for all who want to work
2. Helping the poor
4. Protecting our country from its enemies
5. Fighting crime
5. Fighting pollution
7. Keeping prices down
8. Providing a good education for all
9. Protecting the rights of blacks and other minorities
10. Protecting the rights of women

2
THE UNITED STATES AND THE OLD COUNTRY

PRESIDENT JIMMY CARTER TALKS ABOUT MAKING THE WORLD A BETTER PLACE IN WHICH TO LIVE

President Jimmy Carter was in the White House from 1977 to 1981. Since then he has written five books and organized his presidential library, the Carter Presidential Center in Atlanta, Georgia.

We wrote to President Carter and asked how kids could help make the world a better place in which to live. Here is the question and President Carter's answer.

Question: People think that kids are going to grow up and change the world—make it a better place in which to live. What changes do you think kids should try to make?

President Jimmy Carter: There is always a need to break down barriers between people and to make new friends, even with those who are quite different from us. Sometimes they live nearby and sometimes in foreign countries. This will help to ensure world peace and encourage us to share our wealth and freedom with others. In doing so, our own lives will be more exciting, adventurous, and happy.

Jimmy Carter, 39th president of the United States (The Carter Center)

SENATOR JOHN GLENN TALKS ABOUT PEACE AND FREEDOM AROUND THE WORLD

In 1959 John Glenn was chosen as one of the first seven astronauts in the United States space program. On February 20, 1962, he became the first American to orbit the earth, completing three orbits during a 5-hour flight. His spacecraft was the *Friendship 7*. Before he was an astronaut, Glenn was in the Marine Corps. He fought in two wars—World War II and the Korean War—and won many medals, including the Distinguished Flying Cross.

John Glenn, one of our first astronauts, is now a United States senator. (NASA)

Today John Glenn is a United States senator from the state of Ohio. Senator Glenn was asked for his thoughts about peace and freedom around the world, and how kids can help to work toward those goals. Here is what he had to say.

When I made three orbits in *Friendship 7*, I looked down and saw our earth, a beautiful blue green ball, spinning silently against the vastness of space. As I looked over whole continents, I was reminded that all the boundaries we have created between nations are artificial, and that many of the problems we have today are caused by these artificial separations.

I hope that kids who are growing up today will do all they can to overcome the divisions of our world. It is important that each of us do everything we can to learn more—not only about science and history and math, but also about how individuals and nations can live together safely and peacefully. I hope that many of you will study the languages of nations whose people seem strange to us, and I hope that many of you will consider careers in public service. Most of all, I hope that all of you will start right now trying always to be friendly and fair with others, and practicing the democracy that is so important to ensure peace, freedom, and security for all people on earth.

OUR ETHNIC HERITAGE

Our land was once empty of people. The ancestors of Native Americans (Indians) were the first to arrive. They crossed a land bridge from Asia to America thousands of years ago. Even if our roots are different, we all come from travelers, travelers from every other part of the world. Every American has an ancestor who came from somewhere else.

You can read this chapter in two ways. First, you can read it to discover something about the mix of people who are Americans. Second, you can read it to find out something about your ancestors, the people in your family who lived before you. Finding out where your ancestors came from may take a little work. Of course, you yourself may have come from another country. In that case, you know a lot about it already.

Many people who came to the United States from Europe in the 1800s settled in New York City's Lower East Side. This is the view south on Orchard Street in 1898. (Byron, Museum of the City of New York)

This cartoon, "Welcome to All!" appeared in the magazine Puck *on April 28, 1886. The signs give some reasons why people wanted to come to the United States. (The New York Public Library)*

THE OTHER COUNTRY

You might like to find out something about your roots. The first thing to do is learn where your foreign ancestors came from and when. If your parents or grandparents came from another country, try talking to them.

QUESTIONS TO ASK

1. Why did you come to the United States?
2. What was it like in the country you came from?
3. Did you come planning to stay or to return to the old country?
4. Who came with you?
5. How old were you when you came?
6. What happened on the way over?
7. How much money did you have with you when you landed here?
8. Could you speak English?
9. What did you do for a living in the old country? How did you make a living here at first?

10. Where did you live when you first came?

11. Where did you meet your husband or wife? Where was he or she from?

12. How was the United States different from the country you left?

13. Did you miss your native country? Why? Do you miss it now?

14. When did you decide you were a real American?

15. Would you go back to the old country for a vacation? What would you do there?

16. What were weddings like in the old country? Holidays?

17. How were girls in your family treated? Boys?

18. Who decided things in your family—the man or the woman?

19. Are there any old diaries or journals in the family that I could read? Old photographs? (Look on the backs of photographs for writing that tells who the people are. Get the person to whom you are talking to tell about the people in the photos.) Family Bible?

20. Do you know any crafts, dances, or stories from the old country?

Try to find out about the people in your family who came here from other countries. Fill in the blanks on a chart like this.

Ancestor's name: _____

Born where and when: _____

Date came to U.S.A.: _____

Age came to U.S.A.: _____

Reason for coming: _____

You may have some problems finding information. For many reasons, the trail may end before you learn anything about your ancestors who came from other countries. Some countries don't exist anymore or have changed their borders. Many early inhabitants came here as slaves or servants. Their records may be lost. Family names may have been changed. Some immigrants traveled first to another country, perhaps from Germany to England, then to the United States. Until 1868, records were sketchy. Children who have been adopted may have trouble finding their "real" ancestors. However, you probably will be able to find at least one ancestor.

A LIST OF OTHER COUNTRIES

Here is a list of 34 countries and regions from which people have come to live in the United States. (People who come into a new country to live are called immigrants. Those who leave a country to live somewhere else are called emigrants.) The list includes all those countries from which at least 200,000 immigrants arrived between 1820 and 1978. We have included Native Americans and Africans, too, although most of them did come before 1820. And we have given a section to the Jews, who have a special history as immigrants and as citizens of many countries.

In the early years of the United States, most immigrants came from Europe. Recently, most have come from Asia. Because so many people have emigrated from India and Indochina recently, we have added those places too.

If a country from which your ancestors came is not listed, it can be for two reasons. The number of immigrants from the country may be less than 200,000, or the country may have been part of still another country.

EUROPE

AUSTRIA (AUSTRIA-HUNGARY)

After World War I (1914–1918), Austria-Hungary became the countries of Austria, Yugoslavia, Serbia, Hungary, and Czechoslovakia.

NUMBERS Between 1820 and 1978, 4,315,000 people came to the United States from Austria-Hungary and the countries it became.

Hungarian-Americans in costume (Milwaukee County Historical Society)

LANGUAGES German, Croatian, Slovenian, Magyar, and Czech

FACTS Living in the United States was seen as the answer to their problems by many Austro-Hungarians who were poor and landless. "Here one is a dog, in America a gentleman," said one poor farmer. There is a Hungarian saying: "Meat, plenty of meat in America."

Austrians are known for their music. Wolfgang Amadeus Mozart, who wrote *The Magic Flute,* was Austrian. In summer a famous music festival is held in the city of Salzburg. The Vienna Boys' Choir, begun in 1498, is the oldest Austrian musical group. It still exists.

The evil Dracula, the human vampire, lived in Transylvania, once part of Austria. (That is, he lived there in his creator's mind. Dracula, of course, was not a real person.)

BELGIUM

Belgium became an independent country in 1831.

NUMBERS From 1820 to 1978, 203,000 Belgians came to the United States.

LANGUAGES 5,500,000 Belgians speak Flemish (a language like Dutch); 4,500,000, French; and 150,000, German. Flemish-speaking Belgians are called Flemings. French-speaking Belgians are called Walloons.

FACTS Michael Gilhooley, a Belgian, wanted to go to the United States very

Girls raise the Danish flag at International Language Villages (pages 67–69). (René Paulsen, Concordia Language Villages)

much. In 1919, when he was 14, he managed to sneak aboard and hide on a ship going from Belgium to New York. By the time he was found, it was too late to turn the ship around. At first the Americans in charge of letting people into the country were going to send him back. Then some Americans offered to take care of him and he got to stay.

DENMARK

NUMBERS From 1820 to 1978, 364,000 Danes emigrated to the United States. The peak emigration time was the 1880s, when 88,000 Danes came here to live.

FACTS Vitus Bering, a Dane sailing for Russia, discovered that America and Asia are divided by water. Racine, Wisconsin, founded by Danes, was called Dane City. Guess where danish pastry came from.

German-American kids do a German folk dance at the White House. (Michael Evans, The White House)

FRANCE

NUMBERS Many French came here a long time ago. In 1790, 55,000 French lived in the United States. From 1820 to 1978, 751,000 French people emigrated here. In the early days they taught dancing, fencing, and good manners. They made wigs and ran restaurants. Louis Philippe, later king of France, spent time in Philadelphia.

FACTS Many early explorers were French. Samuel de Champlain is said to have named Vermont by saying, *"Voilà les monts verts"* ("There are the green mountains").

The first European child born in Manhattan, Jean Vigne, was French. The year was 1614.

Many people of French ancestry live in Louisiana. They speak a French dialect called Cajun. Their ancestors came to Louisiana from Acadia in Canada.

GERMANY

Until about 1870 there was no Germany, except in people's minds. Before that, the land we call Germany today was a group of many little states. Each had its own laws.

NUMBERS In colonial times 200,000 Germans came here. From 1820 to 1978, 6,978,000 Germans emigrated to the United States. German emigration peaked from 1850 to 1890.

FACTS   Most of the early German colonists went to Pennsylvania. The first group of 13 families came in 1683 to Philadelphia. They were the ancestors of the Pennsylvania Dutch, who are not Dutch, but German.

In the 1800s thousands and thousands of Germans left their country to come to the United States. Many of them became homesteaders. They developed nearly 700,000 American farms.

In World War I, early in the 20th century, Americans fought the Germans. At home, some people took out their anger at the enemy on Americans with German ancestors. They wanted to hear of nothing German. They changed the names of things that had German names. Sauerkraut became "liberty cabbage." Hamburger became "Salisbury steak." A dachshund was called a "liberty hound." People named Muller changed their name to Miller; the Schmidts became the Smiths. The German language was not taught in school. Less anti-German feeling was directed against Americans of German ancestry in World War II.

To the Germans we owe hot dogs, hamburgers, pumpernickel bread, pretzels, and sauerkraut.

The covered, or Conestoga, wagon used by pioneers who went west came from Germany.

We can also thank Germans for youth hostels, chains of cheap places for young travelers to stay. These were started in the early 20th century in Germany by a teacher. He got the idea when he and his pupils, who were on a hike, got caught in the rain, were refused a place to stay in a barn, and ended up sleeping on beds of straw in a school. Youth hostels were the teacher's answer to the problem.

GREAT BRITAIN

Great Britain includes England, Scotland, and Wales. The ancestors of the British came from many places in Europe. They, like Americans, are a mix.

NUMBERS   In 1760, 1,500,000 British people lived in the American colonies. From 1820 to 1978, nearly five million more arrived. The big wave came from 1860 to 1880. In those years more than one of five immigrants was British.

FACTS   The very famous immigrants who arrived on the *Mayflower* were 101 English settlers. Many Americans claim them as ancestors. Welsh miners came to work in the mines in Pennsylvania. Scottish weavers worked in the mills that made cloth in the Northeast.

A long Welsh word, *LLANFAIRP WLLGWYNGYLLGOGERYCHWY RNDROBWLLLLANTYSILIOGOG OGOCH*, means "St. Mary's Church in the hollow of the white hazel near a rapid whirlpool and the Church of St. Tysilio near the red cave." It may be 51 letters in Welsh, but in English it's even more—58!

To the British we owe our language, much of our law, and part of our culture. Porridge and bagpipes were originally Scottish.

GREECE

Greece is a southern European country made up of many islands and a mainland.

NUMBERS   From 1820 to 1978, 655,000 Greeks arrived in the United States. Arrivals peaked from 1891 to 1920. By 1909, one of five Greek men of working age was in the United States.

FACTS   First to come were men planning to return to Greece after they made money. Some of the money was needed to pay their sisters' dowries. (A dowry is money or goods that a woman must bring with her to her marriage.) Greeks worked as sailors, railroad workers, cooks, and in many other jobs. A group in the early 1900s came to Florida to fish for sponges.

The pita bread sandwich is a Greek invention. If you'd like to make one yourself, you can learn how on page 80.

The idea of democracy began in Greece.

IRELAND

It wasn't until 1921 that the Irish won their freedom from the British. Northern Ireland is still a part of Great Britain.

NUMBERS   From   1820   to   1978, 4,723,000 Irish emigrated to the United States.

LANGUAGES   English and Irish (Gaelic)

FACTS   Before the American Revolution, many Irish Protestants who had

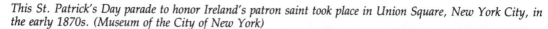

This St. Patrick's Day parade to honor Ireland's patron saint took place in Union Square, New York City, in the early 1870s. (Museum of the City of New York)

New York City's Little Italy, an Italian-American neighborhood on the Lower East Side, at the turn of the century (Library of Congress)

once been Scottish came to the mountains of Kentucky and Tennessee. Because they stayed by themselves and didn't see many other people, they kept their old way of speaking. It is like going back in time to hear them.

Later, many Irish came to the United States because living in Ireland was very hard. It was worst in the 1840s when the potato crop was ruined by a potato blight, a plant disease. Since potatoes were the main food of the Irish, the blight was a disaster. Out of four million Irish, one million died of hunger and another million came to the United States. From 1820 to 1850, more than four out of ten of the immigrants who came to the United States were Irish. Some immigrants brought a bit of Ireland's earth and spilled it on the ground when they arrived.

ITALY

In 1870 Italy became one country. Before that, what we know today as Italy was several states.

NUMBERS From 1820 to 1978 more than five million Italians emigrated to the United States. The peak was 1880 to 1914. During those years, four million Italians emigrated to the United States.

FACTS At least four famous early explorers of the Americas were Italian.

Members of an Italian immigrant family, just landed in the United States, look for their baggage. (International Museum of Photography)

An Italian artist painted the inside of the Capitol dome in Washington, D.C. His name was Constantino Brumidi.

Poor villagers also came to the United States. They said, "Whoever owns the land has everything." "At eight or nine years of age, if not sooner, the peasant child is old enough to bend his neck to the yoke and to fix his eyes upon the soil," wrote Angelo Pelligrini in *Immigrant's Return*.

Italian immigrants helped build skyscrapers and bridges. When they had made enough money, some went back to Italy to live. When someone complained that Italians took dollars back to Italy, Woodrow Wilson, a president of the United States, said, "But they left the subways."

To Italy, of course, we owe both ravioli and Italian opera.

Christopher Columbus, one of the first Europeans to discover America, sailed under the flag of Spain. John Cabot, whose name in Italian was Giovanni Caboto, sailed under the English flag. Amerigo Vespucci gave his first name to the new land—America. Giovanni da Verrazano discovered what is now New York City in 1524. The Verrazano Narrows Bridge from Staten Island to Brooklyn is named after him.

In the 1720s Italian glassblowers arrived in Georgia from the Italian city of Venice, to make trinkets to trade with the Indians.

THE NETHERLANDS

NUMBERS   From 1820 to 1978, 359,000 Dutch emigrated to the United States. Of Dutch-born Americans, more than one of four lives in California.

FACTS   In 1609 Henry Hudson discovered the Hudson River for the Dutch East India Company.

The Dutch invented scalping and taught it to the Indians.

To the Dutch we owe the Dutch door and windmills. American barns are a contribution of the Dutch and Germans.

You can visit the Dutch Museum in Holland, Michigan.

NORWAY

NUMBERS   The total number of Norwegians who came to the United States from 1820 to 1978 is 856,000. At the peak of emigration, the 1880s, more than one of ten Norwegians came to the United States to live.

FACTS   The first European to see America was probably Norwegian. His name was Leif Eriksson, and he sailed to North America in A.D. 1000, nearly 500 years before Columbus.

Most of the early Norwegian settlers were farmers. They built sod huts for houses.

At Corning, New York, Norwegian glass workers and glassblowers began a modern glass industry.

Norwegians founded 19 colleges here—Saint Olaf College in Northfield, Minnesota, for example.

Smorgasbord is a Norwegian buffet popular in the United States.

The Norwegian-American Museum is in Decorah, Iowa.

Tadeusz Kościuszko, 1746–1817, Polish hero in the American Revolution, painted by Paulin Miedzielsky (National Portrait Gallery, Smithsonian Institution)

POLAND

Poland is a country that has been conquered more than once. But Poland has had its own separate government from the end of World War I.

NUMBERS   From 1820 to 1978, more than 500,000 Poles came to live in the United States.

FACTS   There were 1,000 Poles in the Revolutionary army in the American War of Independence. Among them were Casimir Pulaski and Tadeusz Kościuszko, called "the greatest son of liberty . . . that I have ever known" by Thomas Jefferson.

From 1870 most immigrant Poles were poor peasants who settled in the cities. They worked in the factories, mines, and steel mills. In early Pennsylvania coal mines, Polish children worked 10 hours a day, six days a week.

PORTUGAL

NUMBERS   From 1820 to 1978, 446,000 Portuguese emigrated to the United States.

FACTS Ferdinand Magellan, whose ship was the first to sail around the globe, was Portuguese, sailing under the flag of Spain. Portuguese explorer Juan Rodríguez Cabrilho was the first European to arrive in California.

In the 1800s the Portuguese left the islands of Portugal for New England, Hawaii, and California to hunt whales, fish for tuna, and farm. In New England they worked in cotton mills, on farms, and on fishing boats.

The ukulele is a Portuguese musical instrument. Many people think it's Hawaiian, but it's not.

SPAIN

NUMBERS   From 1820 to 1978, 259,000 Spaniards emigrated to the United States.

FACTS   Spain sent Christopher Columbus on his voyage to the Americas. In 1513 Juan Ponce de León went to Florida. Alvar Núñez Cabeza de Vaca was shipwrecked off the Texas coast and walked all the way to Mexico City. The Spanish discovered the Mississippi River and the Grand Canyon. In 1565 they founded St. Augustine. Juan de Oñate led 400 soldiers, plus cattle, to New Mexico in 1598. They were looking for the Seven Cities of Gold, and they found the Pueblo and Navajo Indians.

Santa Fe, San Diego, Monterey, San Francisco, and Los Angeles were once Spanish cities. In the Kingdom and Province of New Mexico, which included Texas, lived Spanish settlers, workers, landowners, and priests.

The Spanish brought the horse, the cow, Churro sheep, citrus fruits, grapes, figs, olives, and grasses to the New World.

SWEDEN

NUMBERS   Between 1820 and 1978, 1,272,000 Swedes emigrated to the United States.

FACTS   In the 19th century, many Swedes had "America fever." Those who had come to the United States sent back glowing reports. For example, they said that the rivers "ran with syrup" instead of water. One person even said, "In America the hogs eat their fill of raisins and dates that everywhere grow wild, and when they are thirsty they drink from ditches flowing with wine." It was said that it was bet-

Scandinavian immigrants pose before their house in Hendricks, Minnesota, in the 1880s. (Minnesota Historical Society)

Russian immigrants, members of the Mennonite religious group, lived briefly in this house in Kansas. (Library of Congress)

ter to be a pig in the United States than to be a person in Sweden.

To the Swedes we owe the log cabin, trolls, and skiing. We also owe to them the ombudsman, a person who listens to complaints and does something about them. He may or may not be a government official.

SWITZERLAND

NUMBERS From 1820 to 1978, 349,000 Swiss emigrated to the United States.

LANGUAGES Two in three Swiss speak German, one in five speaks French, one in ten speaks Italian, and one in 100 speaks Romansh.

FACTS To the Swiss we owe yodeling and Swiss cheese.

RUSSIA AND THE SOVIET UNION

In 1917 the people of Russia went to war against their czar, a kind of king. The new country that finally came about from that revolt was called the Soviet Union. The Soviet Union is an enormous land. It is made up of many countries that were once independent.

To earn enough money to live on, whole families of immigrants worked together making artificial flowers. (Jessie Tarbox Beals, Museum of the City of New York)

NUMBERS From 1820 to 1978, more than three million Russians and Soviets came to the United States. The arrivals peaked between 1903 and 1907, when 457,000 Russians came to the United States.

LANGUAGES People in the Soviet Union speak at least 33 languages and dialects.

FACTS Early in the 1800s, Russians in the fur trade came over the Bering Sea to Alaska. Russia sold Alaska to the United States in 1867, for about $7 million.

Babushkas are Russian grandmothers. They wear head scarves, which are called babushkas too.

From Russia and France came the ballet.

THE AMERICAS

CANADA

NUMBERS From 1820 to 1978, 4,105,000 Canadians emigrated to the United States. Most have come since the middle of the 1800s. It makes sense that many immigrants are Canadian. After all, we share a border—a long one—with Canada.

FACTS Most Canadian immigrants have been French speaking. They worked in shipbuilding and lumbering and in cotton mills. In the 19th century many children worked in textile mills, making cloth.

CUBA

Cuba, an island, lies 90 miles from the Florida coast. In 1895 the Cubans rose up against Spain, which then owned the island, and the United States helped. Cuba won, the Spanish left, and Cuba became free. In 1959 the people again overthrew the government.

NUMBERS From 1820 to 1978, 525,000 Cubans arrived in the United States to become citizens. Since 1978, 275,000 more have come.

FACTS Many Cubans have come to the United States by boat and settled in Miami. So many have settled there, in fact, that it is called Little Havana after the capital of Cuba. In 1980, 125,000 Cubans arrived by boat in what became known as the Mariel boat lift.

Many Cubans can trace their ancestry to Africa, India, China, or Spain.

MEXICO

During the 16th and 17th centuries the Spanish conquered the Native Americans in what is now Mexico. It was not until 1820 that Mexico became free from Spain. From 1846 to 1848 Mexico and the United States fought a war. When Mexico lost, it also lost a big piece of land to the United States—all of what is now Texas, New Mexico, Arizona, California, Nevada, and Utah, plus part of Colorado. There were then 75,000 Mexicans living in that area. They were allowed to become American citizens. Almost all of them did.

NUMBERS From 1820 to 1978, 2,124,000 Mexicans moved to the United States.

These Canadian voyageurs *are canoeing through rapids.* Voyageurs *worked carrying men and goods for fur companies. (Public Archives of Canada)*

This figure photographed in Rosario Chapel in Santa Fe, New Mexico, is called La Conquistadora, *Spanish for "Lady Conqueror." (Robert H. Martin, Museum of New Mexico)*

FACTS   American music and food with Mexican roots include mariachi music, tacos, tamales, and tortilla chips.

The farming and mining methods, law, and architecture of the Southwest have been influenced by Mexicans.

WEST INDIES

The West Indies includes the Greater Antilles (Hispaniola, which includes the Dominican Republic and Haiti; Jamaica; Puerto Rico; Cuba, discussed on page 49); Lesser Antilles (Virgin Islands, Leeward Islands, Windward Islands, Trinidad, Barbados, and Tobago); and the Bahamas. Most of the West Indies were once colonies belonging to countries in Europe.

NUMBERS   From 1820 to 1978 at least 724,000 West Indians emigrated to the United States. The largest numbers came in the 1900s. From 1960 to 1984, 15 of every 100 immigrants to the United States were from the West Indies.

FACTS   Jamaica was a British colony. Nine of ten Jamaicans are black. About 250,000 Jamaicans live in New York City, more than in any other city anywhere, except Jamaica's Port-au-Prince.

The people of the Dominican Republic are Spanish speaking. There are 500,000 to 650,000 Dominicans in the United States. More than half live in New York City. In fact, there are more Dominicans there than in any other city but Santo Domingo, which is in the Dominican Republic.

Haiti is French speaking. Most Haitians who came to the United States live in Miami and New York. At the end of the 1970s, it was said that there were 300,000 Haitians in the United States, most on the East Coast.

The people of Trinidad and Tobago speak a language that is basically Spanish but influenced by Indian and Chinese languages.

Until the end of World War II most West Indians in the United States were blacks. They worked in the Northeast as needleworkers, cigar makers, doctors, dentists, lawyers, businessmen.

Reggae (Jamaica) and calypso (Trinidad) are West Indian.

ASIA

CHINA

NUMBERS   From 1820 to 1978, 528,000 Chinese came to live in the United States. Arrivals peaked from 1860 to 1880. Then, from 1924 to 1943, the American government would not allow any Chinese to emigrate to the United States.

FACTS   In 1848 Chinese heard about Gum San, the Mountain of Gold, which had been found in the United States. They joined thousands of others in the California Gold Rush. The Chinese on the West Coast were called the Celestials because the Chinese Em-

Chinese miners are on the right, while other miners are on the left. Notice how differently the two groups dressed. (California State Library)

pire was known as the Celestial Empire of China. To get to the United States they traveled 7,000 miles by ship, almost ⅓ of the way around the earth.

Because they wore their hair in a braid, they did not look like the other miners. Some non-Chinese miners picked on them. Driven away from the mines, many Chinese started laundries or restaurants. Others became coolies, or workers.

From 1862 to 1869 Chinese helped build the transcontinental railroad for $1 a day and board. Sometimes they worked in baskets lowered on a rope over gorges in the mountains. They worked in tunnels under 15 feet of snow.

Chop suey, made from leftovers, was created by a Chinese-American.

Chopsticks and firecrackers are Chinese inventions. So is india ink, believe it or not!

INDIA

Most of India was once a colony of Great Britain. It became free in 1947.

NUMBERS   From 1820 to 1975, 107,446 Indians came to the United States. Six in ten of these came after 1970.

FACTS   In 1985 the National Spelling Bee in Washington, D.C., was won by Balu Natarajan, 13, born in India. At home, he spoke Tamil, an Indian language. He beat 167 others by spelling the word *milieu.*

To India we owe the sari, curry, and the spices it is made from—cumin, cloves, fenugreek, coriander, and cardamom, for example. The games of chess, Parcheesi, and badminton are also Indian. Zero, perhaps the most important number, was an Indian idea.

INDOCHINA

Indochina includes Vietnam, Cambodia (Kampuchea), and Laos. The land was first ruled by China. From the late 1800s until 1954, France ruled a large part. Later, war began between

An Indian woman wearing a sari (Karie Miller)

North and South Vietnam, with the United States on the side of South Vietnam. The war ended in 1975. The North Vietnamese won. Most Indochinese who have emigrated to the United States were refugees from war.

NUMBERS From 1820 to 1978, 114,000 Vietnamese came to live in the United States. Nine of ten Indochinese emigrants are Vietnamese. The largest numbers arrived from 1975 on. In that year, a "babylift" brought 2,500 Vietnamese orphans to the United States. In 1976 the Laotians started coming. Later, in 1978, more people escaped from Indochina, most in boats. They were called the boat people. Many finally were allowed to settle in the United States. By 1980 there were 261,714 Vietnamese in the United States.

FACTS Many Vietnamese practice more than one religion. A person can be a Buddhist and a Catholic at the same time.

JAPAN

From 1650 to 1850 Japan cut itself off from other countries. It was called the Empire of the Rising Sun. No Japanese came to the United States to live. Then an American, Matthew Perry, helped make a business treaty with Japan. In 1868 the Japanese government opened the country to the world. In 1886 Japanese citizens were finally allowed to emigrate.

A Japanese-American mother and her children wait to be taken to a detention camp. (National Archives)

NUMBERS From 1820 to 1978, 406,000 Japanese immigrants came to the United States. Arrivals peaked from 1891 to 1924. In 1980 seven out of ten Americans of Japanese descent lived in California or Hawaii.

FACTS Those who came from Japan are called *Issei*. Their children are called *Nisei*. Their children's children are called *Sansei*. Their children's children's children are called *Yonsei*. *Kibei* are children born in the United States who go to school at least part of the time in Japan.

Most of the early Japanese immigrants were young men. Marriages for

Japanese-Americans took as many belongings with them as they could when they were ordered from their homes to detention camps during World War II. (National Archives)

them were arranged by mail with Japanese girls who sent photographs. These girls were called picture brides. In 1920 this practice was outlawed by Japan.

On December 7, 1941, the Japanese Air Force attacked Pearl Harbor in Hawaii. They killed or hurt 3,000 Americans. The president of the United States declared war on Japan. The Japanese were called the Yellow Peril.

Many Americans thought Japanese-Americans were spies for Japan. They imagined foolish things. Example: Japanese gardeners planted flowers in American gardens in the shape of an arrow. The arrow pointed to airports and defense plants to show Japanese planes where to put their bombs. This was not true.

The president set up camps to which 110,000 Japanese-Americans were forced to go. The camps were fenced with barbed wire and guarded by soldiers. Meanwhile, Japanese-Americans who made up the United States

442nd Regimental Combat Team in the United States Army fought bravely. They got more medals than any other military men in United States history. In 1944 Japanese-Americans were allowed to leave the camps. They had lost almost everything they had, and the American government paid them 10¢ for every dollar they had lost.

We owe haiku, flower arranging, kimonos, and kites to the Japanese.

KOREA

The country of Korea is at least 4,000 years old, 20 times as old as the United States. It is a small country, and it has been ruled by many other nations. In 1910 the Japanese took it over and called it Chosen, with the accent on the second syllable. They kept it until the end of World War II. After the Korean War it was divided into North and South Korea.

NUMBERS   From 1820 to 1978, 247,000 Koreans came to live in the United States. Many went to Hawaii to live and work as farmers. In 1985, 35,255 Koreans arrived, many of them doctors and farmers.

THE PHILIPPINES

The United States won the Philippine Islands from Spain in the Spanish-American War in 1898. However, Filipinos were not considered citizens of the United States. Instead, they were thought of as "nationals" or "wards." In 1946 the Philippines became an independent nation.

NUMBERS   From 1820 to 1978, 390,000 Filipinos emigrated to the United States. In 1980, there were 774,640 Filipino-Americans in the United States, most in California and Hawaii.

LANGUAGES   Spanish, English, Pilipino (Tagalog)

FACT   The yo-yo comes from the Philippines.

TURKEY

NUMBERS   From 1820 to 1978, 385,000 Turks emigrated to the United States.

FACTS   Armenia is now a part of the Union of Soviet Socialist Republics and Turkey. Armenians say their land was the Garden of Eden. They came to the New World as traders. The first Armenian to arrive was called Martin the Armenian. He was a tobacco grower and merchant in Virginia. Others made silk and ornaments to be traded to the Indians.

Armenian farmers brought varieties of grapes, figs, apricots, and Persian melons to the United States.

Most Armenians belong to the Armenian Gregorian Church, founded about A.D. 300 by Saint Gregory the Illuminator. Saint Gregory talked the king, his cousin, into making Armenia the first Christian nation.

EARLY ARRIVALS

NATIVE AMERICANS (AMERICAN INDIANS)

NUMBERS   In 1500 there were at least one million Native Americans. By 1890 there were only 200,000. By 1970 there were nearly 800,000 Native Americans and more than 34,000 Eskimos and Aleuts.

FACTS   The first Native Americans walked over a land bridge from Asia to get to North America thousands of years ago. By the time Europeans came, some of the Native Americans were living in tribes with as many as 10,000 people. Most did not believe people could own land. Tecumseh, a great chief said, "Sell a country? Why not sell the air, the great sea, as well as the earth?"

It was not until 1924 that Native Americans were made citizens of the United States. And it was not until 1948 that the last state, Arizona, gave them the right to vote.

To Native Americans other Americans owe peanuts, popcorn, chewing gum, tomatoes, potatoes, beans, rubber, tobacco, and some medicines. Certain ideas in the United States Constitution came from the Six Nations of the Iroquois.

Freed American slaves founded Liberia in Africa in the 1820s. The country became independent in 1847. The people in this group bound for Liberia were from Arkansas. (Library of Congress)

AFRICANS

NUMBERS In 1790 there were 750,000 people who came from Africa or had African ancestors in the United States. By 1850 there were four million.

FACTS Africans did not come to the United States in great numbers from 1820 on. However, many Africans came earlier to the United States and to the colonies. Some came with the explorers. At the colony of Jamestown in Virginia were 20 Africans.

Beginning in 1645 Africans were caught and sent to America as slaves. Most were from the western part of Africa. They were from various tribes— Akim, Ashanti, Bantu, Dahomean, Efik, Fanti, Fida, Hausa, Ibo, Kru, Mahi, Mandingo, and Popo. The Fanti, Ashanti, and Akim were from the Gold Coast. The Ibos lived near the Niger River. Mahis, Popos, and Fidas came from Dahomey. Most were sent to the southern colonies.

A prince of the Ibo tribe named Olaudah Equiano (Gustavus Vasa) was captured to be a slave when he was only 11. He wrote of his terrible experiences as a slave. When he first saw the slave ship, he was so horrified that he fainted.

It was not until 1863 that slavery was outlawed in the United States.

Blues and jazz have African roots.

JEWS

The Jewish nation came to an end in A.D. 67. In that year the Romans forced the Jews to flee from Jerusalem. The Jewish state did not exist again until 1948, when Israel was created. In the meantime, the Jews went many places and became citizens of many countries.

Judaism today is a religion, a culture, a nation, a way of thinking. Jewish religious law is written in the Talmud. The spiritual leader of a group of Jews is called a rabbi (teacher).

NUMBERS At the start of the American Revolution there were 2,000 to 3,000 Jews in the United States. In 1880 there were 250,000. Arrivals peaked from 1880 to 1924. In those years 2,378,000 Jews came to the United States.

LANGUAGES Hebrew, the language of the Old Testament of the Bible; Yiddish, a combination of Hebrew and German; Ladino, which was spoken by the Jews of Spain.

FACTS The Jewish Pale of Settlement was established by Catherine the Great of Russia in 1792 in eastern Poland. Russian Jews were forced to live there in all-Jewish villages. Between 1881 and 1910 Polish Jews in the Pale of Settlement fled to the United States to escape pogroms (mass killings).

With their rabbi, these Jewish boys study the Torah, Jewish wisdom and law. (Museum of the City of New York)

In Russia in the late 1800s, Jews were not allowed to own land or sell liquor. Only a few were accepted as students by universities.

Before and after World War II, many Jews entered the United States as refugees escaping the Nazis in many European countries.

SOME FAMOUS AMERICAN IMMIGRANTS

ATLAS, CHARLES (Italian), strongman, went from a "97-pound weakling" to "the world's most perfectly developed man."

AUDUBON, JOHN JAMES (Haitian), naturalist and painter, studied and painted the birds and other wildlife of North America.

BARYSHNIKOV, MIKHAIL (Soviet), ballet dancer and director of the American Ballet Theatre, defected to the United States.

BEMELMANS, LUDWIG (Austrian), writer and illustrator of children's books, is best known for the Madeline books.

BETHUNE, JOHANNA GRAHAM (Scottish), started Sunday schools.

BETTELHEIM, BRUNO (Austrian), expert on raising children, hated school when he was a kid. In 1939, after being in two Nazi concentration camps, he came to the United States. He says, "There are no perfect parents and no perfect children, but every parent can be good enough." Dr. Bettelheim does not believe in spanking, teaching reading, or Little League. He does believe that children should be listened to.

John James Audubon, 1785–1851, painted by Jules Lion (National Portrait Gallery, Smithsonian Institution)

BORGE, VICTOR (Dane), movie actor, pianist, and comedian, spoke, for his first English sentence in a movie, "You'll burn for this, you rat."

CABRINI, MOTHER FRANCESCA (Italian), the first American saint, came to the United States with six other nuns from the Order of the Sacred Heart in 1899. They opened orphanages for Italian children in New York and other parts of the United States.

EINSTEIN, ALBERT (German-Jewish), Nobel Prize-winning physicist and genius, was best known as the first to state the theory of relativity. He escaped the Nazis in World War II.

EVINRUDE, OLE (Norwegian), inventor, made the first outboard motor.

EWING, PATRICK (Jamaican), basketball player, is the center for the New York Knickerbockers.

FOX, MICHAEL J. (Canadian), TV and movie actor, has starred in such movies as *Back to the Future*.

FUNK, CASIMIR (Polish), biochemist, is given credit for discovering vitamins.

GARVEY, MARCUS (Jamaican), black activist, said as a schoolboy, "I was not made to be whipped." He meant he was not made to be whipped by his teachers. At the age of 14 he was sent to work with a printer as an apprentice (learner-worker). He came to the United States in 1916 and founded the Universal Negro Improvement Association (UNIA). The UNIA had millions of members. It owned a church, newspapers, restaurant, hotel, and the Black Star steamship line. Garvey was the first to say that black is beautiful. He wanted to bring together the 400 million blacks in the world.

GERSTENZANG, LEO (Polish), invented Q-tips in 1923 when he saw his wife use a toothpick and cotton on their baby.

HALL, PRINCE (Trinidadian), an ex-slave, fought at Bunker Hill in the American Revolution.

HERBERT, VICTOR (Irish), composer and conductor, wrote *Babes in Toyland*.

JACOBI, ABRAHAM (German-Jewish), started the first children's clinic in the United States in 1860. Dr. Jacobi taught that children's diseases are different from adult diseases.

JONES, MARY HARRIS (MOTHER) (Irish), labor leader, fought against child labor.

John Muir, 1838–1914, painted by Orlando Rouland (National Portrait Gallery, Smithsonian Institution)

LAFITTE, JEAN (French), pirate and smuggler, helped Americans in the battle of New Orleans in the War of 1812.

LEE, BRUCE (Chinese), movie star and expert in the martial arts, starred in many films, including *Enter the Dragon*.

LOEWY, RAYMOND (French), designer, died in 1986, age 92. He created the Coca-Cola bottle and the eagle symbol for the United States Postal Service. By age 16 he had a business selling model planes. In 1919 he came to the United States with $50 in his pocket. It was he who, as a consultant to the United States Manned Space Program, insisted that the space vehicle *Skylab* have portholes for looking out to see the earth.

MARTINEZ, RAUL (Cuban), mayor of Hialeah, Florida, became the first Cuban-born mayor of a United States city.

MEIR, GOLDA (Russian-Jewish), prime minister of Israel at age 71, was born in the Soviet Union, but left at age eight to come to the United States with her parents. When she grew up, she migrated to Palestine, where she helped found Israel.

MUIR, JOHN (Scottish), naturalist, helped establish Yosemite and Sequoia national parks and more than 1 million acres of forest reserves.

PUPIN, MICHAEL (Yugoslavian), physicist and inventor, came here at age 15 with 5¢. He produced the first short-exposure X-ray photos and helped develop radio.

ROCKNE, KNUTE (Norwegian), was the football coach of Notre Dame University.

SALAZAR, RUBEN (Mexican), activist, fought for the rights of Mexican-Americans, especially children.

SCHURZ, CARL (German), politician, was part of an uprising in Germany that failed. He had to escape to Switzerland through a sewer to the Rhine River. In 1852 he came to New York. A friend of President Abraham Lincoln, he became a United States senator and secretary of the interior. He fought against bad treatment of Native Americans and for saving public lands and forests. His wife started the first United States kindergarten.

SCHWARZENEGGER, ARNOLD (Austrian), body builder and movie actor, was Mr. Universe in both 1967 and 1970. He has starred in many films, such as *Conan the Barbarian*.

SHAHN, BEN (Soviet), artist, came to the United States from Russia at age eight. As a boy he chalked drawings of sports heroes on sidewalks. As a grown-up, he painted a mural of the history of American immigrants, among other things.

SIKORSKY, IGOR (Soviet), invented the helicopter.

SKOURAS, SPYROS (Greek), film executive, with his brother, began a chain of movie theaters. He was president of Twentieth Century-Fox, which produced *Miracle on 34th Street*.

SUTTER, JOHN (Swiss), owned Sutter's mill, where the California Gold Rush began.

Phillis Wheatley, c.1753–1784, in 1773, the year her volume of poetry was published (Library of Congress)

VESEY, DENMARK (Virgin Islander), tried to start a slave rebellion in the 1820s in the Carolinas.

VON BRAUN, WERNER (German), a leader of the rocket and space industry, helped to design the ship that landed men on the moon.

WEISSMULLER, JOHNNY (Austrian), actor and athlete, played Tarzan in the movies and won three gold medals for swimming in the Olympics.

WHEATLEY, PHILLIS (African), poet, was brought to Boston on a slave ship at age eight. She learned to read English, Latin, and Greek.

YANN, LIN (Cambodian), came to the United States as a refugee and placed second in a spelling bee at age 12.

An 1880s train carrying immigrants to new homes in the United States (Minnesota Historical Society)

THE BIG WAVE

Between 1880 and 1920, 23 million immigrants, mostly from Europe, came to the United States. Why did they come? Most immigrants came to make more money. Life was hard in their native countries. Sometimes the weather was bad and crops did not grow. Or crops were hit by disease. This was true in the terrible potato famine of the 1840s in Ireland and other countries, also discussed on page 43. Farmers would leave the land and come to the city, where there were often too many people already. When there was not enough work in the city, they often emigrated to the United States. Here land was very cheap, or free, and people were needed to work.

Not all the workers who came to the United States planned to stay. Some wanted to stay just long enough to make money to buy land in the country they were born in. They were called birds of passage. They often worked for a *padrone*, a go-between who arranged work for them and took money for it. The *padrone* knew how to speak their native language as well as English. Bad *padrones* took too much money from the workers. Some *padrones* got children to come to the United States as singers and acrobats, then kept most of what the children made.

Women sometimes traveled alone to the United States to work. Many of them had jobs as servants. Some used the money they made to buy tickets for their families or boyfriends to emigrate too.

Of course, reasons other than more money brought immigrants. War. Lack of freedom to practice religion. An earthquake or tidal wave or volcano. Too many taxes. Fear of disease. Some immigrants came to go to school or to have an adventure.

Usually the immigrants traveled deep down in the ship, in *steerage*, the cheapest place. There were no showers and no dining rooms. It was very crowded and smelly. Many people went up on deck to sleep. The trip lasted from two weeks to two months.

After 1892 most immigrants landed in New York, at Ellis Island. After an okay from officials on the island, they went by ferry to the city, 1 mile away. After that, they might move on to another part of the United States.

Those who came from the same culture tended to stay together, creating, for instance, areas known as Chinatown and Little Italy in a number of cities. Immigrants moving on from cities tended to search out places like the places they came from. For instance, if their country had a cold winter, they often went north.

THE STATUE OF LIBERTY:
THE MEANING OF FREEDOM

The history of the Statue of Liberty is very interesting to all people, and especially to Americans. She stands tall in New York Harbor and welcomes ships to the shores of the United States. The man who thought up the idea for this statue was a Frenchman named Frédéric Auguste Bartholdi. Who would have guessed that this lighthouse would someday mean liberty and freedom to millions of people? In fact, the real name of the Statue of Liberty is *Liberty Enlightening the World*.

In November 1875, Bartholdi started

The Statue of Liberty has symbolized freedom for millions of immigrants to the United States. (National Park Service)

The Statue of Liberty was the first thing people saw when they came to the United States and entered these waters. She gave immigrants coming to this new land hope for a new beginning. When they saw the Statue of Liberty, some prayed, some cried, some laughed, some cheered. Parents lifted up their babies so that they could see her.

Bartholdi often told a story about how he got the idea for the statue. When he was a young student living in Paris, France, there was a wall, built to keep out enemy soldiers. One night a young French girl carrying a torch jumped over the wall and screamed, "Forward!" The enemy soldiers shot and killed her. Bartholdi was shocked. Many years later he remembered the unknown girl with the torch in her hand, and this gave him the idea for the statue.

Bartholdi used his wife as the model for the shape of the statue and his mother as the model for the statue's face. Frédéric Bartholdi said his biggest goal in life was "to have my name written at the feet of all people who have had good ideas."

After many years, bad weather and pollution started to ruin the Statue of Liberty. The United States, with the help of the French people, began to rebuild it. After spending $265 million to fix the statue, the United States planned a big party. On July 4, 1986, the country celebrated the 100th anniversary of the Lady who still stood tall in New York Harbor. The four-day Liberty Weekend had the largest fireworks

to build the statue in France. The statue was 151 feet tall and weighed 225 tons. It was made of copper that was pounded into shape with hammers by many men. It was not until April 22, 1886, that the statue was finally finished. Afterward, the Lady, as the statue was later called, was taken apart piece by piece. She was then sent as a gift to the United States. Each part of the Statue of Liberty was put back together on a waiting pedestal on Liberty Island in New York Harbor. Everyone agreed that this spot was the best place to put the Lady.

show in the history of the United States and the largest street fair ever held in New York City. A group of "tall ships" and warships, some 40,000 in all, floated around the statue. More than 200 airplanes flew overhead on this special day.

The party had some 20,000 performers playing instruments, singing, and having fun. More than 250 banjo players, a 1,500-member drill team, 1,000 violinists, and a 500-piece marching band were there. Big-name singers like Frank Sinatra and Kenny Rogers performed for the crowds.

On Ellis Island, Supreme Court Justice Warren Burger announced that on July 4, 1986, 22,000 people had become American citizens. President Ronald Reagan ended the four-day weekend party by pushing a special button to light up the new "Miss Liberty." The light that had already shown the way for millions of people was once again lighting the way for even more people wanting to find freedom and a new life in America.

For more about the statue, see page 316.

SLEEPING ON THE FIRE ESCAPE

Immigrant children in New York City in the time of your great-grandparents often lived in buildings called tenements. A tenement apartment usually had a toilet in the hall, used by at least two families. Inside the apartment the sink often doubled for washing dishes and faces. Next to it stood a tub in the kitchen for the family baths. It was fitted with a lid to provide counter space by the sink. Water was heated on the stove. In summer the tenements were hot. Children slept on the roof or the fire escape.

Orphans and runaways lived in homes run by the Children's Aid Society. At one of them a bunk cost 6¢, breakfast cost 6¢, and supper cost 6¢. The kids were expected to behave. A sample notice on the wall: Boys Who Swear and Chew Tobacco Cannot Sleep Here.

The hurdy-gurdy man plays for children in a New York City immigrant neighborhood. (Museum of the City of New York)

An immigrant child takes a bath in the sink.
(International Museum of Photography)

In 1903 in New York City's Public School Number 1, there were kids from 25 countries. (In Los Angeles today more than 100 languages are spoken in the public schools.) It was hard in school for kids who came to the United States speaking no English. Special courses in English were given for them. Even so, a 12-year-old kid who spoke no English could end up in first grade.

After elementary school, kids were taught job skills. The Children's Aid Society had trade schools. Boys learned things like shoemaking, printing, sign painting, basket making, cleaning buildings. Girls learned sewing, cooking, dressmaking, hatmaking, typewriting.

Kids under 14, by law, were supposed to be in school. Not all were. Children as young as eight years old worked. They worked in factories, laundries, stores. They fetched packages, carried coal, sold things, and ran errands. With homemade shoeshine kits, they shined people's shoes. Boys and girls both sold newspapers. Children also sold matches, shoelaces, and ribbons. With the rest of their families, children sometimes worked at home. They rolled cigars or made clothes or artificial flowers.

Still, kids had fun. They chased fire trucks, had secret clubs, and pitched pennies against buildings. They played stickball, a game like baseball. Bases were marked with chalk on sidewalk and street.

Said Sophie Ruskay, an immigrant child: "Neither my friends nor I played much with dolls. Since families generally had at least one baby on hand, we girls had plenty of opportunity to shower upon the baby brothers or sisters . . . the love that would otherwise have been diverted on dolls. Besides, dolls were expensive." Sophie Ruskay, *Horsecars and Cobblestones* (New York: A. S. Barnes, 1948).

"Like all kids, immigrant children could get in trouble. From a tenement window, they let down a weight on a string to conk the head of someone, then pulled it up before he could see it. Or they stretched a string across the sidewalk, the height of an adult head, and lifted hats off the heads of men walking along." Samuel Chotyinoff, *A Lost Paradise* (New York: Alfred A. Knopf, 1955).

A COUPLE OF HOURS IN THE UNITED STATES

After a dinner of lasagna (Italian), you start on your homework. You want to get a better grade than the C your teacher gave you for yesterday's homework. (ABCs for grades were first used by Swedes. They were probably first adopted in the United States at Augustana College in Rock Island, Illinois.) At least you are getting an A in PE. (German-Americans pushed for physical education in American schools.) On the radio is some jazz. (Blacks, maybe drawing on their African culture, created jazz.) After you take your sauna (Finnish), you go out on the patio (Mexican, Spanish). You start to do the homework you didn't do the night before, thankful for the eraser on your pencil. (John Eberhard Faber, a German, was the first to attach erasers to pencils.) After a while it gets dark so you go inside and turn on the light. (Nicolas Tesla, responsible for the use of AC electricity in the United States, came here from Austria at age 28.) A friend calls you on the telephone. (The telephone was invented by Alexander Graham Bell, born in Scotland.) The friend wants to know if you have a book from the public library. (Andrew Carnegie, another Scottish-American, believed in and spent his fortune on public libraries.) Isn't it good to be an American?

INTERNATIONAL LANGUAGE VILLAGES

When you speak a foreign language well, you are, in a way, given another life. It's like stepping into another world. The best place to learn a foreign

Using an ancient Viking method, a boy learns to fire clay at the International Language Villages. (Neil Larsen, Concordia Language Villages)

language is in a country where that language is spoken. For example, the best place to learn Danish is probably in Denmark.

But you don't have to travel that far. You can learn a foreign language and go to summer camp, too, at the International Language Villages in Minnesota. Nearly 60,000 young people already have. About 3,000 kids, ages seven to 18, go each summer. You have your choice of nine foreign languages and cultures, each with its own village: Norwegian, Swedish, Finnish, Danish, Chinese, German, Russian, Spanish, French. There is also a French- and German-Swiss Village.

At International Language Villages,

you go through customs, take a foreign name, and use a passport. You change your American dollars for the money of the country. For example, in the French Village, you might take the name Jacques (if you are a boy) or Marie (if you are a girl). The franc is the official money.

People who are native speakers act as counselors. The new language comes easily as you make friends, keep score in a game, talk to people in the store, and ask for certain foods. You make and eat the food of the country. Examples: Chinese wonton, a Spanish gaucho barbecue, and French brioche. You learn history, songs, and dances. Holidays of the country are celebrated: French *le branle*, Swedish *Midsommar* with smorgasbord and dancing around a maypole, *la Armada Invencible* (Spanish). Folk arts and crafts include pottery, weaving, Chinese calligraphy, French bobbin lace making, and Danish Christmas decorating.

If you are in the Russian Village you learn that your friends pull your ears instead of spanking you on your birthday. You play chess in Russian. In the Chinese Village you may learn the Chinese mountain dance. In the Finnish Village you might learn log rolling or a Finnish stick game.

Two days are set aside, one in July and the other in August, for International Day. Campers from all villages gather to share languages, foods, arts and crafts, songs and dances, and gifts. A New Games Festival is a main event. There are parachutes and a 6-foot earth ball. Everybody wins.

Programs: one week, for ages seven to 11, in French, German, Norwegian, and Spanish; two weeks, for ages eight to 17, for all villages; four weeks, for ages nine and up, in German and Russian.

If you don't have enough money to go, you may be able to get a scholarship through a service club, the PTA, or an ethnic group. Language Villages offer a few scholarships based on need. You may write to them (See page 341).

International Language Villages
Concordia College
Moorhead, MN 56560

FOLKLORICO DANCING

Mexican-American children perform folklorico dancing in California and other places where many Mexican-Americans live. In one dance, the iguana, children imitate a lizard; in another, the quetzal, they imitate a bird with a huge crown of feathers. Sometimes the children move like horses or deer. Each region of Mexico tends to have its own dance style, but all the dances have a Spanish and African background in common.

Mothers and children work on costumes. Ribbons that float in the air decorate the dresses, which are already fancy. Parts of the costumes may have special meanings. An apron, for instance, signals a good cook.

KURDS

The Kurds are a mountain people with their own history, culture, and language. Today Kurds live in four countries of the Middle East. Several thousand have emigrated to the United States.

In the Kurdish kingdom of Media long ago, the kings lived in palaces on top of hills. Around their palaces they had seven gardens built, one inside the other—like onion rings! A wall circled each garden, and each wall was a different color: gold, silver, red, and so on. The gardens were called *pairidaeza*, which means "walled all around." The gardens were so beautiful that the ancient Greeks thought, if there were a place for people's souls to go after death, that place should be as beautiful as those gardens. Our word *paradise* comes from this Greek thought about the Kurdish gardens.

A Kurdish girl (I. C. Vanly, The Kurdish Program)

The word *tulip* means "turban" in the Kurdish language. Because tulip flowers look so much like the big turbans the Kurds wear on their heads, the word became the name of this beautiful flower as well.

The costumes worn by Kurds are very colorful. The cloth they use is covered with wildflower designs. Often the colors don't match, but that's Kurdish. They also make salad from fresh flowers.

Last, but not least, here's a Kurdish children's song.

> *Pomegranate and jam*
> *God let the rain fall*
> *For the sick and the poor*
> *God let the rain fall*
> *Bald head of the spring*
> *O bride of the rain*
> *Pray water the crops*
> *Give us meals of past days.*

PEN PALS

You can be friends with someone who lives in another country without ever leaving your hometown. You can do it by getting into a pen pal program. Several groups will put you in touch with someone your own age in a foreign country. They charge only a small fee. When you write, include a self-addressed, stamped envelope (See page 341).

Student Letter Exchange
308 Second Street, N.W.
Austin, MN 55912

Write for free information. Letters will be in English. You get to choose age (12 and up) and continent: Europe, Africa, Asia, Australia, or the Americas. If you are under 12 but over eight, you can write to someone in the United

States. Sometimes whole classes in school write to pen pals. But you can do it on your own.

World Pen Pals
1690 Como Avenue
St. Paul, MN 55108

"We are the generation of children who have never known peace. We wish to speak to you for the millions of boys and girls who do not want to see more war. . . . Please remember the children everywhere." These are words from a letter written in 1950 by ninth-graders from Minneapolis, Minnesota. They sent it to the president of the United States and to people in the United Nations. The result was World Pen Pals. Today kids from 175 countries all over the world write to kids in the United States.

You should be more than 12 years old to join World Pen Pals. The group will put you in touch with kids from other countries. You can't ask for a spe-

When you write to a foreign pen pal, ask questions about his or her country. (John Wanchik)

cific country. You *can* ask for a boy or girl. However, a girl who asks for a boy pen pal may get a girl instead. Your pen pal will write in English.

TIPS FOR WRITING TO A PEN PAL

1. When a group sends you the name of someone to write to, write first. Don't wait for your new pen pal to write to you.
2. Use clear handwriting, or type. Put your name and complete address on both the letter and the envelope. Spell out the name of your street, city, and state. Include U.S.A. at the end of the address.

3. Before you write, find out where your pen pal lives and something about his or her country. Ask questions about your pen pal's country. However, don't be *too* nosy about his or her life. In some places, people are less ready to tell about their feelings right away. Write about your family, your town, what you like to do. Think hard about what

might be interesting about your life. You can talk about hobbies, sports, pets, games, or something special about your town or state. You might tell what you do on a typical day. Give details. Remember that what seems usual to you may seem unusual to someone in another country.

4. Send your letter by airmail. Otherwise, it can take more than six weeks for your letter to get to your new friend.

5. When you get an answer to your letter, write again right away.

6. Learn some words in your pen pal's language.

7. After you and your pen pal have sent a few letters back and forth, you can send little presents to each other.

8. If you visit your pen pal's country or your pen pal comes to the United States, try to meet face-to-face.

FOLKLORE, PROVERBS, AND RIDDLES

Lore from other countries traveled to America with the immigrants. Here's a sampling. What lore have you learned already?

FOLKLORE

GOOD LUCK AND BAD LUCK

It's bad luck to

□ start anything on Tuesday. (Greek sponge fishermen in Florida)
□ whistle if you are young. (Japan)
□ sweep the floor on New Year's Day. If you do, you sweep out the luck and will have fights all year. (Japan)
□ bring a hoe in the house, drop a book and not step on it, count the stars, rock an empty chair, meet someone left-handed on Tuesday, watch a person move out of sight, spin a chair around on one leg, dream of eating cabbage, sit on a pair of scissors or on a trunk, open an umbrella in the house. (Great Britain)

It's good luck to

□ see a squirrel cross your path, dream of silver money, get white flowers on your birthday, eat peas on New Year's Day, find a cricket on the hearth, look at the new moon over your left shoulder, catch a falling star, make a wish on a white horse. (Great Britain)

If you dream about camels traveling in a single file, it means that angels are coming down from heaven. (Syria)

To scare away witches (*brujas*) and fairylike creatures (*gente de chusma*), make a cross on the wall with mustard. (Mexico)

If your left eye jumps, you are going to laugh. If it's the right one, you are going to cry. (Afro-American)

To get rid of warts, tie a knot in a string for each wart and bury the string under a bridge in a wet spot. Or count the warts and they will disappear. Or cut a notch on a fig tree for each wart and tell no one about it. (Creole)

Sneeze once a day, you'll miss something; twice, you'll get kissed. (Creole)

On Halloween Night cut up two sets of the letters of the alphabet and float them in water. The ones that are face-up in the morning are the initials of the person you will marry. (Great Britain)

Bald-headed babies are the smartest pupils. Step on your books to keep from missing lessons. Sleep with your textbook under your pillow, and you'll know your lessons the next day. If you sing in bed, you'll wet the bed. Bathe a baby in dirty dishwater to keep it healthy, or put a rabbit's foot or bag of sulfur around its neck. If you have chicken pox, a chicken flying over you will cure it. To keep a baby from getting colic, blow smoke on its stomach or give it hot water from a shoe. If you want your crops to grow, run around naked in the field after sowing the seed. (Great Britain)

PROVERBS

SPANISH-AMERICAN

Some people chase the rabbit, and some others come to watch. The ones that run get the fever; the others get the benefit.

BRITISH

Dunghills rise and castles fall.

PENNSYLVANIA DUTCH

Roasted pigeons will not fly in one's mouth.

NORWEGIAN

From children and drunks, one will hear the truth.
Necessity makes the devil eat flies.

YIDDISH

It is fated.

Let God care for the morrow.

Better a blow from a wise man than a kiss from a fool.

One fool can ask more questions than ten wise men can answer.

When a fool throws a stone into the garden, ten wise men cannot get it out.

Better the child cry than the father.

There is no such thing as a bad mother.

GULLAH (Southern coastal dialect)

A good run is better than a bad stand.

Every grin teeth don't mean laugh.

Every shut eye don't mean sleep.

RIDDLES

MEXICAN

And it is
And it isn't
What is it?
Thread.

PENNSYLVANIA DUTCH

What kind of stones do you usually find in the water? Wet ones.

POLISH

Why does the dog wag the tail? Because the tail can't wag the dog.

SOME WORDS FROM OTHER LANGUAGES IN AMERICAN ENGLISH

AFRICAN banjo, goober, gumbo, jukebox, juke joint, voodoo

CHINESE chop suey, chow mein

DUTCH boss, coleslaw, cookie, dope, Santa Claus, sleigh, stoop, waffle

ESKIMO malamute, mukluk, parka

GERMAN delicatessen, frankfurter, nix, pretzel, sauerkraut, semester, zweiback

HAWAIIAN hula, ukulele

JAPANESE kudzu, tycoon

SPANISH avocado, bonanza, pueblo, sombrero, stampede, vamoose

ETHNIC THINGS TO DO

One of the best ways to find out about people is to do the things they do. Ethnic groups in America still practice cooking, crafts, dances, arts, and sports that they enjoyed in the old country. We have chosen a few ethnic activities for you to try. Remember that each group has many others. For instance, Japanese activities also include flower arranging, kite making and flying, practicing karate, and more. You can find other activities in books in the library. A good book is by Phyllis and Noel Fiarotta, *The You and Me Heritage Tree: Children's Crafts from 21 Traditions* (New York: Workman Publishing Company, 1976).

YOGA (INDIA)

Yoga, a Hindu discipline, is very old. It is meant to benefit the mind as well as the body.

BREATHING   "Life is in the breath; therefore, he who only half breathes, half lives," according to a yogi proverb. When you breathe in, don't pull in your stomach. Stick it out instead. This gives you more oxygen. Breathe through your nose. It filters out dust and dirt.

NECK ROLL   Let your neck go limp. Pretend you are a rag doll. Roll your head from side to side.

DEEP RELAXATION   Lie on your back on the floor, eyes shut, hands at your sides. Breathe slowly. Allow your muscles to go limp. This is a good exercise for going to sleep easily.

COBRA POSE   Lie face down with your feet together, forehead on floor and hands under your chest. Breathe in and raise your head and chest while keeping your stomach on the floor. This exercise makes you feel fearless.

WORRY BEADS (GREECE)

When the Greeks are worried, they calm themselves by flipping or counting their worry beads. To make some, here's what you need.

15 to 25 beads about the size of a pea
one larger bead about the size of a
small cherry (optional)
a sturdy piece of leather or cotton
string about a foot long

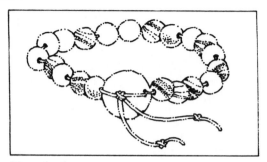

Worry beads

Thread the beads on the string. Then tie the string ends together in a knot, leaving about an inch of string ends and some space between the beads and the knot. Tie this knot around the large bead, if you use it. Tie an additional knot near each string end.

Think of fancy ways to flip the beads. Find something to worry about!

SEVEN STONES (EGYPT)

This game was remembered by Nabil Saad Rageh, recorded by Carol El-Shaleb, and appears courtesy of the Wiliam G. Abdalah Memorial Library.

Divide players into two teams. The field is a diamond with four bases. Stack up seven stones at Base C. Team One stands behind this base. Team Two comes up to bat. One player from Team Two stands at Base A and throws the ball at the seven stones, trying to scatter them as widely as possible. Once the player has thrown, he tries to run around the bases before Team One has picked up all the stones and stacked them again. Once the stones are stacked, the players on Team One try to tag the runner out by throwing the ball at him and hitting him while he is off base. Once he reaches a base, he is safe. If he gets all the way around to Base A, he scores a home run. It

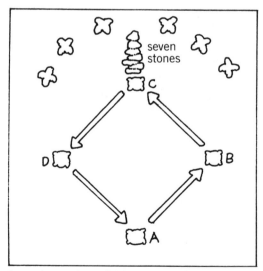

Seven Stones (x = fielder)

counts one point. The next batter is up. After three outs, Team One comes up to bat. Agree on the number of innings before you start playing.

CHOPSTICKS (ORIENT)

The Chinese, Japanese, and Vietnamese often eat their food with chopsticks instead of forks. The practice began in China, and the Japanese adopted it almost 2,000 years ago.

Use the thin ends of chopsticks to pick up your food. It is impolite to point with chopsticks.

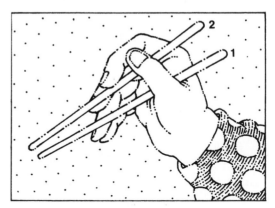

How to hold a set of chopsticks

THE BASIC MOVES

1. Hold a chopstick in the hollow between your thumb and first finger, palm up. Rest the thinner end of the chopstick against your fourth finger. This stick remains rigid.
2. Rest the second chopstick against your first and second fingers and hold it with your thumb. The two thin ends of the chopsticks should meet.
3. Move the second chopstick back and forth, like a bird's beak. Your first and second fingers do the guiding. The first stick remains rigid, remember!
4. Now try to eat some peas.

WALTZING (AUSTRIA)

The waltz was once considered a naughty dance. This was because the partners danced so close together. You need waltz music, which has three beats to the measure. The boy and girl face each other. The boy holds the girl's right hand with his left hand. He puts his right hand at her waist. She puts her left hand on his right shoulder. Each move of the step is made to a beat of the music, starting out on the first beat, which is the strongest.

THE STEP FOR BOYS

1. Stand with feet together. Now take a step straight ahead with your left foot.
2. With your right foot, take a step out to the right, ending up with your feet about a foot apart.
3. Now bring your left foot up next to your right.
4. Take a step backward with your right foot.

5. With your left foot take a step backward to the left, ending with your feet about a foot apart.
6. Now bring your right foot up next to your left.
7. Repeat 1–6.

THE STEP FOR GIRLS

It's the same, but start out with the right foot and move backward when the boy moves forward and forward when the boy moves backward.

SAND PAINTING (NATIVE AMERICANS)

Native Americans of the Southwest use sand painting in ceremonies and in helping people get well. A Navaho medicine man, for instance, makes a circle 10 to 12 feet in diameter. Then he "paints" with sand colored white, blue, yellow, black, and red. The painting may be of Mother Earth, Father Sky, Dawn Boy, Sun and Moon, Dontso the Fly, or some other power or creature. The medicine man chants as he works. He touches the picture first and then the sick person. This way he transfers powers from the one represented in the painting to the sick person.

Here are some things you need to make a sand painting of your own.

1. Fabric dye in some of the following colors: white, blue, yellow, black, and red (Native Americans used crushed flowers and charcoal to make their dyes.)
2. Clean fine white sand
3. Dye pots (Plastic ice-cream containers are good.)
4. Old newspapers

Dye the sand, following the directions on the fabric dye box. Dry on the newspapers.

Make an outline of a design or work freehand. The sun and moon, a thunderbird, a geometric star—these are all good design ideas. Take a handful of sand and trickle it in the outline.

PRESSED FLOWERS (IRELAND)

Place flowers, weeds, and grass between two sheets of wax paper and press them in a book. Be sure it is heavily weighted on top and allow at least two weeks for it to sit. Cover pieces of cardboard with colored paper, arrange your pressed beauties, glue them down, and cover with plastic wrap.

EASTER EGG (EASTERN EUROPE)

Using a pin, make a little hole in the more pointed end of an uncooked egg. Then make a bigger hole in the more rounded end. Holding the egg over a dish, blow out the inside, with the small hole to your mouth. Without using soap, rinse off the egg. Let it dry.

Using a light-colored crayon, draw lines, like belts, around the egg. Make zigzags between the lines. Add other designs, like dots, snowflakes, stars, or flowers. Write *Wesolego Allelujah* (Polish for "Happy Easter"). Paint in the spaces with Easter egg dye or red and yellow food coloring. Add some black ink for accent. Let dry. (Thanks to Irene Piotrowski of United Polish Women of America.)

The Ukrainians decorate Easter eggs the same way the Poles do and call them pysanky. *(Ukrainian Museum)*

CRÊPES (FRANCE)

1 cup milk
2 tablespoons butter
3 beaten eggs
½ cup flour
½ teaspoon salt
1 teaspoon baking powder

Heat milk and butter in saucepan. Let cool a bit, then beat in eggs, flour, salt, baking powder. Beat until it is smooth, like paste. Let the batter stand *at least* 1 hour. Grease and heat a 4-5-inch skillet. Pour in batter in a thin layer to coat the bottom of the pan. Tilt the pan to make sure the batter covers the bottom. Cook 1 minute. Loosen and turn over the crêpe to brown the other side. Eat with butter and sugar or jam.

Thanks to Eugenia Poulin, R.S.M., and Dr. Claire Quintal, *The French Experience in America*, produced by the Rochambeau Education Committee and the Rhode Island Heritage Commission.

TACOS (MEXICO)

tortillas (package)

jar of salsa

YOUR CHOICE OF THE FOLLOWING
    INGREDIENTS

can of refried beans, heated up

hamburger, cooked

olives, sliced

jack cheese, shredded

tomato, cut up small

lettuce, shredded

avocado, mashed (Peel the avocado, take
    out the pit, put the flesh in a bowl,
    and mash it with a fork.)

anything else that suits your fancy

Heat tortillas one at a time in a dry skillet,
on both sides, so you can bend them easily.
Now fill them with whatever you choose.
Put the filling in the middle of the tortilla.
Fold the unfilled sides over the filling.

HAIKU (JAPAN)

A haiku is a poem without rhyme. It
can be about anything. It has three
lines. The first has five syllables, the
second seven syllables, and the third
five syllables. Here is an example.

Petals fall slowly
Into the shimmering pool
I follow them down.

Try writing a haiku verse.

PITA BREAD SANDWICHES
(GREECE AND MIDDLE EAST)

1 package pita bread

YOUR CHOICE OF THE FOLLOWING
    INGREDIENTS

hummus (a spread made with chick-
    peas)

tomato, chopped up

cheese, cut up or shredded

green onions, chopped

cucumber, chopped

and anything else that strikes your fancy

Put a combination of fillings inside the pita
bread "pocket." Eat.

T'AI CHI CH'UAN (CHINA)

T'ai Chi Ch'uan, T'ai Chi for short, is a martial art, a physical and mental discipline. In China and other parts of the Orient, many people do T'ai Chi every day, even when they are very old.

Doing T'ai Chi in China (R. Brook Madigan)

Here is a basic move from T'ai Chi. It is called the Golden Rooster. Lift your right leg in front of you, knee bent. Raise your right arm over your right leg at the same time. It's as if the arm is pulling the leg up with an unseen string. Breathe in as your leg rises. Drop your elbow a bit. Relax the knee a bit too. Bring your arm and leg down. Do the same thing with your left leg and arm.

Usually, many moves are strung together to make a harmonious, dance-like sequence.

BLUES CHORDS (AFRICA)

The blues, a black American song style, has roots in Africa. Blues chords sound different from those in standard popular music. Try playing them on a piano or other instrument. You could even use them to make up a song. Blues songs are ordinarily sad. Often they are about broken hearts.

LIMBO (WEST INDIES)

You need a long pole, some West Indian music, and any number of players for this dance game. To begin, hold the pole crossways at the eye level of the tallest player. The dancing players pass under the pole in single file. Each bends over backward to keep from hitting the pole. Every time the line goes under the pole, lower it a bit. If a player fails to pass under the pole without hitting it, he's out. The winner is the last one left.

ETHNIC QUESTIONS

Can one American be more "American" than another? When people come here from foreign countries, they have choices about how "American" they will become. One choice is to hold on to the old ways as much as possible. People who make this choice tend to live with other people from the old country. Instead of Big Macs and Cokes, they eat the food from the old country. English remains their second language, if they learn to speak it at all. Another choice is to become as "American" as possible. Some immigrants reject their former land. It's like cutting off part of themselves. Children often become "American" faster than their parents. This makes for a gap between the two generations. Still another choice is to try to hold on to the old ways *and* learn new ways. Which is best? What does it mean to be "American" anyway? Is it more "American" to eat with a fork than with chopsticks? Does that question have an answer?

Should foreign-born students be taught in their native language as well as in English? On the yes side, they will learn more quickly this way. They won't have the double burden of learning subjects *and* a new language at the same time. After a while, their English will become good. Then they will move into classes with the other children. On the no side, classes like this hold up the progress of foreign-born children. They will learn English more quickly in English-speaking classes. The language of the United States *is* English. It's not fair to students to pretend that it isn't.

How many foreigners should be allowed into the United States to become citizens? Some people think that too many foreigners are bad for the country. We have too many people already, they claim. Besides, they add, foreigners take away jobs from people who were born here. They are afraid that the country will lose its American character if too many immigrants come in. Other people think that new people bring in new and valuable ideas. The United States, they say, is a big country with lots of room. As for jobs, foreigners will do, for less money, jobs that Americans born here don't want. (But is *that* fair?) How open should our borders be?

3
LISTS

20 STAPLES ON THE GROCERY LIST FOR THE SAN DIEGO ZOO

The San Diego Zoo in California is one of the world's best zoos. More than 3,200 animals live there. It takes a lot of food to feed all of the animals. The cost to buy the food is more than $520,000 a year. Here is just part of a year's grocery list.

1. 715,000 crickets
2. 390,000 tiny mealworms
3. 65,268 tomatoes
4. 62,640 pounds of mackerel
5. 62,240 pounds of sweet potatoes
6. 61,250 pounds of jumbo carrots
7. 56,680 mice
8. 49,320 heads of lettuce
9. 45,240 pounds of bananas
10. 24,480 papayas
11. 14,520 ears of corn
12. 13,500 pounds of Dog Chow
13. 10,800 pounds of rolled barley
14. 5,764 dozen eggs
15. 3,450 pounds of giant sunflower seeds
16. 2,825 pounds of spanish peanuts
17. 2,265 bushels of apples
18. 1,720 pounds of Cat Chow
19. 410 tons of hay
20. 240 pounds of yogurt

See page 215 if you'd like to adopt one of the zoo's animals, and page 288 if you'd like to visit.

Every day, hundreds of pounds of food are fed to the animals at the San Diego Zoo. (Ron Garrison)

THE 15 MOST POPULAR ICE-CREAM FLAVORS

Here, in order of popularity, are the 15 top-ranking ice-cream flavors, according to the International Ice Cream Association. Note: Tin Roof Sundae and Cherry are tied for tenth place. Praline Pecan and Heavenly Hash are tied for 13th place.

1. Vanilla
2. Chocolate
3. Neapolitan
4. Vanilla Fudge
5. Cookies 'n' Cream
6. Butter Pecan
7. Chocolate Chip
8. Strawberry
9. Rocky Road
10. Tin Roof Sundae
10. Cherry
12. French Vanilla
13. Praline Pecan
13. Heavenly Hash
15. Chocolate Almond

Vanilla is the most popular ice-cream flavor in the United States. (John Wanchik)

25 NAMES FOR GROUPS OF ANIMALS

When we talk about a group of geese, we call the group a gaggle of geese.

Here are some other names for groups of animals.

1. colony of ants
2. sloth of bears
3. swarm of bees
4. clutter of cats
5. brood of chickens
6. bed of clams
7. murder of crows
8. brace of ducks
9. gang of elks

10. school of fish
11. skulk of foxes
12. troop of kangaroos
13. litter of kittens
14. leap of leopards
15. pride of lions
16. plague of locusts
17. watch of nightingales
18. company of parrots
19. string of ponies
20. nest of rabbits
21. crush of rhinoceroses
22. pod of seals

These kids are riding on a string of ponies. (R. Brook Madigan)

23. flock of sheep
24. knot of toads
25. pack of wolves

12 FAMOUS BOY SCOUTS

1. Henry "Hank" Aaron, baseball player
2. Neil Armstrong, astronaut
3. Gerald Ford, United States president
4. John Glenn, United States senator
5. Bruce Jenner, Olympic decathlon winner
6. John F. Kennedy, United States president
7. John Ritter, actor
8. Alan Shepard, astronaut
9. Steven Spielberg, film director
10. Mark Spitz, Olympic swimmer
11. Peter Ueberroth, commissioner of baseball
12. Hershel Walker, football player

Gerald Ford, former president of the United States, is also a former Boy Scout. (Boy Scouts of America)

Do you know who was the Chief Scout of the World? Find out on pages 149–155.

15 FAMOUS GIRL SCOUTS

1. Lucille Ball, actress
2. Geraldine Ferraro, congresswoman and first woman candidate for U.S. vice president
3. Carrie Fisher, actress
4. Peggy Fleming, Olympic ice skater
5. Dorothy Hamill, Olympic ice skater
6. Mary Tyler Moore, actress
7. Pat Nixon, First Lady
8. Sandra Day O'Connor, justice, United States Supreme Court
9. Debbie Reynolds, actress
10. Cathy Rigby, Olympic gymnast
11. Gloria Steinem, author and feminist
12. Dr. Kathy Sullivan, astronaut
13. Marlo Thomas, actress
14. Cheryl Tiegs, model
15. Barbara Walters, TV commentator

Actress and singer Debbie Reynolds is one of the most famous Girl Scouts. (Girl Scouts of the U.S.A.)

Do you know who was the Best Girl Scout of Them All? Find out on pages 147–149.

PRESENTS FROM THE HEART: 17 GIFTS THAT COST NOTHING—OR NOT VERY MUCH

1. With a certificate, offer yourself as someone's slave for a day.
2. Make up a book of coupons, each coupon promising something: breakfast in bed, giving the dog a bath, baby-sitting, mowing the

lawn, for example. (Don't promise what you already owe. That is, if it is your job to take out the trash, don't promise that.)

3. Get a picture of someone's favorite TV star free by writing to the program. You can call the local TV station to get the address.

4. Call a radio station and ask for someone's favorite song to be played. Have his or her name mentioned. Make sure the person is around to hear it. You might want to tape it.

5. Paint a picture. Adults love art by children.

6. Write a poem about the person. Put it in a balloon and mail it. Tell the person to blow up the balloon and pop it to find the poem.

7. Write your own messages for custom fortune cookies.

8. Build a homemade kite.

9. For a birthday or other occasion, make a poster and tape it on a door—or on the refrigerator! Or make a banner and hang it across a room on string.

10. Make a cake. Use animal crackers, little candies like M & M's, nuts, and other goodies to decorate it. Write a message on a little piece of paper and attach it, like a flag, to a straw. Stick it in the cake.

11. String popcorn for the Christmas tree or to drape like crepe paper. Let the popcorn get stale before you string it.

12. For a different kind of birthday poster, take a favorite snapshot to your camera store, where it can be blown up to poster size. The snapshot could be a picture of the birthday person. Be sure to ask at the camera store how much the poster will cost.

13. Order pencils with someone's name on them at a stationery store or through the mail. You need to get these in advance. You can also buy balloons, rubber stamps, and bookplates with names on them.

14. Save up a lot of pennies and wrap them in a fancy way.

15. Make a penny tree. Put pennies in little cloth bags and hang them all over a tree branch in a pot.

16. Give candy bars in a fancy box.

17. Pick out a pet, like a goldfish.

HOMEMADE WRAPPING

For wrapping paper, use the Sunday comics, maps, aluminum foil, or napkins. Or use your computer to make paper with a repeat message.

Instead of a box, use a cardboard tube wrapped with paper to look like a firecracker. Or put a little gift in a big box, add something (like a few pennies) that will rattle, then wrap.

If you want, you can decorate a big paper bag, put the gift in, and tie the bag with bright string or ribbon.

More people live in China than in any other country in the world. This street scene in Shanghai, one of China's biggest cities, is typical. (R. Brook Madigan)

THE WORLD'S 20 MOST POPULOUS COUNTRIES IN 1986

1.	China	1,050,000,000	7. Japan	121,500,000
2.	India	785,000,000	8. Nigeria	105,400,000
3.	USSR	280,000,000	9. Bangladesh	104,100,000
4.	United States	241,000,000	10. Pakistan	101,900,000
5.	Indonesia	168,400,000	11. Mexico	81,700,000
6.	Brazil	143,300,000	12. Vietnam	62,000,000

13. West Germany	60,700,000	17. France	55,400,000
14. Philippines	58,100,000	18. Thailand	52,800,000
15. Italy	57,200,000	19. Turkey	52,300,000
16. United Kingdom	56,600,000	20. Egypt	50,500,000

THE TOP 15 KINDS OF RESTAURANTS

A group called the National Restaurant Association made a list of the most popular kinds of restaurants in the United States. Look what kind placed first! Is your favorite on the list?

1. Pizza
2. Hamburger
3. Ice cream
4. Oriental
5. Family style
6. Mexican
7. Café
8. Chicken
9. Fish/seafood
10. Steak
11. Barbecue
12. Doughnut
13. Italian
14. Delicatessen
15. Sandwich

20 FRIGHTENING PHOBIAS

A phobia is a fear of one special thing. Scientists have named more than 700 phobias. Here are 20 of them.

PHOBIA	FEAR OF
1. acrophobia	heights
2. ailurophobia	cats
3. apiphobia	bees

If you are afraid of this cat, you have ailurophobia. *(Ming Chen)*

PHOBIA	FEAR OF
4. arachibutyrophobia	peanut butter sticking to the roof of the mouth
5. botanophobia	plants
6. ceraunophobia	thunder
7. chromophobia	certain colors
8. claustrophobia	enclosed places
9. clinophobia	going to bed
10. dentophobia	dentists
11. gephydrophobia	crossing bridges
12. linophobia	string
13. noctiphobia	night and darkness
14. photophobia	bright lights
15. pyrophobia	fire
16. topophobia	performing (stage fright)
17. triskaidekaphobia	13 people around a table
18. verbophobia	words
19. xenophobia	strangers
20. zoophobia	animals

THE 10 SPACES THAT PLAYERS LAND ON THE MOST WHILE PLAYING THE "MONOPOLY" BOARD GAME

The MONOPOLY board game is a favorite in the United States. It is sold by Parker Brothers. Which spaces do players land on the most? A teacher at Iowa State University once asked his computer to answer that question. Here is what the computer figured out. Illinois Avenue came in first.

1. Illinois Avenue
2. Go
3. B. & O. Railroad
4. Free Parking
5. Tennessee Avenue
6. New York Avenue
7. Reading Railroad

8. St. James Place
9. Water Works
10. Pennsylvania Railroad

See page 180 to find out how often families play MONOPOLY.

Do you know which space on the MONOPOLY board players land on most? (© 1935, 1985 Parker Brothers, Division of Kenner Parker Toys Inc.)

THE 15 MOST POPULAR FUN ACTIVITIES

The United States Bureau of the Census asked thousands of Americans, 12 years and older, what they like to do in their spare time. Here, in order of popularity, are the top 15 activities.

1. Swimming
2. Walking for pleasure
3. Visiting zoos, fairs, or amusement parks
4. Driving for pleasure
5. Picnicking
6. Sightseeing
7. Attending sports events
8. Fishing
9. Bicycling
10. Boating
11. Running or jogging
12. Attending concerts, plays, or other events
13. Camping
14. Playing in outdoor team sports
15. Playing tennis

Visiting a zoo is a favorite fun thing to do in the United States. (St. Louis Zoological Park)

THE 10 MOST COMMON LAST NAMES IN THE UNITED STATES

(Are they in the order you would have guessed?)

1. Smith
2. Johnson
3. Williams
4. Brown
5. Jones
6. Miller
7. Davis
8. Wilson
9. Anderson
10. Taylor

30 FAMOUS LEFT-HANDED PEOPLE

1. Earl Anthony, bowler
2. Dan Aykroyd, comedian
3. Robert Blake, actor
4. Bill Bradley, United States senator
5. Carol Burnett, comedienne
6. Prince Charles, heir to the British throne
7. Jimmy Connors, tennis player
8. Leonardo da Vinci, artist
9. John Dillinger, bank robber
10. Albert Einstein, physicist
11. Gerald Ford, 38th president of the United States
12. Dorothy Hamill, Olympic ice skater
13. Goldie Hawn, actress
14. Isaac Hayes, composer
15. Jack the Ripper, murderer
16. Sandy Koufax, baseball pitcher
17. Paul McCartney, singer and composer

Albert Einstein, one of the world's most famous scientists, was left-handed. (National Portrait Gallery, Smithsonian Institution)

18. John McEnroe, tennis player
19. Kristy McNichol, actress
20. Michelangelo, artist
21. Marilyn Monroe, actress
22. Pelé, soccer player
23. Pablo Picasso, artist
24. Richard Pryor, comedian
25. Robert Redford, actor and director
26. Don Rickles, comedian

27. Babe Ruth, baseball player
28. Wally Schirra, astronaut
29. Mark Spitz, Olympic swimmer
30. Casey Stengel, baseball manager

Did you know there's a club just for left-handed people? See page 134 for details.

30 THINGS AND
HOW LONG THEY LAST

How long do things last before they have to be replaced? Here is a list of 30 things and the average life of each. Remember, the time given is an average. You will have many of these things in your home. Some of them may last longer than the times given here; some of them may not last so long.

1. Automatic washing machines — 8 years
2. Baseball gloves — 10 years
3. Bathing suits — 2 years
4. Bathroom scales — 10 years
5. Bathroom towels — 2 years
6. Bicycles — 10 years
7. Boys' shoes — 1 year
8. Calculators — 10 years
9. Children's coats — 2 years
10. Children's underwear — 1 year

This boy's baseball glove should last for about 10 years. (John Wanchik)

11.	Dishwashers	10 years	21.	Pocket knives	20 years
12.	Earrings	5 years	22.	Refrigerators	15 years
13.	Electric stoves	6 years	23.	Sewing machines	20 years
14.	Eyeglasses	5 years	24.	Socks	1 year
15.	Hair dryers	10 years	25.	Steam irons	7 years
16.	Ironing boards	15 years	26.	Stereo sets	10 years
17.	Ladders	20 years	27.	Suitcases	20 years
18.	Mirrors	20 years	28.	Toasters	10 years
19.	Paint job inside a house	5 years	29.	Tuxedos	5 years
20.	Pianos	25 years	30.	TV sets (color)	12 years

THE NUMBER OF TELEPHONES IN EACH OF 15 COUNTRIES

The United States has more telephones than any other country in the world. Here are 15 countries chosen at random and the number of telephones in use in each country in 1984.

1.	United States	182,558,000
2.	Japan	58,000,000
3.	France	29,370,000
4.	Italy	21,680,000
5.	Canada	16,200,000
6.	Australia	7,400,000
7.	Mexico	5,410,000
8.	China	5,150,000
9.	India	2,600,000
10.	Israel	1,302,000
11.	Iraq	500,000
12.	Kenya	216,000

13.	Paraguay	64,000
14.	Madagascar	38,000
15.	Honduras	33,000

40 NAMES AND WHAT THEY MEAN

GIRLS' NAMES

1. Alice — truth
2. Barbara — mysterious stranger
3. Beulah — she who will be married
4. Bridget — mighty and strong
5. Carol — joyous song
6. Cynthia — moon goddess
7. Dorothy — God's gift
8. Holly — good luck
9. Iris — rainbow
10. Jennifer — fair lady
11. Linda — beautiful
12. Margaret — pearl
13. Maxine — the greatest
14. Melissa — honey bee
15. Natalie — child of Christmas
16. Philippa — lover of horses
17. Regina — queen
18. Sarah — princess
19. Vanessa — butterfly
20. Violet — shy

BOYS' NAMES

1. Adam — man of red earth
2. Arnold — strong as an eagle
3. Boris — fighter
4. Calvin — bald
5. Cameron — twisted nose
6. Duke — leader
7. Elmer — famous
8. Eric — kingly
9. Garrett — mighty spear
10. George — farmer
11. Jethro — outstanding
12. Kenneth — handsome
13. Merle — blackbird
14. Montgomery — mountain hunter
15. Murray — sailor
16. Neal — champion
17. Ronald — mighty ruler
18. Sherwin — fast runner
19. Warren — game warden
20. Wayne — wagon maker

This boy's name means "kingly." Can you guess what his name is? (John Wanchik)

Before he became a famous singer, Elvis Presley once worked as a truck driver. (A & C Archives)

25 FORMER JOBS OF 25 FAMOUS PEOPLE

1. Desi Arnaz, bandleader and comedian — birdcage cleaner
2. Robert Baden-Powell, founder of Boy Scouts — spy
3. Warren Beatty, actor — bricklayer's helper
4. Richard Boone, actor — truck driver
5. Carol Burnett, comedienne — hatcheck girl
6. Glenn Campbell, singer — cotton picker
7. Johnny Carson, comedian — magician
8. John Chancellor, TV newscaster — hospital orderly
9. Sean Connery, actor — coffin polisher
10. Bill Cosby, comedian — shoe salesman
11. Howard Cosell, sports announcer — lawyer
12. Clint Eastwood, actor — gas-station attendant
13. Clark Gable, actor — lumberjack
14. James Garner, actor — gas-station attendant
15. Adolf Hitler, dictator — artist
16. Dustin Hoffman, actor — toy demonstrator
17. Bob Hope, comedian — boxer
18. Walter Matthau, actor — boxing instructor
19. Bob Newhart, comedian — accountant
20. Patricia Nixon, First Lady — telephone operator
21. Elvis Presley, singer — truck driver
22. Robert Redford, actor and director — oil-field worker
23. Babe Ruth, baseball player — bartender
24. Barbra Streisand, singer — theater usher
25. Lily Tomlin, comedienne — waitress

Kids from all over the country compete in the Scripps Howard National Spelling Bee. (Greg Smith)

12 WINNING WORDS IN THE SCRIPPS HOWARD NATIONAL SPELLING BEE

Every year kids from all over the United States go to Washington, D.C., to compete in the Scripps Howard National Spelling Bee sponsored by newspapers across the country. To learn more about the contest, turn to page 130. Here are some of the words kids have spelled to win in Washington.

1. acquiesced   agreed to something without arguing
2. condominium   an apartment that you can own in a building or a town house you can own on shared land
3. croissant   a crescent-shaped roll
4. hydrophyte   a plant that lives in a wet environment
5. incisor   a tooth used for cutting
6. luge   a sled for one person that is ridden by lying on the back
7. narcolepsy   a condition that makes a person fall suddenly into a brief deep sleep
8. onerous   burdensome
9. propylaeum   an entrance to a temple or group of buildings
10. psoriasis   a skin disease
11. sarcophagus   a stone coffin
12. shalloon   a lightweight wool material used for the linings of coats

18 NOISE LEVELS

Sounds, or noises, are measured in decibels. The louder the noise, the higher the number of decibels. Sounds over 85 decibels, heard over a long period of time, can hurt the human ear and even cause permanent hearing loss. Here are some decibel levels to expect, many in our everyday lives.

DECIBELS

1. Rustling leaves — 20
2. Whispering — 25
3. Normal conversation — 60
4. Riding in a car — 70
5. Minibike — 80
6. Standing in a factory — 85
7. Electric shaver — 85
8. Screaming child — 90
9. Passing motorcycle — 90
10. Diesel truck — 100
11. Jackhammer — 100
12. Power lawn mower — 105
13. Sandblasting — 110
14. Live rock music — 90–130
15. Air raid siren — 130
16. Gunshot — 140
17. Jet engine — 140
18. Rocket launching pad — 180

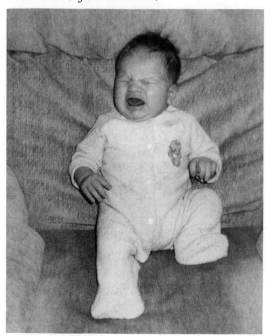

The noise level of this crying baby is high—90 decibels. (Sylvia Zebrowski)

12 FAMOUS SPORTS QUOTES

1. "When the going gets tough, the tough get going."—Knute Rockne, football coach

2. "The game isn't over till it's over."—Yogi Berra, baseball player

3. "I am the greatest."—Muhammad Ali, boxing champion

4. "I keep both eyes on my man. The basket hasn't moved on me yet."—Julius Erving, basketball player

5. "Pro football is like nuclear warfare. There are no winners, only survivors."—Frank Gifford, football player

6. "A ball player's got to be kept hungry to become a big-leaguer. That's why no boy from a rich family ever made the big leagues."—Joe DiMaggio, baseball player

7. "Winning is not the most important thing: it's the only thing."—Vince Lombardi, football coach

8. "The bigger they come, the harder they fall."—Bob Fitzsimmons, boxing champion

9. "Nice guys finish last."—Leo Durocher, baseball manager

10. "My greatest strength is that I have no weaknesses."—John McEnroe, tennis player

11. "For when the One Great Scorer comes to write against your name,/He marks—not that you won or lost—but how you played the game."—Grantland Rice, sports writer

12. "If we win the national championship, so what? It sounds cornball, but that's the way I feel. . . . My best team will be the one that produces the best doctors, lawyers, fathers, and citizens, not necessarily the one with the best record. Let's keep it in context."—Joe Paterno, college football coach

Muhammad Ali, one of the greatest boxing champions of all time (A & C Archives)

25 ANIMALS AND HOW LONG THEY LIVE

(ON THE AVERAGE)

1. Beaver	5 years	
2. Camel	12 years	
3. Cat	11 years	
4. Chicken	7 years	
5. Chimpanzee	20 years	
6. Chipmunk	6 years	
7. Cow	11 years	
8. Dog	11 years	
9. Duck	10 years	
10. Elephant	35 years	
11. Fox	9 years	
12. Giraffe	10 years	
13. Goat	12 years	
14. Gorilla	20 years	20. Mouse — 3 years
15. Guinea pig	3 years	21. Pig — 10 years
16. Hamster	2 years	22. Rabbit — 7 years
17. Horse	22 years	23. Sea lion — 12 years
18. Kangaroo	7 years	24. Squirrel — 10 years
19. Lion	12 years	25. Tiger — 16 years

Elephants usually live about 35 years. (R. Brook Madigan)

12 REAL NAMES OF 12 REAL PEOPLE

Crazy as it seems, these names are real. They belong to real people who live all over the world.

From: John Train, *Remarkable Names of Real People* (New York: Clarkson N. Potter, Inc., 1977).

1. Mac Aroni
2. Doctor Doctor
3. Bathsheva Finkelstein
4. Heidi Yum-Yum Gluck
5. O. Hell
6. Memory Lane

7. Major Minor
8. A. Moron

9. Luscious Pea
10. Cardinal Sin

11. Frank N. Stein
12. Cigar Stubbs

25 PER CAPITA INCOMES AROUND THE WORLD

How rich and how poor are people in different countries around the world? Calculating yearly per capita income is one way of judging. You take all the money earned in one country in one year and divide that number by how many people live in the country. The answer is the yearly per capita income. Not every person in a country gets that exact amount of money. Some people get more; some people get less. The money amounts listed are averages, in United States dollars. The figures are those for the year 1986, and the countries were chosen at random.

14.	Israel	$ 5,609
15.	USSR	$ 2,600
16.	Mexico	$ 1,800
17.	Cuba	$ 1,590
18.	Egypt	$ 686
19.	China	$ 566
20.	Vietnam	$ 189
21.	India	$ 150
22.	Bangladesh	$ 119
23.	Cambodia	$ 100
24.	Chad	$ 88
25.	Laos	$ 85

1.	Qatar	$35,000
2.	Sweden	$14,821
3.	Switzerland	$14,408
4.	United States	$13,451
5.	Canada	$13,000
6.	Denmark	$12,956
7.	Norway	$12,432
8.	Saudi Arabia	$11,500
9.	Japan	$10,266
10.	West Germany	$ 9,450
11.	Iceland	$ 9,000
12.	Australia	$ 8,280
13.	France	$ 7,179

These children live in India, one of the poorest countries in the world. (R. Brook Madigan)

Samuel Langhorne Clemens is the real name of the famous writer Mark Twain. (National Portrait Gallery, Smithsonian Institution)

25 REAL NAMES OF 25 FAMOUS PEOPLE

1. Allen Stewart Konigsberg	Woody Allen, actor and writer
2. Dianne Belmont	Lucille Ball, actress
3. Robert Segal	Robbie Benson, actor
4. Henry McCarty	Billy the Kid, outlaw
5. David Robert Jones	David Bowie, singer
6. George Alan O'Dowd	Boy George, singer
7. Martha Jane Burke	Calamity Jane, frontier woman
8. Cherilyn Sarkesian	Cher, singer and actress
9. Jacob Cohen	Rodney Dangerfield, comedian
10. Henry John Deutschendorf, Jr.	John Denver, singer
11. Issur Danielovitch	Kirk Douglas, actor
12. James Baumgarner	James Garner, actor
13. Ehrich Weiss	Harry Houdini, magician
14. Arnold Dorsey	Engelbert Humperdinck, singer
15. Reginald Kenneth Dwight	Elton John, singer
16. Joseph Levitch	Jerry Lewis, comedian
17. Madonna Louise Ciccone	Madonna, singer
18. Edson Arantes do Nascimento	Pelé, soccer player
19. Prince Roger Nelson	Prince, singer
20. Theodor Seuss Geisel	Dr. Seuss, author
21. LaDonna Andrea Gaines	Donna Summers, singer

22. Annie Mae Bullock   Tina Turner, singer
23. Samuel Langhorne Clemens   Mark Twain, author
24. Marion Morrison   John Wayne, actor
25. Steveland Judkins   Stevie Wonder, singer

SPEEDS OF 12 LAND ANIMALS

MILES PER HOUR (MPH)

1. Cheetah   70
2. Lion   50
3. Quarter horse 47.5
4. Coyote   43
5. Rabbit   35
6. Cat   30
7. Human being   27.89
8. Elephant   25
9. Squirrel   12
10. Pig   11
11. Spider   1.17
12. Garden snail   .03

The cheetah, the world's fastest land animal, can run at 70 mph. (San Diego Wild Animal Park)

Some birds can move much faster. The fastest-moving bird is the peregrine falcon, which can swoop down at 217 mph. The slowest-flying bird, the American woodcock, moves at 5 mph.

4
SPORTS, GAMES, TOYS, CAMP, AND CLUBS

YOUNG CHAMPIONS

Many of the world's best athletes are kids. Many champion skiers, tennis players, figure skaters, and swimmers were only a few years old when they began practicing their sports. And some gifted young athletes have set sports records or established "firsts" before they hit their teens. Here's a list of some of the youngest athletes and their notable feats.

ABLA ADEL KHAIRI became the youngest woman ever to swim the English Channel, at age 13 in 1974. It took her 12 hours and 13 minutes.

MARKUS HOOPER, however, was the youngest person ever to swim the English Channel. He did it at age 12 in 1979.

BILL BOLAND became the youngest jockey to win the Kentucky Derby, at age 16 in 1950. He rode Middleground to victory.

FRANK WOOTEN was the youngest recorded jockey ever to race, at age nine. A South African, he was an English champion jockey from 1909 to 1912.

RICHARD JOHN KNECHT did 25,222 sit-ups at age eight in 1972. It took him 11 hours and 14 minutes.

KAREN YVETTE MUIR became the youngest person to break a world record, at age 12 in 1975. She broke the record for the women's 100-meter backstroke with a time of 1 minute, 8.7 seconds.

A kid-built rocket blasts off! For rocket clubs to join, see pages 135–136. (Estes Industries)

When she was 11, Metha Brorsen became the youngest person to win a world rodeo title. (International Professional Rodeo Association)

HORACE RAWLINS became the youngest player ever to win the U.S. Open Golf Tournament, at age 19 in 1895.

JENNIFER AMYX became the youngest person ever to finish a marathon, at age five in 1975. She ran the Johnstown, Pennsylvania, marathon in 4 hours, 56 minutes, and 35 seconds.

HAL COHEN set a record with 598 straight basketball free throws, at age 17 in 1975. It took him approximately 90 minutes.

JOE NUXHALL became the youngest player ever to play with a major league baseball team, at age 15 in 1944. A left-handed pitcher, he played for the Cincinnati Reds.

RAMON FONST won an Olympic gold medal in fencing for Cuba, at age 17 in 1900.

EDOARDO MANGIAROTTI of Italy, another fencer, also was 17 when he won two Olympic gold medals in 1936.

NADIA COMANECI became the first Olympic gymnast to be awarded a 10—a perfect score—at age 14 in 1976. She received seven perfect scores overall at the Montreal Olympics.

METHA BRORSEN became the youngest person to win a world rodeo title, at age 11 in 1975. She won the cowgirls' barrel racing event in International Rodeo Association competition.

SHANE GOULD broke every women's freestyle swimming record from 100 to 1,500 meters before she was 16. She grew up in Australia and retired in 1973.

MARJORIE GESTRING became the young best woman ever to win an Olympic gold medal, at age 13 in 1936. She won the women's springboard diving event.

JOY FOSTER became the youngest person to win an international competition, at age eight in 1958. From Jamaica, she won the singles and mixed doubles table tennis championship.

BORIS BECKER won his first Wimbledon tennis championship, at age 17 in 1985. From West Germany, he won again in 1986 at age 18.

CHARLOTTE "LOTTIE" DOD, however, was the youngest Wimbledon tennis champion. She won at age 15 in 1887, and again the next year, and three times in a row—in 1891, 1892, and 1893.

TRACY AUSTIN became the youngest pro tennis tournament winner in 1977. She had turned 14 one month before her victory in the Avon Futures of Portland Tournament.

AARON KRICKSTEIN became the youngest winner of a men's Grand Prix tennis tournament when he won the Israel Tennis Center Classic in Tel Aviv, at age 16 in 1983.

23 WAYS TO KEEP FROM GETTING HURT

1. Do stretching exercises at the beginning and end of exercise. Don't bounce. Stretch your muscles slowly. Feel them loosen. Stop before they hurt.
2. If you play on a team, get in shape a couple of months before the season starts. Talk to the coach about ways of exercising to do this.
3. Don't play sports when you are sick. Your illness can become worse. You can also pass it on to other team members. A person who plays when sick is *not* a hero.
4. Don't play sports when you are too tired.
5. Don't play when you are hurt. Don't tape up an injury and play anyway. Watch out for these signs of injury:
   bleeding
   inability to think straight
   passing out
   numbness
   change in looks of a body part
   a joint that wobbles
   sound of ripping or tearing when you are hurt
   swelling
   pain
   limited movement of a joint
   Tell the coach that you are hurt. See a doctor if your injury is serious.
6. The only safe treatment for injury (before you see a doctor) is ICE.

Stretching before you exercise helps prevent injuries. (R. Brook Madigan)

Be careful on playground equipment. (St. Louis Zoological Park)

That means I for ice, C for compression, and E for elevation. Put the injured part above the level of your heart. Place a wet cloth or elastic bandage on it. Put a plastic bag of crushed ice on top of *that*. Wrap it all in a bandage. Leave on for 25 or 30 minutes.

7. Don't take drugs meant to make you play better. In fact, don't take drugs at all unless a doctor prescribes them for you.

8. Play with, and against, kids who are like you in skill and size.

9. Try not to play "like the big guys." That is, don't be violent. Avoid butting heads in football. It's not legal anyway.

10. Always wear the gear recommended for a sport when you play it. Make sure it fits right and doesn't need fixing. Wear it the way it is meant to be worn. If you are a boy, wear a jock strap when you play sports.

11. Take care of your feet. Wear clean socks without holes. Make sure your shoes fit.

12. Keep clean to avoid skin problems. Shower often. Keep your sports clothes washed.

13. Clip your fingernails short. Long fingernails can cause eye injuries.

14. Never wear jewelry of any kind when playing sports. It can catch on things, and you may be hurt. This includes rings and watches, not just necklaces, bracelets, earrings, and pins.

15. Check the playing field and take away anything that players can fall over. Kids can get hurt stumbling over bikes and lawn mowers, for instance.

16. Run with your feet turned in, not out.

17. To avoid Little League elbow, don't throw curve balls or too many fast balls. Follow through after releasing the ball. Don't pitch when your arm is tired. Ask to be taken out if each pitch makes your arm hurt.

18. To avoid other "overuse" injuries like tennis elbow or swimmer's shoulder, use proper motions and rest when it hurts.

19. Use sunscreen lotion if you are spending time in the sun. Be careful to choose a screen with a number high enough to protect you. Make sure it contains PABA (para-amino-benzoic-acid). Apply the screen again every 2 or 3 hours. If you are not used to the sun, stay

out in it no more than 15 to 20 minutes the first day. Add 15 to 20 minutes' more time in the sun the next day and the next. Build up slowly.

20. Use polarized sunglasses to avoid sunburned eyes. Wear sunglasses when fishing to keep from getting a hook in your eye.

21. Don't swim in a thunderstorm.

22. To keep from having heat stroke or heat exhaustion, dress in light clothes. Wear a hat. Drink plenty of water. Don't overdo.

23. Ride your bicycle on the right-hand side of the road. Pay attention to traffic lights and stop signs. Wear a bicycle clip or rubber band to keep your pants leg from catching in the gears.

KID LORE

Kids have their own special lore. Lore includes sayings, beliefs, and customs. It can vary by region.

HIDE-AND-SEEK   What do *you* say when it's time for all players to come in?

Bee, bee, bumblebee,
Everybody come in free.
Allie, allie in come free.
Allie, allie oxen free.
Allie, allie in-fan-tree.

BASEBALL   Some kids say if you hit the trademark with the ball, the bat will crack. This is not true.

SIGNALS   Kids call "times" with crossed fingers. This can mean, "Please stop the game so I can get a drink." It can also mean, "I have called a bigger kid a name and don't want trouble."

Kids who want to claim something say "dibbs" or "dubbs on it" or "I hock it" or "sooks."

GOOD LUCK   (not guaranteed)
Find a penny dated the year you were born.
Put a penny in your shoe.
See a rainbow.
Cross your fingers and make a wish when you see a mail carrier or a red truck.
Cross your fingers until you see a dog.
When riding through a tunnel in a car, ask the driver to honk. Then raise your right hand and make a wish.

KID DAYS   On Toesday kids stamp on one another's toes. If a kid walks with toes in the air, it's not fair to stamp on them.

On Weddingsday if a boy touches a girl they will get married.

WHO WILL YOU MARRY?   Ask a girl the

names of four cars, four colors, four boys, four dates, etc. Write them down in order in a set of boxes, as shown. Then ask her at what age she'll marry. If she says 21, for instance, count off 21 squares and cross off the 21st. Count across the squares, left to right, and skip squares once they're crossed out. Keep doing it until one item is left in each category to tell the story. For instance, she will drive a Pinto, marry Joe, wear a lavender wedding dress, and get married in 2020. Boys can change the choices and play too.

Pinto	Mustang	Cadillac	Mercedes
Tom	Bill	Joe	Fred
Blue	Red	Yellow	Lavender
1990	1995	2001	2020

MARBLES

Here are some classic marble games that kids like to play.

POTS Make a circle on the ground. Each player puts the marbles he or she wants to bet inside the circle. Each player shoots in turn. He keeps all the marbles he can hit with his marble from outside the circle. If his marble stays in the circle, he gets another turn.

BOMBSIES Play like Pots, but drop the marbles from above. Each player gets one shot each turn.

MARBLE SHOE Pitch marbles at a shoe. The first player to get a marble inside the shoe gets one marble from each of the other players. Then the game starts over.

LINE The shooter tries to make his marble stop as close to a line as he can without touching the line. Marbles that touch don't count. The one who comes closest each round gets to keep all the other marbles played in that turn.

Here is some classic marble jargon that kids like to use.

If you call "spans" before someone else says "no spans," you can move your marble a hand's length closer to the target.

The shooter may be about to make a fudgie—or maybe not. (R. Brook Madigan)

"Bombs" gives you the right to a drop shot.
When you call "changies," you can change one marble for another.
"Fudgies" are mistakes.

"Cages" means you claim the right to backstop with your hand.
"Slippants" is what you say when your finger slips.

JUMP ROPE RHYMES

Gypsy, gypsy, please tell me
What my husband's first initial will be.
A, B, C, D, E . . .

Grace, Grace, dressed in lace,
Went upstairs to powder her face.
How many boxes did it take?
One, two, three, four . . .

Mama, Mama, I am sick,
Call the doctor, quick, quick, quick.
How many pills must I take?
One, two, three, four . . .

Alice, where are you going?
"Upstairs to take a bath."
Alice with legs like toothpicks
And a neck like a giraffe.
Alice in the bathtub,
Alice pulled the plug;
Oh, my goodness, oh, my soul,
There goes Alice down the hole.

Bubble gum, bubble gum, chew and blow (Blow bubble.)
Bubble gum, bubble gum, scrape your toe (Drag toe.)
Bubble gum, bubble gum, tastes so sweet
Get that bubble gum off your feet (Slap bottom of shoes.)

The Jackson Five went to France
To teach the children how to dance,
A heel and a toe and around you go,
A heel and a toe and around I go,
Salute to the captain, bow to the king,
Turn your back on the ugly old queen.

Can you make up a jump rope rhyme for these two girls? (John Wanchik)

MAKING WIND TOYS

PAPER AIRPLANE   You make this plane by folding. Once you have finished it, you can test it and change the angle of the folds to make it fly in different ways.

1. You need tape and a piece of stiff paper 8½ x 11 inches in size. A piece of thick typewriter paper will do.

A finished paper airplane

2. Fold the paper in half lengthwise and then open it out again with the inside of the fold up.
3. Pull the upper corners of the paper forward and down until they touch the fold line and form triangles. Fold in place.
4. Flip the paper over. Pull the outside folds of the triangle forward and down until they line up on the middle fold line. Fold in place.
5. Again, pull the outside folds forward and down until they line up on the middle fold line. Fold in place, but let these last folds pop up to be the wings.
6. All the folds, except the last for the wings, become the plane's body. Tape them together.
7. To fly the plane, hold it by its body at the middle and push.

PINWHEEL   This is an old toy.

1. You need a pin and a square piece of paper at least 6 inches on each side.
2. Draw diagonal lines from each paper corner to the one across, through the center. Measure 3½ inches in on the line from each corner and then cut to that point. Fold each corner tip to the center. Overlap the tips. Catch and hold the tips with a straight pin stuck through the center.
3. Blow on the pinwheel. It should turn.

4. With the point of the straight pin, put the pinwheel on a stick or on your hat or on the fence!

Pinwheel design (United States Patent Office)

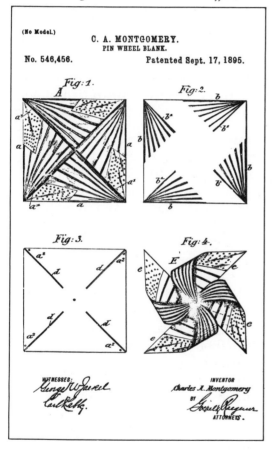

PARACHUTE

1. You need a square handkerchief or piece of thin plastic, some string, and a weight, like a key.
2. To each of the four corners of the square, attach a piece of string at least as long as one side of the square. Knot the strings together. Tie your weight to the knot.
3. Put the weight in the center of the handkerchief and throw the whole thing straight up in the air. It should drift back to the ground. If it falls too fast, use something lighter as the weight.

BULLROARER This is an old toy that grown-ups hate and kids love.

1. You need a piece of cardboard 2 by 8 inches. Twist the cardboard slightly by taking the 2-inch ends, one in each hand, and twisting the ends in opposite directions, one toward you and the other away from you.
2. Put a hole in one end, tie a string through it, and swing the bullroarer around your head. It should make a weird noise.

THE STORIES BEHIND TOYS

There was a time when children had only things such as gourds, animal bones, and rocks for toys. They used gourds as rattles, bones for dice, and rocks as balls. But, by several thousand years ago, kids did have real toys. For

Barbie® and Ken® in 1987 (Mattel, Inc.)

instance, kids in old Egypt had balls, pull toys, rattles, and tops. And kids in old Greece played with yo-yos. Cards, kites, dominoes, and balloons were first used in Asia and are very old.

The earliest dolls used as toys have been found in ruins of ancient Rome. One wooden doll wore bracelets and had legs that could move. Another was made of rags, maybe by a child.

In the American colonies in the 1600s kids played with wooden dolls, animals, and carts. Pioneer children had rag dolls and cornhusk dolls. They built toy log cabins from corn cobs. Native Americans invented the cradle gym: Native American women hung wooden hoops and other objects over babies' cribs to keep them happy.

About 75 years ago American kids were playing with sleds (Flexible Flyers), building blocks, clay, games like Fish Pond, magic tricks, toy stoves, and toy tool chests.

TEDDY BEARS   Theodore (Teddy) Roosevelt was president of the United States. While hunting in Mississippi in 1902, he saw a bear but didn't shoot it. Many newspaper cartoons featured this. Morris Michtom, who owned a toy shop, saw one of these cartoons. It gave him an idea. He made a toy brown bear with legs that moved. Its name? Teddy's Bear. He asked Roosevelt if he could use his name—Teddy. Roosevelt agreed. By 1906 there were many, many teddy bears. Michtom went on to start the Ideal Toy Corporation.

BARBIE DOLLS   Barbie is about 30 years old—no teenager, even though she looks like one. In 1959 Ruth Handler saw her little girl Barbie playing with teenage dolls. Barbie liked them better than baby dolls. She dreamed of being like them, of being queen of the prom. Most teenage dolls at the time were paper dolls. Mrs. Handler thought a solid teenage doll would be popular. She and her husband, Elliott, talked about it, and he agreed. They made the doll in their garage and named her after their daughter. Clothes for the doll even had little zippers.

Some people said Barbie would never sell, that kids liked baby dolls. But, as we know, they were wrong. Barbie, all 11½ inches of her, *was* popular. And she was no baby. In the first eight years of Barbie's life, more than $500 million worth of Barbie dolls were sold. Two million people joined Barbie Fan Clubs. Soon the Handlers were making other dolls—Barbie's family and friends. Ken was named after the Handlers' son. Then there were Skipper, Stacey, Midge, and Francie.

Through the years Barbie has become rich with stuff: playhouses, campers, patios, wardrobes, tents. In 1986 she started her own rock band that plays on a Hot Rockin' Stage. The stage has dressing rooms. The band members have frizzy hair. Barbie is lead singer, of course. She has four backup singers, including her boyfriend, Derek. Ken is not in the band. They travel in a Rocker van with a tape recorder and mike. A four-song tape comes with each Rocker doll. One song is "Dressin' Up."

LIONEL TRAINS   Born in New York in 1880, Joshua Lionel Cowen liked to tinker. When he was seven, he made a model train of wood. Then he tried to fit it with a steam engine. The engine blew up and ruined the kitchen wallpaper. That was the last that Joshua played with trains for a while.

Later, he put a battery inside a tube with a light bulb at the end. He used it in a flower pot to light up the plant. He gave the rights to it to someone else. The tube became the Eveready flashlight.

Finally Cowen went back to trains. By then he was quite grown-up. His first train was a model railroad flatcar with a motor. He sold it for $6 with 30 feet of track. Soon there were other cars. Cowen named his company Lionel. By 1903 Lionel was selling an electric trolley, a derrick motor car, and a locomotive. By 1910 there were train engines, coach and Pullman cars, gondolas, cattle cars, boxcars, cabooses, coal cars, oil cars, and baggage cars.

There were tunnels and train stations to go with the trains.

Today Lionel trains even have cars loaded with tiny milk cans and logs. Telephone poles stand at the edge of the tracks. Signalmen come out of houses and wave flags.

MATCHBOX CARS   In 1952 a hot-selling toy was a model of a royal coach. It was just like the one Elizabeth II of England rode in on her way to be crowned queen. It was only 5 inches long. The company that made it sold a million in one year. Soon they were making other things: cement mixers, dump trucks, and road rollers. The toys were packaged in boxes used for wooden matches. They sold all over the world.

Matchbox models are very precise. The tires, for instance, have tiny treads. The company always has 75 models—ambulances, pony trailers, beach buggies (You name it).

SILLY PUTTY   In 1945 General Electric workers were trying to make some-

The Lionel Rail Blazer includes a saddle-tank locomotive, a boxcar, a flatcar, and a crane. (© 1988 Lionel Trains, Inc.)

How long will the hula hoop keep spinning?
(Wham-O)

thing that could replace rubber. One of them, James Wright, dropped boric acid into a test tube of silicone oil. The result bounced. Adults liked to play with it. It bounced better than a rubber ball. It stretched. If stretched too hard, it snapped. If pressed against a newspaper, it would "pick up" print.

A shop for kids called the Block Shop started selling the stuff under the name Silly Putty. It outsold everything but crayons. Pete Hodgson bought the rights to sell it. He packed it in plastic eggs so that he could ship it in egg cartons. Soon kids were buying Silly Putty.

There was a problem though. It got into kids' hair and clothes. It got stuck in rugs. And once there, it stayed. In 1960 Hodgson brought out a nonsticky Silly Putty.

The astronauts on *Apollo 8* were given Silly Putty in silver eggshells. Pete Hodgson called Silly Putty the "toy with one moving part." The same company made Moonshine. It was like Silly Putty, but it was green and glowed in the dark.

HULA HOOPS   Australia is the home of the Hula Hoop. A toy company named Wham-O brought it to the United States. In the late 1950s Hula Hoops were crazily popular. Wham-O made 2,000 a day, but they were not enough. All over the United States, people were spinning hoops around their middles. One champion could spin 14 at once. Then suddenly the craze was over. Nobody wanted Hula Hoops anymore. In 1965 Wham-O tried a new kind of Hula Hoop—the Shoop Shoop Hula Hoop. It had ball bearings inside.

COOTIES   In the late 1940s Herb Schaper was doodling ideas for fishing lures. He got an idea for a plastic bug to take apart and put together. His first bug looked fierce. Later bugs were tamer looking. The bugs became Cooties, and Cootie became a game. When players throw a certain number on a die, they can add parts to their Cooties. The first to finish his or her Cootie wins.

LEGOS   Danish carpenter Ole Kirk-Christiansen lived in a poor village of potato farmers. To make a living, he began making handmade toys and selling them door-to-door. He did pretty well. His four sons went into business with him. Soon they were selling a big selection—300 animals, dolls, and other toys.

One day Godtfred, the third son, talked to a shopkeeper who said that most toys had no purpose. Godtfred saw he was right. He went back to the factory and thought about it overnight. While building a house with some plastic building blocks, it came to him: If the blocks could be locked into one another, kids could build fancier things. So Lego was born. The word *Lego* comes from the Danish words for "play well."

With their own kids, the Kirk-Christiansens worked out ideas for Legos, including the knobby surfaces for locking pieces together. The Lego system came out in 1954. It was a big success.

The poor little village is now a rich factory town. One kid who came to visit was disappointed that the factory was not made of Lego bricks. So Godtfred had a city built of Lego bricks. Its 600 buildings are all under 3 feet tall. The city is called Legoland, of course!

TINKERTOYS Charles H. Pajeau first made Tinkertoys in 1914 in Evanston, Illinois. Watching kids play with pencils and empty spools gave him the idea. He made the first Tinkertoys in a rented garage. They didn't sell, so he hired some little people to dress up as Santa's elves and play with the toys in display windows, one in Grand Central Station in New York City and the other in a department store in Chicago. Tinkertoys became popular after that.

ERECTOR SETS Erector sets could be the oldest American building toy. A. C. Gilbert, a pole-vaulting champion, also owned part of a magic company. In 1911, on his way to New York City on the train, he was thinking about making toys. He saw a building going up along the tracks. Presto! The idea for the Erector set. The idea wasn't so easy to carry out. Gilbert made cardboard girders in different sizes and shapes. Then he had someone make them in steel. Finally, everything worked. Gilbert's ad slogan was "Hello, boys! Make lots of toys!" Erector sets do have enough parts for girls as well as boys to make lots of toys. There are girders, bolts, wheels, panels, pulleys, gears, axles, motors. From them you can make a robot or a drawbridge or a moon car.

Look what Tinkertoys have become!

SAND CASTLES

Real stone castles are built to last forever, but sand castles usually last only a day. The tide comes in and licks at their walls. Soon they melt away. That's partly why they are fun to build.

Big sand castles—group projects—can weigh from a ton to tens of thousands of tons. Sometimes tractors are used to pile up the sand. In 1977, 20,000 people built a sand castle that was 12 miles long. At the Canadian Open Sandcastle Competition in White Rock, British Columbia, as many as 200,000 people come to watch. Building sand castles can be big-time. Kids

Marissa shows how to drip an edge on a castle wall. (John P. Edwards)

can carry water on a big sand castle project. Or they can stomp down the sand in a big mold with their bare feet. But projects don't have to be big. Kids can make their own smaller sand castles.

First, find a good place to work, away from crowds and the lifeguard tower. You don't want your castle stomped before it's built. Be sure to pick a flat area for building. Next, find the tide line. At the tide line you will see a line of stuff like seaweed, shells, and junk. The good sand for making castles is between the tide line and the water. Here the sand is firmer. It has been smoothed by the tide. Grab a handful of sand. If it is too dry to hold together, move closer to the water's edge. If water leaks from the sand, move farther away from the water's edge.

DRIP SAND CASTLES   These are easy to make, but you need fine, not coarse, sand. Brown sand with some mud in it is best. To test, take a handful of the *dry* sand on the beach. Hold it, then drop it. If some sand stays on your hand, the sand is probably okay for making drip castles.

Fill a bucket halfway with wettish sand. Take out any little stones, shells, or junk. Add water to make the sand soupy, but not so watery that it is flat on top. Fill the bucket with water the rest of the way. Grab a handful of sand from the bucket. Form your hand into a shape like an ice-cream cone. The sand is the "ice cream." Hold it tight, then loosen your little finger enough to let some sand out. With practice, you can learn to use both hands at once and move your hands in a circle. You can also use a kitchen funnel or a plastic bottle upside down with the bottom cut off. The sand should fall into a shaggy pile. You soon have a castle with some towers taller than others. Other tools: spoons, baster, cake decorating tools, modeling toys.

MOLDED CASTLES   You need cups or other containers that are wide at the top and narrow at the bottom. Paper cups of various sizes are good. So are gelatin molds, buckets, pots, and cans with both ends off. The sand should be wet enough *almost* to run off the edge of a scoop (but not soupy). Pick out shells and other junk. Find or make a flat place on the sand for your castle and pick a spot for the first tower. Pack your tower container and smooth the top. Turn the container over on the smooth place you have picked. Be quick. Hit the ground pretty hard. Now raise the container, slowly and straight up. If the sand doesn't come out, put the container down again and tap it. Keep adding towers and watch your castle grow.

OPEN-MOLDED CASTLES   Hold a board in place like a wall. Pack sand against it. Or put two boards down like two walls, parallel and close together, and pack sand between them. A sloped wall lasts better though. Put molded towers in each corner. Use old teacups to make molded tops for your towers. Decorations? Use cookie cutters and potato mashers. Stretch a string along the wall and cut in to make a *string-course*, a decoration from the Middle Ages, five hundred or more years ago. You can make windows by pushing a square object into the walls.

BRICK CASTLES   You need matchboxes, ice-cube trays, bread pans, or other molds of the same shape. The sand should be fairly hard, like soft clay. Pack the mold. Let it sit for a little while. Now tap it out on a hard, smooth place. Keep making these bricks until you have as many as you think you will need. Make a flat, smooth place to build on. Use a mason's trowel, egg turner, or table knife to lift your bricks and put them in place.

SCULPTED CASTLES   These are harder to make. You need a big pile of sand, packed down hard. Then you carve the castle out of it. It is best to work from the top to the bottom.

These are the basic ways of building sand castles. Of course, you can use all the methods to make one castle, and besides castles you can make other things: monsters, space cities, animals. If you like, use objects from the beach for decoration: shells (monster eyes), seaweed (monster hair), rocks (monster noses).

SUMMER CAMP: HOW TO CHOOSE ONE AND BE HAPPY THERE

Some kids really love camp, while others have an awful time. Choosing the right camp and knowing what to expect and how to prepare for it can make a difference. Here are some guidelines.

DAY CAMP OR RESIDENT CAMP? It's important to choose a camp that suits *you*. If you are young and have never been away from home, you might want to go to a day camp. When you go to day camp, you spend evenings, nights,

Horseback riding at River Way Ranch Camp (River Way Ranch Camp)

and weekends at home. You go back and forth to camp each weekday. Day camps offer sports, arts and crafts, field trips, and other activities.

You *live* at a resident camp. That means you sleep there. A typical stay is one week or two, but at some resident camps you can stay longer—even all summer. Resident camps are for children ages seven to 16.

WHAT KIND OF RESIDENT CAMP? At a *general* resident camp, you try many different sports, crafts, and other activities. At some general camps, you can choose one or two activities you really like. An instructor helps you become more skilled in these. You might choose tennis, for instance. Your instructor might help you with your forehand a couple of hours a day. That way you would learn a basic tennis skill but get a chance to do other things.

At a *specialty* camp you really concentrate on learning the skills of one activity. You spend up to 6 hours learning skills and the rest on other activities. Some examples of specialty camps: baseball, football, sailing, tennis, computer, horseback riding, gymnastics, theater, dance, bicycling, foreign language, weight loss, crafts, music, figure skating, soccer, art, basketball, mountain climbing, science. There are also camps for disabled children and those with other special problems.

Waterskiing at River Way Ranch Camp (River Way Ranch Camp)

QUESTIONS TO ANSWER WHEN CHOOSING A SPECIFIC CAMP Once you have decided on the kind of camp you want, you and your parents can choose a specific one. Answer these questions.

1. How much can we spend? Day camps are cheapest. Resident YMCA or church camps usually don't cost much. Specialty camps cost the most. Find out what you get for the fees. Sometimes camps charge extra for many things, so the cost is higher than it seems.

2. Do I want to go to an all-girl or all-boy or coed camp? If the camp is coed, girls will sleep in all-girl cabins, boys in all-boy cabins.

3. Should the camp be close to home or faraway? If you are afraid of being homesick, it might be wise to be close to home. But if you want to see new and interesting places, a faraway camp could be best for you.

4. What else about location matters to me? If you like the water, you might like to be near a lake or ocean. If you want to climb, a camp in the mountains would be a good choice.

5. What activities are important to me? These can include swimming, field hockey, hiking, squash, animal care, archery, theater, arts and crafts, roller skating, BMX motocross, baseball, lacrosse, aerobics, dance, ceramics, nature study, guitar, soccer, music, sailing, horseback riding, karate, tennis, golf,

fencing, softball, canoeing, photography, computers.

Write down a short description of the camp you want. Here's an example: "General resident camp, no more than $100 a week. Coed. In mountains, no farther away from home than 50 miles. Should offer swimming, computers, guitar."

Now make a list of camps that fit your needs. The American Camping Association (ACA) sells *A Guide to Accredited Camps,* a listing of about 2,200 camps all over the United States. You can get it by writing.

American Camping Association
Bradford Woods
Martinville, IN 46151

They will let you know how much the guide costs. Be sure to enclose a self-addressed, stamped envelope (See page 341). You can also call ACA's toll-free number, 1–800–428–CAMP, to order by credit card. Or use the guide at the public library.

You can write to the association below for *Guide for Selecting a Private Camp.*

Association of Independent Camps
60 Madison Avenue
Suite 1012
New York, NY 10010

Now, for the camps that fit your needs, try to find the answers to another set of questions:

1. Have the teachers taught children before?
2. Is there a doctor on the staff? (This is particularly important for weight-loss camps and camps for children with medical problems.) Is the doctor there most of the time?
3. Is the director of the camp there every day?
4. Does the camp have insurance to protect campers?
5. Is the staff well qualified? Counselors are usually college students age 19 and over. They should have been campers themselves, like children, be patient and kind, and be able to teach skills. There should be one counselor for every seven to ten children. Your counselor sleeps in your tent or bungalow and eats with you.
6. Do campers and counselors tend to come back each year? Talk to people who work at the camps on your list. Talk to people who have been to camp there. If the camp holds an open house, try to go.

APPLYING TO CAMP   You should apply as long as a year but no less than four months before camp starts. You will need to fill out an application giving your name, address, phone number, grade, favorite activities. Applications have a section for parents to fill out. This includes medical questions.

WHAT TO TAKE WITH YOU   Camps usually give you a list of things to bring

Water sports are part of the fun at the Salvation Army's Camp Allegheny. (The Salvation Army)

might even address the envelopes before you go to camp.

WHAT GOES ON AT CAMP?   At camp you make your own bed, clean up the cabin, maybe help in the kitchen or garden from time to time. At most camps there's no TV to watch. Instead, you learn how to light a campfire, pack and carry a knapsack, swim, and find your way in the woods. You get to know trees and wild animals. Some nights you may sleep outside.

A Typical Day

7 A.M.–9 A.M. flag raising, cleanup, breakfast
9 A.M.–12:30 P.M. activities (swimming, arts and crafts, and so on)
12:30 P.M.–2 P.M. lunch and rest
2 P.M.–3 P.M. more activities
3 P.M.–4 P.M. swimming
4 P.M.–6 P.M. free time
6 P.M.–7 P.M. dinner
7 P.M.–9:30 P.M. games, plays, scavenger hunts, campfires, songs, and stories

that can include blankets, sheets, a pillow, pillowcases, flashlight, writing paper, stamps, postcards, pens and pencils, T-shirts, shorts, bathing suit, sweatshirts, jeans or long pants, sweaters, sneakers, tennis shoes, Top-Siders, rain slicker or poncho, hairbrush and comb, jacket, pj's, bathrobe, slippers, socks, underwear, rubber sandals, toothbrush, toothpaste, soap, soap dish.

You might also want to bring insect repellent, sun block lotion, and ChapStick. Books and playing cards, perhaps. *Don't bring* radios, video games, and watches. General camps provide sports equipment. You should bring your own to a specialty camp.

Name labels should be sewn in all your clothes. Otherwise, yours may get mixed up with someone else's in the wash.

Make sure you have addresses for the people you plan to write. You

Often there is a special week or weekend of games involving the whole camp.

It's easy to make friends at camp. After all, you eat, sleep, and play with other kids all day and night long. Some kids like to go to camp with a friend or brother or sister. Often camp leaders let them stay together. But the point is to meet new people.

Many camps have a "buddy system"—you and another camper stick together, watch each other for safety. When the counselor whistles, you grab your buddy by the hand and hold your hands up.

SOME TIPS FOR HAVING A GOOD TIME Get into the camp spirit. That means, get into getting along well with others. Be friendly and nice to shy people. If you are shy, try to talk to one other person.

If you are homesick or unhappy, talk to the counselor or director. Keep busy in camp activities. Go to them all. Write lots of letters home. Don't make your letters too sad. Tell about the good things as well as the bad ones. Give camp a chance.

Try to learn at least one new thing each day.

If people tease you, it doesn't mean they don't like you. Teasing is part of camp. You might get offered candy that is really soap. Somebody might steal your clothes when you are in the shower. (If so, get someone to bring you your clothes or run to your cabin dressed in the shower curtain.) You could find your bed short-sheeted. (To short-sheet a bed, you put on the bottom sheet, then turn it up from the bottom so it looks like the top sheet.) Complain only if the teasing is too much.

Obey the rules. These are some usual ones.

No gum, candy, or bare feet
No swimming except when swimming is scheduled
No talking after lights out

CLUBS AND CONTESTS

Everybody can be good at something, the saying goes. Look at this list of clubs and contests, and you'll believe it. Can't jump rope? Try training a frog!

It may seem to you that no one else is interested in the same things as you. That's almost certainly not true. It may be true that no one in your neighborhood shares your interest though. That's why national clubs exist. They give you a way to talk or write to other people with the same interests. Sometimes you *will* find those people live in your town.

National clubs often do a great deal for members. Some offer big meetings every year, pen pal exchanges, magazines, and newsletters. Look through the list below for a club of people who share your interests. If you don't find one, that doesn't mean there is no such club. Ask your librarian how to look for a club formed around your interest. If you decide to write, be sure to include a self-addressed, stamped envelope (See page 341).

BRAIN GAMES AND CONTESTS

American Checker Federation
3475 Belmont Avenue
Baton Rouge, LA 70808

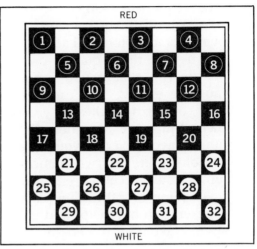

Checkerboard and checkers ready for play to begin

WHAT IT IS National checker tournaments have been held since 1907. The American Checker Federation, begun in 1948, is the official group running national tournaments in the United States now. It also helps sponsor contests by mail and the contest for World Champion. Kids can play through the group's youth program. For advice and materials, write the national youth program director at the address above.

RULES These are the group's official rules of play.

1. The checkerboard should have green- and buff-colored squares. The checkers themselves are red and white. The squares should be numbered on the board, if you are a beginner, so that you can follow the plays.
2. The checkers are placed on the dark (green) squares. Red checkers start on squares number 1 to 12. White checkers start on squares number 21 to 32.
3. Players choose colors by draw. The player with the red checkers has the first move. Players should change colors at each new game to keep the play fair.
4. Play only on the green squares.
5. If you touch a checker, you have to move it. If you move a checker halfway or more across the space, you must make that move.
6. In an *ordinary* move, the checker is moved from its square to one of the neighboring squares on the board. The neighboring square must be empty, and the move must be *forward*. That is, on the board that's pictured, the only red checkers that you can move are 9, 10, 11, and 12. Checker 9 can move only to squares 13 and 14. Checker 10 can move only to squares 14 and 15. And so on. (A checker gets its number from the square it's on.)
7. It's a good idea to move toward the center of the checkerboard in the first part of a game. In general, red's best opening move is 11 to 15. Protect the double corner as long as you can.

8. A *capturing* move is a jump from a green square over a square on which a piece or a king of the other color sits. The square you jump over should be forward and one of the neighboring squares on the board. The square you jump to must be empty. You can't jump over your own checkers. If you can then jump over another of the other player's pieces, you have to do so. If there are two chances to jump, you can choose either one. If you jump over the other player's checker, you have captured it and should take if off the board.

9. All possible jumps must be made.

10. When a checker reaches the row farthest ahead, it becomes a king. Spaces on the king row are 1 to 4 for white and 29 to 32 for red. When a checker makes a move into the king row, that move ends. No further move with the king is possible on that turn. A king is crowned by another checker of the same color. The other player does it.

11. The king can move either backward or forward.

12. You win when all the other player's checkers are off the board or are blocked so they can't move.

The American Checker Federation has fliers giving more detailed rules, tips, and checker problems.

United States Chess Federation
186 Route 9W
New Windsor, NY 12550

WHAT IT IS "Chess Makes Kids Smart" is a slogan coined by the United States Chess Federation. This club is for everyone interested in the game of chess.

HOW TO JOIN Kids can join U.S. Chess. You can join on your own, at any age. Perhaps, however, the best way is through a school program with an adult sponsor. The group offers—free—a *Guide to Scholastic Chess* that tells how to start such a club. Ask an adult who would like to lead your group to write United States Chess Trust to learn more. The trust is part of the federation.

WHAT YOU GET All members get a chess magazine. It lists top players by age group (under eight, nine–ten, eleven–twelve, thirteen–fourteen, and so on) and tells about computer chess, great chess games, and chess meets. It also includes chess lessons. You can join United States Chess without getting the magazine though. That costs less. The group will also rate you for your skill in chess and send free fliers on how to play. There are special prices on chess sets, boards, and clocks.

If you have a school group with an adult sponsor, the group will get *School Mates* newsletter with news about national scholastic championships and other activities. *Pawn & Queen and In Between* teaches kids in grades 3 through 6 about chess. This set of 18 four-page workbooks covers the rules of the game.

ACTIVITIES Any member can play in tournaments. There are two kinds.

Over-the-board tournaments are played face-to-face. United States postal chess is played by mail. Through the magazine, you can find a chess pen pal and play nontournament chess by mail.

MOVES OF THE CHESS PIECES

King moves one square in any direction.

Rook (or Castle) moves along the line of squares up or down, but cannot jump over anything in the way.

Bishop moves the same as the rook, but on the diagonal.

Queen moves like both rook and bishop.

Knight moves two squares up and one across (either way) *or* two squares down and one across (either way) *or* two squares across (either way) and one up *or* two squares across (either way) and one down. It can jump over other pieces.

Pawn moves one square straight ahead and cannot go backward. As an opening move, the pawn can move one or two squares. When capturing another piece, the pawn moves one square along the diagonal.

THE CONTESTS   Each year the United States Chess Federation sponsors national contests. For kids, there are three: (1) National Elementary Chess Championship (kindergarten through grade 6), (2) National Junior High Chess Championship (kindergarten through grade 9), and (3) National High School Championship (kinder-

Chess player Yvonne Krawiec, World Youth Champion, girls under 12 (U.S. Chess Federation)

garten through grade 12). Elementary school children can enter any one of the three.

CONTEST RULES   To enter, you must be in school and in the United States Chess Federation. You are matched with players at your own level. However, you don't play with kids from your school, and you don't play the same kid twice, Everyone plays all the rounds. Each player can win one trophy. There are trophies for good playing and for the best score in your grade and rating.

TIPS FOR YOUR FIRST TOURNAMENT from the United States Chess Federation

1. Don't expect to win every game.
2. Ask for help from the director and other players if you need it.

3. You have to use a chess clock. This gives you a certain amount of thinking time for the whole game. You can use the time any way you want. That is, you can take 1 minute for some moves and 2 minutes for others.

4. You need to write down moves—both yours and your opponent's.

5. You must bring your own equipment. Kings must be between 3 and 4 inches tall.

6. You play all rounds.

7. It's a good idea to know the rules very well.

Scripps Howard National
Spelling Bee
1100 Central Trust Tower
P.O. Box 5380
Cincinnati, OH 45201

WHAT IT IS   The first National Spelling Bee was held in 1925. Now more than eight million students vie to win local contests so they can go to Washington, D.C., for the National Bee each spring.

HOW TO ENTER   You must be sponsored by a newspaper near you. You must not have gone beyond eighth grade at your school finals. You must be under 16 years of age at the start of the national finals.

RULES   In local contests, you may be asked to write words or spell them out loud or both. At the national contest, you must spell words out loud. You can ask that a word be repeated and used in a sentence. You can ask its meaning and what language it comes from. Until there are two kids left in the contest, if you miss a word you're out. Then it goes this way: If one kid misses a word, the second kid gets a chance to spell the word. If he is wrong, the contest goes on. If he is right and can spell the next word right, he wins. If he spells the second word wrong, the first kid gets a chance at it. The official dictionaries are *Webster's Third New International Dictionary* and *9,000 Words: A Supplement to Webster's Third New International Dictionary*. For a list of some winning words, see page 99.

PRIZES   First prize is $1,000. Altogether, more than $10,000 in prizes is given away.

COLLECTING

Ben Franklin Stamp Clubs
United States Postal Service
475 L'Enfant Plaza
Washington, DC 20260

WHAT IT IS   This club of young stamp collectors is named after Benjamin Franklin, who was the first postmaster general of the United States. It began in 1975. More than seven million children and teachers have belonged to a Ben Franklin Stamp Club.

HOW TO JOIN   Many schools and libraries have Ben Franklin Stamp Clubs. The clubs are for students in grades 3 through 7.

WHAT YOU GET   At the beginning of the school year, each club gets a kit with membership cards and a sign-up poster. Newsletters come every other month. Each member receives a *Treasury of Stamps Album.*

ACTIVITIES   Through the club you can trade stamps, go on tours of the post office, and go to local stamp shows and fairs. The main office in Washington, D.C., will lend films to your club. There is also a club-to-club pen pal program.

Junior Philatelists of America
P.O. Box 15329
San Antonio, TX 78212-8529

WHAT IT IS   Philatelists are postage stamp collectors. Collecting stamps is a good way to learn about different places and different times. Junior Philatelists, founded in 1963, is run by and for young people 21 and under. It can help you learn about the hobby.

HOW TO JOIN   You can join the group even if you are a beginner. Junior stamp clubs can join as chapters.

WHAT YOU GET   The group will send

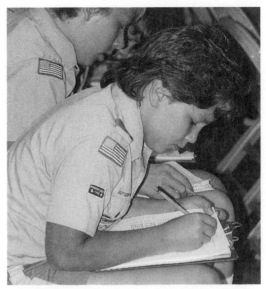

A Boy Scout takes a test in coin collecting at a Merit Badge Clinic. (The American Numismatic Association)

you a free packet of 20 worldwide stamps. All you have to do is send a long ($4^1/8 \times 9^1/2$ inch), self-addressed, stamped envelope (See page 341) and mention *The Macmillan Book of Fascinating Facts.* The club's newsletter has tips, puzzles, a pen pal service, and a stamp exchange with kids from other countries. For example, in the November–December 1986 issue, two kids from the People's Republic of China wrote to start a stamp exchange. Every two or three years a special book of members comes out. It can help you find people near you who have interests like yours. The club also has auctions. In addition, if you have a stamp you can't identify, send it to the above address. The club will send it back to you, telling you what it is.

Children play stamp bingo at the Ameripex '86 exhibition. (Ron Schramm, Ameripex)

NATIONAL MEETING   The American Philatelic Society has events and awards for kids at its yearly stamp show in August.

>   Young Numismatists
>   American Numismatic
>   Association
>   818 North Cascade Avenue
>   Colorado Springs, CO 80903-
>   3279

WHAT IT IS   Have you ever held a coin in your hand and wondered who held it before you? What it bought? If so, you may be a numismatist without knowing it. Numismatists collect coins, paper money, and other tokens. Imagine, a 1947 quarter could once have belonged to your grandmother, a president of the United States, a famous baseball player. It could have paid for apples or computers. Coins have been used for at least 2,500 years. Many old coins are sold for under $1 each. Some ancient Roman coins are priced at under $5.

HOW TO JOIN   To join Young Numismatists you should be 11 years old or more.

WHAT YOU GET   At national meetings the club holds coin auctions just for kids. Some adults give coins for the auction that you can buy at low cost. As a member you get a monthly magazine with a section for kids. The magazine gives 13 awards each year for writing, speaking, and showing coins. The club gives scholarships to the ANA summer seminars at Colorado College in Colorado Springs, Colorado, and kids can borrow books about coins and coin collecting from the ANA library.

ACTIVITIES   You can join the Roman Coin Project through which you can earn Roman, Byzantine, and Greek coins. There are activities through which you can learn about coin collecting. For instance, you can take part in a home-study course or in Boy Scout coin-collecting merit badge clinics held at meetings.

At the Youth Booth of the 1986 annual American Philatelic Society STaMpsHOW, kids learn how to use tongs to handle stamps.(American Philatelic Society)

HORSES

United States Pony Clubs
329 South High Street
West Chester, PA 19382

WHAT IT IS Started in 1929, Pony Clubs are strictly for kids. The name of the group can give you the wrong idea. Although some young members may ride ponies, most Pony Club members ride horses. The riding style is English.

HOW TO JOIN You do not need to own a horse. However, you must be able to get one to ride. You also need a helmet approved by United States Pony Clubs, leather boots or shoes with heels, and other proper clothes for riding. Age? It depends on the club, but most accept kids eight and older.

RATINGS As a member, you are rated according to your skill in horseback riding. D1 stands for safe riding at walk and trot. The highest D rating is D3. Kids with this rating can ride at a can-

ter, jump, and do even more. Riders with even more skill are given other ratings.

ACTIVITIES Meetings are held all year. When the weather is not too cold, kids and horses learn several kinds of riding, including sports on horseback. Clubs hold rallies (contests of skill). Some clubs offer camps, trail riding, games, show jumping, and tetrathlon. (Tetrathlon is an event in which kids swim, shoot, run, and ride.) In winter the horses stay in their stalls, and the meetings, held inside, consist of talks and quizzes. All year long kids learn how to take care of horses, first aid included. They also learn the use and care of saddles and other gear.

NATIONAL MEETING Every year, usually in August, the national group holds championships in horseback-riding skills. This is followed by a Pony Club Festival.

JUGGLING

International Jugglers
Association
P.O. Box 29
Kenmore, NY 14217

WHAT IT IS Juggling is a skill that is nearly 4,000 years old. Children as young as three can learn how. If you are taught in the right way, you can learn to juggle three things at once in one lesson. (Enrico Rastelli, who died in 1931, could juggle ten things at once.) This club was started in 1947.

HOW TO JOIN All you need is an interest in juggling. And the fee, of course.

WHAT YOU GET Members get a card showing they are members, *Juggler's World* magazine, an IJA decal, and more.

NATIONAL MEETING The national meeting lasts six days. You can see hundreds of jugglers all juggling at the same time.

Anthony Gatto juggles in Rome, 1985. He was named "The Greatest Juggler in the World" when he was only 11 years old. (Nick Gatto)

LEFT-HANDEDNESS

Lefthanders International®
P.O. Box 8249
Topeka, KS 66608

WHAT IT IS Alexander the Great was left-handed. So is former Beatle Paul McCartney. A list including other famous left-handed people appears on pages 94–95. If you're left-handed, too, you can join this club.

WHAT YOU GET The club will send you a magazine that has a children's pull-out section with stories, puzzles, and other activities. On the "Letters" page you might find a left-handed pen pal. The club also has left-handed stuff you can order by mail, like school supplies (pens, pencils, rulers). Some of the things might surprise you: books on how to play the guitar and do fancy lettering left-handed; left-handed playing cards, scissors, notebooks, and even toothbrushes.

PLANES AND ROCKETS

Academy of Model Aeronautics
1810 Samuel Morse Drive
Reston, VA 22090

WHAT IT IS   Robert "Hoot" Gibson, a space shuttle pilot, has made model planes. So has astronaut Neil Armstrong. So did the Wright brothers. Both kids and adults build model planes. Some become (or are) pilots. The Academy of Model Aeronautics began in 1936. It has 2,000 clubs and 125,000 members, some of them kids. You can get a list of clubs by writing the AMA. From the list, you can choose the club nearest you. Many of these clubs have AMA CUB programs for kids.

WHAT YOU GET   When you join, you get the monthly magazine *Model Aviation*. You can apply for AMA youth scholarships. You have a place to fly your planes and a chance to enter contests.

ACTIVITIES   If you are in an AMA CUB program, you get to build an easy model and learn to fly it. From there, you can go on to build harder models. There are four kinds of models: indoor, free flight, control line, and radio control. Indoor models are very light and only for flying inside. Free Flight (FF) models fly free outdoors. The third kind, Control Line (CL or UKIE), is flown on the end of a wire or string. The last type, Radio Control (RC), is controlled from the ground by a transmitter that sends radio signals to the model. The model has a radio receiver in it. It costs quite a bit of money.

Models can be powered by wind, with rubber-band motors, with fuel engines, with jet or rocket power. They are built from light wood or plastics.

You can enter your plane in an AMA contest. You will be judged on how long the plane stays up, how well it flies, how fast it goes, how far it goes, and so on. Some events are races.

NATIONAL MEETING   Each summer the AMA sponsors the National Model Airplane Championships. They last a week.

National Association of Rocketry
182 Madison Drive, Dept. JB
Elizabeth, PA 15037

Rocketeers are about to launch a parachute rocket. (Estes Industries)

WHAT IT IS If you love rockets and space shots, this may be for you. As a member, you make and fly model rockets.

HOW TO JOIN You may find an NAR club already exists through your school or through Scouting or through 4-H. If not, you need only five members to start your own NAR section.

WHAT YOU GET

1. A monthly magazine, *American Spacemodeling*, with plans, tips, news of contests and sports launches (This is a bit hard for kids to read.)
2. A copy of the United States Model Rocket Sporting Code ("Pink Book") with rules for competitions
3. Chances to win patches and other awards
4. Chances to buy pamphlets, plans, books, transfers, patches

Getting ready to shoot off a rocket (Estes Industries)

5. For second-year members, money off on model rocket and hobby supplies from makers
6. Insurance

ACTIVITIES Members build models of rockets. The newest thing is space modeling, making models of rockets that have gone into space. You can buy easy kits in hobby stores or through the mail. As you become more skilled, you can build models from scratch. Model rocket engines, designed to be safe, are for sale in hobby stores.

Once models are built, your club can meet to try them out. Of course you try to see whose model flies highest. You can also try parachutes or payloads like raw eggs on your rockets. You can have contests to see whose rocket can land closest to a certain spot. Some kids enter their models in science fairs. NAR members can join the NAR-TREK program. This is a way for someone who has already built rockets to learn more. NARTREK is planned so that you work at your own pace.

CONTESTS The NAR sponsors national and international contests. You can set flight records.

NATIONAL MEETING The national meeting is held in August. You can compete in the United States Model Rocket Championships.

INTERNATIONAL CONTEST The World Model Rocket Championships are sponsored by the FAI, the French arm of the group.

PUPPETS

Puppeteers of America, Inc.
Membership Office
#5 Cricklewood Path
Pasadena, CA 91107

WHAT IT IS This national group of people interested in puppets has been around since 1937.

HOW TO JOIN Kids under 15 can be junior members, with all rights except the one to vote.

WHAT YOU GET Members get the *Puppetry Journal*, a book of members, and newsletters. You can rent films and videotapes from the club's audio-visual library. The Puppetry Store sells books, plays, and other things. Clubs hold meetings and festivals.

NATIONAL MEETING The summer festival lasts six days. It includes shows, workshops, and an exchange store.

RACES

Canadian Turtle Derby
P.O. Box 212
Boissevain, Manitoba
Canada R0K 0E0

WHAT IT IS At the Canadian Turtle Derby, very slow animals (turtles, of course) race one another. Their human owners urge them on.

RULES Bring your own turtle or get one at the contest. Be sure yours is at the turtle stable before the race starts. Children's turtle races are included.

WHEN Held every July, the races last three days.

International Frog Derby
Box 383
Rayne, LA 70578

WHAT IT IS Although many other places sponsor frog-jumping contests, Rayne calls itself the Frog Capital of the World. To get into frog jumping, you need a frog. It's the frog who competes, not you. The winning frog is the one who can jump farthest.

WHEN The Annual Frog Festival in Rayne takes place the third weekend in September. If you can't go there, look for a frog-jumping contest in the area where you live.

RULES   Your frog must measure at least 4 inches, nose to tail. No little green tree frogs are allowed. You can use a bullfrog, toad, or spring frog. You cannot feed your frog hot sauce. The frog is allowed 60 seconds to reach the finish line, 20 feet from the starting blocks. Each frog has three jumps, with 15 seconds and no more for each jump. The judges measure how far it is from where the frog starts to where it lands on the third jump. As you can guess, a frog who jumps zigzag doesn't do too well. You cannot jump up and down, shout, blow on the frog, or do anything else to make him jump. And you cannot touch the frog after the first jump.

Mini-Minnow Triathlon and
Fun Races
California Rivers
P.O. Box 1140
Windsor, CA 95492

WHAT IT IS   Kids can enter this contest. It mixes mini-kayaking, a triathlon, and fun races. The triathlon starts with a 4-

Paddling a kayak to win at the Mini-Minnow Triathlon and Fun Races (Ann Dwyer's California Rivers)

mile paddle down the Russian River in mini-kayaks. The racers then run 1½ miles. After that they bicycle 4 miles. If that's too much, try the fun races, like the Marshmallow Race. Or the K-9, with a paddler and a dog. Or the Four Hands—two people, no paddles, and a mini-kayak.

The All-American Soap Box Derby
789 Derby Downs Drive
Akron, OH 44306

HISTORY   One summer day in 1933, three boys were racing wooden cars down a hilly street in Dayton, Ohio. The cars were homemade and had no engines. Myron E. Scott, a photographer for the Dayton *Daily News*, saw the boys. He took their picture and asked if they would like to race for prizes. Of course they said yes. On the next Saturday many boys showed up to race.

The race was a big hit. The photographer called it a soapbox derby because many of the cars were made of boxes used to pack soap. The boys had used other kinds of crates too. Most wheels were borrowed from roller skates. That summer a citywide race was held, complete with parade. There were 362 drivers and 75 prizes. The officials divided the children by the kinds of cars they drove and by age (under 11 and 11 to 16). Newsreels were shown in movie theaters. Soapbox derby racing became popular. The first All-American Soap Box Derby was held in 1934. In 1935 the derby was moved to Akron, Ohio.

Matt Wolfgang won the All-American Soap Box Derby and became world champion in 1982. (All-American Soap Box Derby)

FACTS   Robert Turner from Indiana, who won in 1934, was only 11 years old. His time was 58.4 seconds. He beat Jack Colopy, whose car cost just 55 cents.

Although a girl raced in 1933, girls were not officially allowed to enter the derby until 1971. The first girl to win the derby was 11-year-old Karen Stead of Pennsylvania, in 1975. She raced even though she had hurt her thumb in a water-balloon fight. Her time was 27.52 seconds. In 1986 all three finalists were girls.

The average speed of a soapbox derby racer is 35 mph.

Derby racers believe in luck. To help them win, kids have carried a pet duck, rabbits' feet, four-leaf clovers, baby shoes, a pair of lucky pliers. One nailed a horseshoe to his racer.

One kid got the idea for the shape of his racer from watching a drop of water fall. His car was long at both ends.

For speed, racers have shaved off their hair and greased their bodies. These things are now against the rules.

Harold Zoellner, who raced in the 1940 derby, made the body of his racer from a furnace pipe.

The track in Akron is 953 feet long. It has three lanes, with lines to help drivers stay in the proper lane. Walls on each side are covered with rubber so that kids whose cars go out of control won't get hurt. The track starts off steep, then levels out.

RULES   There are two classes, divided by age. Children nine to 12 can enter in Junior Division. The combined weight of car and driver in Junior Division can be no more than 220 pounds. Kids 11 to 16 can enter in Senior Division. The combined weight of car and driver in Senior Division can be no more than 250 pounds. Kids ages 11 and 12 can race in either division.

The drivers must make their own cars. Kids racing in the Junior Division get help from their parents. They buy a Junior Kit Car from the derby that will give them a start. It contains official

Becky Watson of Salem, Oregon, and her soapbox racer weigh in at the All-American Soap Box Derby. (All-American Soap Box Derby)

axles and patterns for building the car. Kids racing in the Senior Division can build their cars from scratch or with a Senior Kit Car. In some places there are soapbox derby groups that hold clinics in building racers.

Drivers must wear helmets, trousers, shirts, and tennis shoes. Cars must be safe. Drivers must follow rules of good sportsmanship.

The derby holds local races. The winners go to the national meet.

Each kid races two times. The finish is photographed after each race to see how far ahead of the loser the winner was. After the first race, kids exchange lanes. The winner is the kid who has won by the most. Here's an example. John wins the first race by 3 yards, beating Barry. Barry wins the second race by 4 yards, beating John. Barry wins the heat.

Officials at the race use special flags. The checkered flag is waved to show the heat winner. Solid green means the track is clear. Solid red tells you to stop because the track is not clear.

Drivers can win special awards for their car designs and for fastest time in a heat. Winners of races receive prizes like racing clothes and skateboards. The winners in Senior Division get college scholarships.

HOW TO BEGIN   Write to The All-American Soap Box Derby at the national address given at the beginning of this story. Ask for a list of rules and the name of your regional director.

RADIO

Archie Radio Club
The American Radio Relay
League
225 Main Street
Newington, CT 06111

WHAT IT IS   Radio "hams" are people who love fooling around with two-way radio. Certain radio bands are set aside just for their use. They talk by radio only to other hams all over the world. There are one and a half million of them. Hams are not CBers. Hams radio other people from rooms, not trucks.

True hams have enough radio skills to get an Amateur Radio License. You get this from the Federal Communications Commission (FCC) of the United States government. There are five grades. To get the novice (beginner's) license, you need to know how radio works, the United States government rules for hams, and Morse code at five words a minute. The license is free and lasts ten years.

HOW TO JOIN   Boys and girls can join the Archie Radio Club. You need a "rig" (radio equipment). Your rig should have a radio receiver for listening and a transmitter for talking. It should also have an antenna to pick another signal up from the air or send your signal out. You also need a "radio shack" for your radio station. In the early days most people kept their stuff in a real shack or shed in the backyard. Now most keep

it in the house, but the name radio shack has stuck.

WHAT YOU GET   If you join the Archie Radio Club, you get a membership certificate, an Archie Radio Club ID sticker, and a chart of radio bands, to help you find stations. The American Radio Relay League offers books, tapes, and courses to help you study for a license.

ACTIVITIES   Hams are given a call sign that tells where they are located. They also have a personal ID. Hams can link with telephones through Autopatch. And there are also computer-ham radio links. Through a computer Packet Mailbox you can leave a message for a ham who isn't there. A ham satellite called Oscar (Orbiting Satellite Carrying Amateur Radio) transmits messages.

Ham radio operators work out a problem. (David Greer, WE4K)

Hams work with police and other groups to make up plans for disasters like tornadoes and earthquakes. When a disaster happens, hams provide radio networks so the police and other groups can talk to one another. They also provide such networks for walkathons, bikathons, and marathons. For instance, hams help with the New York City Marathon and the torch run for the Olympic Games. They take no pay for this. And hams call other hams, just to talk. Through this hobby you can make friends around the world.

There is also a club for handicapped hams.

Courage HANDIHAM System
Courage Center
3915 Golden Valley Road
Golden Valley, MN 55422

SPORTS

Police Athletic League (PAL)
200 Castelwood Drive
North Palm Beach, FL 33408

WHAT IT IS   In the 1930s one of a gang of kids threw a rock through a window. A cop, Lieutenant Ed W. Flynn, saw it. He liked kids. He wanted to reach them, not punish them. That day he hunted up the head of the gang and asked him what made the kids act up. The head of the gang had an answer. He said that there was nothing to do and no place to play, so the kids got in trouble. Lieutenant Flynn thought about it. And then he did something: He started a baseball team. That was the beginning of the Police Athletic League (PAL). Now PAL includes arts and crafts, dance, music, drama, reading, gardening, field trips, and more. The programs are run by police officers.

HOW TO JOIN   Check in your phone book for the Police Athletic League. Or call the police department.

CONTESTS   PAL has national tournaments in baseball, basketball, boxing, hockey, and girls' softball. They are held at various times of year.

PAL sponsors basketball teams. (National Association of Police Athletic Leagues, Inc.)

Speed Rope Jump Contest
2504 Duncan Road
Bloomer, WI 54724

WHAT IT IS   This contest has been held every year since 1960 in Bloomer, the Jump Rope Capital of the World. The top five boys and girls get to enter the finals. First- and second-place winners get trophies. Other finalists get medals. All who enter get a patch. Age groups are grades 1 and 2, grades 3 and 4, grades 5 and 6, grades 7 and 8, high school, adult. Only two entries are allowed from each school district. Some kids who have entered could jump 54 jumps in 10 seconds.

RULES   The rope must be ¼-inch manila rope. You can't do anything to it to make it heavier. It can have taped ends or handles. No gloves are allowed. You jump for timed 10-second periods. You get two tries. Each pass of the rope under your feet counts one point. The higher count of the two tries is your score. There is no point if the rope catches, but the count goes on from the number of jumps made before the catch.

How many times can you jump in 10 seconds? Without missing, of course! (John Wanchik)

World Junior Frisbee® Disc
Contest
Wham-O, Inc.
835 East El Monte Street
P.O. Box 4
San Gabriel, CA 91778-0004

WHAT IT IS   This contest is sponsored by the makers of the Frisbee and other companies. It is for boys and girls un-

der 16. To get to the regionals, you need to compete at local events. They are run through park and recreation departments. The world finals are held in October.

RULES   Kids are divided into four groups: boys 11 and under, boys 12 to 15, girls 11 and under, girls 12 to 15. At local events all kids who score 15 or more points get to go to the regionals. At the regionals, the top boy and top girl get to go to the finals. You can use most Wham-O Frisbee discs except the

This boy shows one right way to throw a Frisbee. (John Wanchik)

heavy ones. Prizes are United States Savings Bonds.

The events:

1. *Distance Flight* You get five chances. The two best throws are counted for points. You can throw the Frisbee any way you want—overhand, backhand, and so on.
2. *Accuracy* You throw 10, 15, and 20 yards through a target from different angles.
3. *Catching* You try three of each catch: behind the back, between the legs, behind the head, on the finger. You get two points for each good catch. The most you can get for each kind of catch is four points. At the World Finals, the event will be freestyle instead.

Additional events at the World Finals:

1. *Maximum Time Aloft (M.T.A.)* You throw a Frisbee into the air and catch it. Five tries are allowed, with the two best counted. You get points according to how long the Frisbee is in the air.
2. *Disc Golf™* You play nine holes of Disc Golf. The game is played like regular golf, but with a Frisbee rather than a ball and club.
3. *Freestyle* Each person does a 3-minute act with music.

TWINSHIP

International Twins Association
P.O. Box 28611
Providence, RI 02908

WHAT IT IS This group for twins everywhere was begun in 1934. You can join if you are either an identical or a fraternal twin. Identical twins are not exactly the same, but came from the same egg. They are always of the same sex. One of four sets of identical twins are mirror twins. That is, the right side of one is the same as the left side of the other. Fraternal twins came from two eggs. They do not have to be of the same sex. They look no more like each other than any other two kids in the same family. Every year in the United States, 33,000 sets of twins are born. One set in three is identical.

NATIONAL MEETING   The yearly meeting is held on Labor Day weekend. There are prizes for Most Alike Girls, Most Alike Boys, Most Alike Mixed Twins, and for Most Unalike Females, Most Unalike Males, Most Unalike Mixed Twins.

FORMING YOUR OWN CLUB

Why not form your own club? Clubs are fun, even though some don't last very long. Who knows? Maybe your club will really catch on. Read the stories of the founders of two famous worldwide clubs on pages 147–155. And here are some practical tips.

1. Before you get together, decide what kind of club to have. People have had clubs for studying nature, computers, stamp collecting. Make sure there is no other club in town like it. Some clubs are simply secret clubs, not formed around an interest at all.

2. Have a contest for choosing a name and motto for your club. A good name can bring in members. If you have a computer club, for example, a good name might be GIGO Club, for "Garbage In, Garbage Out." You can also have a special password and handshake.

3. Make up an emblem (a kind of picture that tells what your club is about). The Couch Potato Club might

have a potato as an emblem, for example. You can have this made into a rubber stamp. Members can stamp their lunch boxes, notebooks, and hands.

4. Make rules about who can belong. Don't be too choosy. Remember that lots of kids join clubs and drop out. So you need more members at first than you think. Invite your best friends to the first meeting. Those at that meeting are charter members.

Kids meet to plan a club. (John Wanchik)

5. At the first meeting, make up a list of rules for your club. These might include when meetings will be, how many members have to be at a meeting to take a vote, what offices you will have (president, treasurer, and so on), and how long officers will serve.

   Vote on people "just for now" to lead the meeting and to take notes. Decide when your first official meeting will be. Think about good times to have it. You don't want to have a club meeting when too many kids are at baseball practice, for instance.

6. At the next meeting, vote on the rules. Also choose a president, vice-president, secretary, and treasurer. Get members to name people for each office. Remember that the officers should be able to do their jobs. The secretary, for instance, should write well and fast. Hold a secret vote on each officer. Decide how much dues will be. The dues should not be so high that kids can't afford to join. They shouldn't be so low that the club is always short of money.

This is how most people run club meetings.

The president calls the meeting to order.

The secretary calls roll to see who's there.

The secretary reads the minutes (a report of what happened at the last meeting).

The treasurer makes a report on how much money the club has and how much it spent and brought in since the last meeting.

Someone collects dues.

Members of the club discuss and vote on old business (things they have talked about before but haven't decided on).

Members of the club discuss new business.

There is a club activity. (A joke club might have a round of joke telling. Stamp collectors might hold an auction.)

The members decide on when and where to hold the next meeting.

Everyone helps to clean up.

If you want to advertise your club, read the article on advertising on page 372.

The Couch Potato Club can hang this banner when it meets.

THE BEST GIRL SCOUT OF THEM ALL

JULIETTE "DAISY" GORDON LOW (1860–1927), FOUNDER OF GIRL SCOUTS IN AMERICA

THE "UGLY" BABY Although she was named Juliette, almost everyone called her Daisy. Her mother, who had not wanted another child, said Daisy was "ugly as ten bears." Daisy wasn't really ugly. She had a long thin nose, freckles, and light brown hair. Daisy was the second of six Gordon children. They lived in Savannah, Georgia. Although the family was not rich, they had horses, dogs, a cow, and a cat. The children and their cousins, as many as 20 altogether, spent summers with their aunt.

Daisy was a tomboy. Once she had her hair braided with taffy, a kind of sticky candy. Another time she managed to glue her fingers to a soap dish. Daisy liked horseback riding, acting, drawing, and making paper dolls. She never could spell very well. Even so, she liked writing. When she was eight or nine, she wrote a poem called "The Piggy." Here are the first two verses:

I was passing by a pig-stye,
When I heard a piggy say,
I would like to live in Rubbish
Forever and a day.

But his mother she reproved him,
"You're an idle little sot."
Then the Piggy answered rudely,
"Now, you hush up, I'm not."

Daisy was also very loving. She slept with her dolls to keep them warm, and she saved stray animals.

THE HELPFUL HANDS When Daisy was 14, her family sent her to boarding school in Virginia. From there she wrote her mother, "Mama, I can't keep all the rules. . . . I'll keep clear of the big scrapes but the little ones I can't avoid." She stayed in Virginia two years.

At 16 Daisy started a club called Helpful Hands. The members were supposed to make clothes for the children of a poor family, and Daisy was to teach them to sew. There was a prob-

Juliette Gordon Low, founder of the Girl Scouts, and Lord Robert Baden-Powell, founder of the Boy Scouts (Girl Scouts of the U.S.A.)

lem though. Daisy herself didn't know how to sew. The club was nicknamed Helpless Hands.

LITTLE-SHIP-UNDER-FULL-SAIL   Later, Daisy went to a girls' boarding school in New York where the students wore black aprons and were not allowed to speak to boys. In spite of that, Daisy managed to get married, in 1886. Her husband, Willy Low, was rich and Scottish. The marriage didn't last.

She lived in Scotland and England and traveled in Europe, India, and Egypt. People who knew her said she was full of energy. Native Americans had named Daisy's great-grandmother Little-Ship-Under-Full-Sail. There were those who said the name fit Daisy too. In any case, she wasn't much like other women of her time.

From the age of 21 she was deaf, but she didn't let it stop her. She painted, made models. She built a forge and made iron gates herself. Sometimes she wore vegetables in her hats. Her filing system for bills to be paid shows her sense of humor. There were four sections—This Year, Next Year, Some Time, Never.

Daisy loved animals. Her pet mockingbird sat on her shoulder and took her pen away when she tried to write. Her gray parrot, Polly Poons, slept on her chest at night. Blue Bird, her South American macaw, followed her around like a dog.

GIRL SCOUTS   In 1911, when she was about 50 years old, Daisy met Sir Robert Baden-Powell, who started the Boy Scouts. They quickly became friends. Baden-Powell's sister Agnes had worked with the Girl Guides. Daisy started a company of seven Girl Guides in Scotland, out in the country. One of the girls had to walk 6 miles to get to the meetings. At each meeting the girls had tea, learned to make knots, knit, cook, give first aid, read maps, and signal. Later, Daisy began another group of Girl Guides in London, England.

In 1912, back in Savannah, Daisy called a friend and said, "I've got something for the girls of Savannah, and all America, and all the world, and we're going to start it tonight." That "something" became the Girl Scouts of the U.S.A. It began with 18 girls, who at first called themselves Girl Guides. In 1913 the American groups were given the official name of Girl Scouts. They were like the Girl Guides, but not exactly the same. The first uniforms for the Scouts were blue skirts and middy

Girl Scouts studying photography (Girl Scouts of the U.S.A.)

blouses with light blue ties and big black hair ribbons. Because the uniforms tended to get dirty quickly, the color was changed to khaki.

Daisy wanted girls to think big. In her time, people thought a woman bold to plan to be a doctor or pilot. Not Daisy. Girl Scouts earned badges in flying airplanes, farming, and sending telegrams. Daisy also thought girls should know how to live in the wild. She went camping with the Girl Scouts and swam with them in a big bathing suit with bloomers. Around the campfire, she read the girls' palms and told ghost stories. Her uniform included a broad-brimmed hat, a knife, and a tin cup and whistle that hung on her belt.

Daisy once brought Girl Scout honor pins to a meeting in an old tomato can and stood on her head to show off the new Girl Scout shoes she was wearing. Her style shows in the *Girl Scout Handbook,* where she wrote, "Boiling water is useful to dip your sardine into if you want to get his skin off, but do not dip him into the teakettle."

"THE BEST GIRL SCOUT OF THEM ALL"   By 1927 there were more than 150,000 Girl Scouts in the United States. In that year Daisy died. She was buried in her uniform. In its pocket was a message from the National Board of the Girl Scouts. It read, "You are not only the first Girl Scout, but the best Girl Scout of them all."

GIRL SCOUTS TODAY   Now there are nearly three million Girl Scouts. For a list of some famous Scouts, see page 88.

THE CHIEF SCOUT OF THE WORLD

LORD ROBERT BADEN-POWELL (1857–1941), FOUNDER OF THE BOY SCOUTS

LORD "BATHING TOWEL"   When he was a boy, he was nicknamed Stephe because his real name was Stephenson. He had red hair, freckles, and twinkling eyes. His father, a professor at Oxford University in England, died when Stephe was only three years old. He had six brothers and sisters and two stepbrothers. The children's mother took them for walks in the woods. She told them the names of plants and showed them how to watch animals. At the country houses of their uncles, aunts, and grandparents, the children swam, skated, and rode ponies. They looked at the stars through their grandfather's telescope.

At home Stephe made up plays for

Lord Baden-Powell with a chest full of medals
(Boy Scouts of America)

his brother, sister, and himself. He acted the funny parts. With both hands, he drew comic strips, painted, and made kites and model boats. When he was eight, he wrote,

Law's for Me When I Am Old

I will have the poor people to be as rich as we are, and they ought by rights to be as happy as we are, and all who go across the crossings shall give the poor crossing sweepers some money and you ought to thank God for what he has given us. . . .

At 11 Stephe went to school in London. The other boys could never tell if he was serious or joking. He liked to make fun of things, and sometimes of people. He was good at thinking up antics. Here's an example: On Shrove Tuesday in England, people eat pancakes with lemon juice in honor of the holiday. At Stephe's school the students were given the pancakes with two lemon halves. But they didn't eat the lemons; they had a lemon-peel fight instead. For one of the fights, Stephe showed up wrapped in padding from head to foot. Only his twinkling eyes showed. "Let the battle commence!" he shouted.

Stephe was not a good student. In fact, he once placed 19th out of 19. One of his teachers said, "Seems to me to take very little interest in his work." Another said, "Pays not the slightest attention except in one week at the beginning of the quarter." His French teacher reported, "Could do well, but has become very lazy; often sleeps in school." However, Stephe was good as an actor and a goalkeeper in football, an English game different from American football. The other members of his club, the Druids, called him Lord Bathing Towel.

Outside the playing fields was a woods called the Copse. Here Stephe went to be alone. Hiding in trees from his teachers, he pretended to be a trapper or Native American scout. He watched animals—foxes, deer, rabbits, squirrels, rats, and birds. Later he said it was there that he found his soul.

THE WAR HERO   When it came time to go to college, Stephe applied to Oxford, where his father had taught.

Charles Lutwidge Dodgson was a professor of mathematics there. (Under his other name, Lewis Carroll, Dodgson wrote *Alice's Adventures in Wonderland*.) Dodgson found out, as did the other professors, that Stephe knew "little or nothing" about his subject. So Oxford turned him down.

The army *did* accept him. Stephe, now known as B-P, joined the 13th Hussars, a cavalry unit. He served in India and Africa and did well. But it was as the hero of Mafeking that B-P made his name. By then, 1899, he had made colonel. For 217 days his soldiers held off the enemy Boers. Trapped in the town, they made dummy forts to fool the Boers. In sight of the Boers, they put on games and plays to show they weren't worried. In the plays B-P was the clown. One of the other men at the fort started a Mafeking Cadet Corps of boys age nine and up. The boys carried military messages, delivered mail to civilians, worked in the hospital, and acted as lookouts. In the end, the English outlasted the Boers. The siege was over May 17, 1900. B-P came home a hero.

Once home, he wrote a book called *Aids to Scouting* that, though meant for adults, was very popular with kids. Boys and girls wrote to him asking how they could be scouts.

B-P BEGINS THE BOY SCOUTS In 1904 B-P was asked to inspect the annual review of the Boys' Brigade. The Boys' Brigade had been started in 1883 in Scotland by a Sunday school teacher named Smith. B-P saw 7,000 boys drilling with toy guns in front of an audience of 11,000. It looked like an acting out of war. Even though he was a soldier (or maybe because he was), B-P did not like what he saw. He thought the boys should learn to be brave and have a sense of adventure, perhaps like the Mafeking Cadet Corps. It seemed to him they should learn to act on their own, not as a group following orders. So B-P told Smith that he had some ideas that would bring ten times as many boys into the Boys' Brigade. Smith was interested.

In the summer of 1907 B-P and 21 boys camped on Brownsea Island, in Dorset, England. (In those days, usu-

Lord Baden-Powell on the cover of Boys' Life *in 1929 (Boy Scouts of America)*

Sea Scouts at camp in Florida decipher a map. (Boy Scouts of America)

ally the only people who camped were soldiers or explorers or hunters traveling overseas.) The boys were from different walks of life. Each came to camp knowing three knots, as B-P had requested: reef knot, sheet bend, and clove hitch. Under a flagpole flying the British flag, the Scouts slept and ate in tents: They were divided into four patrols: Curlews, Ravens, Wolves, and Bulls. Each boy wore a streamer of tape in his patrol's color. Patrol leaders car-

ried a white flag with a picture of the patrol's animal and the badge that became the Scout badge.

Each morning B-P woke up the boys with a blast from an African war horn. During the day they played scouting games like deer stalking or whale hunting. They learned first aid, distance judging, and use of a compass. They learned to light a fire with only two matches. B-P told them stories around the campfire. He also taught them a

Zulu marching chant. "Eengonyama!" he would shout, and the boys would answer, "Invooboo! Ya-boh! Invooboo!" The boys would get so excited they would start dancing. Each night one patrol went out in the woods to sleep under the stars. With them they took flour, potatoes, meat, tea, coats, blankets, and matches. There they kept watch until 11 P.M.

"THE BRUSSELS SPROUTS"   *Scouting for Boys* appeared in 1908. It was a boys' version of *Aids to Scouting*. In it were stories, history, games, the Scout motto "Be Prepared," and the Scout law. There were tests for earning Scout badges (none for Tenderfoot, five for Second Class, seven for First Class) and three Badges of Honor. There were patrol calls, secret signs, and a Scout salute. There were skills: tracking, pioneering, camping, getting to know animals and birds, pathfinding, signaling, learning first aid and how to be physically fit.

To write his book, B-P had taken ideas from Native Americans, Zulus, and Japanese. He wanted boys to learn to observe and to use their reason. They could practice observation by noticing the things in shop windows, for instance. Learning to observe would make them kinder, he said, because it would teach them to read other people's feelings. All the things he talked about could be done in small groups. Six boys would be in each group, or Boy Patrol. One boy would lead the patrol. Four to ten patrols would form a troop under a scoutmaster.

Soon there were thousands of Boy Scouts in Britain. They stood out in their uniforms—broad-brimmed hats, colored scarves around the necks, and shorts. Other boys made fun of them by shouting, "Here come the Brussels Sprouts, the stinking, blinking louts."

But boys joined the Scouts anyway, and in 1910 Scouting came to the United States because of a good deed. When Chicago publisher William D. Boyce visited London, a Boy Scout helped him find his way. When Boyce tried to tip him, the Scout refused. Boyce decided Scouting was good for boys. He was so impressed, in fact, that he started the Boy Scouts of America on his return.

GIRL GUIDES AND GIRL SCOUTS   A girl wrote to B-P.

> Dear Sir,
> If a girl is not allowed to run, or even to hurry, to swim, ride a bike, or raise her arms above her head, can she become a Scout? Hoping that you will reply.
> Yours sincerely,
> A Would-Be Scout

As the letter said, girls were expected to act like ladies in those days. And acting like a lady meant not hurrying or running or doing other "boyish" things. But in 1909 at the Crystal Palace Rally for the Scouts, there were seven

Boy Scouts on a hike figure out their route.
(Boy Scouts of America)

On board a ship to the United States in 1912, B-P met a woman named Olave Soames. He married her. A Boy Scout wrote to him about his marriage.

> I am dreadfully disappointed in you. I have often thought to myself, "How glad I am that the Chief Scout is not married, because if he was he could never do those ripping things for boys." And now you are going to do it. It is the last thing I should have expected of you. Of course, you won't be able to keep on with the Scouts the same as before, because your wife will want you, and everything will fall through. I think it is awfully selfish of you.

B-P wrote back that Olave was as excited about Scouting as he was. And it was true. She worked with the Girl Guides starting in 1916.

girls in white blouses, blue skirts, and long black stockings. They called themselves Girl Scouts. And more than 6,000 girls had written in to be Boy Scouts. So B-P started the Girl Guides (British Girl Scouts). He put his sister Agnes in charge.

In 1911 B-P met Juliette Low. They knew many of the same people. Both liked to draw and model things. She worked with the Girl Guides in Scotland and London. And it was she who started the Girl Scouts of America. By 1926 there were more than 150,000 American Girl Scouts and leaders.

CUB SCOUTS Smaller boys wanted to be Scouts too. So B-P did something for them. In 1916 his book, *The Wolf Cub's Handbook* came out. It was built around Rudyard Kipling's *The Jungle Book*. In a year there were nearly 30,000 Wolf Cubs.

CHIEF SCOUT OF THE WORLD In 1920 the first Boy Scout Jamboree was held in London. The Boy Scouts of America made B-P Chief Lone-pine-on-the-skyline and gave him a war bonnet. And 500 Wolf Cubs made a circle and gave a mighty grand howl. At the end, even though B-P had not expected it, a boy made a speech. He said, "We, the Scouts of the World, salute you, Sir Robert Baden-Powell—Chief Scout of the World." A mighty cheer went up. B-P raised his hand in the Scout salute. All linked arms and sang "Auld Lang Syne." The four Scouts carried B-P around the arena.

"I HAVE GONE HOME." In 1941 B-P died. Olave wrote about his death in her diary and ended it with the Scout trail sign for "I have gone home"—a dot inside a circle.

BOY SCOUTS TODAY   Today there are over 4,500,000 Boy Scouts. For a list of some famous Scouts, see page 87.

5
WORDS AND LANGUAGE

STORIES BEHIND COMMON WORDS

AMERICA   In 1497 an Italian, Amerigo Vespucci, sailed along the shores of a new land. He called it *Mundus Novus,* "The New World." Years later a German geographer, drawing a map for a book he was writing, decided to name the new land America after Amerigo Vespucci. The land Vespucci sailed by and the geographer named after him was South America. Later, North America, where the United States is located, was also named after Amerigo Vespucci. Today we are called Americans after Amerigo's first name. If the geographer had chosen Amerigo's last name instead, we might be called Vespuccians.

BIKINI   A French fashion designer named Louis Reard invented the first bikini in 1946. It was very tiny—only 129 square inches of cloth held together by two strings. He named the bathing suit after Bikini Island, the place in the Pacific Ocean where the United States had tested atomic bombs in 1946. Reard read about those bomb tests and probably liked the sound of the word *bikini.*

At first people were shocked by the two-piece bathing suit. Some countries passed laws forbidding women to wear them. Before long, however, bikinis became very popular. A song was even written about them—"Itsy Bitsy Teenie Weenie Yellow Polka-dot Bikini."

Boonfellows gather on the playground. Boonfellow is a lost word meaning "friend." See pages 164–165 for more lost words. (John Wanchik)

GOBBLEDYGOOK   The word gobbledygook, "language that is confusing and means nothing," was made up by Maury Maverick, a congressman from Texas. He was upset by the written reports he received from the people who worked for him. The reports were full of long, important-sounding words, but the words made no sense. Maverick thought that people should write in a simple manner. He wrote a letter to his employees and told them not to write any more "gobbledygook." He said, "Be short and say what you're talking about. Anyone using the words *activation* or *implementation* will be shot."

GRAHAM CRACKERS   These sweet, rectangular whole-wheat crackers are named after Sylvester Graham, a Presbyterian minister, who first made them in the 1830s. Graham wanted people to change their eating habits. He was against meat, white bread, and alcohol in people's diets. He said everyone should eat more fruits, vegetables, and whole-wheat bread. Some of his ideas were strange. For instance, he thought that eating mustard or catsup would make a person crazy. One famous writer called Graham "the poet of bran meal and pumpkins." However, his graham crackers and some of his ideas about food and diet have been praised by modern-day doctors and scientists.

GUILLOTINE   The guillotine is a machine with a heavy blade that rises and drops between two posts. During the French Revolution, it was used a lot to cut off the heads of prisoners sentenced to death. The machine was named after a French doctor, Joseph Guillotin, even though he didn't design and build it. Before the guillotine, condemned prisoners were either hung with a rope or killed with a sword. Dr. Guillotin said that those methods were too painful and too slow. He suggested that a machine be built to behead the prisoners. A carpenter who worked for the king of France made the machine, but most people thought of Dr. Guillotin as the inventor and called the machine by his name. Thousands of people died unjustly under the guillotine's blade. Dr. Guillotin wished he had never thought of the killing machine.

GUNG HO   Gung ho is a Chinese saying that means "work together." An American, Lieutenant Colonel Evans F. Carlson, learned the saying while in China from 1937 to 1939. During World War II, he used the slogan but changed its meaning to "ready to go." Carlson was a marine and the leader of Carlson's Raiders. They fought in battles on Guadalcanal. All of the soldiers in Carlson's Raiders were proud that they were always gung ho, "ready to go." Today gung ho usually refers to a person who is very enthusiastic and always ready for whatever may happen.

GYMNASTICS   Gymnasts perform gymnastics in a gymnasium. All of these words have come down to us from the Greek word *gymnos*, which means "naked." In ancient Greece the men and boys did all of their exercises in the nude. They even ran in Olympic track meets without any clothes. The Greeks believed that nudity was healthy.

KALEIDOSCOPE This tubelike toy makes beautiful shapes and patterns, using mirrors and bits of colored glass or plastic. After David Breuster invented the toy in 1817, he read through a dictionary of Greek words to figure out a name for his invention. He picked the words *kalos*, "beautiful"; *eidos*, "form"; and *skopos*, "watcher." He put them together and got *kaleidoscope*, "watcher of beautiful forms."

LEOTARD Acrobats and ballet dancers wear this one-piece, tight-fitting garment. It was named after a 19th-century Frenchman, Jules Leotard, who first made and wore the costume. Leotard was a trapeze artist and circus star who amazed audiences with his somersaults. His leotard was sleeveless and cut low at the neck.

LEVI'S Levi's, also called blue jeans, date back to the days of the California Gold Rush in the 1850s. A young man named Levi Strauss came to San Francisco to sell canvas material for tents and wagon tops. He wanted to save enough money to stake a claim and dig for gold. He heard many hardworking gold miners and railroad workers complain about how easily their pants tore and wore out. So Levi took some of his brown canvas material and sewed a pair of "tough" pants. Soon everyone wanted a pair of the "strongest pants in the West." To make the pockets sturdy enough to hold gold ore, Strauss put copper rivets on the corners. The popular pants were called Levi's and sold for 22¢. Later, Levi Strauss switched from canvas cloth to denim and dyed the pants blue.

OK *OK* means "all right." It was first used by the OK Democratic Club. This group was formed in 1840 to support the re-election of President Martin Van Buren. The president, who was born in Kinderhook, New York, was nicknamed Old Kinderhook. OK, from the first letters of his nickname, was used in the club's name and was their password. Today OK is used around the world by speakers of many languages.

ROBOT In 1922 a Czechoslovakian writer, Karl Capek, wrote a play called *R.U.R. (Rossum's Universal Robots)*. In the play, lifelike robots do the work of

The word robot *came from this play*, R.U.R. (Rossum's Universal Robots). *(New York Public Library at Lincoln Center)*

General Ambrose E. Burnside invented a new hairstyle for men. Can you guess what it was? (National Portrait Gallery, Smithsonian Institution)

all-night gambling game. He was hungry but didn't want to leave the game. So he ordered his servant to bring him some slices of roast beef between two slices of bread. Two slices of bread with a filling has been known as a sandwich ever since. See page 197 to learn about the names of different kinds of sandwiches.

SIDEBURNS   Sideburns are growths of hair down the sides of a man's face in front of his ears. The man who made them famous was Ambrose E. Burnside, a general in the Union Army during the Civil War. Even though he wasn't a great soldier, he was popular and his picture was in many newspapers. Many men copied his bushy sideburns and clean-shaven chin. At first the new style was called ''burnsides,'' but somehow the word got reversed to ''sideburns.'' After the war General Burnside (who also had a big mustache) went on to become the governor of Rhode Island and a United States senator.

human beings, but before long become monsters and overpower their human masters. Capek took the name robot from the Czech words *robota*, which means ''work,'' and *robotnik*, which means ''slave.''

SANDWICH   The sandwich was born on August 6, 1762, at five o'clock in the morning. At that time an Englishman named John Montagu, the fourth Earl of Sandwich, was playing cards in an

SUNDAE   An ice-cream sundae can have many toppings—syrup, nuts, fruit, and whipped cream. The first sundae was made in an ice-cream parlor in Two Rivers, Wisconsin, in the 1890s. One day a customer asked to have chocolate syrup poured over his vanilla ice cream. The owner of the ice-cream parlor said the syrup would ruin the taste of the ice cream, but the customer wouldn't take no for an answer. Soon many customers wanted syrup on their ice cream, and other ice-cream parlors began to serve the new ice-cream dish.

The sundae got its name in an ice-cream parlor in the nearby town of Manitowoc. George Giffy, the owner, would serve the unusual ice-cream dish only on Sundays because he considered it a special order. That's how the ice-cream dish became known as a sundae. Nobody knows how the spelling of *Sunday* was changed to *sundae*.

POPULAR PUNS

A pun is a joking way of saying something by using (1) a word that has two different meanings or (2) a word that sounds the same as another one with a different meaning. Here are some fun puns.

Two spiders that get married are called newly webs.

There was a sign on a cage of canaries in a pet shop. It said, "For Sale. Cheep."

Little rivers that run into the Nile in Egypt are called Juveniles.

The doughnut said to the cake, "If I had as much dough as you have, I wouldn't be hanging around this hole."

Boxers and carpenters love to eat pound cake.

A clumsy man in Alaska accidentally stabbed himself with an icicle. He died of cold cuts.

When the baby of a king cries a lot, he is called the Prince of Wails.

The old woman put wheels on her rocking chair because she wanted to rock and roll.

A sleeping bag is really a knapsack.

A very pretty actress was hired to play Joan of Arc in a movie, but she got fired.

When a little dog gets real cold, he turns into a Pupsicle.

One cabbage said to the other cabbage, "Two heads are better than one."

People who go bowling seem to like it. They always have a ball.

If you put two ducks and a cow together, you get quackers and milk.

An operation isn't funny unless it leaves the patient in stitches.

WHAT TO NAME YOUR DOG

Here is a list from Carolyn Boyce Johnes's book *Please Don't Call Me Fido*. How many puns can you spot?

Bulova, a good name for a watchdog (or maybe Timex, Casio, or Swatch?)
Underdog

Sir Love-a-lot
Biter of Enemies
Dog
Calculator, for a three-legged dog—"Put down three and carry one."
Tide, for a dog who can't decide to come in or go out

WEBSTER AND HIS DICTIONARY

Noah Webster is best known for his dictionary, but he was also a famous lawyer, politician, and weather forecaster. He was born on October 16, 1758, in West Hartford, Connecticut, the son of a country farmer in a family of two governors, John Webster of Connecticut and William Bradford of Massachusetts.

Webster read a lot of books as a boy. By 1774 he was ready to enter Yale University. He graduated in 1778, taught school, and then practiced law. Later in his life Webster became very interested in writing. In 1793 he founded and edited two newspapers in New York City, *American Minerva* and *The Herald*. He retired from the newspapers in 1803 to spend *all* his time writing his first dictionary.

After years of hard work, Webster published *A Dictionary of the English Language* in 1806. The first dictionary had about 37,000 words. Almost 5,000 of those were "new"; they had never been seen before in other books. *Skunk, hickory, chowder,* and *applesauce*—these were among the new words. They gave new meanings to an old language. Webster kept adding new and better words to make his dictionary better.

After Webster died in 1843, George and Charles Merriam got all the rights to his dictionary. Since 1831 the Merriam brothers had run a printer's office and bookstore in Springfield, Massachusetts. When their revision of Webster's dictionary came out in 1847, it was an overnight success. By the mid-1920s, the company the Merriam brothers began was spending over $1,300,000 a year just to update its dictionaries. Today this company sells about 30 different kinds.

It is a giant job to keep up with the growing number of words in the English language and to decide which words will make it into a new dictionary and which ones will not. How do words find their way into dictionaries? Merriam editors find words to add to the dictionaries simply by looking for them. Merriam-Webster workers spend time every day reading books, newspapers, and magazines. These people are looking for new words that may or may not have been printed before. They are also looking for new meanings of old words. Once a new word or a new meaning is found, the word is marked in the text and its meaning is written down. The marked words go to the typing area, where they are both stored in a computer and printed on 3-inch × 5-inch index cards. People are also paid to listen for new words and new meanings on English-language programs on radio and television.

The English vocabulary is constantly growing. People always need new words because they have new experiences and new ideas to describe. Science gives many new words to the English language. Words like *moonwalk*, *quasar*, *pulsar*, and *black hole* are just a few of them. Life-styles have also supplied new words, such as *flower people*, *preppy*, *hippie*, *yuppie*, and *teeny-bopper*. The sports world has added

These are just some of the card files at Merriam-Webster, a well-known publisher of dictionaries. (Merriam-Webster, Inc.)

touchdown, *home run*, *basket*, *keying*, *key player*, and *designated hitter*. Show business has given a lot of words: *video*, *shoot-em-up*, and *spaghetti western*. New foods have also found their way into dictionaries. Words like *corn chip* and *sloppy joe* have been added from everyday language.

However, it is one thing for a word to get into the language and quite another for it to get into a dictionary. The definitions found in the Merriam-Webster dictionaries are taken from the millions of marked words on the index cards. All these marked words are filed alphabetically. When a new dictionary is being written, a worker will pull all the cards for a new word, sort them out, and then read them carefully to make sure that the meanings are correct. Then a definition is written for each new word. If a word has a questionable meaning, it is put aside until a later time.

Almost 150 years have passed since George and Charles Merriam began selling Webster's dictionary. No matter how many words may come along in the English language, the Merriam-Webster Company will welcome them.

LOST WORDS

Words don't last forever. Words people stop using are left out of dictionaries. After a while people forget about those words. They are "lost."' Why do people stop using certain words? Mostly, other words come along to take their places.

A writer, Susan Kelz Sperling, looked through a lot of old books and dictionaries to find lost words. She wrote a book about them, for adults, called *Poplollies and Bellibones*. She also wrote a book about lost words for kids. It is called *Murfles and Wink-a-peeps*.

Here are some of the lost words that Susan Kelz Sperling brought back to life. They are fun, and it is sad that they are no longer used. They sound wonderful when you say them out loud. Try to make up sentences and stories

This girl is a good example of a bellibone. *(John Wanchik)*

with these words. But, remember, most people won't know what you are saying! You'll have to teach them!

bellibone	lovely girl, both pretty and good
blob-tale	tattletale
boonfellow	friend
fellowfeel	to share another person's feelings
flesh-spades	fingernails
hufty-tufty	show-off, person who brags

lip-clap	kiss
lubber-wort	junk food
merry-go-sorry	story that makes you feel both happy and sad
murfles	freckles
poplolly	special loved one
sparrow-fart	very early in the morning, daybreak
tuzzy-muzzy	bouquet of flowers
wink-a-peeps	eyes

GROOVY SLANG

Do you understand the following story? It is written in the English language, but with a lot of slang. Slang is part of everyday conversation. It includes both new words and new and different meanings for old words. If you don't know—or cannot figure out—some slang in the story, just look at the minidictionary that follows it.

It was Saturday night, and Joe was on a bummer. Everybody thought he was an egghead, a deadhead, a real Robinson Crusoe. Should he hit the books or hit the high school shindig? He decided to make the scene.

Joe played it cool when he blew in to the whooper-dooper. He shelled out a rutabaga to get in. First he saw Jimmy, the beanpole, shooting off his bazoo about his father, a legal beagle. Then he saw Sylvester—Mr. Macho—a real shrewd dude all decked out in red shades. The chicks were gussied up, thick as thieves, and doing a lot of gum beating.

What a bunch of tackheads and schmucks. This was amateur night, and Joe was getting the heebie-jeebies. He decided to vamoose, hit the road in his puddle jumper, and head for home. Better to hang out by the idiot box than spend a night with a bunch of nincompoops. That's the way the cookie crumbles!

SLANG DICTIONARY

amateur night	night that is not top quality
bazoo	mouth

beanpole	tall, skinny person
blew	arrived casually
bummer, on a	in a state of depression
chicks	girls
cool, played it	acted relaxed, not nervous
deadhead	boring person
decked out	dressed up
egghead	very smart person
gum beating	talking about unimportant things
gussied up	well-dressed
hang out	to spend one's time
heebie-jeebies	being scared or nervous
hit	go to
hit the road	to drive away
idiot box	TV
legal beagle	lawyer
macho	strong, he-man type of guy
nincompoops	foolish, uninteresting people
puddle jumper	small car
Robinson Crusoe	person who spends a lot of time alone
rutabaga	one dollar
scene, make the	go to a certain place
schmucks	rude, silly people; jerks
shades	sunglasses
shelled out	paid
shindig	social gathering, like a party or a dance
shooting off	talking too much
shrewd dude	male who dresses well
tackheads	dumb people
That's the way the cookie crumbles	That's the way life is, and there's not much you can do to change it.
thick as thieves	close together in a small group
vamoose	to leave
whooper-dooper	big party or dance

Beanpole

COCA-COLA LANGUAGES

Coca-Cola is the number-one-selling soft drink in the world. It is sold in more than 155 countries around the globe. More than 335 million times a day, people ask for a Coke. And altogether they ask for it in 80 different languages. Here is what a label on a can of Coca-Cola looks like in just eight of these different languages.

For more facts about Coca-Cola, see pages 60, 177, and 196.

1.
2.
3.
4.
5.
6.
7.

1. Arabic
2. French
3. Japanese
4. Thai
5. Spanish
6. Chinese
7. Hebrew
8. Polish

(The Coca-Cola Company)

RIDICULOUS RIDDLES

A riddle is a question or problem that is hard to figure out or understand. How many of these riddles can you answer? Look at the end of the list if you give up or want to check your answers.

1. What has eight legs, two arms, three heads, and wings?
2. When is a black bear most likely to enter your house?
3. Why do hummingbirds hum?
4. What state asks the most questions?
5. Why does an elephant have red toenails?
6. What most looks like half a watermelon?
7. How can you keep a rooster from crowing on Sunday morning?
8. What month doesn't tell the truth?
9. If your uncle's sister is not your aunt, what relation is she to you?
10. What is even more interesting than a talking dog?
11. How can you evenly divide 16 apples among 17 hungry people?

12. What has four wheels and flies?
13. What happens when you give a cat a lemon?
14. With what can you fill a barrel to make it lighter?
15. What happens to girls who swallow bullets?

ANSWERS

1. A man on horseback with a canary on his hand
2. When the door is open
3. Because they don't know the words to the songs
4. Why—oming
5. So he can hide in a cherry tree
6. The other half
7. Kill it on Saturday night.
8. Ju—lie
9. Your mother
10. A spelling bee
11. Make applesauce
12. A garbage truck
13. You get a sour puss.
14. Holes
15. Their hair comes out in bangs.

GRAFFITI

Since the beginning of time, people everywhere have written their names and messages on walls and monuments, trees and rocks, fences and poles. They may not even have known how to write, but they drew something—like a heart with initials inside it. We call these writings graffiti, which means "scratchings" or "scribblings" in Italian.

Some science experts think that the cave drawings of Stone Age man, who didn't have a written language, are really graffiti. The Bible tells us about the handwriting on the wall, "Mene, Mene, Teckel, Upharsin," that predicted the downfall of the last king of Babylon. And when Mt. Vesuvius erupted in A.D. 79, burying Pompeii in volcanic ash, that city's graffiti were preserved for all time. All over the walls of Pompeii, people had written messages, political slogans, and things like "Serena loves Isadore."

Besides public walls, other popular places for graffiti are graveyards, prisons, and bathrooms—probably because they are places where people are usually alone. In the Roman catacombs, an underground network of tunnels where the early Christians were buried, over half a million graffiti messages have been found. In the Tower of London, the walls are covered with the names of famous prisoners. Graffiti in public bathrooms are usually not very interesting, but every so often you see something funny. If

This wall covered with graffiti stands near a freeway in Los Angeles. (R. Brook Madigan)

you ever study Latin, you will learn the famous words of Caesar: *Veni, vidi, vici,* or "I came, I saw, I conquered." In a bathroom in New York City someone wrote, "Veni, vidi, weewee."

In central Tennessee there is a tree with the following words carved on its trunk: "D. Boon Cilled A. Bar in The Year 1760." As you can see, Daniel Boone sure couldn't spell!

During World War II there was an imaginary character named Kilroy who became famous because of graffiti. Everywhere they went, United States soldiers scribbled, "Kilroy was here." Kilroy's name turned up everywhere: on deserted islands in the Pacific Ocean, under the Arc de Triomphe in Paris, on the Statue of Liberty's torch in New York Harbor. At a peace conference to end the war, Stalin, the Soviet dictator, returned from the bathroom and asked, "Who is Kilroy?"

The New York City subway has been a popular place for graffiti. At first, people wrote on the walls and on advertising posters inside the subway cars; "Jesus shaves" was on an ad for razor blades. Then, in the summer of 1972, teenagers began to write in spray paint all over the outside of the subway cars, signing their gang names with great frills and swirls. That is against the law, but some people considered it art, and whole subway cars were moved to museums.

A lot of people don't like graffiti, because the words mess up good, clean spaces. The city of Stockholm, Sweden, has a special wall for graffiti. It is painted over fresh every day, ready for new messages. Some schools provide blackboards and chalk for students to write down whatever they want. It's easy to erase a blackboard.

Graffiti can be playful, creative, and funny. Here are some good examples.

A bird in the hand can be messy.
When in doubt, worry.
Repeal the law of gravity.
Forest fires prevent bears.
The world is flat.—Class of 1492

AMAZING ACRONYMS

An acronym is a special abbreviation, or contraction. It is a word formed from the first or first few letters of a series of words.

AWOL	Absent Without Official Leave
COMSUBCOMNELM-COMHEDSUPPACT	Commander, Subordinate Command, United States Naval Forces Eastern Atlantic and Mediterranean, Commander Headquarters Support Activities. (This 26-letter acronym is the longest in the English language.)
LASER	Light Amplification through Stimulated Emission of Radiation
NASA	National Aeronautics and Space Administration
NATO	North Atlantic Treaty Organization
NUT	National Union of Teachers (in Great Britain)
OPEC	Organization of Petroleum Exporting Countries
PAL	Police Athletic League
RADAR	Radio Detecting and Ranging
SCUBA	Self-Contained Underwater Breathing Apparatus
TARFU	Things Are Really Fouled Up (military slang)
UNICEF	United Nations International Children's Emergency Fund (now United Nations Children's Fund)
WAC	Women's Army Corps
ZIP	Zone Improvement Plan (United States Post Office Zip Code)

LIVELY LIMERICKS

The word *limerick* comes from the name of a town and county in Ireland. A limerick is a funny poem that is five lines long. Here are some popular ones to share with your friends.

There was a young fellow named Paul
Who attended a fancy dress ball.
They say, just for fun,
He dressed up as a bun,
And a dog ate him up in the hall.

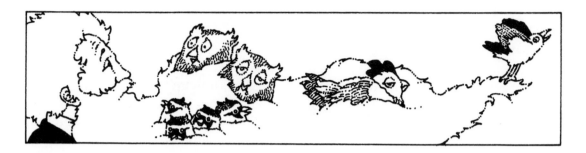

There was an old man with a beard,
Who said, "It is just as I feared!
   Two owls and a hen,
   Four larks and a wren
Have all built their nests in my beard."

There once was a young man named Hall
Who fell in the spring and the fall.
   'Twould have been a sad thing
   Had he died in the spring,
But he didn't—he died in the fall.

There was a young lady of Niger
Who smiled as she rode on a tiger.
   They returned from the ride
   With the lady inside
And the smile on the face of the tiger.

There was a fair maid from Decatur
Who was known as a red-hot potato.
   To the jungle she went
   On mission work bent,
Where a dozen fat savages ate her.

There was a fat lady of Clyde
Whose shoelaces once came untied;
   She feared that to bend
   Would display her rear end,
So she cried and she cried and she cried.

There was a young lady of Lynn,
Who was so uncommonly thin
   That when she essayed
   To drink lemonade
She slipped through the straw and fell in.

There was a young maid who said, "Why,
Can't I look in my ear with my eye?
   If I give my mind to it,
   I'm sure I can do it,
You never can tell till you try.

There was a young lady named Stella
Fell in love with a bowlegged fella,
   The venturesome chap,
   Let her sit in his lap
And she fell clean through to the cella.

There was an old man of Blackheath,
Who sat on his set of false teeth;
   Said he, with a start,
   "O Lord, bless my heart!
I've bitten myself underneath!"

There was a young lady of Kent,
Whose nose was most awfully bent.
   One day, I suppose,
   She followed her nose,
For no one knew which way she went.

A LANGUAGE ONLY ONE MAN CAN SPEAK

There is only one man in the world who can speak the Oubykh language. His name is Tevfik Esenc, and he lives in the farm village of Haci Osman in Turkey.

More than 150 years ago, at least 50,000 people in Turkey could speak Oubykh. But after the Crimean War, many Turkish people moved to other places and learned new languages.

Today language scientists from all over the world visit Tevfik Esenc, who is 84 years old. He is a farmer and lives in a hut with a dirt floor. Tevfik has three sons, but none of them can speak Oubykh.

Language scientists are very interested in Oubykh because it is much different from other languages. The English language has 30 different sounds. Oubykh has 80 different sounds. In Oubykh there are four different ways to say the letters *sh*.

Scientists tape record Tevfik's speech and then try to figure out how to spell the words. They have had to use different alphabets to write down the strange language. Someday the scientists hope to write an Oubykh dictionary.

The people in Tevfik's village are not interested in learning Oubykh. When Tevfik dies, the language will die with him.

TONGUE TWISTERS

Can you twist your tongue well enough to say these tongue twisters? You have to say them fast!

Rubber baby-buggy bumpers
She sells seashells by the seashore.
Three gray geese sat on the green grass grazing.
They say shoes and socks give Susan quite a shock.
Tom threw Tim three thumbtacks.
A big black bug bit a big black bear and the big black bear bled blood.
The sixth sick sheik's sixth sheep's sick. (The *Guinness Book of World Records* says that this is the hardest tongue twister in the world.)

Peter Piper picked a peck of pickled peppers.
Did Peter Piper pick a peck of pickled peppers?
If Peter Piper picked a peck of pickled peppers,
Where's the peck of pickled peppers Peter Piper picked?

STORYTELLING IN JONESBOROUGH

Once upon a time, hundreds of storytellers came from all around to a little town in Tennessee. For three days and three nights, they told stories—wonderful stories. People from miles around came to listen. It was a magical time. On the evening of the last night, everyone walked up to an old cemetery and gathered around a campfire. For hours chills went up each spine as all listened to ghost stories and tales of goblins and monsters.

This is not make-believe. Every year in early October, the National Storytelling Festival is held in Jonesborough, Tennessee. More than 4,000 people come to the event and listen to hundreds of storytellers do what they do best—tell stories. The festival lasts for one long weekend. In big circus tents about 15 very good storytellers spin their wild and woolly tales. In another spot called Swapping Ground, anyone can tell a story.

You've never seen and heard stories told like this before. The storytellers use their hands and their eyes and their whole bodies to relate their tales. Their voices get loud, get soft, and sometimes fade away. The stories have wonderful names—"Orange Cheeks," "Monkey's Paw," and "The Hairy Woman." They are funny, sad, and scary.

On the last night of the storytelling weekend, everybody really does walk up to the Old Jonesborough Cemetery to listen to ghost stories. They all sit on blankets and huddle close together to hear about ghosts, demons, and monsters. In the deep, dark night they get scared witless!

Every year more and more people come to the storytelling festival in Jonesborough. Those who have been before come back because they have had such a good time. If you would like more information about this event, you may write.

National Storytelling Festival
P.O. Box 309
Jonesborough, TN 37659

6
ODD FACTS

AMAZING TRIVIA FACTS FROM A TO Z

AIR Every day you breathe about 70,000 cubic inches of air.

ANIMAL ON TRIAL The trouble started when a chimpanzee smoked a cigarette in front of a crowd of people in South Bend, Indiana. The year was 1905, and there was a law against smoking in public in South Bend. The chimpanzee was arrested, taken to a courthouse, put on trial, found guilty, and fined a small sum of money. The chimpanzee belonged to a man who was traveling with a carnival. He paid the fine, and the chimpanzee was let go.

AUTHOR The youngest person to write a book and have it published is Dorothy Straight of Washington, D.C. She was four years old when she wrote *How the World Began* in 1962. It was published two years later.

BAMBOO Bamboo grows very fast. In just one day it can grow 3 feet.

BATHTUBS In 1885 only one in six American families had a bathtub. Most Americans did not have a bathtub until after World War I. For a long time people thought indoor plumbing was unhealthy. They would use a bathtub only if a doctor said it was all right. The earliest bathtubs were made of zinc or wood or rubber. In the Wild West some people used a portable bathtub made of canvas. It unfolded and fit around the neck while a person sat in a chair.

BEAN BRANDING Tons of vanilla beans are grown in Madagascar, a big island off the eastern coast of Africa. To stop thieves from stealing them, some farmers brand each small vanilla bean! Cows in the United States are branded

This beautiful Fabergé egg made of gold is decorated with diamonds. The coach fits inside! For more about such eggs, see pages 177–178. (Peter MacDonald, The Forbes Magazine Collection)

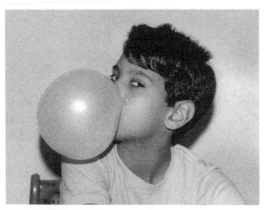

*This bubble was blown from Blibber-Blubber.
(R. Brook Madigan)*

with designs, but vanilla beans are branded with numbers.

BLOODHOUNDS Bloodhounds have a wonderful sense of smell. When it comes to finding lost people, the bloodhound is the best dog for the job. Every day a human being sheds about 50 million skin cells. You can't see these cells; they fall like invisible dandruff. Also, a human being makes about 30 to 50 ounces of sweat a day. Even if you have just taken a bath, there are bacteria on your body that mix with the skin cells and the sweat. The combination gives you a scent. Everywhere you go, your scent falls on grass, bushes, and other things. Even if *you* can't smell anything, a bloodhound can. For many years bloodhounds have followed the individual scents of missing people and have saved the lives of children and adults. As one dog expert says, "A bloodhound that is following a scent on a trail just won't quit."

BUBBLE GUM   The first bubble gum was invented in 1906 by Frank Henry Fleer of the Frank H. Fleer Corporation. He called the pink stuff Blibber-Blubber. However, the gum didn't hold together, and the bubbles were too wet and broke too fast. In 1928 Walter Diemer, who worked for the Fleer Corporation, came up with a much better kind of bubble gum. It held together when chewed and made a nice dry bubble that lasted much longer than Blibber-Blubber's. Diemer called the new gum Double Bubble. According to the *Guinness Book of World Records*, the largest bubble ever blown was 22 inches across. It was made in 1985 by a woman in Fresno, California.

BULLS   In the bullring, the matador shakes his red cape at the bull, and the bull goes crazy when he sees the red color. True? Not so. Bulls are color-blind. They get stirred up by the movement—the motion—of the cape, not the color red. The cape could be yellow, purple, green—any color would work as long as the matador moved the cape around. Most matadors, however, like to use red capes.

COBWEB PAINTING   Painting pictures on cobwebs has been an art since the 18th century. However, today there are not very many artists who can paint pictures on cobwebs. It takes a lot of time, and it's very difficult. First, the artist has to gather up the cobwebs on frames. Then the artist has to clean out any dirt and soot. Finally, it takes lots of time and care to paint a picture with a very soft brush. The cobwebs are very delicate and many of them break. The finished pictures are usually small— about 2 inches square.

COCA-COLA Coca-Cola, the world's most popular soft drink, has a secret ingredient called 7X. While most of the ingredients that make up Coke are listed on its label, 7X is not. Only two people who work for Coca-Cola know what makes up 7X. They are not allowed to travel together, because an accident might hurt or kill both of them. However, the secret formula for 7X is written down. The recipe is in a safe-deposit vault at the Trust Company of Georgia. For more facts about Coca-Cola, see pages 60, 167, and 196.

CRYING The only animals that cry are human beings.

CULLINAN DIAMOND The largest diamond ever found was the Cullinan Diamond. It was 3,106 carats—more than 1¼ pounds. The Cullinan Diamond came from a mine in Pretoria, South Africa. It was sent by mail to England's King Edward II. When he first saw the diamond, the king wasn't very impressed. He said, "I would have kicked it aside as a lump of glass if I had seen it on the road." The Cullinan was cut into 105 diamonds. The largest stone cut from the Cullinan was the 530-carat Star of Africa, which is one of the British crown jewels.

DOG BITES Every day in the United States 2,466 children are bitten by dogs.

Dogs also bite 28 United States mail carriers every day.

DREAMS When you sleep, you dream about one-fifth, or 20 percent, of the time. For example, if you sleep one night for 8 hours, you dream about 96 minutes of that 8 hours. Sometimes we remember our dreams; sometimes we forget them.

DUMB THIEF On the night of November 22, 1978, an 18-year-old broke in to a house in Baltimore, Maryland. The owner was home, and the burglar demanded all her money. She had $11.50. The thief was so mad that he ordered her to write him a check for $50.00. When the woman asked for his name, the thief spelled out his real name for her. After he left, the woman called the police and gave them the name of the burglar. Two hours later the police caught the very dumb thief.

EASTER EGGS Have you ever heard of an Easter egg that costs over a million dollars? In Russia, during the rule of the czar Alexander III, a man named Carl Fabergé made 53 Easter eggs for the czar to give away as gifts. These weren't ordinary Easter eggs; they were beautiful works of art. The eggs were decorated with gold and silver, diamonds and pearls, and other valuable jewels. Inside each egg was a surprise. One egg held a small gold carriage with crystal windows and diamonds all over its surface. Another egg contained a flower basket with diamond roses and other flowers, all with

Thomas Alva Edison was one of the world's all-time great inventors. (Edison National Historic Site)

jewels in the petals. Other surprises inside the eggs were singing birds, pictures, and royal crowns. Sometimes it took more than a year to make just one of Fabergé's Easter eggs. Today each egg is worth a lot of money, but the art collectors who own them don't put them up for sale very often.

EATING　It is a good idea to take a rest after eating. It helps to digest your food. If you become very active after eating, some of the blood around the body organs that digest food moves to other parts of your body. Without the right amount of blood, your food is harder to digest. In many European countries, stores and businesses close for 2 hours after lunch. Everybody goes home for a rest and comes back to work later in the afternoon.

FEARS　More than 3,000 Americans were asked, "What are you most afraid of?" The number-one answer was "speaking before a group." Next came "heights." "Insects and bugs" and "money problems" tied for third place.

FINGERPRINTS　Because everybody's fingerprints are different, fingerprints are a good way of identifying people. Even the FBI, which has collected more than 169 million fingerprints, has never found two that are alike. However, some experts say it is *possible* for two fingerprints to be the same, but the odds are against it. The chance that two fingerprints will be identical is one in about 64 billion.

G.E. SNAKE　In 1986 a married couple in Gainesville, Florida, found a snake in their backyard. It had swallowed two 15-watt light bulbs. They brought the snake to a veterinarian named Dr. Elliot Jacobson. Dr. Jacobson, who called the snake G.E., said the snake probably thought it was eating two big chicken eggs. The doctor operated on the snake and squeezed out the light bulbs in about 45 minutes. After the operation, G.E. was put on a heating pad and given soft food and Gatorade.

HAIR　Most Americans have brown hair—about 70 percent of them. About 15 percent have natural blond hair. Next come those with black hair—

about 10 percent. The smallest group have red hair—just 5 percent. For more about hair, see page 202.

HEIGHT The American man grows to be about 5 feet 8 inches tall. The American woman stands about 5 feet 4 inches tall. Of course, these heights are averages.

INVENTOR Thomas Alva Edison was one of the world's great inventors. Over his lifetime he patented 1,093 inventions. One scientist said Edison's inventions were worth about $25 billion. To learn more about Edison the inventor, see page 309.

JOKES Johnny Carson is one of this country's favorite comedians. His TV program "The Tonight Show" has run for many years. It is estimated that he has told about 638,645 jokes on his show.

KISSING The world's longest kiss took 17 days, 10½ hours. It ended on September 24, 1985, in Chicago. The two people who kissed were Eddie Leven, age 30, and Delphine Chra, age 26. The longest kiss in a movie was in the 1941 film *You're in the Army Now.* Two of the movie's stars, Jane Wyman and Regis Toomey, kissed for 3 minutes and 5 seconds.

LAUGHING DISEASE In the country of New Guinea a tribe called the Fore has been struck with a very strange disease. It is called kuru, or the laughing disease. People who get the disease can't stop laughing and giggling. Kuru is very serious: Those who get it always die. Doctors think the disease is caused by a virus, but they don't know how to cure it.

LAWS Some states have very old laws that make no sense today. These are laws most people have never heard of. Nobody gets arrested for breaking them, but they are still "real" laws. For instance, in Kentucky it is against the law to carry an ice-cream cone in your pocket. In New York it is against the law to shoot a rabbit from a moving trolley car. In Idaho one person is not allowed to give another person a box of candy that weighs more than 50 pounds.

LIBRARY BOOK In 1823 a man in Cincinnati, Ohio, checked out a book from the University of Cincinnati Medical Library. He forgot to return it. His great-grandson returned the book in 1968— 145 years later. The library staff figured out that the fine for the overdue book was $2,264. Luckily, the great-grandson did not have to pay the fine.

LIGHTNING STRIKES Roy Sullivan, a forest ranger in Virginia, was struck by lightning seven times in his life. He was hit in 1942, 1969, 1970, 1972, 1973, 1976, and 1977. His hair was set on fire twice. He also had burns on his eyebrows, shoulder, stomach, chest, and ankle. One time Sullivan was driving when he was hit, and he was knocked 10 feet out of his car. He said, "Lightning has a way of finding me. When a storm blows up, I put my wife and kids in the living room and sit in the kitchen, scared." In 1983 Sullivan died at the age of 71, but his death had nothing to do with lightning.

LOST DOG   In 1923 a family from Silverton, Oregon, went to Indiana on a vacation. They took their English sheepdog Bobbie with them. The dog got lost, and the family went home without him. Six months later, Bobbie showed up at the family's house in Oregon. He had traveled almost 3,000 miles. An animal group later traced Bobbie's trip. He had crossed rivers, deserts, and mountains. From time to time, families along the way had helped him. At the end of his trip, Bobbie was very skinny and his legs were swollen. But he had found his way home.

MEAT EATING   Americans eat a lot of meat. In a lifetime, an American who lives to be 70 years old will eat 880 chickens, 14 beef cattle, 23 hogs, 35 turkeys, 12 sheep, and 770 pounds of fish. These numbers are, of course, averages.

MINISKIRTS   When miniskirts became popular in the late 1960s, the government of Greece outlawed them. The government said that women's and girls' dresses could not be more than 14 inches above the ground. Policemen in Greece carried tape measures to make sure no one was breaking the rule.

MONOPOLY   Families that own the board game MONOPOLY play the game about nine times a year, on the average. To find out which spaces players land on most frequently, see pages 92–93.

MULE ELECTION   In 1938 a mule named Boston Curtis was elected to a local office in Milton, Washington. The mule's election was a joke planned by the mayor of Milton. He said most people don't pay any attention to whom they vote for in an election. To prove his point, the mayor secretly put the mule's name on the ballot. The mayor was right. The mule won the election.

NOSE PRINTS   People can be identified by their fingerprints. How can valuable show dogs be identified? Trainers and breeders take nose prints of the dogs. Nose prints are better than paw prints.

OSTRICH EGG   The ostrich is the bird that lays the largest egg. An ostrich egg is 6 to 8 inches long and weighs about $3\frac{1}{2}$ pounds. Its shell is very thick. It takes about 40 minutes to hard-boil an ostrich egg.

OVER 100   Americans live longer now than they ever did before. Today there are about 37,000 Americans over the age of 100. The oldest United States citizen was Charlie Smith of Florida, who died in 1979. He claimed he was born in Liberia in 1842 and therefore was 137 years old in 1979. Smith came to the United States as a slave and lived in Texas, Georgia, and Florida for most of his life. He worked at many different jobs. Nobody knows for sure if he was

137 years old when he died, but he was very old.

PANGRAM A pangram is a sentence that uses all the letters in the alphabet at least once. Here is an example of a pangram: The quick brown fox jumps over a lazy dog.

PLACE NAMES Some places in the United States have very strange names. Here are just a few such places: Sleeping Giant, Connecticut; Kissimee, Florida; Coffee Pot Rapids, Idaho; Crummies, Kentucky; Monkey's Eyebrow, Kentucky; Whynot, Mississippi; Tightwad, Missouri; Double Trouble, New Jersey; Knockemstiff, Ohio; Bowlegs, Oklahoma; Cut and Shoot, Texas; Looneyville, West Virginia.

POPULATION Every day more than 200,000 babies are born in countries all over the world.

POUNDS OF MONEY How much does $1 million weigh? In $100 bills, it weighs 20 pounds. If a bank robber wanted to steal $1 billion in $100 bills, he would have to carry away 10 tons of money.

ROBINSON CRUSOE There was a real-life Robinson Crusoe. His name was Alexander Selkirk. In 1704 he was a sailor on a ship passing off the coast of Chile in South America. Selkirk had a fight with the ship's captain and asked to be put ashore on one of the tiny Juan Fernandez Islands, which was deserted. Selkirk lived there for four years and four months before he was rescued and returned to England. A writer in England, Daniel Defoe, heard about Selkirk and how he had lived on the island. In 1719 Defoe wrote a book called *The Life and Strange and Surprising Adventures of Robinson Crusoe*. What happened to Defoe's hero, Robinson Crusoe, wasn't exactly the same as what happened to Alexander Selkirk. Defoe made up a lot of things. However, Defoe did get his book idea from the real-life adventures of Selkirk.

SAFETY PIN Walter Hunt, an American, invented the safety pin in 1849. He did it one evening in a hurry—in only 3 hours—because he owed somebody $15 and needed the money the next day. He sold his invention for $400 flat and paid his debt. That was a big mistake. The person who bought the invention got very rich. Hunt never made another penny for his work.

SINGING DOGS About one dog in a thousand can sing. One of the most

Pete the Pup, who starred in the Our Gang *comedies, liked to sing "Jeannie with the Light Brown Hair." (A & C Archives)*

This stone money is found on the islands of Yap in the Pacific Ocean. (Flora Wallechinsky)

famous singing dogs was Benjy of Brookline, Massachusetts. His favorite song was "Raindrops Keep Fallin' on My Head." Another famous dog singer was Pete the Pup, who starred in Our Gang comedies. He liked to sing "Jeannie with the Light Brown Hair."

SNORING   More men than women snore. An overweight person is more likely to snore than a thin person. People snore more in the summer than in the winter. The older you get, the more likely you are to become a snorer. About one person in eight is a snorer.

SNOWFLAKES   On January 28, 1887, giant snowflakes fell on the Coleman Ranch at Fort Keogh, Montana. They were 15 inches across and 8 inches thick. A mailman who saw the snowflakes said they were "bigger than milk pans."

SPEAKING   When you speak just one word, you use 72 muscles.

STOMACH PAINS   In 1960 an American man checked into a hospital. He complained about stomach pains. Later the doctors operated on him and found 258 unusual things in his stomach. Among the things the doctors removed were 26 keys, 39 nail files, 88 coins, and 3 pairs of tweezers.

STONE MONEY   The strangest money in the world is found on the islands of Yap in the Pacific Ocean. The money is in the form of large, doughnut-shaped stones. The smallest stones are 6 feet across; the largest stones are 12 feet across. Many years ago the stones were the only kind of money on Yap. Today the people on the island do use United States dollars for everyday purchases, but they still use the stones to buy large items. Because the stones are so heavy, nobody can ever steal them. Some weigh over a ton each.

STREET NAMES   What is the most popular street name in the United States? According to the United States Post Office, the most popular is Park. In second place is Washington. In third place is Maple.

TALLEST MAN   Robert Wadlow of Alton, Illinois, holds the record for being the tallest human being in the world. He was 8 feet 11 inches tall. Born in 1918, he was 6 feet tall by the time he was eight years old. When Wadlow stopped growing at age 21, he weighed 491 pounds. He died at age 22.

TIGHTROPE WALKER   In 1859 a French acrobat strung a 1,300-foot rope across Niagara Falls. His name was Charles Blondin, and he had an incredible sense of balance. With a crowd of people watching, he walked from one side of the falls to the other on the rope. Then he walked across the rope on stilts. Then he walked across with his feet in a gunnysack. At one point he carried a little stove out onto the rope and cooked an omelet. For more about daredevils at Niagara Falls, see page 315.

TINY TOWN   In 1925 the schoolchildren of Springfield, Missouri, decided to build a miniature town in a park there. During school hours and in their spare time, the students laid out a whole town on a 6-acre space. In two months they built more than 400 little buildings, each one-twelfth the size of a regular building. There were schools, barbershops, gas stations, and a YMCA. People came from miles around to walk through the beautiful Tiny Town, which is what the students named it. Three months after it was finished the students had to take Tiny Town apart.

TOILET   The name of the man who invented the flush toilet was Thomas Crapper. He lived in England. The queen of England was so impressed with his invention that she made him a knight—Sir Thomas Crapper.

TOOTHBRUSH   The toothbrush was invented around 1770 by a prisoner in England's Newgate Prison. The prisoner, William Addis, had a lot of time to think while in jail. He cleaned his teeth the way most people did in those days—by rubbing them with a rag. One day Addis saved a small bone from a piece of meat he had eaten for dinner. He made holes in the bone, glued bunches of bristles into the holes, and the first toothbrush was born! When Addis got out of jail, he made and sold his new invention and was very successful.

TREE HOUSE   In Africa some people live inside a tree. The tree is called a baobab. Its trunk is 30 feet thick. After digging out the inside of the tree trunk, the people move in and set up housekeeping. The baobab is the world's best

This strange tree is called the baobab. People in Africa sometimes dig out the insides of the trunk and live inside the tree. (Australian Overseas Information Service)

tree house. It also grows in Australia, India, and Madagascar.

TUXEDOS   Renting and buying tuxedos is big business in the United States. Men spend hundreds of millions of dollars every year to rent tuxedos. More than $100 million is spent by men who buy their own. This very dressy, formal suit can cost as little as $140 or as much as $3,500.

WORDS   A child first entering school knows about 3,000 words. By the time a child grows into an adult, he or she uses 10,000 to 20,000 words when speaking or writing and can understand another 30,000 to 40,000 words when reading or listening.

X-RAY VISION   Disguised as Clark Kent, Superman sometimes looks through his eyeglasses when using his X-ray vision. Why don't his glasses melt? They don't melt because they were made from the windshield glass in the space capsule that brought the baby Superman to Earth from the planet Krypton. Superman made the glasses himself from the special glass.

ZIPPER   An engineer in Chicago invented the zipper in 1891. The first one was used on a pair of shoes. Before zippers, people used buttons, hooks and eyes, laces, and buckles on their shoes and clothes. Some dresses had as many as 30 buttons. The fly on a pair of men's pants had as many as 15.

RED, WHITE, AND BLUE: 50 QUESTIONS AND ANSWERS ABOUT THE UNITED STATES

You'll find the answers at the end of the questions. Hint: A state can be the answer more than once.

QUESTIONS

1. You could be fined $300 for picking a wildflower in this state. Name the state.

2. What is the only state that is divided into two parts?

3. What state was named after an American president?

4. In what state will you find the oldest, tallest, and largest trees?

5. What is the only state in the United States that grows coffee and pineapples?

6. What state has the shortest ocean coastline?

7. What state has a lake that contains more than four times the amount of salt found in oceans?

8. There is only one state where houseflies cannot live. What is that state?

9. In what state can you hunt for diamonds and keep all that you find?

10. Only two states in the United States grow a wild plant that eats meat. Name the states.

11. What state is called an island but isn't?

12. What state has the cloudiest place in the United States?

13. What state has the world's largest canyon?

14. What was the first state in the United States?

15. In what state can you play outside in the sunshine for 20 hours a day during the summer?

16. What state had the very first drive-in movie theater?

17. The first national park in the world, Yellowstone National Park, is mostly in what state?

18. What state has an island only about 2 miles away from the Soviet Union?

19. A town in this state used to mark off its streets with buffalo bones. What state is it?

20. What state has a river that sings?

21. What state grows the most potatoes?

A park ranger in Sequoia and Kings Canyon National Parks shows children a cross-section of a sequoia tree. In what state are these parks? (National Park Service)

22. What state has more lakes than any other state?

23. What state makes the most breakfast cereal in the world?

24. Most of us play games with marbles. Where do you think most of them come from?

25. Which state produces the most milk, cheese, and butter?

26. What state inspired the song "America the Beautiful"?

27. What state is the smallest?

28. What state grows the most peanuts in the United States?

29. In what state would you find the biggest popcorn factory in the United States?

30. What state makes the most wooden toothpicks?

31. Where would you find the heads of four presidents carved in the side of a mountain?

The Grand Canyon is the world's largest canyon. Where is it? (National Park Service)

32. What state has the most people living in it?

33. You will find a town named Springfield in almost every state, but which state has Springfield as its capital?

34. Where is the lowest and hottest place in the United States?

35. Which state grows the most mushrooms?

36. What state was Davy Crockett born in?

37. Where did the Pilgrims land?

38. What state gets the least amount of rain?

39. Where would you find the snowiest place in the United States?

40. Where would you go to see the most famous horse race in the United States?

41. What state was part of Massachusetts for over 100 years?

42. You can visit this state's capital only by airplane or boat. What state is it?

43. Where is most of the United States's gold kept?

44. In what state will you find the largest city in the United States?

45. In what state did women first get

the right to vote?

46. What state produces the most food?

47. In what state did Americans figure out how to make a rocket to carry people to the moon?

48. In what state were Daniel Boone, Abraham Lincoln, and Muhammad Ali born?

49. Which state has the most tree farms?

50. Where did the Pony Express riders start their ride?

ANSWERS

1. Colorado
2. Michigan
3. Washington
4. California (Bristlecone is oldest; redwood is tallest; sequoia is largest.)
5. Hawaii
6. New Hampshire
7. Utah (the Great Salt Lake)
8. Alaska (It's too cold for flies to breed.)
9. Arkansas (in Crater of Diamonds State Park)
10. North Carolina and South Carolina (The plant is the Venus's-flytrap.)
11. Rhode Island
12. Oregon (In Portland, it is cloudy about two days out of every three.)
13. Arizona (the Grand Canyon)
14. Delaware
15. Alaska

16. New Jersey
17. Wyoming
18. Alaska
19. Kansas
20. Mississippi (The Pascagoula River makes a sound like bees flying.)
21. Idaho
22. Florida (30,000 lakes)
23. Michigan (in Battle Creek)
24. West Virginia
25. Wisconsin
26. Colorado
27. Rhode Island

Davy Crockett is an American hero who died in the battle of the Alamo in Texas. In what state was he born? (National Portrait Gallery, Smithsonian Institution)

These diamonds were discovered in a state park where you get to keep any diamonds that you find. In what state is this park? (Arkansas State Parks)

28. Georgia
29. Iowa
30. Maine
31. South Dakota (Mount Rushmore)
32. California
33. Illinois

34. California (Death Valley)
35. Pennsylvania
36. Tennessee
37. Massachusetts
38. Nevada
39. Washington (on Mt. Rainier)
40. Kentucky (the Kentucky Derby)
41. Maine
42. Alaska (There are no roads to the capital city of Juneau.)
43. Kentucky (at Fort Knox)
44. New York (New York City)
45. Wyoming (in 1869)
46. California
47. Alabama (at the Alabama Space and Rocket Center)
48. Kentucky
49. Mississippi (Fooled you—not Washington or Oregon!)
50. Missouri

SURPRISING FACTS ABOUT OUR PRESIDENTS

Presidents are people too. There are many funny, sad, and surprising stories about their lives. Here are some little-known facts about some of the men who have been president of the United States.

FALSE TEETH   By the time he was 57, George Washington had lost all of his teeth. His first set of dentures, or false teeth, was made of wood and ivory. Even wearing them, his face looked funny because his cheeks still caved in. An artist who was painting a picture of Washington had to stuff his cheeks with cotton to make them look normal. Washington tried many different kinds of false teeth. One pair was made of lead. Another pair was made of cow's teeth. All of the dentures were painful. The first president of the United States did not smile very much.

MOTHER TROUBLE   George Washington's mother, Mary Ball Washington, was always complaining about money, even though her son George bought her a house and gave her money all the time. Still she asked for more and told George's friends that he was cheap. Once she even wrote to government leaders and told them she needed money because her son was not taking good care of her. The president was very upset and embarrassed by his mother's complaining.

WET WALLS IN THE WHITE HOUSE
President John Adams was the first president to live in the White House. He and his wife, Abigail, moved in on November 1, 1800. The White House wasn't quite ready. The rooms were very cold, some of the stairways still hadn't been built, and many of the walls had just been plastered and were still wet. The president had to order his staff to bring in many stacks of wood to make fires to dry out the walls.

THE PET MOCKINGBIRD   Thomas Jefferson, the third president of the United States, had a pet mockingbird. He kept it in a cage in his office until he was alone. Then Jefferson let the bird out to fly around the room. The president taught the mockingbird to sit on his shoulder while he worked and to peck food from his lips when he ate. When

Jefferson went upstairs to bed, the mockingbird followed, hopping up the steps, one by one.

THE INVENTOR   Even though he was a very busy president, Thomas Jefferson still found time to work on inventions. Over his lifetime he came up with dozens. He built a revolving chair and a revolving music stand. He also made a pedometer—a gadget that measured how far he walked—and a walking stick that unfolded into a chair. One of his inventions, a new kind of plow for farming, won a gold medal at an exhibit in France.

THE SHORTEST PRESIDENT   At 5 feet 4 inches, James Madison was the short-

George Washington and his mother did not get along this well very often. (Library of Congress)

est of all American presidents. He weighed about 100 pounds, his hair was brown, and his eyes were blue. A shy man, he spoke in a quiet, low voice.

SWIMMING WITHOUT A BATHING SUIT When he was president, John Quincy Adams liked to "skinny-dip"—go swimming with no clothes on. He got up 2 hours before sunrise, walked to the Potomac River, hung his clothes on a tree, and jumped in the water for a fast swim. Usually nobody was around, but once in a while things went wrong. One morning someone stole his clothes and he had to ask a young boy to go to the White House for more. Another time sneaky lady reporter Anne Royall followed him to the river. She had found out about the president's secret swims. While he was swimming, she took his clothes off the tree and sat on them. President Adams, still in the water, saw her and asked what she wanted. Anne Royall said she wanted a special interview with him and she wouldn't get off his clothes until he agreed. The president had no choice. Up to his chin in the water, he answered questions for the lady reporter. Finally she left and Adams got dressed and walked back to the White House.

A BULLET IN HIS BODY The seventh president of the United States, Andrew Jackson, fought a duel in 1806, before he became president. A man named Charles Dickinson said terrible things about Jackson's wife, Rachel, and Jackson challenged him to a duel. The two men met, stood back to back, and walked eight steps before turning to fire their guns. Dickinson shot first, and a bullet hit Jackson's chest. Then Jackson fired and hit Dickinson in the stomach. Dickinson died. Jackson lived, but the bullet was never taken out of his body because it was too close to his heart.

FATHER OF THE MOST CHILDREN John Tyler, our tenth president, had more kids than any other president. He was married twice; his first wife died. With his first wife, Letitia, he had eight children—three boys and five girls. Tyler's second wife, Julia, gave birth to seven children—five boys and two girls. Altogether he was the father of 15 children.

HORSE EATING WHITE HOUSE GRASS Zachary Taylor had a favorite horse named Whitey. He rode the horse when he was a general in the Mexican War. When Taylor became president in 1849, he brought Whitey with him to the White House. The horse was allowed to run around and eat the White House lawn.

MARRIED HIS TEACHER When he was 19, Millard Fillmore could barely read and write. He had grown up on a farm and spent most of his time working instead of going to school. He went back to school and was lucky enough to get a wonderful teacher, Abigail Powers.

He fell in love with her and later married her. Fillmore went on to become a schoolteacher, a lawyer, and the president of the United States.

A BACHELOR IN THE WHITE HOUSE Only one president never got married. He was James Buchanan. He had planned to marry, but his fiancée died when he was 28. His niece Harriet Lane lived in the White House and acted as First Lady during his presidency.

THE TALLEST PRESIDENT Abraham Lincoln was the tallest president. He stood 6 feet 4 inches tall and weighed about 180 pounds. He had very long legs and arms.

THE LITTLE GIRL AND THE BEARD In 1860 an 11-year-old girl named Grace Bedell wrote a letter to Abraham Lincoln, who was then trying to be elected president of the United States. She wanted him to win the election and tried to give him some helpful advice. Grace told him to grow a beard because his face was too thin and whiskers would make him look better. Lincoln wrote a very nice letter back to Grace. He did win the election, without a beard, but started to grow whiskers shortly after. He was the very first president to grow a beard.

DREAMED ABOUT HIS OWN DEATH Before he was killed, Abraham Lincoln had a nightmare. He dreamed he was walking through the White House and heard a lot of crying. When he asked

Of all United States presidents, William Howard Taft weighed the most—over 300 pounds. (Library of Congress)

someone what was wrong, he was told that the president was dead. A week later, on April 14, 1865, Lincoln was shot to death at Ford's Theater in Washington, D.C.

SEWED HIS OWN CLOTHES Andrew Johnson, the 17th president of the United States, was once a tailor, a person who makes and fixes clothing. He even had his own shop in Greeneville, Tennessee. Once, while governor of Tennessee, he made a suit for the governor of Kentucky. Until he became a congressman in Washington, D.C., he made a lot of his own clothes. Johnson was always proud of being a tailor. He was one of our best-dressed presidents.

ARRESTED FOR SPEEDING Ulysses S. Grant was caught speeding in his horse and carriage in the streets of Washington, D.C. The policeman who stopped him started to arrest him but changed his mind when he saw that the driver was the president of the United States. Grant told the policeman, "Do your duty," so the policeman took the horse and carriage to the police station and Grant walked back to the White House. The president later paid a $20 fine. This wasn't his first speeding ticket. He had been caught twice before.

BORN WITHOUT A NAME   The mother of Ulysses S. Grant couldn't decide what to name her new baby. At first she liked the name Albert but then decided against it. For a whole month the baby didn't have a name. Finally she chose Hiram Ulysses Grant. Years later,

when Grant was ready to enter West Point, he didn't want to be embarrassed by his initials, H.U.G. He changed his name to Ulysses S. Grant for the initials U.S.G.

NO BOOZE IN THE WHITE HOUSE President Rutherford B. Hayes was against drinking alcohol. He and his wife, Lucy, never touched a drop and would not allow any to be served in the White House. Instead, lemonade and other soft drinks were served at White House dinners and parties. Because of this, the president's wife got the nickname Lemonade Lucy.

HANGED TWO CRIMINALS One of Grover Cleveland's jobs, before he was president, was sheriff of Erie County, New York. As sheriff, he also had to be executioner. Twice he had to put a noose around a man's neck and spring the death trap. Both men had been convicted of murder.

AFRAID OF THE LIGHTS   Electric lights were first put in the White House in 1891, when Benjamin Harrison was president. He and his wife were so afraid of the new invention that they wouldn't touch the light switches. They asked the servants to turn the lights on and off. If the servants weren't around, they slept all night with the lights on!

GOOD TIMES IN THE WHITE HOUSE Theodore Roosevelt's family had *fun*

President and Mrs. Theodore Roosevelt and their six children posed for this photograph during Roosevelt's first term. (Harvard College Library)

while living in the White House. The 26th president had six children. They walked on stilts and rode bicycles in the halls of the White House. They had pillow fights and roller-skating contests. The children had many pets, including dogs, cats, rabbits, birds, and raccoons—even a black bear and a calico pony named Algonquin. Once, Archie, one of the boys, was sick. The other kids figured out a way to sneak the pony into Archie's bedroom. They got Algonquin into the house, put him in the elevator, and took the pony for a ride, all the way to Archie's room on the second floor.

During World War I, when Woodrow Wilson was president, sheep "mowed" the White House lawn. (Library of Congress)

BOXING MATCHES IN THE WHITE HOUSE Theodore Roosevelt loved sports. He liked horseback riding, wrestling, swimming, tennis, rowing, and hiking. He really enjoyed boxing. When he was president, he boxed in the White House gym. One time he even fought John Sullivan, the heavyweight champion of the world. However, in 1904 he was hit in the left eye during a fight with an army officer. Four years later he was blind in that eye, but he kept his injury a secret for many years.

STUCK IN THE BATHTUB President William Howard Taft was the heaviest of all the presidents. He carried between 300 and 350 pounds on his 6-foot frame. One day he got stuck in the White House bathtub. After that he ordered a special bathtub, just for him.

Four regular-size people could fit into the tub.

SHEEP ON THE WHITE HOUSE LAWN During World War I most of the White House gardeners were drafted into the army. President Woodrow Wilson ordered that a small flock of sheep be placed on the lawn to eat, or "mow," the grass. The sheep did their job well—a little too well: They also ate some of the flowers and plants. Mrs. Wilson sold the wool from the sheep, made over $100,000, and gave the money to the Red Cross.

HATED HIS LOOKS President Woodrow Wilson did not like his looks. He had big ears, a long face, and wore glasses. Most people thought he looked just fine, but he thought he was homely. He did have a good sense of humor and once wrote a poem about his looks.

For beauty I am not a star
There are others more handsome by far
But my face I don't mind it
For I am behind it
It's the people in front that I jar.

THE PRACTICAL JOKER   President Calvin Coolidge played practical jokes. One of his favorites was to press all the buttons on his desk and then hide behind his office door. Soon, everybody—secretaries, the Secret Service, his servants—raced into the office. Then Coolidge would pop out from behind the door and say, "I just wanted to see if everyone is working."

VASELINE FOR BREAKFAST?   No, he didn't eat it. He had it rubbed on his head while he ate his breakfast in bed.

President Woodrow Wilson thought himself homely and wished for better looks. (Library of Congress)

That's what President Calvin Coolidge did with Vaseline petroleum jelly. Nobody is quite sure why.

SECRET CHINESE CODE   President Herbert Hoover and his wife, Lou, spoke Chinese. They had learned the language years before while living in China. Whenever the Hoovers wanted to tell each other something secret in front of guests, they spoke Chinese. It almost always worked.

THE STAMP COLLECTOR   The 32nd president, Franklin D. Roosevelt, had many hobbies, but his favorite was stamp collecting. He had 40 stamp albums and more than 25,000 stamps worth $200,000.

THE MOST FAMOUS WHITE HOUSE DOG   President Franklin D. Roosevelt and his Scottish terrier, Fala, were always together. Each morning, the president gave Fala part of his own breakfast. Fala especially liked bacon and muffins. Sometimes, however, Fala caused trouble, even though he didn't do anything wrong. During the years of World War II, Roosevelt made secret trips to different places. He usually took Fala with him. As soon as the dog needed to go for a walk, the trip was no longer secret. If people saw Fala, they knew that Roosevelt was nearby.

LOTS OF PRESIDENTIAL RELATIVES   By blood or by marriage, Franklin D. Roosevelt was related to 11 other presidents: George Washington, John

Adams, James Madison, John Quincy Adams, Martin Van Buren, William Henry Harrison, Zachary Taylor, Ulysses S. Grant, Benjamin Harrison, Theodore Roosevelt, and William Howard Taft.

THE NAMELESS INITIAL The *S* in Harry S Truman is really a name, not an initial. When Truman was born, his parents couldn't agree on his middle name. Both of his grandfathers had names beginning with *S*. Which should they choose? So that they wouldn't hurt anyone's feelings, the parents decided to use *S* as a middle name. It didn't stand for the name of either grandfather, and it didn't have a period after it.

THE YOUNGEST PRESIDENT John F. Kennedy, the 35th president, was the youngest man to be elected president of the United States. He was 43 years old.

ONE PRESIDENT'S TOAST TO ANOTHER When he was president, John F. Kennedy invited a group of Nobel Prize winners to dinner at the White House. Every one of the guests was a genius. At the dinner table Kennedy made a toast: "I believe this is the most extraordinary collection of talent, of human knowledge, that has ever been gathered at the White House, with the possible exception of when Thomas Jefferson dined alone."

KING OF THE TOOTHBRUSHES President Lyndon B. Johnson liked presenting

President Franklin D. Roosevelt here let a young friend pet Fala, his Scottish terrier. (FDR Library)

gifts to people. His favorite was an electric toothbrush. He said, "I give these toothbrushes to friends for then I know that from now until the end of their days they will think of me the first thing in the morning and the last at night."

WORKED AS A MALE MODEL Before he became a lawyer, Gerald R. Ford had a number of different jobs. For a short time he was a park ranger at Yellowstone National Park. He was also a male model. In 1940 he and a friend modeled winter sports clothes for an issue of *Life* magazine. In 1942, dressed in a navy uniform, Ford made the cover of *Cosmopolitan* magazine.

THE OLDEST PRESIDENT Ronald Reagan was the oldest man to be elected president. When he took the oath of office, he was 16 days short of age 70.

FOOD FACTS

APPLES   Apples are 84 percent water.

BANANA SPLIT   The most miles of banana splits ever made were eaten on August 8, 1984, at the Addison County Field Day in New Haven, Vermont. Exactly 17,654 banana splits in separate dishes touched each other in eight rows that totaled 2½ miles in length. Over 8,000 people were on hand to eat the miles of splits.

COCA-COLA   This soft drink was first made in 1886 by pharmacist John Pemberton of Atlanta, Georgia. He made the syrup as a cure for headaches and hangovers. A worker at his store added carbonated water to the syrup and made the first Coke. For more facts about Coca-Cola, see pages 60, 167, and 177.

DOUGHNUTS   The first doughnuts (with holes) were made by a baker's helper, 15-year-old Hanson Crockett, in Camden, Maine, in 1847. He couldn't get his fried cakes to cook in the middle, so he cut out the soggy centers and made the first ring doughnuts.

HAMBURGER   Raw chopped-meat patties were first seasoned and cooked in Hamburg, Germany. The Germans called them *deutsche,* or beefsteak. In the United States they were first called Hamburg steaks and later hamburgers.

The first major hamburger chain restaurant was White Castle, which was started in 1921. The White Castle hamburger was a thin 2½-inch square and sold for just 5¢.

HONEY   Honey is the only food that does not spoil. Honey found in Egyptian tombs tasted very good, even after sitting for thousands of years. A honeybee makes 154 trips to make just 1 teaspoonful of honey. In order to gather a pound of honey, a bee flies a distance equal to more than three trips around the world. There are more than 250 different flavors of honey in the United States.

HOT DOG   A Chicago newspaper cartoonist named Tad Dorgan came up with the name hot dog. In 1906 Dorgan went to a baseball game in New York's Polo Grounds. He drew a cartoon of the frankfurters served there, making them look like dachshund dogs on buns. Beneath the cartoon he wrote "hot dog," and the new name stuck.

KETCHUP   Ketchup, or catsup, originally came from China. The Chinese made a spicy sauce of fish broth and mushrooms and called it ketsiap. Sailors brought the sauce to England, where tomatoes were added. From then on the name for this sauce was ketchup. Believe it or not, ketchup was once sold as a medicine. Way back in the 1830s one company in the United States sold a product called Dr. Miles's Compound Extract of Tomato.

LEMON   The custom of serving a slice of lemon with fish goes back to the Middle Ages. It was believed that if a person accidentally swallowed a fish bone, the juice from the lemon would dissolve it.

LIFE SAVERS   Life Savers came about by accident. In 1912 Clarence Crane, a candy maker from Cleveland, Ohio, took a new candy recipe to a pill factory to have the candy pressed into discs. The machine goofed and pressed the candy out in little rings. Crane liked the new look. It reminded him of a life preserver. He decided to go ahead and sell the new candy and call it Life Savers. Life Savers are one of the top-selling candies in the United States. Between 1913 and 1980, more than 29,651,840,000 rolls of Life Savers were sold. If that many rolls of candy were placed end to end, their holes would form a tunnel stretching to the moon and back three times!

POPSICLE   At first the Popsicle was called the Epsicle. It was named after its creator, Frank Epperson of San Francisco, California. One cold night in 1905 he happened to leave a glass of lemonade on his windowsill with a stirring stick in it. The next morning the lemonade was frozen on the stick in what was called an Ice Lollipop, then an Epsicle, and finally a Popsicle.

Doughnuts have been an American favorite since they were first made in 1847. (R. Brook Madigan)

POTATO CHIPS   The first potato chips were made by George Crumb, a chef working at the Moon Lake Lodge in Saratoga Springs, New York. One evening in 1835 a customer kept sending his french fries back to the kitchen, complaining again and again that they were too thick and too soft. Finally, Crumb took a potato, sliced it very thin, and fried it. The potato chip was born.

RICE   Rice is the main food for half the people of the world.

SANDWICH   Different kinds of sandwiches have different names. For example, a "grinder" is called that because of the grinding movement the mouth makes to eat it. The "hero" sandwich gets its name from the hero-size appetite needed to eat one. And the "submarine" sandwich has a shape that is like a submarine. You can read about the word *sandwich* on page 160.

HOW LONG DO THINGS TAKE? A QUIZ

In 1977 Stuart A. Sandow wrote a book called *Durations: The Encyclopedia of How Long Things Take.* The book is full of wonderful facts about how long many things take to happen. For instance, the book tells you that it takes an hour to print $392,000 of MONOPOLY money, 103 seconds for a blue shark to swim a mile, and one year for light to travel 5 trillion miles. Listed on the right are ten different "things." Each one matches up with a certain "time it takes" listed below. See how many you can get right! Answers are given at the end.

a. 6 seconds   f. 2 seconds
b. 4 seconds   g. 3 seconds
c. 1 second   h. 10 seconds
d. 8 seconds   i. 5 seconds
e. 9 seconds   j. 7 seconds

How long does this man have to stay on the bucking bronco in order to qualify for a rodeo event? (International Professional Rodeo Association)

1. The time it takes to qualify in a rodeo by staying on a bucking bronco or bull in the riding events
2. The time it takes a small hummingbird to beat its wings 70 times
3. The time it takes the sound of thunder to travel a mile
4. The time it took for the shortest Olympic performance on the balance beam
5. The time it takes to hear the echo of a sound that bounces off a wall 1,100 feet away on a cold day
6. The time it takes to say the McDonald's Big Mac tongue twister: "Two all beef patties, special sauce, lettuce, cheese, pickles, onions, on a sesame seed bun"
7. The time a professional basketball team has to advance out of its back court after the other team has scored
8. The time it takes for a sky diver's static-line parachute to open
9. The time a lion tamer keeps his head in a lion's mouth during his act
10. The time it takes to allemande left or do-si-do during a square dance

ANSWERS
1 = d; 2 = c; 3 = i; 4 = e; 5 = f; 6 = b; 7 = h; 8 = a; 9 = j; 10 = g

THE REAL AMERICAN COWBOY

The cowboy is often pictured in movies and on TV as someone who packs a gun and settles quarrels with shootouts in the main street of town. The real American cowboy did not live this way. He did not shoot anyone who stood in his path and was rarely an outlaw running from the sheriff. The real cowboy usually owned a gun that he hardly ever carried and was not very good at shooting. There were many kinds of cowboys: working cowboys, show cowboys, and *sometimes* outlaw cowboys.

Large numbers of real cowboys lived and worked from around the end of the Civil War in 1865 through the 1880s. In those years cattle ranching was a way of life in the American West. About half the land in the United States was used to raise cattle by 1885. The cowboy was a rugged, important person who did hard, backbreaking work to help provide food for the nation.

Most people do not know that one in every seven cowboys was black. Before the Civil War many blacks worked as cowboys on Texas ranches because they were slaves. During the 30 years after the Civil War, about 5,000 of these black cowboys rode out of Texas to leave slavery behind and look for a new and better way of life. Some cowboys were Mexican, and others were Native Americans. Most white cowboys were southerners, some were midwestern-ers, and a few were English.

America's first working cowboys lived on Texas land where, after the Civil War, ranchers had a big supply of beef but no place in Texas to sell it. Texas ranchers had to get the cattle to

Nat Love was a typical cowboy in the early American West. About one in seven cowboys was black. (Library of Congress)

the nearest railroads, which were in Kansas, in order to ship the cattle to the East Coast of the country, where beef was needed. The cowboys had to push the cattle hundreds of miles along cattle trails to reach the railroads. For the most part, being a working cowboy meant going hungry, getting wet and cold, falling asleep in the saddle while watching a herd, and getting yelled at by the trail boss. A cattle drive meant many months of hard times. A herd of cattle traveled about 12 to 15 miles a day.

Cowboys had special dress for the cattle drives. They wore their pants tight to keep them from being caught in the brush. Leather chaps (flaps) were worn over the pants to protect the cowboy from thorns and branches. A vest, usually made from some kind of animal skin, kept the cowboy warm. A large hat with a wide rim sheltered the cowboy's eyes from sun, wind, and rain. The special hat was also used to send messages, fan a fire, or direct a herd of cattle. A bandanna—like the ones bandits used to cover their faces while holding up a bank—worked as a breathing mask to keep out trail dust. Since the working cowboy was seldom on foot, he wore a high-heeled, pointed-toe boot. The heels gave the cowboy a firm hold in the stirrups while on horseback. The pointed toes helped him slip easily into the stirrups when mounting or slip free if he was thrown from his horse.

Another kind of cowboy was the show cowboy. Because the adventures of real cowboys fascinated people, rodeos and Wild West shows came about. The rodeo became very popular around 1900. It usually included different kinds of events that tested a cowboy's skills. A show cowboy could rope a calf, wrestle a steer, ride a bull, or bust a bronco (tame a wild horse). Cowboys often tested their skills against those of other cowboys just to get to brag about who was the best.

The Wild West shows used these contests as part of their entertainment. Buffalo Bill Cody's Wild West Show was one of the most famous. These traveling shows let people in the eastern part of the United States see how the western cowboys lived and played. People watched everything from wild-animal riding to fancy shooting with the famous six-shooter gun.

In real life a cowboy spent a lot of time with his cattle. After a stampede, for instance, it took days to round up all the cattle that had run wild. The work was hot, dusty, and bone breaking. The average working day was 14 hours. The real cowboy often went without a good night's sleep and only on occasion enjoyed any comforts of home. Because he was always on the move, the real cowboy hardly ever had time to marry and settle down. Cowboys became known as rugged, overgrown kids because most real cowboys were young men in their early twenties and some were truly boys.

THE BODY: A WONDERFUL MACHINE

GROWING BIGGER AND BETTER

At birth the average baby weighs about 7 pounds. The baby has a lot of growing up to do to reach adult size. Not only do the arms and legs grow; the nose and ears grow too. The process of growing up takes about 20 years.

Not all parts of the body grow at the same time or at the same speed. Here, with their speeds and timing, are some of the changes that take place without your even thinking about them.

BONES   A baby has 270 to 300 bones—more than an adult's 206. As you grow up, some of your bones grow together. This is called fusion.

Have you ever gently felt the soft spot on the top of a newborn baby's head? It is soft because there is no bone there yet. The two sides of the skull join together to protect the head, becoming one bone in place of two, when the baby is about 18 months old.

Bones are very soft at birth. Soon they begin to harden, thanks to the calcium in milk and other dairy products. But in childhood, bones are still somewhat flexible and may bend—not break—if you have a bad fall. Doctors call such a bending a "greenstick" fracture. (A green stick is a young twig that has not yet hardened into a firm branch.)

Growth is completed when the bones stop growing and the calcium layer of the bone seals. This happens between the ages of 15 and 25. The last bone to fuse is the collarbone. When it does, you have about 206 bones left instead of 270 to 300 that you had as a baby. Sometimes bones fail to fuse, so some people have one or two extra bones. And one person in every 20 has an extra rib bone.

BRAIN   A newborn baby's head is relatively large compared to the rest of the body. So is a newborn's brain, and that

This baby's body will go through many changes before she grows up. (Sylvia Zebrowski)

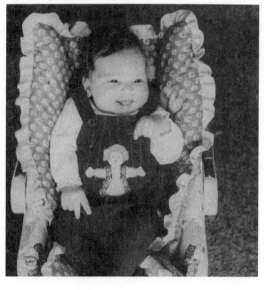

brain also grows faster than the rest of the body. During the first six weeks, the baby's brain doubles in size. By age three the brain is two-thirds the size of an adult's. By age six it is nearly full size, while the rest of the body still has a lot of growing to do.

HAIR   Babies often have only "peach fuzz" on their heads and look bald. There are between 100,000 and 200,000 hairs on a typical adult head. A single hair lives only about two to four years before it drops out and is replaced. The hair on your head is like a forest, with old and new hairs growing side by side. The hair grows about 4 3/4 inches a year, or 25 feet over a lifetime. A man's beard grows a little faster than the hair on his head. There's more about hair on pages 178–179.

EYES   Most babies are blue eyed because the cells for other colors have not yet developed. Between one and two years of age, your eyes turn the color they will stay: blue or green, brown or black. Babies cannot see very well because they cannot focus their eyes; but by about age eight the eyes are giving you your sharpest eyesight.

TEETH   A baby has, of course, no teeth, and a baby's jaws are small compared to the skull. First you develop "milk teeth," or baby teeth; by age four you have about 20 of them. Between the ages of six and 17, the baby teeth fall out. As the jaw grows to make more room, baby teeth are replaced by adult teeth, about 32 in all.

SKIN   A baby's skin is very, very soft. As you grow up, your skin stretches like pie dough and loses that wonderful baby softness. A grown-up's skin is a kind of waterproof sack, with some two million tiny holes in it for sweat glands. It also has places where it is "pleated"—the elbows and knees, so you can move your arms and legs—and places where it is thicker or thinner than elsewhere. It weighs about 6 pounds.

MISSING PARTS AS YOU GROW OLDER

Doctors say you are the healthiest when you are about 15 years old. As you get older, growing stops and getting older begins.

When you cut yourself, you may lose some blood, but the body can replace blood and other cells. Skin cells, for example, are replaced every 19 days;

red blood cells, every three weeks; white blood cells, every four months; kidney cells, every two to four years; and bone cells, every 15 to 25 years.

Brain cells, however, cannot be replaced. Luckily, the 12 billion nerve cells in the brain leave you with some to spare. Over a lifetime you may lose hundreds of thousands of brain cells. By the age of 70 or 80, up to one-quarter of brain cells may have died off.

As you grow older, the eye muscles no longer work so well, and the cornea, the covering over the eye, may get clouded. Many people have to wear glasses later in life as their eyesight gets weaker.

The most common sign of aging is wrinkling. As you grow older, your muscles aren't so firm and your skin loses its elasticity, so it wrinkles. Sometimes the color of the skin changes too. You know how some kids get freckles in the sun? Some older people get blotchy places like big freckles.

The body is such an amazing machine that it can survive with some of its important parts missing—not just a few hairs or teeth either. You may have

Wrinkles, the most common sign of aging

known or heard of someone who lost an arm or a leg and lived a pretty regular life. Did you know that you can survive with only one lung or one kidney instead of the two you start out with? And today doctors perform more and more transplants, so that parts of the body can be replaced if necessary.

SLEEP

If you have a baby brother or sister, you know that he or she sleeps an awful lot. You need less and less sleep as you grow up. Preschool children sleep 10 to 12 hours a night; school children, 9 to 11. When you become an adult, you will probably sleep 7 to 9 hours a night. And some older people sleep only 4 to 6 hours a night.

"TRUE" STORIES THAT ARE UNTRUE (OR PROBABLY UNTRUE)

POCAHONTAS SAVED THE LIFE OF CAPTAIN JOHN SMITH

Captain John Smith was the leader of the English settlers who landed in Jamestown, Virginia, in 1607. During that year he was captured by Native Americans and sentenced to die. As the warriors raised their clubs to kill Smith, a 12-year-old Native American girl ran in between Smith and the warriors. She was Pocahontas, the daughter of Chief Powhatan. Pocahontas saved Smith's life.

Some experts think this story is probably not true. Captain John Smith wrote his first book about Jamestown in 1608. Nowhere in the book did he talk about how Pocahontas had saved his life. Sixteen years later Smith wrote another book, and in that second book he told the story of Pocahontas for the first time. Why did he wait so long to tell such an exciting story?

Among his friends, Smith was known as a great storyteller—someone with a wonderful imagination. In his books there were several other stories about how he had been rescued by beautiful young women. Did he invent the Pocahontas story, or did she really save Smith's life? We may never learn the truth.

Did Pocahontas, the daughter of Chief Powhatan, really save Captain John Smith's life? (National Portrait Gallery, Smithsonian Institution)

HUNDREDS OF WITCHES WERE BURNED IN SALEM

There were witch trials in Salem, Massachusetts, in 1692. Ten young girls in Salem listened to tales of witchcraft told by a slave named Tituba. These girls seemed to be under a spell. They had screaming and crying fits and said that real witches lived in Salem. The girls yelled out the names of the witches, and those people were put on trial. It was a terrible time in Salem. The girls were wrong. There were no witches. But people believed the girls.

Were hundreds of people burned to death in Salem? No, nobody was burned at the stake, but people were found guilty of being witches and were put to death. About 30 were put on trial, and 20 were judged guilty. Nineteen of the 20 were hanged, and one man was pressed to death under rocks.

GEORGE WASHINGTON CUT DOWN A CHERRY TREE

When George Washington was six years old, he got a small hatchet for his birthday. He lived on a farm and found all kinds of things to chop up. One day George's father was very angry. Someone had chopped up a cherry tree so badly that the tree was ruined. George's father said to George, "Do you know who killed that beautiful cherry tree yonder in the garden?" George answered, "I can't tell a lie, Pa. You know I can't tell a lie. I did cut it with my hatchet." George's father was so happy that his son was honest that he didn't punish him.

That is one of the most famous stories about George Washington, the first president of the United States. True?

False. The story was made up by a man named Parson Weems. He wrote one of the first books about George Washington. Weems admired Washington so much that he sometimes invented stories with Washington as the hero. George Washington was a great man—and a hero—but he didn't chop down a cherry tree when he was six years old.

For some surprising facts about George Washington, see pages 188–189.

PAUL REVERE MADE A MIDNIGHT RIDE

Henry Wadsworth Longfellow, a famous American poet, wrote "Paul Revere's Ride." It is the story of how one man named Paul Revere, during the American War for Independence, rode

through the Massachusetts countryside to warn the Americans that British soldiers were coming to attack them. Because of Revere's horseback ride, the American soldiers were ready for the

British attacks. The beginning of Long-fellow's poem:

> Listen, my children, and you
> shall hear
> Of the midnight ride of Paul
> Revere. . . .

Some of the facts in Longfellow's poem are wrong. However, it has become a very popular poem, and many people don't know which facts are true—and which are not.

Here is the real story. Paul Revere did make a midnight ride on April 18, 1775, but he wasn't alone. At first there were two men: Paul Revere, a silversmith, and William Dawes, a shoemaker. Dawes left Boston first and rode to the town of Cambridge. He yelled, "The British are coming!" Revere left later in the day and at midnight arrived in Lexington to spread the same news.

Meanwhile, Dawes met Revere in Lexington, and he and Revere decided to push on to Concord. A third man joined them in Lexington. His name was Samuel Prescott, and he was a doctor. The three men rode off to warn the people of Concord, but all three were stopped by British soldiers. William Dawes was able to turn around and ride back to Lexington. Paul Revere was captured, then released, and walked back to Lexington. William Prescott escaped and made it through to Concord to warn the Americans.

All three men were heroes. All yelled, "The British are coming!" Nobody knows how the poet Longfellow got his facts mixed up. Paul Revere got all the credit. Not too many people remember William Dawes, who rode the most hours, or William Prescott, who made it through to Concord.

BETSY ROSS SEWED THE FIRST AMERICAN FLAG

Here is the story the way it's usually told. In 1776, just before the Declaration of Independence was signed, three important men visited a woman named Betsy Ross. She was a seamstress who lived in Philadelphia. The men were General George Washington, Robert Morris, and Colonel George Ross. All three were members of a flag committee from the Continental Congress. They showed Betsy a drawing of a flag and asked her to sew one just like the drawing. She did, and her flag became the first "Stars and Stripes" flag.

Probably not true. There is no record—no proof—that Betsy Ross was hired to sew the flag. In fact, there was no flag committee in 1776. Betsy did sew some flags, but she made them for the navy. How did the story get started?

It got started in 1870, almost 100 years later. William J. Canby, Betsy's grandson, was giving a speech in Philadelphia and told the story of Betsy Ross making the first flag. He said he had heard the story from his grandmother and from other family members. However, nobody in the family had ever seen Betsy working on the flag, nor had any of the relatives ever seen the finished flag.

The story of Betsy Ross as an American heroine quickly became popular. It was a good one for the 100-year anniversary of the city of Philadelphia, which was coming up. Before long the story was printed in school textbooks. Then everyone believed it was true.

7
SCIENCE

THE PANDA: IS IT A BEAR? IS IT A RACCOON? WHAT IS IT?

PANDA FACTS

The people in China, where the panda lives, have thought of the panda as a god living high up in the mountains.

It was 1869 before Europeans found out that there were pandas.

The panda has a "sixth finger" that looks like a thumb. It is part of the wrist bone and is not a real finger at all, but the panda uses it like one.

Pandas are big eaters. All day long, moving and resting, moving and resting, they eat bamboo. Bamboo is a kind of grass that grows about as tall as two men standing one on the other's shoulders. Pandas eat the food part, not the part like wood. Pandas will also eat meat—mice, for instance—and they eat flowers and grass. Sometimes they steal honey from beehives in villages. Most of their diet, however, is bamboo.

Giant pandas weigh as much as big men—about 200 pounds—but out-eat big men by a lot. Each day pandas eat almost 70 pounds of food! Imagine how much this is. Two apples weigh about a pound, so 140 apples weigh 70 pounds. Could any human being eat that many apples? If you weighed 100 pounds, you would have to eat about 35 apples a day to equal what a panda eats, body weight for body weight. How come pandas don't get very fat? The answer is that their gut belongs to a meat-eater, but they eat vegetable matter. Food goes through a panda's body very fast and doesn't digest very well.

Although pandas live alone and travel alone, they leave signs for one another. They scratch bark to leave

Astronaut Bruce McCandless II space-walks outside the Earth-orbiting space shuttle Challenger. *For more about men and women in space, see pages 244–253. (NASA)*

panda messages. Sometimes they leave behind a smell from their scent glands by rubbing on something with their rear ends.

A baby giant panda weighs about 4 ounces, no more than a couple of small candy bars, and is born to a mother weighing 200 pounds. (If humans were like pandas, a 7-pound baby would have a 5,600-pound mother.) The baby starts eating bamboo when it is 6 months old. It stays with its mother for 18 months.

The giant panda is on the badge of the World Wildlife Fund.

PANDA QUESTIONS

Pandas may be related to bears. The Chinese thought they *were* bears. The Chinese name for panda is *bei-shung*, which means "white bear." Panda blood *is* like bear blood. Then again, pandas may be related to raccoons. Some American scientists have thought so. Nobody knows for sure. Maybe the panda is one-of-a-kind in the animal world.

We don't know when pandas sleep—in the daytime or at night.

We don't know if they hibernate—go to sleep in the winter—like bears.

SAVING THE PANDAS

Pandas live in the bamboo forests of China in the Woolong Natural Reserve, where the mountains are high and rocky. The pandas used to live in lower places too, but people cut down the bamboo forests there to cover the land with farms and towns and cities. That left the pandas nothing much to eat.

Even in the reserve, the pandas may not have enough bamboo. In the winter of 1975–1976 all the umbrella bam-

A giant panda in a Chinese zoo (R. Brook Madigan)

boo for 2,000 square miles died. In 1983 the arrow and fountain bamboo did the same. It is natural for bamboo to die. Bamboo blooms very rarely, sometimes only every 100 years. When that happens, all plants die until new shoots come. The pandas have little to eat. They come down to the lower slopes of the mountains and eat farmers' grain. Still, many die.

The Chinese try to save pandas when the bamboo dies. People go into the mountains to find starving pandas. They catch them with nets and feed them sweet potatoes, sugarcane, meat, and corn. The villagers put out food too, and some is dropped from airplanes. The Chinese have also planted more kinds of bamboo so that it cannot all die out at once.

FAMOUS PANDAS

SU-LIN Ruth Harkness's husband went to China hunting a panda for a zoo, but he died in 1936 before he found one. She went to China herself to finish what he started. With a man called Quentin Young, she traveled 1,500 miles by boat and then hiked into the mountains, where they set out foot traps for the pandas. One day, against orders, a guide killed a panda. Ruth Harkness was very angry. Then in a hollow tree she found a baby panda, probably the child of the dead panda. Ruth Harkness fed the panda from a bottle. She called it Su-Lin, which means "little bit of something cute." Su-Lin came back to the United States in a wicker basket in 1938 and ended up at the Brookfield Zoo near Chicago. After living there a little over a year, she died.

PANDORA THE PANDA Pandora the Panda came to the Bronx Zoo in 1938

as a 24-pound cub. Because she played like a human being, one man thought she was a person dressed up in a skin.

PAN-DEE AND PAN-DUH These two came to the Bronx Zoo in 1939. Pan-duh sat on her own birthday cake.

Giant pandas play on a ladder. (R. Brook Madigan)

MING   Ming was a panda at Regent's Park Zoo, London. When Mary, Queen of England, visited in 1939 Ming grabbed for her umbrella.

LING-LING AND HSING-HSING   In 1972 Ling-Ling and Hsing-Hsing came to the National Zoo in Washington, D.C. The panda cubs turned somersaults and balanced on barrels. In 1983 Ling-Ling and Hsing-Hsing had a baby, but it died after three hours.

ZOO BABIES

No panda was born in a zoo anywhere in the world until 1963. Then finally, a 5-ounce baby was born in Beijing Zoo, China. She was named Ming, which means "brilliant." Since then, more than 30 baby pandas have been born in Chinese zoos.

In 1980 in Mexico City, Ying-Ying gave birth to the first baby panda born in a zoo outside China. Photographers came to take pictures. People came to see the new baby. After seven days Ying-Ying crushed the baby by accident. All the attention had made her too nervous. For two days she wouldn't eat or sleep because she was so sad. Luckily, Ying-Ying had another baby, Tohui, before long. This time she was left alone with the baby. No one stared. All was fine. Tohui lived to grow up. Then in 1983, still another baby was born in Mexico.

ADOPTING A ZOO ANIMAL

You, or a group you belong to, can adopt a zoo animal. When you do this, your money goes toward taking care of it for a year. The animal, of course, stays at the zoo. Often you cannot adopt a specific animal. That is, if you choose to adopt a sheep, your money can go to care for any one of the zoo sheep.

The cost depends on the zoo and the animal you adopt. For instance, at one zoo it costs $50 to adopt a snapping turtle and $1,000 to adopt a tiger. It costs more to feed a tiger!

By adopting an animal, you can free some of the zoo's money for special programs. These include the study of wildlife, saving endangered animals, teaching kids about wildlife, and buying another animal. You get a certificate of adoption and a decal from many adoption programs. Some zoos give

T-shirts, information about your animal, and parties for zoo "parents." The zoos listed below have adoption programs. So does the Popcorn Park Zoo (See pages 426–427). If your zoo is not included, call and ask if it has one.

> Brookfield Zoo Parents Program
> Brookfield Zoo
> 8400 West 31 Street
> Brookfield, IL 60513

Every day, 2,000 animals are fed at the Brookfield Zoo. That's almost a million meals a year. By adopting an animal, you help pay food costs. You get a certificate, a car decal, an iron-on T-shirt decal, and a newsletter. You will also be invited to the Parents Picnic. Adopting a sea lion costs more than $1,000; a kiwi, several hundred dollars. For much less, you can be the parent of a tree shrew, a European harvest mouse, a magpie robin, and other animals.

> Adopt-an-Animal Program
> Columbus Zoo
> 9990 Riverside Drive
> Powell, OH 43065

The zoo pays more than $225,000 a year to feed its animals. If you adopt an animal, you get a certificate, a picture of the animal, facts about the animal, a bumper sticker, a decal, and a T-shirt transfer. You are invited to Adopt-an-Animal Day. It doesn't cost a lot to adopt these animals: gold tetra, hermit crab, pencilfish, talking catfish, yellow stingray, chicken, rock lizard,

Not all the animals at the zoo are real. (© 1985 Chicago Zoological Society)

American toad, barking tree frog, and three-striped poison arrow frog.

> Detroit Zoo
> Zoological Parks Department
> 8450 West Ten Mile Road
> P.O. Box 39
> Royal Oak, MI 48068-0039

You receive a certificate, a card, and an Adopt-an-Animal T-shirt. For not too much money you can adopt these animals: laughing thrush, chicken, frog, newt, turtle, gecko, porcupine, cow, goose, prairie dog, iguana, and swan.

> ADOPT
> Philadelphia Zoo
> 34th and Girard Avenue
> Philadelphia, PA 19104

On the menu for the 1,700 animals at the Philadelphia Zoo are fake ants, chopped meat, and Zoo Cakes. Fake ants are for the anteaters, who won't eat anything they don't think is an ant.

Many zoos allow children to pet some of the animals, like this llama at the Philadelphia Zoo. (Zoological Society of Philadelphia)

Fake ants are made from ground meat and evaporated milk. Zoo Cakes are made of alfalfa-leaf meal, cornmeal, barley, yeast, salt, soybean meal, chicken, cod-liver oil, and water. They are given to bears, monkeys, apes, and other animals. Some meat-eaters get meat, vitamins, and minerals. Animals that eat no meat get a mix of hay, grains, vitamins, and minerals. The turtles' food is put into gelatin so that it will hold together under water.

When you adopt an animal at the Philadelphia Zoo, you get a certificate, adoption papers, and a T-shirt decal. October 18 is ADOPT Parent's Recognition Day, when you meet your zoo-keeper and tour the zoo. On that day,

if your name is drawn, you will get to help feed the animals. Animals you can adopt for not too much money are the fat-tailed gecko, Madagascan tomato frog, African hedgehog, chinchilla, Egyptian fruit bat, southern grasshopper mouse, vampire bat, and paradise tanager.

Riverbanks Zoo Parent Program
Riverbanks Zoological Park
500 Wildlife Parkway
Columbia, SC 29210

There are 800 animals in the Riverbanks Zoo family. When you adopt an animal, you get a Zoo Parent certificate, window decal, and T-shirt iron-on. The head of the zoo will invite you to the yearly Zoo Parent Picnic. It doesn't cost much to adopt a fox squirrel, Tokay gecko, Amazon tree boa, black-bellied seedcracker, Pekin robin, or red-legged honeycreeper. If you have a couple of thousand dollars, you can adopt an elephant. If you don't,

Olga the walrus celebrates Christmas at the Brookfield Zoo. (© 1985 Chicago Zoological Society)

you can share the elephant with other people and split the cost.

Animal Adoption Office
San Diego Zoo
Zoological Society of San Diego
Post Office Box 551
San Diego, CA 92112

The zoo has 3,200 animals to feed. They need papaya for the howler monkeys and hay for the Asian elephants. Some of the animals up for adopting at the lowest rate are the elephant shrew, armadillo, Barbary sheep, green iguana, blue-tongued skink, tiger snake, bearded dragon, Amazon parrot, fairy bluebird, Hawaiian goose, king vulture, and hummingbird. There's more about the San Diego Zoo on pages 85 and 288.

Orca Adoption Program
P.O. Box 945
Friday Harbor, WA 98250

You can also adopt a whale. This program was founded to save the orca, or "killer" whale in Puget Sound, Washington. Once the whale was hunted. The state of Washington put a stop to that in 1976, but now pollution is killing orcas.

You or your group can adopt an orca for about $20. You get a certificate, a picture of your orca, the story of your orca, and a newsletter.

INTERESTING FACTS ABOUT ORCAS

You can tell one from another by the shape of a patch on the back and by the shape of the back fin.

They are not really killers, except of the fish they eat.

Orcas live in groups of families. Each group eats, travels, and plays together. And each group has its own "language" of calls.

When orcas play, they chase one another and jump out of the water.

THE PARADE OF THE GRAY WHALE

WHALE FACTS

Whales live in the ocean, but they are not fish. They are mammals, like humans. Like humans, they breathe air. Like humans, whale babies drink their mother's milk.

What is the largest animal that ever lived? A *whale*, not a dinosaur.

Whales are very smart. They "speak" to one another in a language that varies. Scientists record whale songs, then try to figure out what the whales are saying to one another.

Although whales are big, some of them, called baleen whales, eat very tiny things—shellfish smaller than a fingernail. The whales swim among the shellfish and fill their mouths with the creatures. Then they push out the seawater with their big tongues. A part of their upper jaw, the baleen, hangs down and, like a sieve, traps the shellfish inside. The whales digest the food in their three-roomed stomachs. Even a one-year-old whale eats more than 1,000 pounds of fish a day.

Gray whales are baleen whales. They were once rare, but countries got to-

A gray whale calf that has slid up on its mother's back eyes a human being. (Alisa Schulman)

gether and agreed to stop killing them in 1937. In the United States, whales are kept safe by the Marine Mammal Act.

THE BIG PARADE

Every winter huge gray whales parade down the California coast in a stately procession. They are leaving their summer home in the sea of the far north for their winter home in the south.

In summer in the north, daylight lasts almost 24 hours each day, and the whales keep eating. Although their food is small, the whales eat so much of it that they put on blubber. Blubber is fat that they need to keep them warm in the cold water.

In winter when the ice comes, the whales must leave or be trapped in the ice and die. The trip south takes three months, from October to December. It is 4,000 miles long. Sometimes the whales are far from the sight of land.

Once they arrive in Mexico, the whales breed in lagoons. Their babies are often born in the lagoons, where the water is very salty. The salty water may help to hold the babies up.

In March and April the gray whales make the return trip north. You probably will not see them, though, because then they travel far offshore.

If you live on the California coast and want to see gray whales, the time to do it is October to December. Pick a place where they are known to pass close by and where you can look down. About 15,000 gray whales travel past the coast every year. Sometimes you can see 25 to 30 at once parading by on their southward journey. Some places sponsor whale-watching trips on boats, but whales often travel south close enough to land to be seen from shore.

Since whales must come up for air, you are likely to see them if they come by. Watch for the white plume they make when they "blow." If you're lucky, you may see the whales come up out of the water. For example, when whales want to see what is going on in the air, they stick their heads out for a look. This is called "spyhopping." Baby whales slide up over the backs of their mothers to see what's going on. Sometimes whales breach (leap out of the water), turn over, and then fall back in the water.

This spyhopping gray whale is covered with barnacles and lice. (Alisa Schulman)

FISHY PETS

You can keep a bit of a lake right in your house. How? Have a fish tank, or aquarium. Keeping fish can be simple. It can also be involved. Perhaps the easiest fish to raise are goldfish. Guppies are not too much trouble either.

If you have problems with your fish, talk to the people in the pet store. They are trained to solve problems with fish.

GENERAL RULES

GETTING THE WATER READY FOR FISH Before you buy fish, clean out a couple of plastic jugs. *Don't use soap.* Then fill the jugs with water and leave them in the room where you will keep the fish.

Let the water get as hot or cold as the room. Wait for the chlorine in the water to pass into the air, or else use chlorine remover in the water. (You can get chlorine remover at a pet store.)

When you clean an aquarium, wash everything in it—except the fish! (John P. Edwards)

CHOOSING THE FISH   When you start your aquarium, begin with the fish that are easiest to raise. Add the kinds that are harder to raise later. Add the fish once a week, one at a time.

To make sure of healthy fish, pick those that are swimming, have perfect fins, and do not have any signs of disease. Don't pick those at the top or bottom of the tank in the pet store. Don't pick fish with faded colors. Bring each fish home in a plastic bag with water in it.

CHOOSING THE BOWL   Be sure to get a bowl or aquarium with a wide mouth. Why the wide mouth? More water surface meets the air, so more oxygen from the air gets into the water. Fish need oxygen to live.

WELCOMING THE FISH TO ITS HOME Rinse out the fishbowl. Fill it with the water from the plastic jugs. Leave the fish inside the plastic bag and, without opening the bag, place it in the fishbowl. Do this so that the temperature of the bag water can slowly become the same as the bowl water. After an hour, let the fish out.

BUYING FISH FOOD   The kind of fish food you buy depends on the fish. Goldfish need food made of bits of dried vegetables. Since guppies eat fish, they need food that is mostly meat.

FEEDING   Never overfeed the fish. Why? Old food settles to the bottom of the tank and rots. The rot breeds germs that are bad for your fish. Just put a bit of food on the top of the water. How much is a bit? A pinch of food between your thumb and first finger should do the trick.

CLEANING THE BOWL   Clean the bowl when it gets dirty. Once again, fill your two plastic jugs with water and wait a day. You'll also need a siphon hose and a bucket. Holding one end closed with a finger, fill the hose with water under the tap and then close the open hose end with another finger. Fingers in place on the hose, dip one end in the bowl and the other in the bucket. Now release the fingers. Use the end of the hose in the bowl as a little vacuum cleaner that sucks up the dirt at the bottom of the bowl—with water instead of with air! Leave enough water in the bowl to cover your fish. Stop the flow by pulling the hose from the bowl and letting the last water in the hose flow into the bucket.

You can also use a straw to clean the bottom of the bowl. Get food or other stuff inside one end of the straw, put your finger over the other end, and pull the straw out of the water. Empty the stuff into the trash by taking your finger away from the end of the straw.

When you've drained as much water as you can, take out your fish and sponge the inside of the bowl. *Don't use soap.* While you sponge, your fish can live in the water in the bucket. Use a fishnet to move them back and forth.

Be careful not to disturb the gravel when you pour the clean water in. (John P. Edwards)

When the bowl is clean, fill it with the water from the plastic jugs and put your fish back in.

RAISING GOLDFISH AND GUPPIES

To raise goldfish and guppies, follow the general rules. In addition, with guppies, get a pair, a male and a female. Keep the guppy tank warm, at least 65 degrees F. at night and between 70 and 80 degrees F. in the daytime. If it is cold at night, put a lamp next to the tank. After a while the guppies should have babies. Don't be upset when the big fish eat the little ones.

CITY GARDENS

Just because you live in the city doesn't mean you can't have a garden. Dirt, water, and sun are all to be found in a city, and they are all you need for a garden—a garden that will grow indoors. Wherever you live, you may enjoy gardening indoors.

SOME GENERAL TIPS

Most plants (but not all) grow in dirt. You can make good dirt for plants from ⅓ potting soil, ⅓ sand, and ⅓ vermiculite. You can buy all three at a garden store or buy the sand from a pet store. Don't use beach sand, because it is too salty for plants.

You need pots to hold plants and their dirt. The pots should have drainage. That is, there should be a way for extra water to flow out of the pot at the bottom—a hole! Before you put dirt and a plant in a pot, layer a few small stones or broken pieces of pot at the bottom. Then, holding the plant in the pot with one hand, add dirt around it with the other, packing the dirt lightly. Keep the plant centered in the pot. Fill the pot with dirt to within ½ inch of the rim.

Always work on newspaper so you don't get dirt all over everything.

Most plants need water, but not too much. Too much water can kill them. Don't water the leaves. Water the soil. Add water a little at a time and stop as soon as any runs out the hole at the bottom of the pot. Keep a dish under the pot to catch water drips. Never water soil that's already damp.

Most plants need sun, but not too much. Plants reach for the sun, so turn them around once in a while. That way they won't grow lopsided. Check in a plant book for the amount of sun different kinds of plants need.

DISH GARDEN

WHAT YOU NEED

    3 or 4 carrots
    2 beets
    2 turnips
    shallow saucer or aluminum pan
    (perhaps from frozen food)
    wet sand

TO MAKE THE DISH GARDEN   Cut off the vegetables about 1 inch below their tops. Eat the carrot bottom. Cook the beet and turnip bottoms and eat them too.

Put the wet sand in your saucer or pan dish, about 1 inch deep. Leaves up, bury the cut-off tops halfway down in the sand in the dish.

Keep the garden well lit, but out of direct sun. Lightly sprinkle the dish with water every day.

In about a week green sprouts will show at the tops. In a few weeks, you will have carrot, beet, and turnip leaves.

WORLD IN A BOWL

A terrarium is a tiny earth garden growing in glass. Some terrariums are completely closed off. They don't even need watering. The plants inside the terrarium use the same water again and again. They pull water from the earth, the air pulls water from them, and then the air hits the cold glass top. Water in the air turns to drops on the glass and falls back on the plants and the earth and is recycled again.

The little world has other advantages, besides watering itself. It is screened from pollution, its temperature is very steady, and insects find it hard to get in.

WHAT YOU NEED

a glass bowl with no drainage hole (An old fishbowl will do.)

glass lid or plastic kitchen wrap

tools: small watercolor paintbrush, long-handled spoon

little stones or coarse sand

some charcoal (kind used in aquariums)

soil for terrariums (In a pail, mix together 2 cups potting soil, 2 cups coarse sand, and 2 cups peat moss, shredded.)

shredded peat moss or sphagnum moss (in addition to what's in the soil mix)

decoration (bits of wood, rocks, shells, pinecones, for example)

moss

tiny plants

You can buy tiny plants or find them in a woods, backyard, or field, but don't mix up wild and store-bought plants. If you buy them, choose from golddust, dracaena, nephthytis, tiny evergreens, ferns, ivy, baby's tears, palm trees, African violets. If you find plants outdoors, dig them up with a trowel or spoon and get lots of soil with each plant. Put each one in its own plastic bag or paper cup. Water them when you get home. Make sure the plants look good together.

TO MAKE YOUR TERRARIUM

1. Wash the glass bowl and let it dry. Make sure you've rinsed off all the soap. Wash everything else except the plants.

2. Put enough stones or sand in the bottom of the bowl to cover it to a depth of 1 or 2 inches. You can vary the depth, making a little hill.

The ingredients you need for a terrarium (John P. Edwards)

Make sure that you firmly tamp down the dirt when you put your plants in your terrarium. (John P. Edwards)

spoon to dig little holes for them in the soil and push down the dirt around them once they are in. The moss doesn't need a hole. It can simply be pushed into the soil. Leave the plants enough room.

7. Arrange the decorations.
8. Use the brush to get dirt off the glass.
9. Water the plants with a mister or a bulb sprinkler, the kind used for ironing clothes. Stop when you can see the water going into the sand at the bottom.
10. Let the terrarium sit for a day or two. When you see no more water on the inside walls, cover the terrarium with the lid.
11. Put the terrarium within 5 feet of a window, but not in direct sunlight.

3. Put down a thin layer of charcoal.
4. Add about an inch of peat moss or sphagnum moss.
5. Finish off with 2 or 3 inches of soil, varying its landscaping.
6. Decide where the plants will go. To decide, arrange them in various ways in their little pots in a place about the size of the terrarium floor. Keep bigger plants where they won't hide the little ones. Choose a taller one (a little tree, perhaps) as an accent. Now put the plants in the terrarium. Use the

AFTER YOU FINISH YOUR TERRARIUM

If the terrarium becomes foggy, take the lid off, at least partway. Water once a month. Take out dead leaves and plants. Wipe inside and out once in a while.

Why not put together another terrarium? There are many plants to try in a wide variety of containers. Some people like the challenge of getting the earth and the plants down through the narrow neck of a glass bottle. It takes special tricks and some practice. And remember: If you can't care for more terrariums yourself, they make great gifts!

HOW YOU CAN HELP STOP POLLUTION

Pollution is bad air. It's junk on the streets. It's garbage dumps. It's bad water. It's toxic wastes. It's all sorts of poisons. Much pollution exists because of waste. You can help stop it. Here are some ways to help.

RECYCLING

Newspaper, glass bottles, and aluminum cans can be used again to save trees, metal, and energy. Recycling centers are places where you can take these things. Most recycling centers have rules about how materials are accepted. Usually, these are the rules.

NEWSPAPERS Put newspapers in brown paper bags or tie them in bundles with string. Newspaper can be burned for energy or made into new paper. Most recycling centers do not take other kinds of paper.

GLASS Sort glass bottles by color. Bottles should be clean, with tops off. You can leave the labels on. Bottles can be used again after washing, or they can be melted down for making glass fibers. No window (plate) glass can be taken.

CANS Only aluminum cans are accepted, and most are labeled as such. They should be clean. The aluminum can be used again, to make more cans. Remember, no tin cans.

To recycle garbage, heap up vegetable and fruit peelings in the yard and cover them with dirt. This is a compost heap. Don't include bones or meat scraps. Keep the compost heap a bit damp. In a month or two the peelings will have rotted to make rich dirt. You can use the rich dirt in your garden.

SHOPPING

Buy recycled paper products. They are usually labeled as such.

Whenever you can, buy things that are used or get your old things fixed. When you do buy new things, buy those that will last a long time. Every product thrown away means more of a waste problem.

At the grocery store, ask for paper bags, which can become part of the soil again, rather than plastic bags, which cannot. Or carry a string bag to the store and bring your things home in it.

SAVING ENERGY AND WATER

To save energy, first become aware of all the ways it's wasted.

Don't leave lights on when you don't need them.

Take showers rather than baths. Showers usually take less water than baths.

Walk or ride a bike instead of going by car. Bicycles cost much less to make and use far less material. They don't pollute the air, and they take up less parking space. In rush hour they are sometimes faster than cars.

Put a sweater on instead of turning up the heat.

Every new product means use of energy. Use your imagination to put old things to work. For example, old tires make swings and tunnels in playgrounds.

ACTION

Join a group fighting pollution, or start a group yourself—a kids' group.

If your state does not have a bottle return law, fight for one. Write to your representatives in the state law-making body. Ask them to push for such a law. It takes six times as much energy to make one throwaway can as to make one returnable bottle.

Spread the word on pollution problems. Ask your friends and family to write letters to government agencies.

Start a clean-up-your-city group. You could get a group together to clean up a park or the beach or an empty lot in the neighborhood. (Check with the owner of the property first.) Make sure there is a grown-up to help.

Try to get people to use bikes to go from one place to another. Start a bicycle club. Have a Bike Day, when people use bikes instead of other means of transportation.

Help trees. Trees keep the air clean and fight noise pollution. Adopt a tree in your city. Make sure it has enough water.

Beautiful waterways become ugly from the junk people leave behind. (Steve Delaney, EPA)

Throwing trash from boats can pollute the water. (Steve Delaney, EPA)

Pollution often can't be seen from high above the earth. (Steve Delaney, EPA)

Spraying water from a drinking fountain may be fun, but it wastes a precious resource. (Steve Delaney, EPA)

This boy catches crabs in his net—but crabs can't live if the water is too dirty. (Steve Delaney, EPA)

Trucks and cars leave behind air-polluting gases. (Steve Delaney, EPA)

STORIES BEHIND INVENTIONS OF EVERYDAY THINGS

ALARM CLOCK Levi Hutchins made clocks for a living in the 1700s. In those times people depended on the sun to wake them up, but Hutchins had to get up at four in the morning. It was still dark then, and the sun couldn't wake him. So in 1787 Hutchins invented a special clock. This clock had a gear that tripped the minute hand and started a bell ringing.

BICYCLE In 1790 a Frenchman named de Sivrac made a wooden vehicle called a *célérifère*. It looked like a horse on wheels. It had no pedals. The rider made it go by pushing on the ground with his legs. Karl von Drais, a German, added a way to steer about 1816. Blacksmith Kirkpatrick Macmillan of Scotland added pedals and invented the first "modern" bicycle in 1839. A carved horse's head decorated the front of the frame. It was hard to stop. Other people improved the bicycle over the years.

CHEWING GUM Long ago natives of Mexico chewed chicle, the gum of the sapodilla tree. Then, in 1870, a United States inventor, Thomas Adams, was trying to make something to replace rubber. Chicle gum looked as if it might work, so he was playing around with it. He chewed a piece just for fun, liked it, and began selling it. At first not many people bought chicle gum. It seemed silly just to chew and chew on

something. Then Adams had the idea of asking shopkeepers to give customers a piece of the gum when they bought candy. He also added sugar and flavor to his chewing gum, and it did become popular. By 1890 he owned a huge factory making nothing but chewing gum.

FLEXIBLE STRAW It used to be hard for little children to drink through straws. When they sat at a table, they were too short for their mouths to reach the straw end sticking out of the glass. If they tipped the glass, they could spill the drink. If they bent the straw, the bent place shut off the flow. One day Joseph B. Friedman saw his little girl struggling with these problems. It gave him the idea for a new kind of straw made of plastic with a band of pleats in its middle. This new straw could bend easily. It was the first flexible straw.

FORK Though forks were invented by at least the 1000s, most people didn't use them. They ate with their knives instead. A famous English writer, Jonathan Swift, said, "Fingers were made before forks. . . ." The English thought forks were sissy. Most Asians, of course, use chopsticks. According to one story, a Chinese, offered a fork, said that he didn't want it, because it had been in hundreds of mouths before his, maybe even his enemy's.

ICE-CREAM CONE   There are at least two stories about the first ice-cream cone. (1) In 1904 Charles E. Menches, an ice-cream salesman, visited his girlfriend. He brought her presents: flowers and an ice-cream sandwich. She had no vase, so she rolled up one of the sandwich layers to hold the flowers. Then she made another cone, this one for the ice cream, from the other sandwich layer. (2) About the same year Abe Doumar was selling souvenirs at a fair. He overheard the ice-cream salesman nearby say he had run out of dishes. Doumar suggested making cones from waffles to hold the rest of the ice cream.

PAPER BAG   Mattie Knight began to invent things at age 12. She is most famous for the invention of a machine that would make a paper bag with a flat bottom. She died in 1914 at age 76.

PAPER CLIP   Someone picked up a hairpin on the sidewalk, bent it into shapes, and realized one shape could hold sheets of paper together. There have been paper clips ever since.

RUBBER BAND   Before America was discovered by Europeans, natives in Central and South America, where the rubber tree grows, made rubber balls and other things. A French explorer, Charles de la Condamine, sent rubber to Europe from Peru. People noticed that it made a good eraser. A rubber bottle was turned into the first rubber bands. Thomas Hancock thought of slicing a rubber bottle, as if it were a

John Boyd Dunlop, 1840–1921, who invented tires (Dunlop Tire Corporation)

hollow round of bologna, to make rubber bands for waistbands and garters.

TIRE   In 1888 the little son of John Dunlop, an Irish veterinarian, had a problem. The metal wheels of his tricycle were being damaged by stony streets. To stop the damage, Dunlop invented a tire filled with air. It was wrapped, like a bandage, on the tricycle wheel and was called a "pudding" or "mummy" tire.

TOILET PAPER   In 1857 a man named Gayetty invented a toilet paper with his name on each sheet. It was called Gayetty's Medicated Paper. Five hundred sheets sold for 50¢. That was a lot of money in those days.

Three gentlemen meet under three umbrellas about 200 years ago. (Library of Congress)

One of the first vacuum cleaners, the Model "O" manufactured by the Hoover Company in 1908 (The Hoover Company)

UMBRELLA Umbrellas go back thousands of years. Egyptians carried them. In Burma one of the king's titles was Lord of the Great Parasol. Only the king could use a white one. But the umbrella as we know it—for protection from rain, not sun—was invented in the late 1700s. Sometimes makers put acorns on the handles, thinking acorns would keep umbrellas safe in lightning. (The god of thunder's sacred symbol was the oak tree.) At least one person attached a wire to his umbrella top for the same reason—protection from lightning. The wire trailed after him as he walked along.

People made fun of umbrellas. Those who drove horse-drawn cabs for a living were afraid they would lose business if umbrellas became popular. Umbrellas made it easier for people to walk in the rain. Some people were afraid to carry an umbrella because it might show that they had no carriage. Other people made fun of umbrella users by following them, carrying sieves on broom handles.

VACUUM CLEANER Hubert Cecil Booth invented the first vacuum cleaner that worked and became popular. The problem was how to sift the dust out of the stream of air. He had the idea of sucking the air and the dirt *in*, to a trap that would hold only the dirt. To test if this would work, he put a handkerchief over his mouth and sucked. Dirt was trapped in the handkerchief. The first of his vacuum cleaners, in 1901, was so big it had to be drawn by horses from house to house. It stayed outside and pulled dust from the house with a long hose. Booth's machine was used to clean the blue carpet in Westminster Abbey before the crowning of Edward VII as the king of England in 1901.

WRISTWATCH   The wristwatch was invented in Switzerland in 1790. The first ones were little clocks attached to bracelets. A famous empress, Josephine, wore one covered with pearls and emeralds. German army officers wore wristwatches in 1880. They were more practical in battle. In the time it took to reach for a pocket watch, an officer could get shot.

BEING AN INVENTOR

To be an inventor, you don't have to come up with a world-changing idea. Some of the best inventors think of a better way to make something that already exists.

For example, car windshield shades that look like giant eyeglasses were invented by Abraham Levy of Israel. Over a million were sold in Israel from the mid-1970s to the mid-1980s. The idea came to Levy when he had to park his car in the sun. He knew his car would be hot inside when he came back. He decided to invent something to solve the problem, but his first models didn't work. For instance, he tried a board made of plastic, but it got dirty and didn't fold. Levy worked with lots of shapes and materials before he came up with folding cardboard.

The idea of windshield shades wasn't new with Levy. People before him had tried to make them. Some shades had folding legs and suction

cups. Others rolled down. The earliest shade, invented in 1912, was a gadget with curtains. Levy's was the model that caught on. It was cheap, simple, and easy to make, and people were willing to buy it.

Like Levy, you don't have to know a lot of math and science to be an inventor. An open mind is more important. So is being willing to keep trying. Ask yourself questions: How could something be better? Cheaper? What bothers you about it? Could the bother be changed? What, for instance, might be done to improve a school lunch box? To help with certain parts of homework, could a special computer program be written? What could make housekeeping easier for you, your mother, and your father, besides somebody else to do the work? What is it about yard work that you hate? Can you invent something to make it easier or more fun? How can tools be improved? Remember, good inventions are often the inspirations of lazy people.

Once you have an idea, ask yourself more hard questions: Is it really new? Is it practical? Will people use the invention often enough so that it will make money? Can it be made cheaply enough so that people will buy it? Can many copies of it be made easily? Will it be as good as things like it? The simplest ideas are often the best.

Now it's time to build a model. Attack the most difficult problem first. When something you try doesn't work, learn from it. Ask yourself why it didn't work. That may give you an idea for something else to try. Take your time. When you have a model, tinker with it. Make it as perfect as you can. Test it several times to make sure it works.

When you have finished refining the idea for your invention, draw a picture of it on one side of a piece of paper. Describe it in writing on the other side. Date the paper. Put it in a self-addressed envelope, seal it with sealing wax, and send it to yourself by registered mail. Do not open the envelope. This is your proof that you were the first to think of the idea.

HOW TO PATENT AN INVENTION

Anyone can patent an invention, even a child.

When you have a patent, the United States government gives you the right to make your invention, use it, and sell it. You are the only person who has this right. If someone copies your invention, you can take that person to court.

Over 100,000 people request patents each year. You can get a patent for (1) new and useful inventions or discoveries, (2) new and useful ways of making something better. Most patents are for 17 years.

If you come up with an important invention, perhaps you should ask your parents or guardian to help you patent it. Getting a patent is not simple, and it costs money. Most inventors hire a patent attorney to help them. The patent attorney prepares papers. He arranges for a Patent Office search to see if someone else has already come up with the same idea. He sees the invention through the whole process, which takes a long time. The Patent Office will send you a list of patent attorneys. Write for the *Directory of Registered Patent Attorneys and Agents Arranged by States and Countries.*

Commissioner of Patents and
Trademarks
Washington, DC 20231

Be sure to enclose a self-addressed, stamped envelope (See page 341).

ODYSSEY OF THE MIND

The Odyssey of the Mind (OM) was started in 1978 by Dr. Samuel Micklus, a professor of technology at Glassboro State College in Glassboro, New Jersey. He believes that young people can compete in mental contests as well as in physical ones. The games that make up this special kind of Olympics are "mind games." Micklus believes that the games he dreams up are to be played with the same competitive spirit as sports games.

The idea behind OM is that creative thinking *can* be taught. OM encourages creative problem solving by kids. Micklus thinks there are a lot of problems that need solving in the future and that kids need to be taught how to solve them. Kids get a chance to show off how creative they can be. Some teachers and coaches are surprised to see that the pain-in-the-neck kid sometimes turns out to be one of the smartest and most creative in OM.

The competition in OM is in three divisions: kindergarten through grade 5; grades 6 through 8; and grades 9 through 12. Students must first win a local competition before going on to the national championships.

Most students work on teams. OM teams cannot have more than seven persons. Each team has an adult coach to act as an adviser to the group. Teams and coaches might spend up to five months trying to solve a particular problem. Points are awarded to the teams that do the best; points are also given to teams for the way they present

their creation. Showmanship takes brains too!

Some problems are short, and others are long. Depending on how tough the problem is, you may get minutes—or months—to figure it out. A short-term problem, for example, might be to take a clothes hanger and, in 1 minute, think of as many different things as possible that it could be. One long-term project was to find a new use for a mousetrap. Using a mousetrap as the main body, one student team created

The problem in this OM competition was to build a balsa-wood structure to balance and support heavy weights. (IBM/Odyssey of the Mind)

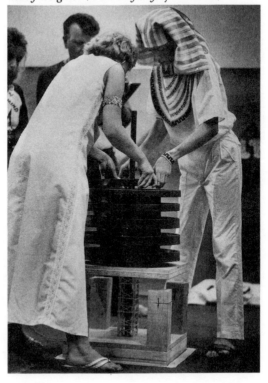

Another OM problem had this solution: a mouse-trap that sets off 49 other mousetraps, rings a bell, raises a flag, and breaks a balloon. (IBM/Odyssey of the Mind)

a movable, big-wheeled "mousemobile." You get a lot more time for this kind of problem.

One of OM's most popular problems for young kids was "Cruppets." In this game kids were asked to write and act out a short play. The students could have five cruppets (puppets) in the play, and each one had to look like someone famous. Older children have had problems like "Earthquake Struc-

ture." Teams were asked to build a structure using balsa-wood strips, no taller than 8 inches and not weighing more than 1/2 ounce. Yet this same structure was supposed to be strong enough to hold very heavy weights! Another problem was "Monsters Menacing Mankind." This problem asked students to build remote-controlled creatures that could battle with creatures built by another team. Micklus is always on the lookout for more problems.

Since 1979 OM has spread to schools all across the United States. Many kids think that this kind of competition is a Super Bowl of the mind. OM tells kids that whether they win or lose, they are already champions in their own minds. Searching for a way to solve a problem can be exciting and fun. If you want more information about the competition, please write for it.

Odyssey of the Mind
P.O. Box 27
Glassboro, NJ 08028

Remember to enclose a self-addressed, stamped envelope (See page 341).

ARCHAEOLOGICAL DIGGERS: DETECTIVES OF THE EARTH

Archaeology is a study of the things of the past. What things? A temple. A piece of garbage. A spinning wheel. A ship. A piece of pollen. A few stones. Almost anything!

Many things archaeologists find are

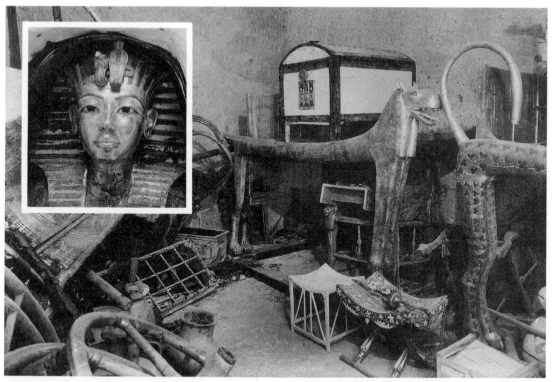

Tutankhamen, a young king of Egypt, lived more than 3,000 years ago. In 1922 archaeologists opened Tut's tomb and found this gold mask and many other things—even a chariot and a horse—inside. (Egyptian Expedition, The Metropolitan Museum of Art)

buried in the earth. If you have ever been around when someone was digging a hole, you know what can happen. Lost and forgotten things turn up—a tool, your sister's Mickey Mouse watch, coins. Things that were lost in the grass got buried in the dirt as time went on. Whole cities and towns can also become buried, and they interest archaeologists. Usually, the farther down they dig, the older the things they find.

When cities and towns burn or earthquakes shake them or people leave them to go someplace else, the build-ings fall down and dirt covers them. Slowly they become buried. But cities can be buried in another way. For example, 1,900 years ago in Pompeii, Italy, a volcano erupted without warning. It happened so quickly that people were caught and the whole town was buried in the volcano's dust. When archaeologists dug up Pompeii, they found things as they had been that day of the eruption. The baker's loaves were still in the oven. A dog was still chained at the door. It was like going back in time.

TREASURE OF TROY

When Heinrich Schliemann was eight years old, he saw in a book a picture of a city in flames. The picture changed his life. The old city in the picture was Troy, set on fire by the Greeks during a war fought partly because of a beautiful woman named Helen. The artist had drawn the picture based on the facts in an old poem written more than 2,700 years ago. No one knew exactly where the city had been. In fact, no one knew if the city had been real. After all, the poet could have made up the story. Heinrich made himself a promise: He would find the lost city of Troy.

When he was 14, he got a job working for a grocer, and when he was older, he went into business and became rich. In 1871, when he was 50, Heinrich was able to start digging for Troy.

From reading the poem and other books, he had a good idea where Troy was, and there he headed. Of course it had to be buried. For three years he and his crew of 150 workmen dug.

They took out 250,000 cubic meters of dirt and junk. That's enough to fill 1,500 houses. He didn't find one city—he found seven! He and his young wife, Sophia, lived in a hut near the dig. It was cold in winter. In summer snakes and mosquitoes bothered them. At night he and Sophia sorted through what had been found during the day—pottery, tools, weapons.

At last the diggers reached the bottom city. Schliemann thought it was the Troy in the poem. One day he spied a piece of copper in the dirt. It was treasure, he thought. He let his workmen go so that they would not know about the treasure and steal it. He and Sophia dug where the copper was, and they *did* find treasure—buttons, vases, cups, two beautiful diadems (thin crowns), and 8,700 gold rings! Shliemann draped Sophia with jewelry and said, "Darling . . . you are wearing the treasure of Helen of Troy." But she wasn't. The city he had found was 1,000 years older than Helen's Troy.

THE FARMBOY AND THE FURNACE

In 1924 a French farmboy of 15, Emile Fradin, was plowing a field. The oxen pulling his plow fell into a hollow. In the hollow, Emile found two bricks stamped with designs. He began to dig. He found a paved floor, some glass, and an ax head. Though he didn't know it, he had unearthed a glassmaker's furnace from the Middle Ages.

THE ANCIENT BULLS

In 1868 a Spanish hunter in a place called Altamira was digging a fox from its hole and found a cave. Twelve years later, an archaeologist, Señor Marcelino de Sautola, decided to dig out the cave some more. While he was working, his daughter wandered deeper into it, carrying a candle. On the walls she saw red and black paintings of animals. Her shouts of *"Toros! Toros!"* ("Bulls! Bulls!") brought her father. The animals she had thought were bulls turned out to be bison. There were also a deer and wild boar. The paintings were at least 20,000 years old.

In 1940, four French boys and a dog named Robot discovered the famous cave paintings of Lascaux. Robot, who was hunting rabbits, went down a hole in the ground. The boys could hear him barking. The dog's owner decided to try to save Robot and went down in the hole too. The other boys followed.

They found Robot, unhurt, in a cave. When the boys lit candles to look around, paintings of bulls sprang out of the dark. It probably had been 15,000 years since a human being had looked at them. There were several caves like this, bright with paintings of horses, bison, swimming stags, a man with a head like a bird, a rhinoceros. Bison and rhinoceroses had not roamed France for thousands of years.

In the caves, besides the paintings, archaeologists found oil lamps the painters had used. They also found paints: ocher, a red- to yellow-colored earth ground and mixed with fat of animals. It may be true that ancient people did not *live* in these caves. Instead, the caves may have acted as centers for religion or magic. The pictures may have had to do with hunting rites. But no one knows for sure. Maybe the ancient people just liked to paint.

SOLDIERS OF CHINA'S FIRST EMPEROR

In Xian, China, in 1974, farmers digging a well found some old life-size figures made of terra-cotta, a kind of clay. The figures were soldiers and looked like real people: Each had its own face. Archaeologists realized that the find was important and began digging. They discovered an underground pal-

ace 3 miles around and 140 feet high— the 2,200-year-old tomb of China's first emperor, built by 700,000 men. The terra-cotta soldiers—almost 7,500 altogether in three burial pits—were present to serve the emperor in the next world.

In the first pit, in rows, like an army

The terra-cotta army buried with the first emperor of China (A & C Archives)

on the march, were 6,000 soldiers, all facing east, plus six four-horse chariots. In the second pit were 1,400 more soldiers, charioteers, soldiers on horseback, and archers using crossbows. The crossbows were rigged to shoot if anyone entered the tomb. The third pit held 73 soldiers guarding leaders riding in a chariot. The terra-cotta figures were once colored brightly, but most of the colors have worn off.

ARCHAEOLOGISTS OF TODAY

Are archaeologists treasure hunters? Yes, they are that and more: They are also detectives and students. They ask and seek answers to many questions: What food did the people grow? What animals did they hunt? What did they believe? How did they trade with other people? How did they write and keep records? What did they think about art? An archaeologist can often tell, from looking at a piece of pottery, for instance, when it was made and by whom.

Many modern archaeologists do what is called salvage archaeology. They get their chance when workers dig into the earth to build something. Here are two examples. In 1913, in Boston, a subway was being built. Wooden stakes were unearthed. Archaeologists figured out that they were part of a fence built more than 4,000 years ago to trap fish. Other parts of the fence have been found since. In New York City, in 1964, three men—a businessman, a lawyer, and a Hopi Indian—dug in dirt that had been thrown up digging for a housing project. They found very old bottles, a doll's head, clay pipes, even a pair of pants more than 130 years old.

Archaeologists don't just dig. They also take pictures from airplanes. From the air they can see shadows of old ditches and walls. Some work underwater, digging up old shipwrecks.

THINKING LIKE AN ARCHAEOLOGIST

Are you thinking of digging for treasures of the past? Before you do, it's a good idea to learn to think like an archaeologist, a superdetective. Put together a collection of common objects—perhaps a clothespin, can opener, sunglasses, dog license, box camera, computer disk, flip top from a soda can, light bulb, and stamp. Now imagine yourself having found them on a dig a thousand years from now. Ask yourself how these objects were used. What are the clues that lead to those decisions?

It's okay to come up with a use that's different from the one you know. For example, it's perfectly logical to think that the flip top was part of a necklace. However, the fact that you have found no chain should make you wonder.

BEING A DIGGER

Diggers are strong and careful. The work they do is very hard, and sometimes it can be boring; but there is almost always something new to be learned. Digging is usually done in the summer when the ground is warm and people are out of school.

Sometimes you can join a dig with archaeologists. Here's how to find out about local digs. Get a copy of *American*

These kids studying finds are taking part in the archaeological program of The Collegiate Schools in Virginia. (The Collegiate Schools)

Antiquity and look at the section called "Current Research." You can find *American Antiquity* at a college library, or you can write to the

American Anthropological Association
1703 New Hampshire Avenue, NW
Washington, DC 20009

or the

Archaeological Institute of America
P.O. Box 1901 Kenmore Station
Boston, MA 02215

Be sure to enclose a self-addressed, stamped envelope (See page 341). For finding out about digs, you can also try the department of archaeology or anthropology at your local college, a museum, an historical society, or an amateur archaeological society.

Other chances for digging come through summer schools and programs. They cost money, sometimes a lot. Here is a sample.

The Cottonwood Gulch Foundation
P.O. Box 14957
Albuquerque, NM 87191 (winter)

P.O. Box 969
Thoreau, NM 87323 (summer)

This program began in 1926. The first members, called Trekkers, traveled in trucks and lived in the wilderness for two months. Now the group offers Prairie Trek Expeditions for boys 12 to 17 and Turquoise Trail Expeditions for girls 13 to 17. There are also family programs. The base camp is at Cottonwood Gulch in the Zuni Mountains of New Mexico. An archaeologist is on the staff to show kids how to dig. Other activities include arts and crafts and learning about rocks, plants, and animals.

The Fenster School of Southern Arizona
8500 East Ocotillo Drive
Tucson, AZ 85715

These pieces of pottery have been identified as black-and-white Gallup. (Cottonwood Gulch Foundation)

Young archaeologists work at a Cottonwood Gulch dig in New Mexico. (Cottonwood Gulch Foundation)

There are two separate programs. If you're over 12 (grade 7 or above), you can go to the six-week summer-school session and study other subjects besides archaeology and anthropology. On the school grounds is a Hohokam Indian site, where you learn to dig. You also map the site and prepare and study what you find. If you live in or near Tucson, you can go to the day camp for kids five to 12. You won't actually dig, but you can visit the site on a hike. When you do, you will learn about the Native Americans who lived

there and the ways their culture is being studied.

Kampsville Archaeological Center
Box 355
Kampsville, IL 62053

The site was inhabited as many as 12,000 years ago and as recently as 700 years ago. There are many layers of cultures in-between. Scientists are rebuilding an ancient village. You can help. You can also help search for some of the more than 75,000 sites in the area. You find objects, like pots and tools. Then you study them to see what they tell about the cultures they are from. You learn how to make stone tools and clay pots. You see how early people made use of stones and plants. For example, they used corncobs for making a fire. You build a Native American house.

How can you go? Get your school to plan a field trip. It must be between the beginning of May and the end of August. You need an adult leader for every ten kids.

Early in August, the center hosts Archaeology Day. That whole day you can tour sites and labs and visit museum displays. The center also offers slide-illustrated lectures and workshops.

The Collegiate Schools
North Mooreland Road
Richmond, VA 23229

The Collegiate Schools offer a summer program. One of the courses is field archaeology. First you learn how to dig and study what you dig up. Then you actually go to a site to work. Only kids who will be at least in grade 6 the following fall can enter the class.

LASERS

Lasers seem to do magic. They can be bigger than your yard or smaller than a dot. Some you can see, and some you

The man at the keyboard is creating laser music. (AT&T Archives)

can't. Lasers can be any color, but each laser is of one color only. Some can make holes in anything. Others can't. What else can lasers do? Show fingerprints that can't otherwise be seen. Weld car parts. Drill holes in the nipples of baby bottles. Do surgery without knives. Read supermarket codes. Transmit phone calls. See viruses that many microscopes can't see, and see them in action. Speed up computers. Make light shows. Make 3-D images that you can put your hand through.

But lasers weren't invented by humans. There is a natural laser in space, above the planet Mars.

And lasers are not magic, but science.

Laser stands for *Light Amplification by Stimulated Emission of Radiation.* Although other scientists had the idea, it was Theodore Maiman who first teased out a laser. In 1960 he made laser light flash from a fake ruby.

Regular light travels out of step in all directions and is of many colors, or frequencies. Laser light travels in step in one direction and is of one color, or frequency, only. Laser light can do the special things it does because of these exciting ways that it is different from regular light.

Here's one way that scientists produce laser light. They start with a glass tube filled with a special gas. Near each end of the tube is an electrical pole. One is positive and one is negative, like those of a battery. There are two mirrors, one beyond each end of the tube, and the mirrors are parallel to each other.

An electric current flows between the poles and causes the atoms in the gas to soak up energy and become excited. From time to time, one of the excited gas atoms will drop back to normal. When it does, it gives off a photon, a particle of light. When that photon hits another excited atom, it causes that excited atom to give off a photon, too, *of the same color* that travels *in the same direction* as the original photon. More and more excited atoms are hit and give off other photons, which all bounce back and forth between the mirrors and cause still more and more photons to be produced. And *all* these photons are the same color and are traveling parallel! During this bounc-

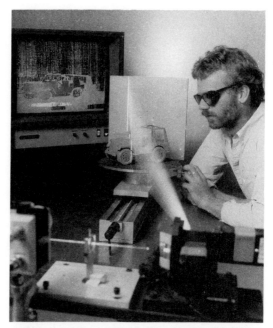

The man can put his hand through the model car because the car is a hologram! (GE Research and Development Center)

ing back and forth, a beam of laser light escapes through one mirror that is somewhat transparent.

A hologram is a record of laser-light patterns. Its name comes from *holos,* "whole," and *gramma,* "message," in Greek. So a hologram is a "whole message." It is a 3-D image made of light. It shows something in the round and looks "real." You can walk around it and see the back of it. A hologram of a child, for instance, has front, back, and sides. From the back you can't see the face, but you can put your hand right through it.

To make a hologram of an object, laser light is split into two beams. One beam is reflected to the object with a mirror and then sent to a piece of film.

The other beam goes right to the film, never touching the object. When the two beams meet again on the film, they make new wave patterns that are recorded on the film as a hologram of the object. To project the 3-D image in space, the hologram on the film is lit by another laser beam.

Holograms are used on stickers and credit cards. They can be made from information fed into a computer. The computer can then supply the information an object would. A hologram can be a model of something that does not yet exist. The books in a whole library can be put on a hologram no bigger than a sugar cube.

DAVID: THE BOY WHO LIVED IN A BUBBLE

David Phillip, the Bubble Boy, was born at 7 A.M. on September 21, 1971. He was called the Bubble Boy because as soon as he was born, he was placed

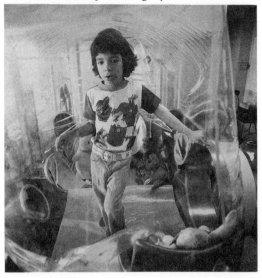

David Phillip, age 5, in one of the bubbles in which he lived (Baylor College of Medicine)

in a sterile plastic bubble, free from dirt or germs to keep him safe. David had a rare disease called Severe Combined Immunodeficiency (SCID). This disease is so serious that even the mildest of germs in the air could have been deadly to David. David would have to live in a bubble either until he developed his own immune system (his body's way of protecting him from attacks by germs) or until modern science discovered a cure for SCID.

Because of David's special health problems, he lived half of his life at home and half at the hospital. David's parents built two special rooms with four separate plastic bubbles. David had a crib bubble where he slept, a supply bubble, a playroom bubble, and a transport bubble. David's transport bubble was used to take him to the hospital and other outside places.

Even though he lived in a bubble, David was a lot like other children. He could be touched by other people, just not without some kind of sterile protection. He played with toys and watched TV. In fact, one of David's favorite pastimes was watching football on TV with his father. David was a Houston Oilers fan. Once David had a special visitor, Houston Oilers running back Earl Campbell.

Like most children, David had favorite foods. He especially liked spaghetti. However, he could only eat foods that came in cans because his food had to be sterile. Foods like ice cream, which David saw advertised on TV, could not be made safe enough for him to eat. Even his birthday cakes were ''off-limits,'' but David did have fun figuring out ways to blow out the candles.

David had some great moments in his life. For example, he became an honorary member of the fire department in the town where he lived. When he was six, he got a wonderful gift from NASA—a special space-bubble suit just like the ones the astronauts wear. With this space suit, David could move inside and outside the house, all by himself. For the first time in his life, David really saw the outdoors! The special suit also made it easier to play with his friends.

David could not go to school, but he had a speaker phone hooked up there and at his house. In this way he could talk to both his teachers and his classmates. Even though David could not see the other students, he made many friends. David was very smart and was a good student.

David, age 6, wears a special space suit made for him by NASA. (Baylor College of Medicine)

David loved his older sister, Katherine. The bubble that David lived in had large rubber gloves. With them, he could reach outside the bubble or someone could reach inside. Katherine and David used the gloves to have boxing matches with each other. She won most of the time. Katherine also kept her younger brother company at night. She slept in the same room, on the other side of the bubble.

David was about nine years old when he first learned he was famous. His parents kept most of the news about him a secret because they thought it might upset him. However, one day he read a newspaper article about his birthday. The next day when David's mother told him to clean up his messy room, he yelled, "I don't have to clean my room. I'm a star!"

After David had lived in a bubble for 12 years, he and his doctors and his family made a life-or-death decision. They agreed, since David had not yet developed his own immune system, to try to give him one. Without taking him out of the bubble, doctors gave David a bone marrow transplant from his sister, Katherine, to share her immune system with him. Everybody hoped that David's body would accept the new immune system, but the transplant didn't work. David soon got very ill.

Now, to try to help David, the doctors had to take him out of the bubble he had lived in all his life. He was afraid to step out into the "real world," but at last he hugged and kissed his family for the first time. David's first request was for a Coca-Cola.

Many doctors worked day and night trying to find a cure for David's problem, but his health got worse. David died after being out of the bubble for only 15 days.

David was a very brave kid. He never cried. He packed his 12 years with a lot of fun and friends in spite of his disease.

The doctors who tried to help David learned a lot about his disease. Today they know more about how to treat other children with the same kind of sickness. Because of David's heroic life, children with this disease will be helped for years to come.

SPACE SUITS: ENVELOPES FOR HUMANS

Being in a space suit is like being in a little Earth. Inside a space suit a person can go anywhere: places without air, for instance. In a space suit people can walk in space or on other planets or the moon. There *are* problems. You can't get "outside." It's not easy to eat or go to the bathroom inside a space suit.

The idea of a space suit has been around for a long time, long before space travel.

THE LEAKY SUIT   In the 1930s Wiley Post, who raced airplanes, wanted to fly high above the earth. The higher he flew, the faster he could go. The air is too thin, up high above the earth, to fly without some kind of space suit. He had a suit made, but it started leaking and blew open at the waist when he tried it out. A second suit was made, but Post had gotten a bit fatter in the meantime. He got stuck in the second suit, trying it on, and had to be cut out of it. These first two suits were made like balloons. The third suit, though, was made in two layers. It worked. Post did not win his next race, however. His plane got engine trouble.

THE MONSTER SUIT   Another space suit was made about this same time by a maker of diving suits. But it, too, had problems. The eye holes moved up when the suit was blown up, and the person inside wasn't able to see out. The diving-suit maker tried another suit made of metal, like a suit of armor. It didn't work either.

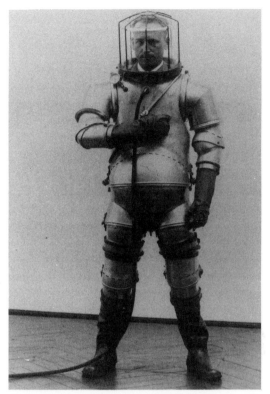

German metal suit of the 1940s (National Air and Space Museum, Smithsonian Institution)

Wiley Post in his two-layered space suit, complete with nozzle below the knee for pumping in air (National Air and Space Museum, Smithsonian Institution)

THE CRANK SUIT   Another weird suit was also designed in the 1930s, by the French. It had a crank in the chest so that the "pilot could control his own air pressure."

THE ARMOR SUIT   In the 1940s a German invented a metal suit. It had joints like a suit of armor and a helmet like a birdcage.

AND THERE HAVE BEEN . . .   a suit with tripod legs and food bins inside, a potato-cell suit like a big sleeping bag, the one-armed suit, and the dog suit that made a dog look like a monster.

TODAY'S SPACE SUITS Astronauts do not usually wear space suits inside the spacecraft. But they must wear space suits when they leave the vehicle to walk in space. The suits weigh more than most people. Some have a power unit for moving around in space. This adds 250 pounds more. (Remember, though, in space things have no weight.) The space suit has a backpack with a life-support system holding oxygen. (Oxygen is part of air. People can't live without breathing it.) It has a two-way radio. A cooling system is built into the underwear of the space suit. And, there *is* a built-in "bathroom."

SPACE TRAVEL

Space is not much like home. The temperature can be as low as −250 degrees F. or as high as 250 degrees F. That's a lot colder than your refrigerator and twice as hot as it gets on a very hot day in the desert. There's no air to breathe, unless you bring it with you. Things in space float, even people. Nothing is up. Nothing is down.

The first live beings to travel in space were not astronauts, but chimponauts. In 1953 two monkeys named Pat and Mike rode a rocket. In 1959 Able, a male monkey, and Baker, a female monkey, traveled in a missile at 10,000 mph. Then in 1961 a chimpanzee, Ham, went up. And Enos, another chimp, went around the Earth twice before John Glenn. Why chimps? They are like humans but much stronger. The project of using chimps in space ended in 1970. Fifty former chimponauts now live at the Primate Research Institute.

Men have been traveling in space since the 1960s. They have been to the moon and beyond. The newest manned spacecraft are space shuttles.

Ham, the first space chimpanzee, parades in front of reporters with his handler after a 5,000-mph ride in space. (NASA)

Columbia rises off the launching pad on April 12, 1981, for the very first space shuttle mission. On board are astronauts John Young and Bob Crippen. (NASA)

They are the first spacecraft that can be used over and over again. Rockets launch space shuttles, but the shuttles land like airplanes. Space shuttles carry people and cargo, up to 65,000 pounds of it, to Earth orbit.

The space shuttle has four parts: the orbiter, the solid rocket boosters, the external tank, and the main engines in the rear of the orbiter. Only the orbiter and main engines go into Earth orbit. The other parts are for lift-off and powered flight.

Scientists and engineers ride in the shuttle. They do experiments in space that can't be done on Earth. For example, the Hubble Space Telescope orbits Earth 310 miles above the clouds. With it, astronomers can see the stars 50 times more sharply and can see seven times farther into space than ever before. The telescope has solar panels that turn the sun's rays into electrical power to run the telescope. Its instruments relay what the telescope sees to people on the ground.

LIFE IN SPACE

The astronauts who live in the space shuttle have no mattresses or pillows. Instead, they sleep in sleeping bags held to a wall. They have to zip themselves in to keep from floating around the cabin. Their arms are held down with a strap.

Astronauts can't eat chili in space. It explodes there. Grains of salt and pepper don't easily shake out in space. If they do, they drift around the cabin. The salt and pepper used in space are liquid. Astronauts eat cookies, peanuts, eggs, peaches, orange juice, rolls, and other things. The food has had most of the water taken out. The astronauts must take a needle and shoot water back in. You can't pour water in space. If you try, it forms into balls that drift around the spacecraft. Food trays have built-in magnets to hold them to the table. Magnetism does the job in space that gravity can't.

Taking a shower isn't easy. In spaceships of the past, one astronaut showered with a water gun while another astronaut sucked up the used water with a little vacuum cleaner. Now the showers are like car washes. A person showers in a sealed box, and a machine sprays water for washing and then air for drying.

When astronauts go to the toilet, they strap themselves in with a seat belt. Pumps take waste away.

Suction cups on the astronauts' shoes hold them to the floor or wall or ceiling. The cups are the only way to stay in one spot. One astronaut worker turned himself over with a screwdriver when he forgot about anchoring before unscrewing a bolt.

Astronaut Henry W. Hartsfield (left), on the space shuttle Columbia, *is tucked in a sleeping bag attached to the wall. If he tried to sleep in an ordinary bed, he might end up floating around the cabin, like the astronaut candidates and doctor (right) practicing how to move in zero gravity. (NASA)*

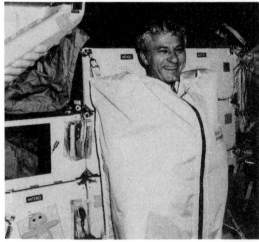

FIRST AMERICAN WOMAN IN SPACE

The first American woman in space was Sally Ride. She was in the eighth astronaut training class in 1978. More than 8,000 people asked to be in that class. Six of the 35 who were finally chosen were women. Sally Ride was one of them.

The training was tough. For instance, Sally was dragged on a rope by motorboat, then dropped 400 feet into the ocean. At age 31, in 1982, she became the youngest astronaut to go into orbit. Her ship was the space shuttle *Challenger*. The trip took six days. Like most astronauts these days, Sally Ride was not a pilot on the shuttle. Instead she was a mission specialist.

Sally Ride has written a book for kids called *To Space and Back*.

Astronaut Sally K. Ride, mission specialist on board the Earth-orbiting Challenger, *talks with ground controllers as she carries out an experiment to help decide if a space factory will work. (NASA)*

SPACE JOBS

The crew on a spacecraft acts as a team. Each person has been highly trained.

If you want to be a pilot, you must be under 40 years old and 60 to 74 inches high. Your eyesight must measure at least 20/100, correctable to 20/20. You need a college degree in mathematics, science, or engineering. You must have commanded a jet aircraft for at least 1,000 hours. Being a test pilot helps.

If you want to be a mission specialist, you need a college degree, just like a pilot. You also need to have studied

Astronaut Ronald E. McNair, mission specialist, shown in a training session, was on board Challenger *January 28, 1986, when it blew up. (NASA)*

biology and to have worked at least three years in a special field. Mission specialists may run machinery, study space, or watch over the health of the crew, for example.

Once you are accepted as a pilot or mission specialist in the space program, the training takes two or three years. You learn to live nearly weightless in a big water tank, wearing a space suit. You study science, mathematics, meteorology, guidance and navigation, astronomy, physics, and computers.

A payload specialist is usually someone who works for the company that manufactures a payload. If you are a payload specialist, your company trains you to work with the equipment and help carry out its purpose. Then you must spend 150 hours at Johnson Space Center learning about the shuttle and other things.

THE *CHALLENGER* TRAGEDY

The first "average citizen" who was to go into space was Christa McAuliffe. She represented the Teacher in Space Project as a payload specialist. A high school teacher from Concord, New Hampshire, she had been chosen from among 11,000 people who applied. She said on the "MacNeil/Lehrer News Hour," "I want to give an ordinary person's view of space, the idea that there's a new way of living out there."

On January 28, 1986, *Challenger* blew up. In it were seven crew members. All were killed. Christa McAuliffe was one of them. The families of *Challenger* crew members plan a science education center in Washington, D.C., as a "living tribute" to those who died. It will be called Challenger Center for Space Science Education. A child who visits the center will learn about space by acting "just like an astronaut."

BUG BOX IN SPACE

In the flights before *Challenger* exploded, crews carried out selected experiments thought up by private citizens and companies. Young people could submit experiments through the National Space Shuttle Student Involvement Project. This was run by the National Aeronautics and Space Administration (NASA) for the National Science Teachers Association.

Todd Nelson explains the Bug Box to astronauts Jack R. Lousma (left) and C. Gordon Fullerton (right). (NASA)

There were rules. The experiment had to be safe, travel in a container, and not take up too much astronaut time.

When Todd Nelson entered the contest, he was 17. His experiment, which was chosen to go up on the shuttle, was called "Insects in Flight Motion Study," or the "Bug Box." Todd wanted to see if insects would fly dif-ferently in space, where there is no gravity. Insects on earth use lots of energy to get off the ground. How much would they need in space? Would the size of their bodies and wings make a difference?

Commander Jack R. Lousma reported on the experiment on TV.

> They sure do make noise. It's hard to sleep at night with them buzzing away. The moths are lively, the bees have gotten stationary, and the flies took to walking. The bees got smart fast. They decided there wasn't any use flapping their wings and going out of control, so they just float around and wiggle their legs.

The astronauts filmed and videotaped the insects. The results showed that the insects did have problems. The flies did best. The bees just floated around.

THE FUTURE IN SPACE

Future space missions will study the Sun, explore Jupiter and its moons, and map Venus. NASA plans a space station to be in place by 1994. Astronauts will build it in space and live in a space orbiter until the job is done. A grid the size of a football field will form the base. On it will be housing, antennas, solar collectors, and three labs— one Japanese, one European, and one American. The shuttle can carry the building materials into space. The materials can float, leashed together and to the space orbiter, until they are put together by the space workers.

Space can be a good place to make

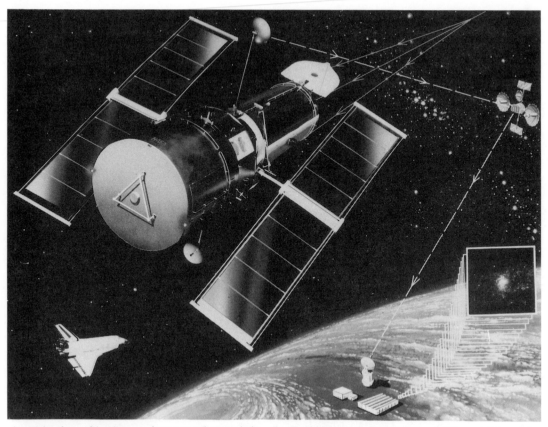

An artist drew this picture of a space telescope before the Hubble Space Telescope (page 247) went into orbit. A shuttle orbiter and a ground tracking station are also pictured, in the background. (NASA)

things that can't be made on Earth—certain chemicals and perfect crystals and perfect glass. Space factories will make the chemicals, grow perfect crystals for electronics use, and make perfect glass for lenses.

Satellites put up by space missions can beam solar energy to Earth. Lunetta, a giant space mirror, will catch and send sunlight to Earth to light city streets. You may carry a wrist tele-phone and call your friend from any-where, with space-satellite telephone setups. Satellites can bring you more TV channels.

Someday people may live in space all their lives. Scientists have designed space cities. Some are shaped like wheels, others like cans. Most spin to give a feeling like that of gravity. Freeman Dyson, a physicist, thinks we can make space colonies and put them in orbit to circle the Sun like Earth. Other scientists see ways to make the other planets into places where people can live.

Gerard K. O'Neill, a physics professor at Princeton University, thinks that, by 2081, 200 million people will make trips into space every year.

A SPACE PROGRAM FOR KIDS

If you like the idea of space travel, you may want to join a Young Astronaut Club. If you do, you get a membership card and decals. You also receive facts about the space program through newsletters and computer updates on what's going on in space. You might also go on a field trip to a space center or a space museum. There are national contests in space activities, with prizes. Some kids go to launches or space camp. You are ranked according to your grade. Kids in grades 1 to 3 are Trainees. Kids in grades 4 to 6 are Pilots. Kids in grades 7 to 9 are Commanders.

How can you join? Your school may already have a group. If not, try to start one. You need a leader at least 21 years old. You can start a chapter with as few as five members. If you are a shut-in or can't start a group at school, you can still belong. Just ask to be a satellite member. For information, write to the national office:

Young Astronaut Program
P.O. Box 65432
Washington, DC 20036

Be sure to enclose a self-addressed, stamped envelope (See page 341).

8
COMPUTERS

A HISTORY OF COMPUTERS

The first digital computer was the human hand when used for counting. The second digital computer was the abacus, a counting machine made of beads strung on wires. As far as we know, the first abacus was used almost 2,500 years ago.

The French mathematician Blaise Pascal invented a calculating machine in the 1600s. It was a little brass box. He called it the Pascaline.

THE FIRST KID GENIUSES AND COMPUTER HACKERS?

When the Englishman Charles Babbage was a boy, he taught himself math and made keys to pick locks. When he grew up, he invented the cowcatcher. There's no doubt he was smart. In the 1800s he came up with ideas for a computer. He never got the chance to build one.

In his mind he saw 100 men doing arithmetic. Just one machine, he thought, could do all their work in less time. First he designed the Difference Engine, a kind of adding machine. Later he thought of a fancier machine, the Analytical Engine. Although rough in form, the Analytical Engine he thought of was like a modern computer. Its many gears and cranks could have done about one addition a second. It had a "store" for numbers in

Playing computer games (pages 270–274) is a good way to learn how computers work. (Atari Corporation)

Parents and children can learn about computers together. Sometimes the kids know more than the adults. (Apple Computer, Inc.)

use. It had a "mill," gears and wheels where the work of adding the numbers could be done. It had a gadget to send numbers between the mill and the store, and it had an input-output gadget. Steam could drive it.

Some of Babbage's ideas came from the French inventor Jacquard's plan to weave patterns in rugs using punch cards. Where Jacquard's holes fitted to patterns in a rug, Babbage's holes fitted to mathematical symbols.

Even though he was the inventor, Babbage could not describe the Analytical Engine so people could understand it. However, Ada Augusta, countess of Lovelace, could. She was a genius and the daughter of the poet Alfred, Lord Byron. She had been a teenage whiz. When a report on the Analytical Engine appeared in French, Lady Lovelace translated it into English. She put in her own notes telling how it worked. Lady Lovelace said that the "Analytical Engine weaves algebraic patterns just as the Jacquard loom weaves flowers and leaves." She also was able to put into words Babbage's ideas of "loop" and "sub-routine." A computer language is named Ada, after Lady Lovelace.

For 40 years Babbage tried to build his Analytical Engine. He ran out of cash, so he and Lady Lovelace tried to win money betting on horse races. No luck. He invented a machine that would play ticktacktoe. This was another money-maker, he thought. He used it in carnivals. None of his schemes for making money worked out. The machine stayed an idea for a long time.

THE INVENTION OF MODERN COMPUTERS

The first electronic computer, ENIAC (Electronic Numerical Integrator and Calculator), was finished in 1946 at the University of Pennyslvania. It weighed 30 tons, used 18,000 vacuum tubes, and had 70,000 resistors and 6,000 switches. It was 100 feet long, 10 feet high, and 3 feet deep—bigger than a small house. It used a huge amount of power. Some people said that when it was turned on, the lights in Philadelphia went dim. It could multiply 500 sets of numbers a second. That might seem like a lot to you when you're doing arithemetic, but it's nothing compared to what a modern computer can do.

By 1975 you could buy a computer with the same power as ENIAC's for $500. Today you can buy a home computer the size of a stereo that can compute better than ENIAC. Twenty times faster, with a bigger memory than ENIAC's, this home computer needs no more power than it takes to turn on a light bulb. If cars had progressed as much as computers, a fancy car today would cost about $2.50 and get 2 million miles to the gallon.

A COMPUTER DICTIONARY

ADA   A computer language for the army, navy, and air force named after Ada Lovelace (See A History of Computers, pages 255–256.)

ACCESS   Way to get facts from computer memory or put them into computer memory

ADDRESS   Where something is stored in the computer's memory

AI   (Artificial Intelligence) Ability of computer or other machine to solve problems or make choices or learn like a human being

ALU   (Arithmetic Logic Unit) Part of the computer that does the arithmetic and compares characters and numbers

BACKUP   Storing of a copy of a program or file in case the original gets lost or ruined

BASIC   (Beginner's All-Purpose Symbolic Instruction Code) A computer language

BAUD   Bits per second

BBS   (Electronic Bulletin Board) A kind of computer club

BINARY NUMBERS   Ones and zeroes, the language used by a computer (0 in the arithmetic you usually use is 0000 in binary code, 1 is 0001, 2 is 0010.)

BIT   (Binary Digit) Smallest piece of information in computer; on or off

BOOTING   Getting the computer started; clearing memory and loading first instructions

BUG   Mistake in computer program or something else gone wrong (How did it get its name? A bug got stuck in a computer, and . . .)

BYTE   Eight bits

CAI   (Computer-Assisted Instruction) Learning at least partly by computers; usually includes computer lessons and worksheets done on the computer

CHARACTER   Letter, symbol, or number

CHIP   Thin slice of the metal silicon with very tiny wires and circuits; types: CPU, RAM, ROM

COBOL   (Common Business-Oriented Languge) A computer language

The "brains" of the computer are under the monitor. (Apple Computer, Inc.)

COMMANDS   What you tell the computer to do, from among the tasks it can carry out and in terms the computer can understand

COMPUTER   Machine that can remember and carry out a plan

COMPUTER LANGUAGE   Set of commands that can be turned into machine-language commands

CONTROL   Part of computer that tells other parts what to do

CPU   (Central Processing Unit) Main part of system; contains ALU (Arithmetic Logic Unit) and CU (Control Unit); control center of computer

CR   (Carriage Return) Sometimes ENTER, key that returns the cursor to the beginning of a new line and does other things besides

CRTL   (Control Key) Special key that, when used with others, controls some things the program does (For instance, CRTL-Z—hitting CRTL and Z—can, in some programs, put a stop to what the computer is doing.)

CURSOR   Means "runner" in Latin; symbol showing where next character will appear on video screen

DATA   Information fed into a computer

DATA BASE   A group of data stored together

DATA PROCESSING   Putting in, storing, using, and putting out information; uses math and reasoning

DEBUGGER   Software to get the bugs out

DEFAULT   A setting in the system or program that will be used unless you change it (For example, the default setting for page length may be 66 lines. You can change to 84 if you want to.)

DIRECTORY   List of all files under one heading

DISK   Stores information; looks like phonograph record; fits into disk drive that spins (The drive both writes on the disk and reads the information on the disk. Of the two types, floppy disks and hard disks, hard disks tend to hold more information.)

DOS   (Disk Operating System) Sets space, keeps track of files, saves files, and controls disk storage in other ways

DOT MATRIX   Name for a kind of printing that makes characters from a grid (For example: HV)

DOT MATRIX PRINTER   Printer that uses a dot matrix

DOWN TIME   When the computer isn't working because there is something wrong with it

ESC   (Escape) A key used with other keys to do certain jobs; sometimes starts the computer going when it seems "stuck"

FIELD   Place in record that stores one kind of data, such as names or dates

FILE   Group of records under single name

FORTRAN   (Formula Translator) A computer language for business and science

FUNCTION KEYS   Special keys that do certain jobs when told to by the software (usually F1, F2, etc.)

GIGO   (Garbage in, garbage out) A computer joke

GLITCH   Something that causes problems in a computer system; a bug's cousin

GRAPHICS   Drawings

HACKER   Someone who likes to use computers and may spend a good deal of time at it; may know a lot about computers

HARD COPY   Printout on paper

HARDWARE   Machine parts of computer—wires, metal, etc.

IMAGING   Taking information and turning it into a picture

INPUT   Part of the computer where information is put in

INPUT DEVICE   Something used to put information inside computer—joystick, keyboard, disk drive, etc. (Input can come from tapes, disks, or cards. It can come from sensors, like thermometers. It can come from someone typing on a keyboard.)

I/O   Input-output

JOYSTICK   Gadget that can be moved to move the cursor, usually either back and forth or up and down

K   1,024 bits of computer memory

KEYBOARD   Input device; like typewriter keyboard

LED   (Light Emitting Diode) Light showing if computer devices are on or off

LIGHT PEN   Tool that you point at computer picture (It gives commands to the spot it is pointed at.)

LISP   (List Processor) Computer language

LOGO   Means "word" in Greek; computer language developed for children; uses "turtle" as input device

MACHINE LANGUAGE   Way of showing in symbols the electrical changes inside computer

MAINFRAME   A big computer, or the place where computer circuit boards go, or the main part of a computer

MEMORY   Place (chips) in computer where information is stored in binary code

MENU   List of choices shown on monitor (You choose what you want the computer to do.)

MICROPROCESSOR   A CPU on a chip or chips

MODEM   (Modulator-Demodulator) Gadget through which you can telephone other computers

MONITOR   Picture screen that shows you information; like TV screen

MOUSE   Pear-shaped device for moving the cursor (You can hold it in your hand.)

NANOSECOND   1/1,000,000,000 (billionth) of a second

NIBBLE   Four bits

OPERATING SYSTEM   Commands to oversee the whole computer system

OUTPUT   Part of computer where information is put out

OUTPUT DEVICE   Takes programs or data from computer and moves them to something else; examples: the screen, printer, or spoken words

PASCAL   Computer language

PC   Printed circuit or personal computer

PILOT   (Programming Inquiry Learning or Teaching) Computer language using simple commands; good for beginners

PIXEL   (*Picture Element*) A dot on the computer screen where a row and column meet (A computer screen is divided by rows and columns.)

PRINTER   Tool that prints out information

PROCESSOR   Part of computer where work is done

PROGRAM   Set of orders telling the computer to do something

PROGRAMMING   Making up a program

RAM   (Random-Access Memory) Storage space (memory) inside computer where data can be stored and from where it can be brought back to the screen quickly (When the power is off, the data is lost.)

RASTER GRAPHICS   Screen scheme that uses pixels; used in color TV

RECORD   Piece of data stored in a file

ROM   (Read-Only Memory) Memory with data stored on it forever; cannot be erased; cannot easily be changed

SOFTWARE   Computer programs

STORAGE   Place where information is stored in computer

STRING   Set of characters that are joined and have meaning (For instance, the word *string* is a string of six characters.)

SYSOP   (System Operator) Person who runs an electronic bulletin board (BBS)

TURTLE   Pointer (input tool) that works something like a mouse.

USER FRIENDLY   Easy to use

VECTOR GRAPHICS   Smooth line computer graphics

WORD PROCESSOR   Computer program or computer with which you can write and edit

BUYING A COMPUTER: A QUESTIONNAIRE

Avoid disappointment after you buy a computer. If someone in your family plans on buying one, everyone who will use it should answer five sets of questions. Think backward about buying a computer. That is, *start* with what you want the computer to do. Ask the first big question.

WHAT ARE WE GOING TO USE THE COMPUTER FOR?

Write down all the answers your family comes up with. Here are some possible answers: write reports for school, do math homework, write letters, play games, use bulletin boards, play around with computer graphics. Try to think of everything. Then you are ready for the second big question.

WHAT SOFTWARE WILL DO THE JOB?

You will probably need some sort of word-processing program. What should it be able to do? Footnotes? Outlines? Lists? Sort items alphabetically?

You may also need a data-processing program. Does your father or mother want to keep records by computer? What kind of records?

There are programs for writing music, for playing around with computer graphics, for learning various subjects, and more.

Next, ask your friends and other people you know who have computers about the special software they use. You might also talk to people in a computer club or go to a computer software store. Computer magazines can help too.

What software will help us do the things we want to do on a computer? What are its flaws? Make a list of the software for each use. Then you are ready for the third big question.

WHAT COMPUTERS CAN RUN THE SOFTWARE?

With your list of software, go to a computer software store. Ask the name of the computers on which each piece of software runs best. You now have a set of brand names. From this list, you can choose one or two computers you might buy. Keep in mind that some computers can be added on to later. That is, you can get more memory or another monitor. Now you are ready for the fourth question.

WHAT MUST WE KNOW ABOUT EACH OF THE COMPUTERS ON THE LIST?

1. Does it have color? Do we need color?

2. How much memory does it have? Lots of memory is important for some games and computer graphics.

3. Does it take hard disks or floppies or both? If you need a lot of memory or do big jobs—write a novel, for instance—a hard disk is useful. However, it is good to be able to copy your work on a floppy. In this case you would have both a hard and a floppy disk drive.

4. What kind of keyboard is best? If you do a great deal of writing, this is an important question.

5. What is the best cursor mover: mouse, light pen, keyboard?

6. Should we buy a clone? Some well-known computers have been cloned. That is, they have been copied by other companies at a cheaper price. How well will the clones work with our chosen software? Can we depend on the clone?

7. How much can we spend? Price differs by the computer and the place you buy it.

Once you know which computer you want, you are ready for the fifth question.

WHAT ELSE DO WE NEED, ALONG WITH THE COMPUTER?

MONITOR   It is like a TV screen and is a must. Most monitors these days come with a full screen so that you can see all you have written on a line. The color can be green, yellow, or white. You will be spending a great deal of time reading things off your monitor. You should have one that will hurt your eyes the least.

PRINTER   Printers can be dot matrix, daisy wheel, or laser. Dot-matrix printers print out letters that are made of

A family buying a computer should keep in mind the needs of all those who will use it. (Radio Shack)

many small dots. They are very fast. Daisy-wheel printers print out letters more like a typewriter's. They tend to be slower. Laser printers do a beautiful job, but they cost a lot.

MODEM   This is the gadget with which you link your computer with the telephone, and from there with other computers. One wire plugs into your phone, the other into your computer. You need a modem for using electronic bulletin boards (BBSs), which are described below.

COMPUTER NETWORKS

COMPUTER CLUBS

People in computer clubs get together to talk over problems and help one another. These clubs are often called users' groups. Most computer clubs are based on one kind of computer or software. In one town, for example, there could be three users' clubs: one for owners of Commodores, another for owners of Apples, and a third for owners of IBM PCs. Club members trade programs they have written. They sell one another used computers and other computer parts. They tell one another how they ironed out the bugs in programs. Sometimes they put out a magazine or newsletter.

To find out about users' groups in your area, ask at your computer store or write to the company that sold you your computer. If there is no users' group in your area, you might want to start one at school. Begin with the people you know who have a computer like yours. To let other kids know what you're trying to do, put an ad in the school paper or on a bulletin board. Tell about the club in front of your class or in assembly. See the section Forming Your Own Club on pages 145–146.

ELECTRONIC BULLETIN BOARDS (BBSs)

An electronic bulletin board (BBS) is another kind of club. It's a club where you may never meet the other members. Instead, you talk through your computers, hooked up by telephone. For this you need a modem, a gadget that makes such hookups possible.

Find out about local BBSs in one of

the fliers given away by computer stores. Some networks list BBSs too. Sometimes computer clubs or businesses run BBSs. However, most BBSs are run by one person—a sysop, or system operator. You could be a sysop, if your parents agree to it. It takes some money. When someone calls, you don't have to be there. Your computer will "answer."

To join a BBS, you usually have to answer an electronic questionnaire. Some BBSs run by local people allow 15 to 20 minutes a day free on their system and unlimited time for a small price. Many have a "chat" mode. That means you can exchange messages with the person in charge of the system. Other BBSs are just for leaving and getting messages. Messages can be open or secret.

You must have a certain kind of computer to join some BBSs. With these you can take programs from the BBS, or download, into your own computer. Also you can put programs from your computer into the BBS, or upload.

Users (members) often pick special names for signing their messages. Here's an example:

Vorkzo Zocktola
From the planet Tondoo
In the land of Zobor

Vorkzo has another "earth" name. He is a young man who lives in Solana Beach, California.

With your own bulletin board, you plan your own set of activities. You can, for example, form a BBS around an idea, like computer game contests. You can have a chess club on a BBS and dare all comers. That way when you lose, no one sees your red face. You can flirt. You can play-talk, based on your "personality" as a member. (Vorkzo often takes the point of view of a non-earthling.) You can also start a debate about something very serious, like pollution or computer crime.

LOCAL AREA COMPUTER SERVICES

Local computer services offer data bases, listings of products, and special services. Some charge. Others don't. Businesses or libraries pay for some.

NATIONAL NETWORKS

You can plug into national networks run from mainframes (big computers) through your telephone. Here, too, you need a modem. Get the latest news, weather report, and sports results. Read movie reviews. Get help with your computer and software. Use some software free. Play games. Learn something new. Look up an encyclopedia article without turning pages or going to the library. (If you join The Source, for example, you can use Academic American Encyclopedia.)

The hitch? It costs money to join national networks, and you are charged a fee every time, based on your use time. If you're lucky, though, you can call on a local or free long-distance number. Sometimes the service is cheaper during nights and weekends. Most services give users an ID number and secret password. You are told how to get on line by dialing a number, then choosing what you want from a menu. When done, you type in OFF.

Kids can join an electronic bulletin board (BBS) or start their own. (Apple Computer, Inc.)

Here is the address of the network mentioned above.

The Source
Source Telecomputing Corporation
1616 Anderson Road
McLean, VA 22102

COMPUTER GRAPHICS

With your computer, you can draw pictures, change their shapes, and do quickly what would take many artists a long time. How does it work? There are two kinds of graphics: raster graphics and vector graphics.

RASTER GRAPHICS A computer program is turned into little electrical signals. The signals go to an electron "gun" behind the video screen. The gun then fires electrons in a pattern at the screen's back surface. The electrons "bring alive" tiny bits of phosphor—bright stuff—on the screen. These bits, or dots, are called pixels. Pictures form on the screen.

The idea of making pictures with dots is not new. Look at the comics in your newspaper through a magnifying glass, for instance. You will see that they are made up of dots of ink. Comics have been made like this for a long time. Raster graphics are often used in video games.

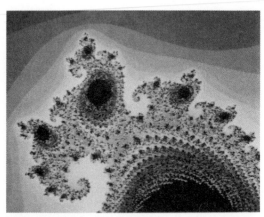

Fractals are computer "pictures" of mathematical ideas. They often look like works of art. (Art Matrix, Cornell National Supercomputer Facility)

VECTOR GRAPHICS Lines are drawn from point to point on the screen. These can make shapes that seem 3-D. Three-D movies are made using computers, laser cameras, and holography.

Moviemakers use computers for special effects. They can create a scene with a computer. The live actor seems to be inside the scene, but he really isn't.

Computers can change the shape of one thing into the shape of something else. A flower can become a dancer. A box can become a sphere. Some movie cartoons can be made this way.

Scientists use computers to change the images of objects in real life to make them easier to see and understand. Computer graphics can help scientists understand patterns of stars and snowflakes, for instance. Computers can make ideas from math into pictures. Sound waves can be changed into pictures by a computer too.

Space-flight photographs can be changed into sets of numbers by a computer. Each number stands for the amount of light given off at that spot in the photograph.

Scientists can tell the computer to make some light colors lighter and some dark colors darker. That way certain things show up better. They can also add false colors to point up certain things.

MAKING YOUR OWN COMPUTER GRAPHICS
With some computers, you can use very fancy computer design to change numbers to dots on a screen. Each number stands for the color and brightness of a pixel.

Computer programs give you a "library" of shapes. You can use the shapes to make up a "solid" thing with the keyboard or a light pen. For instance, you might make a pyramid. The computer will smooth it out and fill it in. Once you have your shape, you can turn it to see it from different angles. If you have made a pyramid, you can look at it from the bottom or from the top or from the sides. You can shrink it or make it bigger. You can fill it with color. You can move it.

Some graphics programs allow you to trace maps and pictures and then make changes in them on the screen.

Even if you don't have a package this fancy, you can probably do line drawing. Check out your word-processing program for this feature. Data-processing programs include ways of changing information into graphs and charts too. These can be useful for schoolwork.

A computer can be your teacher—or you can teach it! (Apple Computer, Inc.)

YOUR MACHINE EDITOR AND SILENT TUTOR: USING YOUR COMPUTER FOR HOMEWORK

A computer can help you learn something new, organize your work, write reports and stories, edit what you have written. It is a wonderful tool.

YOUR MACHINE EDITOR, THE WORD PROCESSOR

Using word-processor software, you can write book reports, stories, and essays. You can keep track of your notes from classes too. A word processor is better than a typewriter or a pen. You can check your spelling and correct it. If you change your mind about the way you have said something, you can edit it. You can move sentences around. There are no smudgy messes on your screen when you get through.

CUT AND PASTE   Most word-processing programs have a "cut-and-paste" feature. This means you can take a whole block of text, "cut" it, move it, and copy it somewhere else. For example, suppose this is what you have written.

> Peasant children 300 years ago in France worked in the fields with their parents. They started this as soon as they could walk. Babies were hung up on a hook in the kitchen. It was hard work. School came second, if at all.

The sentence about babies is in the wrong place. If you were writing with a pencil, you would circle that sentence and show with an arrow where it might go instead. *Then* you would have to re-copy the paper. With your word processor, you can move the sentence. After you cut and copy the sentence, you can put it where you think it belongs. Your screen would look like this:

> Peasant children 300 years ago in France worked in the fields with their parents. Babies were hung up on a hook in the kitchen. They started this as soon as they could walk. It was hard work. School came second, if at all.

Notice that the paragraph still does not make sense. However, it will, with a little easy editing:

> In France 300 years ago, peasant children were not babied. Infants were hung up on hooks in the kitchen because their parents did not have time to watch them. Older children worked in the fields with their parents. They started this as soon as they could walk. It was hard work. School came second, if at all.

Don't think that the computer can do the writing. It is only a tool. What it can do is save you time. You can easily juggle your ideas and try them out in different ways, without recopying! You can quickly play around with crazy ideas. You can let your fancy go. Remember, though, only you can clean up your work and order it neatly. The computer is just a tool. It stops where you stop. It won't finish for you.

OUTLINES AND LISTS   Making outlines and lists is easy on a word processor. Often word-processor programs will renumber your lists when you want to put something in another place. Some have a ready-made outline form you can use.

SPELLING CHECK AND THESAURUS Most word-processing programs will check your spelling for you or help you find the right word, with the thesaurus. Be careful not to rely too much on these two features. They work in a machine-like way. Using them without knowing what you are doing can lead to mistakes in meaning. For instance, one thesaurus gives *fumble* in a list of words meaning about the same as *mistake*. But try *fumble* in the fourth sentence in this paragraph to replace *mistake*. It doesn't work, does it? A word isn't a football!

YOUR SILENT TUTOR

STUDYING   Some programs help you study a subject or a skill. You can buy programs like these at your computer store, or you can use them at your library or school. Here are some examples.

1. LOGO is a computer language developed for children. A "turtle" is your cursor. With commands, you teach the turtle to draw squares and triangles, then fancier designs. LOGO teaches you planning and problem solving as well as computer programming.
2. Rocky's Boots includes 39 games to teach children, age nine and older, ideas of reasoning and computer circuits. You end up building a machine that kicks targets.
3. Odell Lake is a learning game based on a lake, a model world. You are a trout looking for food and trying to keep from being eaten. Luck is written into the game.
4. Bank Street Writer is a word-processing program for children.

The Family Software Catalog, by mothers and educational consultants, lists software by areas such as mathematics, fun with words, mindbenders, and mystery and adventure. Each program's hardware needs are listed. A program is first screened and tested with children to see if it works. If the children like it and learn from it, it can be included in the catalog. Each program is also graded according to how hard it is. Write to this address:

The Family Software Catalog
Evanston Educators, Inc.
915 Elmwood Avenue
Evanston, IL 60202

You can use a computer to do other schoolwork too. With some computers, you can make models of almost anything. These are very useful for learning. They give your eyes something to see that you would otherwise have to imagine in your head or try to draw on paper. For instance, if you are studying chemistry, you can make models of various elements and molecules. If you are studying geometry, you can make a model of a cube and then turn it in many different ways to see how its faces relate.

NOTE TAKING When you store your notes from school on your computer, you can use the word search feature to help you organize your study time. For example, if you have taken notes in class several days in a row for a report on pioneers, these notes may be mixed in with notes on math and science. However, you can tag your notes, when you put them into your computer, with a word like *pioneer*. Then you can easily find them with a word search.

USING YOUR MODEM You can send and receive homework notes. You can plug into information services. Information services sometimes help with encyclopedia or magazine research. This can be useful to you when you must write a report.

GRAPHICS If your computer can do graphics, you can make charts and graphs to illustrate your reports. You can even draw maps on some computers.

COMPUTER GAMES: A FEW FACTS

When Nolan Bushnell was a kid, he liked to figure out how things worked. He played with Erector sets and ham radios. When he grew up, he still liked to fool with games and ideas. Like other college kids, he liked to play Spacewar, the first computer game. It dawned on him that other people might want to play computer games, so he started his own company to make them. It is called Atari. *Atari* is Japanese and means "prepare to be attacked." The word is used in the game of Go, a kind of oriental chess.

Bushnell's first game was electronic Ping-Pong, called Pong. It came out in 1972. To play it, you had to put a coin in a slot. Pong was the first video game operated with coins. Do you remember Chuck E. Cheese, the huge mouse? He is another Bushnell creation. And there

With exciting graphics, you see the ground fall away beneath you as you take off. (Atari Corporation)

are more: a home robot company, an educational TV company, and a string of computer camps for children.

Another Atari game is Breakout. It was designed by Stephen Jobs, who, with Stephen Wozniak, later started Apple Computer.

Space Invaders was invented in Japan. It was very popular there. It was so popular that the Bank of Japan had to make three times as many 100-yen coins as were then around. Why? People needed them to feed into Space Invaders slots to play the game.

Pac-Man is another game that was first Japanese. Its name in Japan is Puck-Man, borrowed from a character in a Japanese nursery rhyme. The rhyme tells of a monster who eats everything. While he does this, he says, "Puck, puck, puck." When the game came to the United States, it was popular here too. After Pac-Man came Ms. Pac-Man, Baby Pac-Man, Pac-Man Plus, Super Pac-Man, Professor Pac-Man, and Jr. Pac-Man.

WANTED: GAME PLAYERS!

Computer games can be played in arcades or on home computers. If you have a modem, you can order up video games through national networks and BBSs.

You can choose your computer games to fit your skills and hobbies. Here's a set of questions that should help you choose.

1. Do you like to playact and solve problems? Try a role-playing game. Adventure games are usually role-playing games. Adventure, based on Dungeons and Dragons, is a famous example.
2. If you enjoy sports, try a sports game. You can play against the computer or against someone else.
3. Are you crazy about chess or checkers? Sharpen your skills on computer board games.

Control your Piper 181 Cherokee Archer from a keyboard with Atari's Flight Simulator. (Atari Corporation)

4. Do you like thinking like a battle chief? Try war games.

5. If you move well and fast, try shoot-'em-up games or maze games.

6. Would you call yourself a space freak? Try space games that seem to take place in other worlds. Such games also test how quick you are—in space chases, for example.

7. Are you an artist or poet or composer? Creative kids like games that allow them to make up their own game or write music.

MAKING UP YOUR OWN COMPUTER GAME

Making up your own computer game can be more fun than playing one that someone else made up. If you belong to a computer club, you might make up a game as a group or have a contest in game making. Bulletin board members often invent their own games for callers to play. (The chances are you won't be able to sell your game to a software company. Most companies don't accept ideas from outsiders.)

THREE BASIC TIPS

1. Make the game easy enough so that players think they can win.

2. Make the game hard enough so that players will stay interested.

3. Try to second-guess the player. That is, choices should make sense.

FROM IDEA TO ROUGH PLAN

Let's say you want to make up an adventure game. Work with the following questions.

WHERE DOES IT TAKE PLACE? Some ideas are a planet in outer space, a diamond mine, a theme park (where you can't tell the real from the fake), a cellar, an attic, a land with no straight lines, or a place where everything moves backward in time.

WHAT IS THE EVENT?   The event could be a need for a rescue, a treasure hunt, or being lost and finding home.

WHO ARE THE CHARACTERS, AND WHAT ARE THEY LIKE?   Three ideas for characters are a dragon that can be defeated only if it eats dead fish but hates fish, a witch who can see only the color blue, and a monster dangerous only in the daytime.

WHERE ARE THE EXITS?   Figure out a kind of maze. If your game takes place in a house, plan the doors to the rooms. Then figure out a difference in the door for each room. One room might have a door that leads to the cellar. Another door might lock every time someone enters that room.

WHAT ARE THE TOOLS A PLAYER CAN USE TO GET OUT OF A JAM?   The player could use a sword, a map, a dead fish, a flask of powerful perfume, or a magic wand that works only with a certain magic word.

FLOW CHARTS

In order to write a computer game, make flow charts.

A circle means start or stop. A square means action. A diamond means place for deciding.

For example, you are on planet Zork. You have a choice of three planets to visit to defeat the evil master of the universe. You can visit Arcland, Flatspace, or Moon. Which do you choose?

Once on your chosen planet, you have further choices.

Arcland: fly, go underground, travel overland
Flatspace (kill the evil rectangle): visit square, circle, or triangle
Moon: ride in a space vehicle or stay in your space suit

Follow the choices on Arcland.

Fly: meet giant orc, get shot down by Arcers
Go underground: visit Stone City, search for diamond mines, or meet giant earthworm
Travel overland: end up in Archouse, Fun Arcade, or Arcer Academy

Let's say you choose to go underground, where you meet the earthworm. You then have two *more* choices: to fight the earthworm or to make friends with it. If you fight the earthworm with a sword, it turns the sword against you and the game is over. If you use the laser gun, you succeed only in wounding the earthworm and end up in jail for it. If you make friends, the earthworm helps you find the end of the tunnel . . . and so on. . . .

Now try making a flow chart for your game. You probably need a large piece of paper to work on.

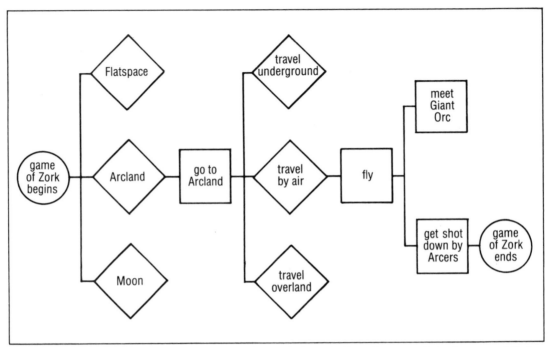

This sample flow chart uses circles, squares, and diamonds (page 273) to plot one path in the game of Zork from start to finish.

PROGRAMMING YOUR GAME

When you get to this point, it is time to think about programming your game. You may need to get some help with this. It is possible to use BASIC, but your game will be slow.

After you have written a program for your game, you might want to send it to *3-2-1 Contact Magazine*. Send the game written out, not as a disk. Include your name, address, age, T-shirt size, and type of computer. The magazine has a computer column in which programs by kids are printed. It pays $25 for each program it prints.

Basic Training
3-2-1 Contact Magazine
1 Lincoln Plaza
New York, NY 10023

DO COMPUTERS REALLY THINK?

How do you know that a bucket with a hole in it leaks? Can a computer figure this out too?

At Epcot Center, Walt Disney World, a Mark Twain robot tells stories. How smart is it?

If a computer can read words out loud, is it intelligent?

What is it to behave in an intelligent way? Some scientists say that there are two signs of intelligent action. One is that it suits the problem. The other is that it cannot be guessed ahead of time.

WHAT ARE SOME TESTS FOR ARTIFICIAL INTELLIGENCE?

Alan Mathison Turing, an English mathematician, made up a game called To Test for Artificial Intelligence. To play it, you need at least two people and a computer. You put one person and the computer behind a screen. The second person sits in front of the screen. He asks a question. He does not know if the computer or the person on the other side will answer. If he can't tell if the answer is given by the computer or the person, and it *is* by the computer, then the computer has artificial intelligence. John von Neumann, another mathematician, asks if a computer can be programmed to make itself. If the answer is yes, artificial intelligence may well be at work.

IS THE BRAIN A COMPUTER?

The brain may come up with answers like a computer, but it is not one really. The human brain weighs about 1 pound. It has 10 billion neurons, body cells of a special kind, many doing special things. There are 1,000 times 10 billion connections between neurons. These fancy networks in your brain can make decisions. The brain does far more than help you do your homework. For instance, it "tells" your hand how to move when you pick something up.

IS A COMPUTER A BRAIN?

The digital computer makes yes or no (1 or 0) decisions. It works in bits, not wholes. To do so it uses math and reasoning. It can sort through data to find data that match. It can store information and then bring it back. Some newer computers are made up of networks. They can remember faces and teach themselves to read. Some computers can make choices. They can move robot "hands" to pick things up. They can find facts that don't exactly match but are alike.

As this is being written, people working with artificial intelligence are finding out new things. Perhaps they are making a computer that is just like a human brain. Have they?

COMPUTERS: GOOD OR EVIL?

Some people think computers are not good for kids. Others think they are the answer to kids' problems. What do you think?

Does using a computer keep you from learning how to get along with other people? The computer never judges you. It never makes fun of you because you give the wrong answer. It never gets angry, and it never gets hurt. This can be considered bad because you might get used to no feelings in response to what you do. On the other hand, it's good because you can feel in control. You can keep working on a problem or skill until you learn it.

Besides, working on a computer is often a group problem. Maybe you and your parents use the computer together. If you do, it can bring you together. If you don't—if you know computers and your parents don't—you might seem further apart. In school, kids often help one another with computer problems. But, some people say, only rich kids can afford home computers, and this adds to the distance between rich and poor.

On the other hand, if you have a computer, it is always there. It can help you learn to stick to a problem and work it through. If a subject is boring, the computer can glitz it up with gimmicks and graphics. Usually it doesn't lie. When you are wrong, it tells you. You can't say the computer doesn't like you. You can't blame it. You can't win it over. Are these features good or bad or both?

Some kids do become so busy with computers that they rarely pay attention to people and may end up shy and lonely. You can make up your own exciting world on the computer, but how much of this is good for you? Can you turn into a data junkie and never realize that there are other ways to learn things?

If you think computers have all the answers, remember what computers don't know—how it feels to have a broken heart, for example, and why cruelty is bad. Remember, too, that if you go off the right track, the computer can't help you the way a human teacher can.

BREAKING IN TO COMPUTERS

Just a word about this: It is against the law. Some kids try to break in to computers to change grades or find secret information. This is just as bad as breaking in to a school office and changing grades or rifling through the files.

9
KIDS' TRIP GUIDE TO THE UNITED STATES

There are thousands of wonderful places to visit in the United States. It is impossible to write about all of them in this chapter. Those listed are here because they are places that kids especially like. It is hoped that not too many of your favorites have been left out. If you want to learn more about any particular place, look at the end of this chapter where the State Offices of Tourism are listed on pages 342–343. For example, if you want more information about the Space and Rocket Center and U.S. Space Camp in Huntsville, Alabama, go to the end of this chapter and find Alabama. Under Alabama, you will see the address for the Alabama Bureau of Tourism & Travel. Write a letter or postcard to that office. Be sure to tell them the name of the place you want to learn more about.

ALABAMA

THE SPACE AND ROCKET CENTER AND U.S. SPACE CAMP, HUNTSVILLE

You can become an astronaut for the day when you visit the Space and Rocket Center. This large space museum has more than 60 hands-on

Yosemite National Park (page 290), one of the most beautiful places on earth (National Park Service)

astronaut-type exhibits. These exhibits will make you feel as if you are on a space shuttle or an *Apollo* flight to the moon. There are plenty of rockets and missiles and Spacelab stations to see. You will also want to visit the Spacedome, a theater where you can watch a movie on a 67-foot screen that totally surrounds you.

The U.S. Space Camp is part of the Space and Rocket Center. This camp is for kids and runs from March to September. The camp lasts a week, and you really get to act like an astronaut—eat space food, wear space suits, and learn all about traveling in space. There are two different programs to join, de-pending on your age. One program is for kids in grades 5, 6, and 7. They get to build and launch model rockets, become "weightless" on a micro-gravity trainer, and use computers and other equipment on Space Station Mission Day. The other program is for kids in grades 8, 9, and 10. They train for two-day simulated shuttle missions in which they work with satellites and go on space walks. The U.S. Space Camp does cost money—about $500 for younger kids and $600 for older kids. To get more information about the camp, you can call a toll-free telephone number: 1-800-633-7280.

ALASKA

DENALI NATIONAL PARK AND PRESERVE

This national park is 6 million acres in size—a little bit bigger than the state of Massachusetts. It is known as one of the world's last wilderness areas and great frontiers. Denali today is almost as wild and unspoiled as it was many years ago when early pioneers explored it. You can see more than 155 kinds of birds and 37 kinds of mammals. One of the most popular is the Dall sheep, with their pure white coats and—on the rams—beautiful curling horns. Denali also has the biggest moose in the world. A full-grown Alaskan bull moose can weigh 1,500 pounds; his antlers alone can weigh 80 pounds.

Denali has wonderful views of quiet lakes, snowcapped mountain peaks, and lots of different kinds of plants. Mt. McKinley—the highest peak in North America—is here, but most of the time park visitors can't see it. That's because it is so high that it makes its own weather and is usually hidden by clouds and fog. You can camp, hike, and fish at Denali, and in the summer you can watch sled-dog shows. But mostly you can just enjoy the wilderness. Be sure to take your binoculars!

Visitors ride mules in the mile-deep gorge of the Grand Canyon. (Richard Frear, National Park Service)

ARIZONA

GRAND CANYON NATIONAL PARK

The word that describes the Grand Canyon of the Colorado River is *awesome*. It is 227 miles long, 10 miles wide, and 1 mile deep. There are three separate areas in the park—the South Rim, the North Rim, and the Inner Canyon. It takes 5 hours to drive from the South Rim to the North Rim! The South Rim is open all year, but snow closes the North Rim, usually from late October until mid-May.

The oldest rock layers in the Grand Canyon date back two billion years. The colors, lights, and shadows in the canyon will truly dazzle you. If you want to go down into the canyon, one way to do it is by mule. A mule-pack trip usually takes a full day. To go on the trip, you have to be at least 4 feet 7 inches tall and weigh under 200 pounds. There are lots of things to do at the Grand Canyon: hikes, junior-ranger education programs, nature walks, and campfire talks.

HEARD MUSEUM, PHOENIX

This museum is dedicated to the Native Americans who live in the southwestern part of the United States. More than 75,000 different objects are here. You will see beautiful baskets, pottery, and pieces of jewelry. There are also different kinds of Indian houses—a Navajo hogan and an Apache wickiup included. Don't miss the kachina dolls carved by the Hopi Indians. The kachina dolls are so interesting and beautiful that many famous people, like actor John Wayne and Senator Barry Goldwater, have collected them. A wonderful slide show—"Our Voices, Our Land"—will teach you all about the life and traditions of the Native

Many kachina dolls are on display at the Heard Museum. (Heard Museum)

Americans who have lived in the Southwest.

ARKANSAS

CRATER OF DIAMONDS STATE PARK, MURFREESBORO

Visitors come here mostly for one reason: to search for diamonds. What you find you get to keep! The diamond field is the only diamond area in North America that is open to the public. Every day two or three diamonds are discovered; every year about 1,000 diamonds are found. The chances that you will find a valuable diamond are not very good, but you will have fun looking! Here is a tip on diamond hunting from the park rangers: "Diamonds have an oily, slick outer surface that dirt or mud will not stick to, so look for clean crystals." When you get tired of diamond hunting, there are campgrounds and picnic areas to enjoy.

MID AMERICA CENTER MUSEUM, HOT SPRINGS NATIONAL PARK

Everything in this museum seems to say, "Reach out and touch me." You can pull, tug, push, spin, pump, twist, and do all sorts of things to the many "toys of science." That's what the museum calls its exhibits. You can launch a hot-air balloon, make bubbles chase one another, walk inside a giant camera, play tick-tack-toe with a computer, make a toy windmill, create a small tornado, and generate electricity. The Lands Alive exhibit lets you form mountains, rivers, and lakes by pumping water and air over and under a piece of land. At the Gas Masher you can try to crush a small amount of air—not too easy to do.

The Energy Coaster has pool balls that bounce, fall, and slide on ramps and lifts and through twists and turns. Test your strength against the Gravity Tower, and see if it is true that what goes up must come down. Don't miss the light exhibit, where you can work with lasers, mirrors, prisms, solar power cells, and holograms. And don't forget to stop by the Hushaby Hot-Air Rocking Chair and the Little Dragon Carpet-Sweep (It has eyes that search for dirt). The Mid America Center Museum is a place where your imagination can run wild!

CALIFORNIA

ALCATRAZ ISLAND, SAN FRANCISCO

Just about everyone who goes to San Francisco wants to ride the cable cars and see the Golden Gate Bridge. But don't miss Alcatraz, the most famous prison in the history of the United States. Built on Alcatraz Island in San

Francisco Bay, "the Rock" was first a military fort but became a federal prison in 1933. Many hard-core criminals were kept here, including Al Capone, George "Machine Gun" Kelly, and Robert "Bird Man of Alcatraz" Stroud.

Rules at the prison were tough. No newspapers or radios were allowed, inmates were not permitted to play cards, and for a while they weren't allowed even to talk to each other. By the time Alcatraz was closed in 1963, 26 prisoners had tried to escape. Most were captured, shot to death, or drowned. However, five escapees were never found, and some people think that they did get away.

Since Alcatraz is a very popular tourist site, you will need to make reservations to visit. A boat leaves from Fisherman's Wharf to take you to Alcatraz Island. On the island you will see the cell blocks where the prisoners were kept, find out how they lived, and hear exciting stories about the most dangerous criminals and the famous escape attempts.

DISNEYLAND, ANAHEIM

If you haven't heard of Disneyland— "the happiest place on earth"—you must have been born on another planet! Disneyland has seven different theme areas: Main Street U.S.A., Tomorrowland, Frontierland, Fantasyland, Adventureland, Bear Country, and New Orleans Square. The rides here are fantastic. Some of the most popular are the Pirates of the Caribbean, the Haunted Mansion, the Jungle Cruise, the Matterhorn, and Space Mountain (The last two are both roller coasters). When you are at the park, you have to see *Captain EO*, a 17-minute 3-D space-adventure movie. It was made by Michael Jackson and George Lucas. *Captain EO* stars Michael Jackson and has many songs, exciting dances, and laser special effects. The space crew in this movie is a strange group, including Hooter—a little green elephant who sneezes wild musical notes through his trunk—and Fuzzball—an orange-haired space monkey with butterfly wings. No matter where you go in Disneyland, you have a good chance of meeting some favorite Disney characters—Mickey Mouse, Minnie Mouse, Goofy, Donald Duck, Snow White, and the Seven Dwarfs.

Can you spot the ketchup and the mustard here in the dining room at Hearst Castle? (Hearst San Simeon State Historical Monument)

HEARST CASTLE, SAN SIMEON

One of America's richest men, William Randolph Hearst, built Hearst Castle. It took more then 20 years to complete. The castle and its three guest houses sit atop Enchanted Hill overlooking the Pacific Ocean. At one time it took 20 gardeners to care for the outdoor plants and flowers. Mr. Hearst even had his own zoo, and animals roamed all over the land. Many famous people— United States presidents, movie stars, and important people from other countries—came to visit Mr. Hearst at his castle. They were very impressed by the art and furniture he bought to decorate his home. Hearst Castle has 165 rooms—including 42 bedrooms, about 40 bathrooms, a movie theater, and two libraries. You'll probably get a big laugh when you visit the dining room. Sitting on a big silver platter are a bottle of ketchup and a jar of mustard. Even though Mr. Hearst was very rich, he didn't believe in being too fancy! Because Hearst Castle is so big, there are four different tours that you can take.

KNOTT'S BERRY FARM, BUENA PARK

Knott's Berry Farm is America's oldest family fun park. It has more than 165 rides, shows, and attractions. There are four theme areas: Old West Ghost Town, Fiesta Village, Roaring '20s, and Camp Snoopy. In Camp Snoopy you can meet Snoopy and his pals—Linus, Lucy, and Charlie Brown. The park's best thrill rides are the Corkscrew (an upside-down roller coaster), Montezooma's Revenge, and the Parachute Sky Jump. At Knott's Berry Farm you can pan for real gold dust, ride in a stagecoach, or watch a Wild West stunt show. When you get hungry, there are lots of different foods all over the park. The most popular is a chicken dinner served at Mrs. Knott's Chicken Dinner

Camp Snoopy, a part of Knott's Berry Farm, has 30 rides and shows. (Knott's Berry Farm®)

Restaurant. Every year more than one and a half million people wait in line to taste this delicious chicken.

MONTEREY BAY AQUARIUM, MONTEREY

This is the world's biggest aquarium. It was built to make you feel that you are down inside the ocean and up close to all the fish and other marine life that live in the water. You will be eye to eye with more than 5,000 sea creatures— dolphins, sea otters, sharks, octopuses, eels, and more. There are two Touch Tide Pools: You can touch the rough skin of a sea star at one pool or run your fingers over the back of a slippery bat ray at the other pool. Bat rays are pretty friendly! Kids especially like the Sea Otter Exhibit. It is two stories tall and lets you watch sea otters as

The touch tide pool at the Monterey Bay Aquarium is full of wonderful water creatures that you can pick up and investigate. (© 1987 Monterey Bay Aquarium)

they dive and play. A guide at the aquarium will tell you all about the life of the sea otter. Because a sea otter eats so much food every day, it costs $10,000 a year to feed just one! Deep-sea divers go into some of the exhibits and swim around while answering questions from the visitors.

REUBEN H. FLEET SPACE THEATER & SCIENCE CENTER, SAN DIEGO

The movies in the Space Theater make you think you have left earth and are moving through space and time. The theater is inside a huge dome so that the movie surrounds you. The sound system has 152 speakers. Every night there is a special laser show set to popular music. The Science Center in the same building has 50 exhibits that don't work unless people make them work. You can move a 500-pound granite block with your own two hands or look through a navy submarine periscope. Stop by the Anti-Gravity Mirror that makes impossible tricks very easy. With its help, you can lift both feet off the ground at once or make your head disappear from your body. At Whisper Dishes you whisper into a dish on one side of a room, and a friend near another dish on the other side of the room can hear you—but nobody else in the room can! Other popular exhibits are Pedal Power and Magic Wand.

SAN DIEGO WILD ANIMAL PARK, SAN DIEGO

More than 2,200 animals roam on the 1,800 acres of the San Diego Wild Animal Park. There are no cages. The Wgasa Bush Monorail Train takes you on a 50-minute safari, and park guides tell you all about the many animals you will see—elephants, antelope, rhinoceroses, lions, ostriches, gorillas, giraffes, zebras. At Nairobi Village you can ride on an elephant, watch an animal show, or start out on the Kilimanjaro Hiking Trail. To get really close to the animals, you can go on a photo caravan. Open-air trucks carry you right into the fields, where you can take great pictures. You have to be 12 years old to go on a photo caravan, and the caravans are very expensive—$35 for kids and $50 for adults.

SAN DIEGO ZOO, SAN DIEGO

More than three million people a year visit this world-famous zoo. It is especially popular because it has many rare and unusual animals. There are cuddly koalas from Australia, long-billed kiwis from New Zealand, wild Przewalski's horses from Mongolia, and pygmy chimps from central Africa. Everybody's favorite animals—lions, tigers, bears, elephants, and giraffes— are also there. Peacocks roam all around the zoo and spread their colorful tails. You can take a wonderful bus tour or go on the Skyfari, a ride that flies you across the zoo. At the Children's Zoo you can watch baby animals being fed with bottles—just like human babies. There are also many baby animals that you are allowed to pet. Altogether the San Diego Zoo has 3,200 animals. There's more about the zoo on pages 85 and 215.

SEA WORLD, SAN DIEGO

Want to be kissed by a killer whale or splashed by a leaping dolphin or squirted by a walrus? Then come to Sea World. This marine zoological park has six animal shows, 30 educational exhibits, three rides, and four aquariums. Kids love the animal shows. Shamu, the 2-ton killer whale, does tricks you won't believe. There are the dolphin show and the sea lion show as well. Visitors are often asked to take part in the animal tricks and stunts. At the Dolphin Petting Pool, you can pet and feed several kinds of dolphins and whales. At Penguin Encounter, you can watch 400 penguins walk over 10,000 pounds of crushed ice and dive and swim in a big pool. San Diego isn't the only place that has a Sea World. There is also a Sea World in Cleveland, Ohio, and another in Orlando, Florida.

SEQUOIA AND KINGS CANYON NATIONAL PARKS

These parks are famous because of their trees. People come from all over the world to see the General Sherman tree in Sequoia National Park. This giant sequoia tree is the largest living thing in the world. It is about 2,200 years old, the trunk weighs about 1,385 tons, and it stands approximately 275 feet tall (about the height of a 16-story building). At ground level the distance around the tree's trunk is almost 103 feet. Some of General Sherman's branches are bigger and taller than other trees. It's hard to tell that this is the world's largest tree because there are so many other large sequoias in these two national parks. You can camp and fish and hike in the parks. There are more than 800 miles of hiking trails.

UNIVERSAL STUDIOS TOUR, UNIVERSAL CITY

This tour gives you a behind-the-scenes look at how movies are made. During the first part of the tour—on a tram—you will be attacked by alien creatures, find yourself in the middle of a laser battle, see the "parting of the Red Sea," watch a flash flood, and be on top of a collapsing bridge. All of that is nothing compared to one of the tour's newest thrills: King Kong. While you are riding along crossing a bridge in the tram, King Kong rises out of a river and tries to tear the tram off the bridge and throw you in the river! King Kong stands 30 feet tall and weighs 7 tons. He comes so close to you that you can smell his banana breath.

The second part of the tour takes place in the Entertainment Center, where there are five different live-action shows: Adventures of Conan,

The King Kong ride at Universal Studios Tour (© 1986 Universal City Studios, Inc.)

Screen Test Comedy Theatre, Western Stunt Show, A-Team Live-Action Show, and Animal Actors Stage. You can easily spend a whole day on the tour. Everywhere you turn, you find action, excitement, and special effects.

WINCHESTER MYSTERY HOUSE, SAN JOSE

The story behind this mystery house is pretty weird. Sarah Winchester, the lady who built the house, was the daughter-in-law of the man who invented the Winchester rifle, "the gun that won the West." Sarah got scared after her husband and baby girl died. She thought that evil spirits were punishing her family for all the people who had died because of the Winchester rifle. She believed that as long as she kept building her house, the evil spirits would stay away from her and she would be safe. For 38 years she had workmen build and add on to the house. They worked 24 hours a day.

What a strange place the house turned out to be. There are 160 rooms with 2,000 doors, 10,000 windows, 40 staircases, and 47 fireplaces. There are doors that open to blank walls, staircases that lead nowhere, secret peepholes, and windows in places that never get light. The house is so complicated that Mrs. Winchester's servants had to use a map to find their way around. Mrs. Winchester was obsessed by the number 13: There are 13 bathrooms, lamps with 13 lights, rooms with 13 windows, stairways with 13 steps, and 13 panes of glass in some windows. She even signed her will 13 times. By the time she died, Sarah Winchester had spent $5 1/2 million on her mystery house.

YOSEMITE NATIONAL PARK

President Theodore Roosevelt called Yosemite "the most beautiful place on earth." It has deep canyons, tall forests, snow-covered mountains, thundering waterfalls, meadows filled with flowers. In the spring and summer you can hike, bicycle, ride horseback, rock climb, or go river rafting. The Junior Ranger Program has special events. In the winter you can ski or ice-skate. When you go to the park, get a copy of the *Yosemite Guide*. There are always a lot of things going on at Yosemite, and this newspaper lists them all—from nature walks to camera/photography talks.

COLORADO

ROCKY MOUNTAIN NATIONAL PARK

When you see the spectacular mountains in this park, you will find it hard to believe that a great sea once covered most of this land. Of course, that was about 100 million years ago! Because of its beautiful scenery, this is one of the top ten national parks in the United States in numbers of visitors per year. Within the park there are 67 mountain peaks that are 12,000 feet or higher. The park is a wildlife sanctuary, and you will see many bighorn sheep, elk, and deer. Horseback riding, hiking, and mountain climbing are the most popular activities in the park. In the summer there are nature-study walks and field trips.

CONNECTICUT

MYSTIC SEAPORT MUSEUM, MYSTIC

A visit here just might make you want to run away to sea. It was in this area, in the 1800s, that some of America's great sailing ships were built. You can go on board three tall ships and see the sails being set, just as they were set more than 100 years ago. There are also 300 smaller boats and ships on display. Every day you can watch people practicing crafts like boatbuilding, blacksmithing, woodcarving, and fireplace cooking. In the summer, kids are invited to play the games played by kids of long ago—hoop-rolling, walking on stilts, pitching horseshoes, and ring toss. A special Children's Museum shows what it was like for kids who went to sea with their parents in the 19th century. You can walk around in the ship's cabin, climb into the sleeping bunks, and play with the toys that those kids took on the sea voyages.

DELAWARE

HAGLEY MUSEUM, WILMINGTON

Hagley is an outdoor history museum on 230 acres along the Brandywine River. It was here, in the 19th century, that much of America's black gunpowder was made. At that time there was no electricity, just water power. About 25 of the homes and mills have been fixed up to look just as they did then. As you walk through the powder mills and yards, the machine shop, and the old schoolhouse, you will feel that you are walking back in time. Powdermen and machinists will show you how to work a waterwheel, a water turbine, and a steam engine. School groups often visit Hagley because the museum has special programs for kids. Students get to pretend that they are living back in the 19th century. They put on special costumes and act like the kids who worked and played back in the days when the gunpowder mills were important to the United States.

FLORIDA

BUSCH GARDENS: THE DARK CONTINENT, TAMPA

This family fun park has an all-Africa theme. There are seven different areas: Timbuktu, Morocco, Serengeti Plain, Nairobi, Stanleyville, the Congo, and Bird Gardens. The park has thrill rides, live entertainment, animal shows and exhibits, shops, restaurants, and games. If you love roller coasters, don't miss the Scorpion in Timbuktu and the Python in the Congo. There are so many live animals here that Busch Gardens is also known as a zoo. At Serengeti Plain you will see almost 500 head of African big game, including lions, zebras, rhinoceroses, and giraffes. You can see the animals by taking a monorail, steam locomotive, or skyride safari.

An elephant taxi ride at Busch Gardens: The Dark Continent (Busch Entertainment Corporation)

SPACEPORT USA, KENNEDY SPACE CENTER

Spaceport USA, part of the Kennedy Space Center, has lots of indoor and outdoor exhibits as well as movies on space travel. You can see a model of the space shuttle, an orbiter from a space shuttle, a lunar rover, plus real moon rocks and astronaut space suits. In the IMAX Theater, you can watch the movie *The Dream Is Alive* on a giant screen that is 5½ stories tall and 70 feet wide. A special stereo sound system lets you feel that you are taking off with the astronauts. After you see all the space exhibits, you might want to take a bus tour of Kennedy Space Center or of Cape Canaveral Air Force Station. Both of the bus tours leave from and return to Spaceport USA.

ST. AUGUSTINE ALLIGATOR FARM, ST. AUGUSTINE

There are 650 live alligators at this farm! It is also a zoo and a museum. There are four exciting and educational shows: the Alligator Wrestling Show, the Snappin' Sam Show, the Reptile Show, and the Alligator Feeding Show. Besides the alligators, you will see crocodiles, bobcats, raccoons, monkeys, pelicans, sheep, ducks, and other animals. You are allowed to feed some of the animals, but not the alligators. The people who work here teach visitors interesting facts about alligators. For instance, did you know that the average alligator lives for 60 to 90 years? And it eats a lot: In the summer months, when it eats the most, an alligator can eat 3,000 pounds of food at

One of the exciting shows at the St. Augustine Alligator Farm (St. Augustine Alligator Farm © 1988)

just one feeding. Alligators are usually fed twice a month.

WALT DISNEY WORLD, ORLANDO

Walt Disney World is the number-one entertainment park in the United States. It is huge—28,000 acres. It includes the Magic Kingdom theme park, Epcot Center, recreation areas and campgrounds, a junior golf course, hotels, and shopping villages. The Magic Kingdom theme park—very much like

Disneyland—has 45 different rides and shows. Epcot Center has two major areas: Future World and World Showcase. In Future World, don't miss Spaceship Earth, World of Motion, Journey into Imagination, and Computer Central. In World Showcase, built around a lake, see the history and culture of ten nations around the world.

GEORGIA

AGRIRAMA, TIFTON

The Agrirama is an outdoor museum that lets you see what farm life was like in the 1890s. You will see a cotton gin, sawmill, turpentine still, blacksmith shop, logging train, pioneer cabin, smokehouse, sugarcane mill, and more. You will also see soap making, quilt making, spinning, and plowing. The people who work at the Agrirama say that kids are always telling them, "My grandparents told me about this kind of life, but I didn't believe them." Sheep shearing, rail splitting, log rolling, barrel making, candy pulling, wagon rides, and cane syrup cooking—these are just some of the special events that go on all year long.

CALLAWAY GARDENS, PINE MOUNTAIN

This is one of the prettiest—and most fun—places in the United States. Since it's called Callaway "Gardens," you have probably figured out that it has plenty of flowers. It does—more than you could ever count. People say that Callaway is a "colorful collection of nature," but this family vacation place has more than flowers. It offers swimming at a beach, horseback riding, playgrounds, bicycling, fishing, cookouts, miniature golf, paddleboats and canoes, rides on a riverboat and a train. In the summer there is a special one-week recreation program for kids. The camp counselors are circus performers with the Florida State University Circus. The circus performers put on a Flying High show every day. In their spare time, they will teach you everything from swimming to roller-skating—and some circus acts.

HAWAII

HAWAII VOLCANOES NATIONAL PARK

All of the Hawaiian Islands were created from volcanic eruptions. On the Big Island of Hawaii, in Hawaii Volcanoes National Park, there are active volcanoes. They are Mauna Loa and Kilauea. Mauna Loa rises 13,677 feet above sea level and was built up by many lava flows. Kilauea's crater is almost 3 miles long and 2 miles wide. When a volcano is about to erupt, people hurry to watch it happen. If you follow safety rules, it is usually okay to watch the eruption. Unlike other volcanoes in the world, Hawaii's volcanoes do not throw out heavy clouds of ash. As you walk through the park, you will see unusual volcanic formations, giant tree ferns, and "steam puffs" that rise out of the ground. You'll also want to see the Footprints Trail—tracks made by a Hawaiian army in 1790 when they weren't able to escape a volcanic eruption. Taking a look at these huge, powerful volcanoes is really an experience to be remembered.

POLYNESIAN CULTURAL CENTER

On the island of Oahu, the Polynesian Cultural Center has seven villages that show how people used to live in Samoa, Tahiti, Tonga, Fiji, Maori New Zealand, the Marquesas, and Hawaii. The cultural center is very big. You can get around by walking or taking a canoe ride or riding a tram shuttle. Some of the many activities to watch are coconut husking, climbing a coconut tree, conch-shell blowing, hula dancing, carving wooden weapons and tikis, net throwing, and coconut-leaf weaving. The people in the villages will teach you how to crack a coconut, how to play bamboo instruments, and how to play lafo—a game like shuffleboard. Every day there is a special

Learning their history at the Polynesian Cultural Center will help you understand the people of Hawaii. (Polynesian Cultural Center)

parade called Pageant of the Long Canoes. And, as soon as you get there, eat some Hawaiian shave ice. There's nothing like it anywhere. Aloha!

IDAHO

SIERRA SILVER MINE TOUR, WALLACE

Go underground and learn how silver is mined. That's what happens on the Sierra Silver Mine Tour. Tour guides will give you a hard hat, put you into a passenger trailer, and take you down into a 1,000-yard tunnel. They will tell you how silver ore used to be mined, using hand drills and mules, and show you the equipment that is used today. Close to the mine is a mining museum with a lot of mining gear and equipment. You can also see a 16-minute slide show about silver mining.

ILLINOIS

ADLER PLANETARIUM, CHICAGO

The planetarium has exciting sky shows featuring the star-studded heavens, nearby planets, and faraway galaxies. There is an exhibit about space exploration, and there is a wonderful collection of old astronomical instruments. Kids especially like the Learning to Use Telescopes area, which shows how a telescope works and gives visitors a chance to practice using a small telescope. Another popular exhibit is the Special Scales area, where you can find out how much you would weigh on another planet. Altogether

You can look at the skies from the Hall of Telescopes. (The Adler Planetarium)

there are three large floors of incredible astronomy exhibits.

MUSEUM OF SCIENCE AND INDUSTRY, CHICAGO

This museum will definitely knock your socks right off! It is one of the best museums in the United States. It covers about 15 acres and has more than 2,000 exhibits in 75 main exhibit halls. Everywhere you turn, there are buttons to push, cranks to turn, and levers to lift. You can take a ride to the center of the earth on the Augernaut, watch baby chicks hatch before your eyes, walk through a beating 16-foot-high heart, and ride in electric cars into a full-size coal mine. You can also go aboard a World War II German submarine, challenge a computer to a game of tick-tack-toe, and see supercold liquids instantly freeze fresh flowers and other objects. Don't miss the Circus Exhibit, which has 22,000 animated figures and a movie shown on a 30-foot screen. And stop by the Money Center, where you can test your money wits with the money-minded computer. You could spend a week at this museum.

INDIANA

THE CHILDREN'S MUSEUM, INDIANAPOLIS

This is the largest children's museum in the world. It is an adventure, and the adventure begins the minute you walk in the door. You can barter for goods in a 1700s French fur trading post, sit in the cockpit of a 200-mile-per-hour Maserati race car, and explore the twisting passageways of an Indiana cavern. Please Touch signs are everywhere. You can pick up animal skulls, snakeskins, bird feathers, shells, and rocks in the Natural Science Gallery. In the Physical Science Gallery you can learn about lasers by ringing bells, pulling pulleys, and lighting up lights. The Prehistory Gallery has a life-size *Tyrannosaurus rex* dinosaur. People at

Kids can help with physical science experiments in the Science Spectrum gallery at the Children's Museum in Indianapolis. (Children's Museum of Indianapolis)

the museum will show you how to dig for real dinosaur bones. Other important things to see are the 2,700-year-old Egyptian mummy, the 1890s firehouse, and the toy trains. Before you leave, take a ride on the carousel, which has beautiful hand-carved wooden animals.

IOWA

LIVING HISTORY FARMS, URBANDALE

Living History Farms is a 600-acre, open-air museum that tells the story of farmers and farming in the Midwest. People who work here dress in old-fashioned clothing and do the routine daily chores of the people who once lived here. The buildings, the ways of planting crops, and the food are the same as they were long ago. Every season is different at the farms. In spring the workers plow the fields and plant crops. Pigs and lambs are born. In the summer hay is made, and in the fall corn is harvested. You will see butter making, milking, spinning, canning, butchering, and much more. You can travel around the farms in carts pulled by tractors.

KANSAS

KANSAS COSMOSPHERE & SPACE CENTER, HUTCHINSON

Another name for this exciting place could be Right Stuff Central. The Kansas Cosmosphere & Space Center is the Midwest's largest space museum. The building, which looks like a lunar module, houses Omnimax Theater, Hall of Space, and a planetarium. The Omnimax does more than just show a movie; its tilted projection dome and six-channel sound system give you a feeling of "being there." The Hall of Space has more than $100 million of space artifacts, including astronaut space suits, a lunar rover, and a scoop that once dug soil from the moon. At the touch of a button, the Astronaut Data Bank will answer questions about your favorite astronaut. The planetarium has many different kinds of shows as well as outdoor sky lectures.

The cosmosphere has a summer camp called Future Astronaut Training Program for students entering grades 7, 8, and 9. You get to wear space suits, eat space food, see what weightlessness is like, and learn how tough it is to go to the bathroom in space! All of your training leads up to T-Minus 0 Day, when you get to launch, carry out, and land a simulated shuttle flight. The summer camp costs about $400.

KENTUCKY

KENTUCKY HORSE PARK, LEXINGTON

If you love horses, you will love the Kentucky Horse Park. There are more than 30 breeds of horses at the park. On the Walking Farm Tour you can watch blacksmiths making horseshoes from red-hot steel, grooms rubbing down horses, and trainers working with horses. You can also ride a park shuttle or horse-drawn carriage through the park. One of the highlights of your visit will be the Parade of Breeds, in which many different horses perform. The park has two wonderful movies on horses and an International Museum of the Horse.

There are more than 30 breeds of horses at the Kentucky Horse Park. (Kentucky Department of Travel Development)

MAMMOTH CAVE NATIONAL PARK

In this park is Mammoth Cave, which has many underground passageways, deep pits, sinkholes, springs, and underground rivers. Altogether there are more than 300 miles of passages—it's the biggest cave system in the world. You can choose from five different tours ranging from ¼ mile in 1½ hours to 5 miles in 6 hours. Kids under 16 must be accompanied by an adult unless they are on the special cave exploration tour for kids from ages eight to 12. No matter which tour you take, you will see sparkling gypsum crystals, colorful stalactites and stalagmites, and other cave formations. Some of the cave rooms are as wide as 200 feet; the tallest dome is 192 feet high. In the very darkest parts of the cave live many rare and unusual animals: eyeless fish, ghostly white spiders, and blind beetles. Be sure to wear sturdy low-heeled walking shoes and take a jacket or sweater with you.

LOUISIANA

ROSEDOWN PLANTATION AND GARDENS, ST. FRANCISVILLE

A visit here will put you in the Old South, before the Civil War. This plantation once belonged to a wealthy cotton planter. He built the mansion in 1835. The house has wonderful antique furniture, paintings, and statues. The plantation's gardens take up 30 acres. The many different kinds of flowers—especially the magnolias—are beautiful. The road leading up to the mansion is lined with giant oak trees. The plantation is a reminder of a time in American history that has been left behind.

MAINE

ACADIA NATIONAL PARK

This park has an unusual combination of ocean and mountain scenery. It includes a large part of Mount Desert Island, the largest rock-based island on the Atlantic coast—more than 40 square miles in area. There are more than 120 miles of hiking trails. Swimming, fishing, and boating are popular in the summer. In the winter there is skiing, ice fishing, ice-skating, and ice boating. More than 500 different kinds of wildflowers grow in the park, and it is a sanctuary for birds and animals. Park rangers conduct naturalist programs and tell you about the park's geology, marine life, and wildlife.

MARYLAND

B & O MUSEUM, BALTIMORE

The B & O (Baltimore and Ohio) Railroad was America's first railroad, and its first tracks were laid right where the museum is today. More than 50 locomotives and a big collection of passenger cars are on display. One of the early passenger cars is a double-decker stagecoach on wheels. Some of the old locomotives are very different from today's, and they have wonderful names: Tom Thumb, Arabia, Hercules, Grasshopper, Dragon, and 10-Wheeler. The most famous locomotive is the 1856 William Mason, which has been used in lots of movies and TV programs. Every day three model trains run around the museum, chugging around tiny hills and blowing their whistles through toy towns.

NATIONAL AQUARIUM, BALTIMORE

You will take "a trip around the world of water" when you visit the National Aquarium. This spectacular seven-level building has over 5,000 creatures and contains over 1 million gallons of water. At Children's Cove you can walk among living exhibits and pick up creatures like horseshoe crabs, spider crabs, sea urchins, starfish, and whelks. At the Atlantic Coral Reef, you will look through 13-foot-high windows to see an underwater rainbow of more than 3,500 fish. At the Open Ocean Tank, there are lemon sharks, sand tiger sharks, sandbar sharks, and nurse sharks. At the Marine Mammal Tray, there are two female beluga whales, Anore and Illamar. These bluish gray whales are very playful and very smart. Both have "chubby" bodies: Illamar weighs 824 pounds, and Anore weighs 786 pounds.

MASSACHUSETTS

THE COMPUTER MUSEUM, BOSTON

In room after room full of computers, the Computer Museum tells the whole history of computers from the very beginning. There are four main exhibit areas and lots of opportunities to work on the computers. You can "paint" a picture on a computer, using 20 different colors; tell a talking computer what to say; compose a tune and listen to a computer play it back; change the computer image of your own face. There are more than 25 different hands-on computer experiences. At the museum's gift shop, you can buy state-of-the-art microchip jewelry and chocolate "chips."

OLD STURBRIDGE VILLAGE, STURBRIDGE

This outdoor living history museum tells the story of everyday life in a small New England town during the years from 1790 to 1840. There are more than 40 buildings, and they were moved here from different parts of New England. There are homes, meeting-houses, mills, a general store, a printing shop, and more. Costumed "villagers" show and tell what early American life was like. You will see waterpowered machines sawing logs into boards, women cooking at the hearth, blacksmiths hitting their anvils, farmers working in the fields during harvest-time. All year there are special events: cider making, haying contest, wool days, harvest weekend, candlemaking, turkey shoot, and maple sugaring.

PLIMOTH PLANTATION, PLYMOUTH

How many times have you read the story of the Pilgrims who came from England in 1620 aboard the *Mayflower* and settled in America? Plimoth Plantation is where it all happened. *Plimoth* is an old spelling for the town that today is called Plymouth. At this wonderful place you learn exactly how those early colonists lived. The best thing about Plimoth is the modern-day Pilgrims. These people, who work at the plantation, dress, talk, and act just like the first Pilgrims. They have stud-

The Mayflower II, *a copy of the ship that brought the Pilgrims to America, is docked at Plimoth Plantation. (Plimoth Plantation)*

ied a lot to be able to act their parts. They will tell you all about why they came to this country, what life was like in England, and how it was crossing on the *Mayflower*. The acting is so good that you will think you are talking to real Pilgrims. Visitors see the Pilgrims plant and harvest crops, take care of animals, prepare food, build houses, and trade for furs. You are invited to join in and grind corn, fetch water, and chop firewood. You will hear lots of Pilgrim trivia. For example, the real Pilgrims didn't eat pumpkin pie and cranberry sauce at the first Thanksgiving. They did eat duck, goose, turkey, cornmeal, and fish.

The *Mayflower II*—a ship modeled after the one that brought the Pilgrims to America—is docked at Plimoth Plantation. You can roam all over the ship to see what it was like for the 102 passengers who sailed the Atlantic for 66 days.

MICHIGAN

BRONNER'S CHRISTMAS WONDERLAND, FRANKENMUTH

Every day is Christmas Day at Bronner's Christmas Wonderland. Bronner's has more than 30,000 Christmas decorations and gifts—trees, ornaments, wreaths, lights, tinsel, Santas. There are 3,000 different kinds of ornaments and 500 kinds of nativity sets from countries all around the world. More than 100 decorated Christmas trees are up throughout the store. The greeting "Merry Christmas" is on hand-blown ornaments in more than 60 languages. There are lights everywhere—100,000 of them. More than 600 animated Christmas figures perform around the "wonderland": Deer fly, Santas ho-ho-ho, carolers sing, and elves make Christmas toys.

HENRY FORD MUSEUM & GREENFIELD VILLAGE, DEARBORN

The Henry Ford Museum & Greenfield Village is the most visited indoor-outdoor history museum in all of North America. There is so much to see and learn that you will think you are walking inside an encyclopedia of American

Visitors at Henry Ford Museum & Greenfield Village can ride a train pulled by a steam engine. (Henry Ford Museum & Greenfield Village)

history. The museum has hundreds of thousands of items: cars, musical instruments, airplanes, locomotives, bicycles, streetcars, steam engines. You'll love to see all the early cameras, TVs, radios, sewing machines, refrigerators, and phonographs. You can pedal a high-wheel bicycle, use a telegraph key, and work a flatbed printing press.

At Greenfield Village you can ride antique cars, a steam train, a paddle-wheel steamboat, and a 1913 carousel. The village has buildings that were moved here from all over the United States. You'll see Thomas Alva Edison's laboratory, from Menlo Park, New Jersey, where the light bulb, the phonograph, and 42 other inventions were born. You can also visit the bicycle shop where the Wright brothers designed and built their first airplane, the house where Noah Webster wrote his American dictionary, and the courthouse where Abraham Lincoln practiced law. Workers in costumes show different arts and crafts like tinsmithing, pottery making, glassblowing, and weaving. The museum and village will show you—in a very fun and exciting way—how our country has changed over the years.

MINNESOTA

THE DEPOT, DULUTH

This remodeled railroad depot has four floors of exhibits, including a doll and toy collection, a fur trading post, and a two-story tree house. Depot Square has more than 20 old storefronts filled with treasures from the past. You can get an ice-cream cone at Bridgeman's ice-cream parlor, watch a silent movie at the Zelda Theater, ride on a trolley, and peek in windows of a saloon and a doctor's office. Don't forget to stop at the railroad museum to see the collection of railroad cars and locomotives.

MISSISSIPPI

FLOREWOOD RIVER PLANTATION, GREENWOOD

This beautiful plantation gives you an idea of what it was like when "cotton was king" in the South. Built in the mid-1850s, the plantation has 26 buildings, including the planter's mansion, the cotton gin, the pottery shop, and the cookhouse. Workers in costume— the planter, the schoolteacher, the potter, the candlemaker—will tell you about life at the plantation. Depending on what time of year you visit, you can watch cotton being planted or pick some for a souvenir. You might also press cane to make syrup or dip a candle. The Cotton Museum is a good place to learn the history of cotton in the South. The museum has a hand-operated cotton gin used to clean cotton after it was picked.

MISSOURI

THE MAGIC HOUSE, KIRKWOOD

Explore a human-size maze. Match wits with a know-it-all computer. Twirl down a three-story, spiraling slide. Touch an electrostatically charged ball and watch your hair fly wildly on end. Leave your shadow hanging on a wall. Crawl, climb, squeeze, and bounce your way through the totally dark Touch Tunnel. You'll find this, and much more, at the Magic House. There are more than 50 "magictivities" here. At the Magic House you can buy a "Guide to the Magic House" that tells you about each magictivity and explains how each one works and why.

MARK TWAIN BOYHOOD HOME AND MUSEUM, HANNIBAL

This is the house where Mark Twain grew up. His real name was Samuel Clemens. His father built the house in 1844. All the exciting things that happened to Mark Twain in this house and in the town of Hannibal gave Mark

Twain the ideas for the stories he wrote in *The Adventures of Tom Sawyer* and *The Adventures of Huckleberry Finn*. Next to the house is a museum that has his books, writing desk, and other personal belongings. The best time of year to visit is the week before the Fourth of July. That's when kids, dressed up like Tom Sawyer, compete in the Fence-Painting Contest. You have to paint fast and neat! At the real Tom Sawyer Fence is a sign that says, "Here stood the board fence which Tom Sawyer persuaded his gang to pay him for the privilege of whitewashing. Tom sat by and saw that it was well done." Other contests that take place are frog jumping, raft racing, and mud volleyball.

MERAMEC CAVERNS, JESSE JAMES HIDEOUT, STANTON

Meramec Caverns is called "the greatest show *under* earth." It has five levels and many "rooms" and passages filled with wonderful sights. Some of the cave formations are 200 million years old. One stalagmite is 200 feet thick, 33 feet high, and 500 feet around. There is a great music and light show at the Stage Curtain—one of the world's largest cave formations. Some of the rooms have names: the Jungle Room, the Echo Room, the Hanging Gardens, the Wine Room. The famous outlaw Jesse James once hid out in Meramec Caverns. After he and his gang robbed a bank or train, they sometimes came here to divide up their money and hide from lawmen. Once a posse trailed the James gang to the caverns but couldn't find them in the darkness.

A cave formation at Meramec Caverns, where outlaw Jesse James once hid out (Art Grossman © 1981)

MONTANA

GLACIER NATIONAL PARK

Thousands of years ago huge glaciers, like giant icy grinding stones, helped create this grand, million-acre place. We now call it Glacier National Park. Its 50 glaciers, 200 lakes, and mile-high peaks will amaze you. You can see and walk on the glaciers. If you follow Going-to-the-Sun Road, you will cross the Continental Divide at 6,664 feet through Logan Pass. The Continental Divide is a water divide. On the west side of it, streams flow to the West Coast. On the east side of it, streams flow to the East Coast.

In the park are 235 species of birds, including eagles and falcons. There are also mountain goats, mountain lions, lynx, grizzly bears, bighorn sheep, and wolves. You can take a day trip with someone who will tell you about the plants and animals. In July thousands of plants bloom. You can row a boat or paddle a canoe on one of the lakes. Or you can explore part of the 700 miles of horseback and foot trails.

The park is closed by snow, usually from mid-October to mid-June.

NEBRASKA

HAROLD WARP PIONEER VILLAGE, MINDEN

Walk through history at the Harold Warp Pioneer Village. The one-room schoolhouse looks as it did back in 1935. The old books, desks, stove, and water pail are still there. The sod hut made of blocks of earth has walls 3 feet thick. In the general store the shelves are stocked with button shoes and calico, old guns, and other old-time wares. A glass cat sits on the cracker barrel to keep mice away. A wooden Indian stands in the window. The Elm Creek Fort, built in 1869, once kept five families safe in the Indian Wars.

Making souvenir brooms at Harold Warp Pioneer Village (Harold Warp Pioneer Village)

On Sundays, for 5¢, kids can ride a merry-go-round that's more than 100 years old. Spinners spin yarn and weavers make cloth right before your eyes. Watch a broom maker or a glass-blower at work. Explore the Pony Express Pumpkinseed Relay Station with its three-horse barn.

More than 30,000 historical items are arranged in order by time in 25 museum buildings. There's everything from airplanes to crystal radios to ice skates to tin toys, and all of these work, some with the push of a button.

NEVADA

HOOVER DAM

In 1905 a terrible Colorado River flood wrecked roads, crops, and buildings in the Imperial Valley. The water lay on the land for more than a year. It was not the first time—just the worst. Once the water drained away, everything became too dry. The answer to the problem was the Hoover Dam. It tamed the river and brought water to the cities.

Finished in 1935, the dam is one of the modern wonders of the world. It was built by more than 5,000 men working day and night for five years. The giant measures 660 feet thick at the bottom, 45 feet thick at the top, 1,244 feet long, and 726.4 feet high.

You can learn about the dam at the Exhibit Building or at the Visitor Center at the Nevada Drug Store in Boulder City.

NEW HAMPSHIRE

MONTSHIRE MUSEUM OF SCIENCE, HANOVER

This hands-on science museum changes all the time and is never boring. There is always something in the Discovery Room to amaze and delight you. In the Outdoor Physics Playground, you can learn about natural forces. The sandbox, for instance, has built-in magnets and is filled with sand rich in iron. In the museum are live leafcutter ants, Stanley the snake, and an electric eel. Outside are nature trails, including a canoe trail. You might get in on an adventure camp or hike.

NEW JERSEY

EDISON NATIONAL HISTORIC SITE, WEST ORANGE

Did you know that Thomas Alva Edison invented wax paper, gum tape, and the first electric voting machine? It shouldn't surprise you. After all, during his lifetime, Edison patented 1,093 inventions. About a third of them had to do with electricity. He once ran electric wires around the walls of his study to kill cockroaches. His favorite invention? The phonograph. His first record was "Mary Had a Little Lamb." At his Invention Factory in West Orange, you can see a phonograph like the one he played it on.

To Edison, and to other people as well, we owe the movies. You can tour a full-size copy of the Black Maria, the first motion picture studio, and watch an early Edison movie.

But there is more than a phonograph and a Black Maria at Edison's workplace. The labs and machine shop at West Orange were stocked with all Edison and his workers might need— "everything from an elephant's hide to the eyeballs of a United States senator," he once bragged. Edison also bragged that he could make anything from a lady's watch to a locomotive in his machine shop. You'll believe it when you see it. He worked here from 1887 to 1931, when he died. Go to the Visitor Center for information.

You can also tour Edison's house, about a mile from the labs. It looks just the way it did when he lived there. The Edison laboratory that was in Menlo Park, New Jersey, is now at Greenfield Village in Dearborn, Michigan.

SIX FLAGS GREAT ADVENTURE (THEME PARK AND DRIVE-THROUGH SAFARI), JACKSON

The Ultra Twister triple-twists you over and under, sideways and down, then spins you backward. It's one of several roller coasters at Six Flags Great Adventure. On the Sarajevo Bobsled, you rocket over 180-degree turns. Riding the Looping Starship is like traveling in space.

If you want something milder, you can climb a giant fishnet to enter a hut and then leave on a slide. When you tire of that, go on safari to see some of the 1,900 wild animals. These include elephants, rhinoceroses, tigers, camels, ostriches, kangaroos, families of lions—animals from nearly everywhere, wandering free.

And there are rock star concerts, a

All aboard for a ride on the Ultra Twister at Six Flags Great Adventure in Jackson, New Jersey! (Six Flags Great Adventure®)

waterskiing show, a puppet show, and dancing dolphins. The show "Evolution" traces the history of rock music.

Six Flags Great Adventure is open from the end of March to the end of September.

NEW MEXICO

BRADBURY SCIENCE HALL, LOS ALAMOS

Here at 5:29:45 A.M. Mountain War Time, July 16, 1945, light burst, the earth rocked, and a roar split the air. A mushroom cloud rolled up. The light was many colors: gold, purple, violet, gray, blue. It lit everything sharply. "It was as though the earth had opened and the skies split," said William L.

Laurence, writer. But scientist J. Robert Oppenheimer said, "I am become Death, the destroyer of worlds." The first nuclear bomb had gone off.

Two years before the blast, scientists came to Los Alamos in secret to build the nuclear bomb. They called their work Project Y. The scientists had code names. The Bradbury Science Hall shows the history of their project. But best of all are more than 35 hands-on exhibits. You can line up a laser and talk to a computer. You can see how lab equipment works. You can watch films on computer graphics and on famous scientists too.

CUMBRES & TOLTEC SCENIC RAILROAD, CHAMA

You may have seen this railroad in the movies. It was a "star" in *The Lone Ranger, Bite the Bullet, Shootout, Showdown, Missouri Breaks,* and *The Good Guys and the Bad Guys.* In the beginning, though, it carried supplies and people to gold and silver mines. Now it is the longest and highest narrow-gauge steam railroad excursion in the United States. The tracks were laid only three feet apart instead of at the standard width of 4 feet, 8$^1/_2$ inches. Why? The narrow tracks could go around sharper mountain curves. Sharp curves make for an exciting ride!

It takes six hours to ride the railroad 64 miles from Chama to Osier, Colorado, and back. The train winds over gorges, whistles through two tunnels, and roars over trestles. It's like railroading in the 1880s. At noon you stop for lunch in Osier.

When you get back to Chama, explore the railroad yards, where coal and water are stored. Coal is burned to boil water into steam to drive the train. The locomotive burns 4,000 pounds of coal and boils 4,000 gallons of water in one hour of travel. The

An exciting ride awaits you on the Cumbres & Toltec Scenic Railroad. (Cumbres & Toltec Scenic Railroad)

wooden coal-loading tower in the yards is the last still working in the United States. You'll also see old rail- road cars: boxcars, flat cars, cabooses, and more. You can ride the train from June to October.

INDIAN PUEBLO CULTURAL CENTER, ALBUQUERQUE

Visit a Pueblo Indian home. Learn how to do Pueblo Indian crafts. Eat Pueblo Indian foods. See ancient Pueblo Indian pottery and jewelry. If you're lucky, watch a Pueblo Indian dance or show in the theater or plaza. The Indian Pueblo Cultural Center holds 700 years of Pueblo Indian history and culture. On the Fourth of July, an Indian Crafts Fair is held.

If you have time, you can also visit the pueblos of the tribes that live near the center. They have dances at special occasions throughout the year. For in- stance, in January or February at the San Juan Pueblo, the comic Deer Dance is performed. In this dance, Apache "hunters" with sunflower-stalk "ar- rows" track "deer." The Zuni hold a Kachina Dance every December. It cheers the end of the old year and the beginning of the new one. All houses built during the year are blessed. The dancers cross the river, then weave through the streets of the pueblo for most of the night. At the Taos Pueblo, there are pole climbing, races, and War Dances.

NEW YORK

CORNING GLASS CENTER, CORNING

The glass time tunnel at the Corning Glass Center takes you through 35 cen- turies of glassmaking. You can see tools chipped from volcanic "glass" by human beings from a time before his- tory was written. The museum wall is a "linear periscope" that brings the outside in with a mirror trick. You won't believe it until you see it. Inside the museum there are 24,000 things made of glass. Some you can touch. There are also games to play. All this is just at the museum.

At the glass center you can see one of the biggest pieces of glass ever made by humans—the first casting of the

200-inch mirror disk for the Mount Palomar telescope in California. It is 2 feet thick and weighs 40,000 pounds. You can also watch a craftsman make tiny animals from tubes of glass. You might even get to blow a glass bubble.

"Light Fantastic" at the Hall of Science and Industry is a giant show controlled by computers. In the hall there are also live shows and push-button exhibits.

And that's not all. Take the glass-covered bridge to the Steuben Glass Factory. See glass red-hot and flowing like honey. Watch skilled teams make things of hot, molten glass.

GENESEE COUNTRY MUSEUM, MUMFORD

Time-travel into the 19th century, more than 100 years back, at the Genesee Country Museum. Here, on 125 acres, people in costume show you what life was like then. See quilts being stitched, cheese being made, cloth being woven, pottery being thrown. Watch the blacksmith at his forge.

Among the 50 buildings are three working kitchens. Watch mothers fix meals as they did 100 years ago. The carriage barn holds 40 horse-drawn vehicles, including a private stagecoach, sleighs, and the world's only 12-horse brewery hitch wagon. See the drugstore, cooper shop (for making barrels), and log cabin. Visit the one-room schoolhouse and the Romulus Female Seminary, where girls studied.

You might help feed the chickens and geese, pet a heifer, see oxen being trained, or learn to milk a goat. Meet Nancy, the Shetland pony. See the flower and vegetable gardens. In one, the Dye Garden, flowers are grown to make dyes for the yarn used by spinners.

In July and August, kids ten to 15 work here, in costume. They help with chores and go to school.

The museum opens the day before Mother's Day and closes the third Sunday in October.

THE MARGARET WOODBURY STRONG MUSEUM, ROCHESTER

From the time she was a kid, Margaret Woodbury Strong collected things. Among them were 18,000 dolls, 300 dollhouses, and *toys*. This museum named for her holds her collection of 300,000 things.

Don't miss the dolls. You'll see jointed wooden dolls, dolls that wet their pants, twin dolls, clown dolls, peddler dolls. There are dolls that play the piano, dance, drink tea, blow bubbles, and walk.

One dollhouse has an elevator that you can pull up and down by a string. Some have little lights that really light.

Some dollhouses are tiny grocery stores.

Among the toys is a school with kids at their desks. A toy fireman climbs up a toy burning building. A toy mill turns, powered by water. You can also see toy steam locomotives, penny banks, and General Grant smoking his cigar.

NIAGARA FALLS

Three falls make up Niagara Falls. The American Falls is 184 feet high and 1,075 feet across. The Canadian (Horseshoe) Falls is 176 feet high and 2,200 feet across. Bridal Veil Falls is the smallest.

Niagara Falls is one of the most exciting natural wonders in the United States. (New York Power Authority)

For more than 100 years daredevils have been trying to master Niagara Falls. Sam Patch dived twice over the falls and lived to tell about it. In 1859 and 1860 the great tightrope walker Blondin walked across the falls on a wire, turned somersaults, and carried his manager on his back. More of his feats are described on page 183. In 1901 schoolteacher Annie Taylor went over the falls in a barrel. She was the first to try. She lived. Others were not so lucky. Today it is against the law to try stunts at the falls.

Here at Niagara Falls, the world's first hydroelectric plant was built. The year was 1895. Now the Niagara Power Project can make enough electricity to keep Chicago powered. You can see and learn about the falls at the Niagara Power Project building or go to Prospect Point Observation Tower, 282 feet high, or see the falls from Niagara Reservation State Park on Goat Island. *Maid of the Mist* boats cruise right to the base of the American Falls and travel into the water below Horseshoe Falls. They run from mid-May to the third week in October.

The falls are lit up at night.

NATIONAL BASEBALL HALL OF FAME AND MUSEUM, COOPERSTOWN

Close to 200 baseball greats are honored here. You'll find life-size wood carvings of Babe Ruth and Ted Williams. In the Great Moments Room are larger-than-life blowups of great baseball players in action. Follow the story of baseball in an audio-visual show. Find out how baseball gloves, bats, and other equipment changed over the years. See what happened in "This Week in Baseball" on TV monitors.

Among the thousands of items is the Abner Doubleday baseball, over 100 years old. Small and homemade, it was found in an attic trunk. The stitched cover is torn open, showing the cloth stuffing. Abner Doubleday, it is said, invented modern baseball.

Each year a game between two major-league teams is held at Doubleday Field down the street.

One of the many exhibits at the National Baseball Hall of Fame and Museum in Cooperstown, New York (National Baseball Hall of Fame)

STATUE OF LIBERTY, NEW YORK CITY

Standing proud and tall in New York Harbor is the Statue of Liberty, one of our country's most visited national monuments. It was the first glimpse of their new land for millions of immigrants in search of a new life. The size of the statue will amaze you. It is 151 feet tall. The arm that holds the torch is 42 feet long. The index finger alone is 8 feet. It is mounted on a pedestal.

Ferries take you to and from Liberty Island. You can see beautiful views of New York City from the island and on the ferry rides. An elevator takes you from the entrance to the top of the pedestal. If you want to go to the top of the statue, walk around inside the crown, and see the view from there, you must walk up 12 stories. There are many wonderful exhibits, including displays of the casts, molds, and tools used to make the statue. In the American Museum of Immigration located in the pedestal, you will learn about the immigrants who came to the United States in the late 19th and early 20th centuries—who they were, how they got here, what they brought with them, and where they settled.

To learn more about the statue, see pages 63–65.

NORTH CAROLINA

TWEENTSIE RAILROAD, BLOWING ROCK

During your 3-mile ride, your train will be robbed (in fun). Indians will attack (in fun). And if you last (of course you will), you can pan for gold. The Tweentsie Railroad spells adventure. This narrow-gauge railroad's real name is ET & WNC (East Tennessee and Western North Carolina) Railroad Company. People used to joke that the initials stood for "Eat Taters and Wear No Clothes." The railroad is more than 100 years old.

You can visit an old-time western town at the railroad stop. If you're hungry, you can eat at the restaurant and then get your dessert at the ice-cream parlor or buy candy at the Fudge Works.

At the Country Fair, scare yourself with the rides and try your luck at the arcade. And that's not all. Stay for a show. You have your choice: the Magic Show, the Country and Western Variety Show, or the Tweentsie Ragtime Review.

The sky ride takes you to a mining town on Mouse Mountain. Try panning for gold. Board a small train into

Mouse Mine No. 9. Visit the petting zoo. And don't miss the Elderberry C. Simcox Rainmaker Show.

Tweentsie Railroad is open from Memorial Day weekend through the end of October. In the spring and fall, though, you can only take the train ride (with no show), visit the petting farm, take the Mouse Mine train, and pan for gold. Everything else is closed.

NORTH DAKOTA

INTERNATIONAL PEACE GARDEN, DUNSEITH (UNITED STATES) AND BOISSEVAIN (MANITOBA, CANADA)

The International Peace Garden was made in the name of peace in 1932. It celebrates the open border between Canada and the United States. You can see flags of both countries made of 1,200 flowers.

Three tours take you into the 2,339-acre garden.

CANADIAN NATURAL DRIVE   Part of this 3½-mile drive is through wild land, where you might see deer, moose, muskrats, and foxes. The 20-minute Lake View Hiking Trail walk takes you past beavers building their dam.

UNITED STATES CULTURAL DRIVE Along this drive, you'll see a clock made of flowers, the Peace Chapel, and the Peace Tower, 120 feet tall.

FORMAL GARDEN WALKING TOUR   The 1½-mile Border Walk takes you past water fountains, pools, and gardens. Every 15 minutes, the sound of bells comes from the Carillon Bell Tower.

OHIO

CLEVELAND HEALTH EDUCATION MUSEUM, CLEVELAND

This fantastic museum will amaze and delight you. It has 200 exhibits, many of them hands-on. While you have a good time, you'll learn how the body works and how to stay healthy. Juno the Talking Transparent Lady explains body systems. Ten miles of flashing lights carry messages through the Upjohn Brain. And there's more, including the Wonder of Life, the World of Microbes, and the Theaters of Sight and Hearing.

KINGS ISLAND FAMILY ENTERTAINMENT CENTER, KINGS ISLAND

A theme park with everything, Kings Island features over 100 rides, shows, and other attractions. Try riding VORTEX, a steel roller coaster that turns you upside down six times, with a 100-foot drop, two vertical loops, a boomerang turn, a corkscrew, and more! Dizzy from that, you can stagger on to the Beast, a huge wooden roller coaster. It has two long hills and two

The chair-swing ride called the Zephyr at Kings Island Family Entertainment Center whirls park visitors 50 feet into the air. (Kings Island)

long tunnels. Ready for more? Scare yourself on one of the other four roller coasters or many other rides.

In Hanna-Barbera Land, you'll find an animated puppet tree, McScrappy's Farm, the Scooby Choo electric train, and a carousel.

The Wild Animal Habitat has more than 350 wild animals. There are elephants, tigers, zebras, rhinoceroses, ostriches, a giraffe, monkeys, and deer. At the petting farm, you can touch animals. And you can watch a sea lion and dolphin show.

More? Live shows, actors and musicians roving around, rock concerts,

night fireworks. There's the Cinema 180 Theater, where films take you into a volcano's crater, on a runaway train, or on a giant roller coaster.

At the Recording Studio, you can make musical videotapes and recordings. Put on a costume, choose from more than 200 songs, pick an instrument, and you're on the air!

Sports fans will like the College Football Hall of Fame. You can play the field-goal-kicking game or computer games.

The park is open from mid-April through early fall.

PRO FOOTBALL HALL OF FAME, CANTON

If you love football, you'll love all 51,000 square feet of the Pro Football Hall of Fame. Canton was the home of the American Professional Football Association, the father of the National Football League (NFL). Jim Thorpe, the first pro football big-name star and a Native American, played on the Canton Bulldogs in 1915. There is a 7-foot-tall statue of him here.

Trace the history of pro football from 1892 to today. See the oldest football that dates from 1895, a 1902 uniform, and the World's Tallest Trophy, over 22 feet high. Visit the Pro Football Adventure Room and the Super Bowl Room.

In the theater you can watch pro football action movies, test your knowledge of football on electronic

question-and-answer panels, and see "16 Fantastic Finishes" on video.

Every year a Hall of Fame Game Day is held here.

If you love football, the Pro Football Hall of Fame is the place to visit. (Pro Football Hall of Fame)

OKLAHOMA

NATIONAL COWBOY HALL OF FAME AND WESTERN HERITAGE CENTER, OKLAHOMA CITY

This is the world's largest museum of the Old West. You can pretend you are living in the West of yesterday. Life-size exhibits include a Native American camp, a mountain man and beaver dam, a cowboy chuckwagon. You can walk through a gold-mine cave and a house built of prairie sod.

There's a complete pioneer town with a general store, livery stable, and hotel. You can play the nickelodeons in the Silver Dollar Saloon, or you can visit the John Wayne Collection.

Among the things he collected are Hopi kachina dolls carved by kachina dancers and given to Hopi children.

Visit three halls of fame: one for the rodeo, one for great westerners, one for great western performers. See End of the Trail, an 18-foot-high statue of a tired Native American warrior on his pony. With sound and light, the Great Map takes you across the United States by trail, pony express route, and railroad. It covers 80,000 square feet.

TSA-LA-GI, THE CHEROKEE HERITAGE CENTER, TAHLEQUAH

"In the fall and winter of 1838–1839, the Cherokees were driven from their homes and pushed along a dreary march westward. Of 16,000 who started that miserable journey, more than 4,000 died along the way from disease, hunger, and exposure. The march lasted nearly a year, and ever after it has been known as 'The Trail of Tears'. . . ." This is how the outdoor summer show at the Cherokee Heritage Center begins. It tells the sad story of the march of the Cherokees from their homes in the East to the West.

The blowgun is demonstrated at Tsa-La-Gi, the Cherokee Heritage Center. (Cherokee National Historical Society)

The National Museum here presents the story of the Cherokees from before written history to now. See ancient Indian things. Watch video shows. Marvel at Indian art.

Walk into old Cherokee life of the 1600s at the Ancient Village. This is not a show put on for you. Everything is as it was in real life then. Warriors may be out hunting or playing stickball against another village. Women may be cooking over open fires or grinding corn with rocks. You may see Cherokees making tomahawks, battle hammers, pottery, beadwork, canoes, or baskets. Sometimes there's dancing in the village square.

OREGON

WASHINGTON PARK ZOO, PORTLAND

At Washington Park Zoo animals live almost as if they are in the wild. At the Penguinarium, Humboldt penguins torpedo at 22 miles an hour in the man-made surf. The chimpanzees have their own island. The elephants play in a swimming pool, and none are chained. The Cascade Stream and Pond Building copies the land of the Cascade Mountains. Here beavers, otters, water ouzels, and trout live as if in nature. You might even see a beaver mother carrying her baby under her arm. In the man-made Alaskan tundra are grizzly bears, wolves, musk oxen, caribou, and more. You can hear a wolf call. You can put your hand on the cold ground, with its field of tiny, furry flowers. In other parts of the zoo, polar bears swim under dark ice, and big cats go fishing.

The Children's Zoo features an animal nursery, children's theater, and electronic learning games.

WORLD FORESTRY CENTER, PORTLAND

A 70-foot tree talks at the World Forestry Center. You can see how a sawmill works. Exhibits include Forests of the World and the Jessup Collection of trees of North America. There's an old locomotive.

Outside you can visit Magness Tree Farm, a working forest. Here Christmas trees are grown, cut, and sawed into logs. Kids going into grades 6 through 12 can go to summer camp at Magness.

PENNSYLVANIA

BUHL SCIENCE CENTER, PITTSBURGH

The Buhl Science Center is an amusement park of science and one of the best science museums in the United States. The house of mirrors turns you into a whole crowd. There are 19 hands-on exhibits about color. In one, if you move your hand, it doubles and triples in blue, green, yellow. Watch chicks hatch; then hold them. Finger paint on the computer. Tell the Puma Robot's arm to etch your initial. The Discovery Lab has lots of up-to-date equipment and hands-on experiments to do. A talking glass lady teaches anatomy and how the body works.

Every day there's a sky show in the planetarium. Its 65-foot dome gives a

A walk-through kaleidoscope at the Buhl Science Center (Buhl Science Center)

360-degree view of the universe. Some evenings, you can see a laserium concert.

HERSHEYPARK, HERSHEY

Have you ever shaken hands with a candy bar? At Hersheypark you can, for this is a theme park built in Hershey, Pennsylvania, home of chocolate. Hershey also calls itself the "Cleanest and Greenest."

Scare yourself witless on the more than 35 rides. Two of the roller coasters are the wooden Comet, more than 1/2 mile long with double drops, and the Sooperdooperlooper, which takes you in a complete circle. Then there are the Coal Cracker Flume, Giant Wheel, and

A favorite thrill ride at Hersheypark is the sooperdooperlooper roller coaster. (Hersheypark)

Dry Gulch Railroad. Try the Ferris wheel or old merry-go-round. Kissing Tower, with kiss-shaped windows, is 330 feet high.

There are seven areas featuring different times and places. For example, in Der Deitschplatz are makers of stained glass and candles.

At the Hersheypark Recording Studio, you can record your voice singing one of 100 tunes.

At Photozines, you can put yourself on your favorite magazine cover.

There are seven live shows, including theater in a barn, rock and roll, a puppet booth, and a dolphin show.

Hersheypark is open Memorial Day weekend to Labor Day.

While you're in Hershey, take a walk on Chocolate Avenue, where the streetlights are shaped like Hershey's kisses, and tour Hershey's Chocolate World to see how chocolate is made.

LANCASTER COUNTY, PENNSYLVANIA DUTCH COUNTRY

Many of the German settlers in Pennsylvania two hundred years ago belonged to special religious sects: Amish, Mennonite, Dunker. Today those who came after them still cling to the old ways. Many refuse to drive cars and travel instead in horse-drawn carts. Their houses are without TVs and telephones. Their children do not go to public schools. They speak a mix of German and English. "Die cow hat uber die fence geyumpt," they might say.

They call themselves the Plain People. The men dress in black suits and wear beards. The women wear dresses fastened with straight pins. The kids dress like the adults. Most Plain People are farmers. They plow their fields with horses or mules, not tractors.

To see Lancaster County, where the Plain People live, start at the People's Place in Intercourse. Here you can see a movie about the Plain People and visit an Amish museum. Don't miss the Feeling Box or Dress-up Room at the museum. Close by you can watch girls sew bonnets and hand dip candles.

From Intercourse, choose among many places.

AMISH FARM AND HOUSE The house has ten rooms. You can see farm animals and crops. During the tour, which takes about half an hour, you learn about the Plain People's way of life.

AMISH HOMESTEAD An Amish family lives and farms here on 71 acres. It dates back to 1744. Take a guided tour.

PENNSYLVANIA FARM MUSEUM You can see how farm people have lived in Pennsylvania for more than 200 years.

There are a one-room schoolhouse, country store, pottery shop, and Conestoga wagon. See bed ropers and tinsmiths at work.

STURGIS PRETZEL HOUSE This is the oldest pretzel bakery. You can take a lesson in how to twist pretzels.

GAST CLASSIC MOTORCARS A Rolls Royce Silver Shadow II, cream colored, once owned by the family of Michael Jackson, is here.

PENNSYLVANIA RENAISSANCE FAIRE The Faire is held seven weekends from the end of August through mid-October. You can see a human chess match, mud show, medieval games, jousting and fencing, jugglers and jesters.

An Amish boy skates to school in Lancaster County, also called Pennsylvania Dutch Country. (Pennsylvania Dutch Convention & Visitors Bureau)

PETER J. McGOVERN LITTLE LEAGUE BASEBALL MUSEUM®, WILLIAMSPORT

Bat and pitch, then watch the instant replay on TV. Test your knowledge of Little League baseball with a computer quiz. See how baseballs and bats and gloves are made. Watch the documentary film *The World of Little League.*

It's been 50 years since the first Little League game. There was one league then. Now there are 7,000. That's a lot of history. You'll find most of that history here. There are highlights of past World Series, exhibits showing how Little League has changed, and much more.

A display of batting helmets at the Little League Baseball Museum (Little League Baseball Museum)

RHODE ISLAND

THE BREAKERS, NEWPORT

In Newport, an old town by the ocean, very rich people once lived, and still do. Newport looks like a very old seaport, which it once was. One of the great estates, the Breakers, was owned by millionaire Cornelius Vanderbilt. The Vanderbilt "Cottage," built around 1900, was used as a children's playhouse. Four wooden posts on the porch are carved in the shape of characters from Dutch folklore. The cottage has a living room and kitchen. The kitchen has a stove, sink, and china cupboard. A big redbrick fireplace has seats *inside* it.

The children's playhouse at a mansion called The Breakers in Newport, Rhode Island (Preservation Society of Newport County)

SOUTH CAROLINA

MIDDLETON PLACE, CHARLESTON

Henry Middleton, president of the First Continental Congress, began these gardens on his river plantation in 1741. Some say it took 100 slaves ten years to complete them. There are terraces, flowers everywhere, and beautiful lakes. Animals roam here—baby farm animals, peacocks, sheep, deer, and black swans. If you're lucky, you might see baby swans riding on their mother's back. If you're even luckier, you might glimpse the ghost of Middleton Place, the Little Gray Lady.

Wagon rides at Middleton Place (Wade Spees)

There's plenty to do. Go on a horse-drawn wagon ride. Catch hens laying eggs. Visit the sugarcane mill. See the pirogues—dugout canoes—used for travel through flooded rice fields. In the stable yard you can watch crafts-men at work spinning and weaving, making shingles, and throwing pots. You can also see people grinding corn and milking cows. Sometimes kids can help turn the hominy mill.

WORLD OF ENERGY, KEOWEE-TOXAWAY VISITOR CENTER, CLEMSON

Hands-on exhibits tell the story of electricity from thunderstorms through atomic power. Play computer games to test what you know about energy. Feel a seam of coal. Go inside a fission chamber. See how energy is made from the atom. You can also tour the place where nuclear-power-plant workers are trained. After you have looked inside, try the nature trail outdoors.

SOUTH DAKOTA

CRAZY HORSE

A huge statue, the largest ever to be made, is being carved out of a mountain in the Black Hills 5 miles north of Custer. It shows the Native American hero Crazy Horse sitting on his horse. When it's finished, it will be 563 feet high and 641 feet long. All four heads on Mount Rushmore could fit *inside* Crazy Horse's head. Four thousand people could stand on Crazy Horse's arm; it is as long as a football field. The horse's head will be as high as a 22-story building. A five-room house could fit inside the horse's nostril.

In the 1940s Sioux chiefs invited the artist Korczak Ziolkowski to carve the statue. The work was begun in 1949. Ziolkowski, hanging off the mountain by a rope, marked out the outline in white paint.

The statue is not yet done. Eight million tons of rock have already been blasted off the mountain. Ziolkowski died in 1982, but the work is going on anyway. Before he died, he said to his wife, Ruth, "You must work on the mountain, but go slowly—so you do it right."

You might get to watch some of the work being done on Crazy Horse if the weather is good. You can also see the Indian Museum of North America and a slide show about the statue. Among other things in the museum are a sweat lodge used for the Sun Dance and a tepee you can go inside.

MOUNT RUSHMORE NATIONAL MEMORIAL

Would you believe Abraham Lincoln's nose to be 20 feet long? It is at Mount Rushmore! Here huge heads of four presidents of the United States have been carved out of the mountain. They are George Washington, Thomas Jefferson, Abraham Lincoln, and Theodore Roosevelt. The heads loom 400 feet above the Visitor Center. The face of each president is 60 feet high. Each eye is 11 feet wide. Over 360 people, many of them miners, worked on the sculpture. Begun in 1927, the Mount Rushmore Memorial took 14 years to finish. First the rock was blasted away to make a rough form. Then carvers

Washington, Jefferson, Theodore Roosevelt, Lincoln—the face of each president carved on Mount Rushmore is 60 feet high. (National Park Service)

hung over the side of the mountain in harnesses or chairs and worked on the details. Over 400,000 tons of rock were blown and chipped off the mountain.

At the Visitor Center, you can see a film about the heads. You can also visit the museum, where the sculptors' tools are on display.

WALL DRUG STORE, WALL

Ted and Dorothy Hustead bought the drugstore at Wall in 1931. Those were bad days for business. The Husteads didn't do too well. Then one day in the summer of 1936, Dorothy had an idea. She heard the cars of tourists driving through Wall. She knew the tourists had to be thirsty from their trip through the desert. Why not give away free ice water and hope the tourists would buy something? The Husteads put up signs saying Free Ice Water— Wall Drug Store. The free ice water worked.

Now 10,000 glasses of water a day are sometimes given away at Wall Drug. Wall Drug signs are everywhere, even in Europe and in Greenland.

But there's more at Wall Drug than ice water. The life-size animated Cowboy Orchestra will play you a tune and make you laugh. See the giant Jackalope—a weird "animal"—and a stuffed bucking horse. Get your picture taken sitting on the stuffed buffalo. Chat with the talking parrot.

At Wall Drug you can buy, among other things, petrified wood, corncob toilet paper, left-handed lariats, cowboy boots, fossils, and crystals. The restaurant offers buffalo burgers and peanut butter pie.

Wall Drug is open all year, but the exhibits are open only from mid-May to October 1.

TENNESSEE

AMERICAN MUSEUM OF SCIENCE & ENERGY, OAK RIDGE

There are 200 exhibits you can play with in this museum. Watch the energy

machine whirl balls by using gravity. Visit Electric City. Amaze yourself with the perpetual motion machine. See atoms on the move. Play computer games to test what you know about energy. Go wildcatting for oil. You can also see movies and other shows.

Energy: The American Experience shows American life and work of the late 1800s and early 1900s in four life-size exhibits. Learn about what it was like to work in a coal mine. See how the car changed the life of nearly everyone in the United States. Find out about what's going on at Oak Ridge now and about future hopes for energy use.

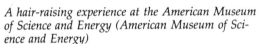

A hair-raising experience at the American Museum of Science and Energy (American Museum of Science and Energy)

GREAT SMOKY MOUNTAINS NATIONAL PARK

The scenery in this park will amaze you with its beauty. Sixteen mountain peaks soar more than a mile high. The smoky haze, which gave the park its name, hangs in the valleys. Flowers like rhododendron and azalea bloom in spring. Leaves turn color in the fall. You might see a wild boar, wild turkey, or deer.

The park is also an outdoor museum where you can see how pioneers lived. There are old log cabins, barns, and working mills from pioneer days. Stop at Sugarlands Visitor Center for information. (On the North Carolina side of the park, stop at Oconaluftee Visitor Center.) There you can find out where the 75 historic buildings are. Don't miss Mingus Mill, a water-powered mill for grinding corn. It makes cornmeal from mid-April through October. At Oconaluftee Pioneer Farmstead, you can see people doing crafts.

If you are from eight to 12 years old, you can become an official Great Smoky Mountains National Park Junior Ranger. All you have to do is fill out a workbook and go to a special program. When you do, you'll find out about a tree that grows on stilts and what a nursery log is. Then you get your Official Junior Ranger Badge.

MUD ISLAND, MEMPHIS

This is how it is on the Mississippi mud! When you're in Memphis, don't miss Mud Island, a river park. You can get there by bridge or monorail. The scale model of the Lower Mississippi is 2,000 feet long—nearly ½ mile. It has bridges, levees, and 20 river towns on its banks. Markers tell about the history of the Lower Mississippi and give other facts. One step equals 1 mile. At the end is a 1-acre copy of the Gulf of Mexico.

Go on board the 1870s steamship *Belle of the Bluffs* and the Union gunboat. Learn stories of river disasters like floods. Go to the River Folk Gallery, where life-size figures of Mark Twain and the keelboat man Mike Fink "talk" to you about what life and work were like on the river. Visit the fresh-

A scale model of the lower Mississippi River is one of Mud Island's main attractions. (Memphis Convention and Visitors Bureau)

water aquarium, where you might see a catfish. Listen to music—jazz, country, blues, rock and roll. Take a ride on a riverboat, and play in Huckleberry Finn's backyard.

MUSEUM OF APPALACHIA, NORRIS

In this mountain village, you can see how Appalachian pioneers lived. On 65 acres sit 30 real mountain buildings. Among them are a log cabin with dirt floor, country store, church, and schoolhouse. You can even see an old-time privy. There are farm buildings too—a barn, corncrib, corn mill, hog house, sheep pen. And there are animals to go with them—lambs, goats, ducklings, chickens.

In the display building, you can see how pioneers made what they needed. You'll see spinning and weaving, shoe-

making, blacksmithing, and the making of Kentucky rifles, baskets, and musical instruments. Don't miss the old lock and key display. You won't believe the many ways to lock things up.

If you come in spring at the right time, you can watch fields being plowed with mules or oxen. At the Tennessee Fall Homecoming, there are many activities: music making, molasses boiling, barrel making, shingle and rail splitting, and having a great old time!

OPRYLAND, NASHVILLE

Of all the theme parks, Opryland has the most music by the most famous musicians. It features a dozen live shows, including country, bluegrass, gospel, and rock and roll. Some of the shows are "Hot Country," "Livin' in America" (rock and roll), and "The Laughing Place" (a 15-minute show for kids). Sometimes you can watch TV tapings.

Opryland also has 21 rides and adventures, including white-water rafting, Tin Lizzies, Wabash Cannonball (a corkscrew roller), and a spinning ride in a dome with flashing lights and rock and roll. Big "G" Kid Stuff is a play area just for kids. You can also see craft making and have your picture drawn by a sidewalk artist. There's a petting zoo. Opryland is open weekends in spring and fall and seven days a week in summer.

TEXAS

THE ALAMO, SAN ANTONIO

At the Battle of the Alamo, 188 people tried to hold out against an attack by hated General Santa Anna's 4,000 men. Davy Crockett was one of the heroes. During the battle, he took his fiddle and, along with a bagpiper, put on a musical to cheer up the men. But on March 6, 1836, it was all over. The Alamo fell, and all its defenders died. Less than two months later, 800 men under General Sam Houston fought against Santa Anna's 1,500 men at San Jacinto. "Remember the Alamo!" they shouted. They won. Texas was free. It was a country by itself—the Republic of Texas—for nearly ten years before it became part of the United States.

Now a chapel is all that is left of the fort. In the museum nearby you can see and hear the story of the Alamo.

The Alamo, where Davy Crockett was a hero (The Alamo, The Daughters of the Republic of Texas)

LYNDON B. JOHNSON SPACE CENTER, HOUSTON

From here, Mission Control talks to astronauts out in space. You can visit Mission Control. Come early. It's first come, first served. At the Visitor Center are craft that have flown in space—moon rockets, launch vehicles, engines, moon buggies. There are famous craft too: the *Mercury* capsule in which Gordon Cooper circled Earth 22 times in 1963 and the *Apollo 17* command module *America* that carried astronauts to the moon in 1972. You can walk through *Skylab* trainers and try on a training helmet. You can watch scientists studying moon rocks. You can see space suits and Mercury star charts.

Films are shown every day.

PERMIAN BASIN PETROLEUM MUSEUM, LIBRARY, AND HALL OF FAME, MIDLAND

This museum celebrates Texas oil. It shows how oil came to be and how people drill for it. You can take a Time Tunnel trip to the bottom of a 230-million-year-old sea. Lifelike figures move, waves lap above you, and actors' voices tell the story. The Marine Diorama has about 200,000 models of ancient sea creatures. It's in 3-D and took two years to build.

At the displays of oil- and gas-well fires, hear the roar and watch the flames of the blowouts. See an old pipeline plane as it seems to fly over oil fields. Turn a windmill fan. Pump an old gasoline pump. Explore a model of an oil rig. Outdoors are the real things—old drilling rigs and gear.

WET 'N WILD, ARLINGTON AND GARLAND

Thrilling wet rides will excite you *and* cool you down on a hot day. Blue Niagara flings you 300 feet, in floods of water, from eight stories high. Hydramaniac drops you down two enclosed tube slides three stories high into a 360-degree twist before splashdown. At Shotgun Falls, 2,000 gallons of rushing water a minute shoot you out a 70-foot slide. Go on Der Stuka, Kamikaze, and Dragon's Tail if you dare. If they're too much, you can rent a raft. At the Wet 'n Wild in Garland is a children's park with fountains and water cannons.

UTAH

ZION NATIONAL PARK

At fabulous Zion National Park, the many-colored rocks have taken on beautiful shapes. Weird-looking rocks called hoodoos look like mushrooms to some people, king's footstools to others. The Watchman and West Temple loom high. Zion Canyon cuts deep through the red rock. Checkerboard Mesa, Lava Point, Emerald Pools, Red Arch Mountain, Mountain of the Sun, Twin Brothers—all are there.

Zion National Park has even more to offer than rock art. You might see roadrunners, mountain lions, bighorn sheep, and mule deer. There are waterfalls, springs, a petrified forest, and—would you believe?—a swamp in the desert! At the Visitor Center is a museum with exhibits and a slide program.

Kids ages six to 12 can become Junior Rangers in summer (June through late August). Kids who go to one session at the Zion Nature Center get a certificate saying they are Apprentice Junior Rangers. Those who go to a session and another event are given an Assistant Junior Ranger badge. Kids who go to three events get a Junior Ranger patch.

VERMONT

SHELBURNE MUSEUM AND HERITAGE PARK, SHELBURNE

Shelburne is an outdoor museum of early New England life. Visit the steamship *Ticonderoga*, a 220-foot sidewheeler that used to run on Lake Champlain. See Colchester Reef Lighthouse. Pretend to be a prisoner in the pillory in front of the jail. Imagine the kids who did the 100-year-old schoolwork on the walls of the schoolhouse. Marvel at the tiny circus parade with dozens of elephants, clowns, and bandwagons. See old toys, dolls, and

A typical building at Vermont's Shelburne Museum and Heritage Park (Einars J. Mengis, Shelburne Museum)

dollhouses. Walk the covered bridge footpath. Watch the waterwheel turn on the sawmill. Enjoy the feel of early New England life.

VERMONT WILDFLOWER FARM, CHARLOTTE

Acres of wildflowers bloom here, all in season—violets and trillium in spring; daisies, black-eyed Susans, poppies, and wild roses in summer; asters in fall. There are ferny nooks, fields in full sun, pathways through woods. Flowers are labeled. Labels give facts about a flower's history and its uses by colonists and Native Americans. You learn about how plants were used as medicines and what plants are poisonous. The labels also tell legends about the flowers. At the shop you can buy black-eyed Susan seeds or an acre of a wildflower mixture. There's a 15-minute slide show, "Wildflowers through the Seasons."

VIRGINIA

BUSCH GARDENS: THE OLD COUNTRY, WILLIAMSBURG

At Busch Gardens, travel back in time to the 1600s in Europe and America. The costumes are old-time; the rides are modern.

OLD ENGLAND   Cross a drawbridge and see a castle. Go to Threadneedle Faire, where you play Veggie Darts, take a lesson in face painting, act out skits with the Talers.

AQUITAINE (FRANCE)   Visit Le Mans raceway and a doll shop.

GERMANY   Learn folk dances and sing along to music in the big hall. Sail the Rhine in a paddle-driven sidewheeler. If you have the nerve, ride the Big Bad Wolf, a roller coaster.

SCOTLAND   Ride the Loch Ness Monster, a double-loop roller coaster 13 stories high with speeds up to 70 mph.

NEW FRANCE (CANADA)   See an old-time trapper's village. Ride Le Scoot Flume, a thrill ride.

At a Bavarian festival hall at Busch Gardens: The Old Country, visitors enjoy German food, dance, and song. (Busch Entertainment Corporation)

SAN MARCO (ITALY) See "*La Festa Italiana*," with folk songs, folk dances, and opera. Rides at DaVinci's Garden of Invention include some in balloons.

INDIAN EAGLE'S NEST VILLAGE (NATIVE AMERICAN) Play in the Ball Crawl, Cloud Bounce, and Punching Bag Forest.

Among the shows are "America on Ice," an ice revue, and "The Enchanted Laboratory," a computer-animated story.

The rat catcher, the town crier, a juggler, a flower girl, and other characters in costume wander the streets. At the Sing-Along recording studio, you can cut a record. In Recollections, make a copy of your shadow with the help of a computer. And don't forget to meet the Budweiser Clydesdale horses.

Busch Gardens is open on weekends from the end of March to the end of October. It is open every day from the end of May to the beginning of September.

COLONIAL WILLIAMSBURG, WILLIAMSBURG

Williamsburg is over 350 years old. Everything is as it was in the old days. It is the real thing. In order to restore it, experts studied old papers and archaeologists carefully dug up the ground.

Among the 88 buildings are homes, shops, and taverns. The jail once held pirates. People dressed in old-fashioned clothes walk through the streets and work at their trades. You can see them make wigs, boots, bread, bricks, cloth, books, baskets, barrels, musical instruments, and more. When you're done watching, you can try on a wig or a three-cornered hat. Then you might take a ride in an ox-drawn cart or a horse-drawn carriage.

You can tour the Benjamin Powell House. You'll find out how a family in the 1700s lived and worked. There are tours just for kids: Time Trippers for kids seven to nine and Young Apprentice Tour for kids ten to 12. Check at the Visitor Center for details.

Every Saturday at noon, April through mid-November, the Junior Fife and Drum Corps goes on parade. Three times a week, mid-March through October, the militia of colonial soldiers gathers at Market Square Green.

WASHINGTON

OLYMPIC NATIONAL PARK

Olympic National Park is a gift of the sea. It's watery, cloudy, mossy, and beautiful. There are piney rain forests, glaciers, lakes, fields of wildflowers, and ocean. Rugged Mount Olympus looms with its cliffs and crags.

In 1900 the park was created as a refuge for elk. You can still see elk here, as well as deer, bears, wild goats, and bald eagles.

The park has 600 miles of trails. Some are self-guiding nature trails. Along the shore, you can study tidepools of sea creatures. On Saturdays you can make sand sculptures.

Kids ages six to 12 can get a Junior Wilderness Ranger certificate in July and August only. All you have to do is sign up at a Visitor Center and go to some activities.

WEST VIRGINIA

CASS SCENIC RAILROAD STATE PARK, CASS

Do you know what it's like to ride an old steam-driven train, the engine's pistons thumping, smoke streaming from the smokestack, whistle screaming? Find out at Cass. The Cass railroad line was built in 1902 to haul lumber. There's a choice of three rides in a train pulled by a 90-ton locomotive. The 8-mile round trip up the steep mountain to Whittaker Station takes 1½ hours. You stop for a picnic lunch in wild country. The 22-mile trip to Bald Knob takes 4½ hours. Bald Knob is the second highest point in West Virginia. The third trip runs along the Greenbrier River. While you're in Cass, don't miss the graveyard of old trains, the country store, and the History Museum.

The railroad runs from Memorial

Ride on an old steam-driven train at Cass Scenic Railroad State Park. (West Virginia Department of Commerce)

Day weekend through October. The Bald Knob train runs only on weekends in the fall.

WISCONSIN

CIRCUS WORLD MUSEUM, BARABOO

Here at Baraboo are the original winter quarters of Ringling Brothers Circus. On one ticket, you get to go to a circus, sideshow, parade, *and* hear calliope and circus band concerts. You can also see a circus museum, Wild West Exhibit, and magic show. You can watch wild-animal training, huge Percheron horses loading and unloading circus wagons, and wire walkers crossing the Baraboo River.

At the one-hour Big Top Circus, you'll be thrilled by Castle's Bears riding motorcycles and doing a Russian dance. There's more: the unicycle act, Liberty Camels, and Lady Lowande on

Happy the Clown performs in the circus street parade at the Circus World Museum in Baraboo, Wisconsin. (Circus World Museum)

the Cloud Swing. There are clowns, of course!

Theater of Illusion, the magic show, features amazing tricks like the Levitation of Princess Karnac, the Amazing Dancing Handkerchief, and the Girl Visibly Pushed through Solid Plate Glass. Don't miss Buffalo Bill Cody at the Wild West Exhibit, and don't miss the Wild Animal Menagerie.

At the museum are old circus wagons and a tiny animated circus. You can see circus posters and old costumes.

Circus World Museum is open from May through the middle of September.

WYOMING

YELLOWSTONE NATIONAL PARK

The home of Old Faithful, Yellowstone has 200 geysers. Mud volcanoes bubble here. Many-colored pools arise from hot springs. Old steam vents make weird sounds. Glass made by a volcano can be found on a mountain. There's a petrified forest. Mountains rise above high tableland. The Grand Canyon of the Yellowstone River cuts through 24 miles of golden cliffs. There's a thundering waterfall higher than Niagara. This is strange and beautiful country.

Of course, you don't want to miss the star attraction—Old Faithful. It blows every 65 to 70 minutes, rising 140 to 150 feet in the air, sending 10,000 to 12,000 gallons of steaming water bursting forth each time.

Mammoth Hot Springs with its pastel terraces, Firehole Lake, and Foun-

tain Paint Pots are only a few of the other wonderful spots in Yellowstone's two million acres.

You can cruise Yellowstone Lake and maybe see a moose. Moose aren't the only animals here. There are also bighorn sheep, black bears, grizzlies, elk, deer, antelope, bison, wolves, flying squirrels, coyotes, eagles, and more.

The park headquarters is at Mammoth Hot Springs, but there are several other Visitor Centers where you can learn what the activities are.

Old Faithful geyser erupts about every 65 minutes at Yellowstone National Park. (National Park Service)

DISTRICT OF COLUMBIA

SMITHSONIAN INSTITUTION

The Smithsonian has 100 million things, more than you can see even in several days. In Washington, D.C., it includes 13 museums and the National Zoo. There is so much you mustn't miss!

THE NATIONAL MUSEUM OF AMERICAN HISTORY Find George Washington's false teeth, the Fonz's leather jacket, and Archie Bunker's chair here. Marvel at a 19-room Victorian dollhouse. See a Model T, a turbo car that won the Indy 500, an old locomotive that makes locomotive sounds. Here, too, are the First Ladies' gowns. Kids nine years and older can go to the Hands-on History Room. Put together a bucket here. See human posture in stays and waistcoats of the 1700s. Try the clothes on. Make a chair. At the Discovery Corners, find out how soldiers lived in 1776 and how electricity works.

NATIONAL MUSEUM OF NATURAL HISTORY AND NATIONAL MUSEUM OF MAN Here are objects from the history of earth and humankind. At the Insect Zoo, watch a tarantula eat its lunch. Visit a living coral reef. See the dead giant squid, 30 feet long, and a 90-foot model of a blue whale. Follow the evolution of the horse. In the Discovery Room, touch petrified wood and woolly mammoth teeth, try on costumes, and smell spices. Listen to the music of Africa. Watch a scene from

Chinese opera. See a dance from India, an Easter Island stone head, a birch-bark canoe, mummies, and dinosaurs.

NATIONAL MUSEUM OF AMERICAN ART Here's art for kids. In the Explore Gallery and the Discover Gallery, statues are for touching, and paintings are hung where you can see them.

NATIONAL AIR AND SPACE MUSEUM The National Air and Space Museum

This lunar module, built for the Apollo moon landing program, is on display at the National Air and Space Museum. (National Air and Space Museum, Smithsonian Institution)

has 270 aircraft, 100 spacecraft, and 50 missiles and rockets. Most are the real thing, not copies. Not all are on display, but you'll see the *Flyer* flown by Orville Wright at Kitty Hawk in 1903, the *Spirit of St. Louis* flown across the Atlantic in 1927, *Skylab,* an *Apollo* command module, and the U.S.S. *Enterprise* from "Star Trek." At the walkthrough *Skylab* Orbital Workshop, you can see how astronauts live in space. The museum has more: a moon rock you can touch, a working model of the flight of the Montgolfier balloon, the idea machine and push-pull game, and the Spacearium, which gives you the feeling of traveling in space.

NATIONAL ZOOLOGICAL PARK   See the giant pandas Ling-Ling and Hsing-Hsing being fed. See page 212 for more about them. They are among the 2,500 animals at this famous zoo. At Zoolab, you can touch things. Try on a wing at Birdlab. Get a feel for reptiles at Herlab.

ANACOSTIA NEIGHBORHOOD MUSEUM Find out about the history of Afro-Americans. There are mini-exhibits and puppet shows especially for kids.

UNCLE BEAZLEY   This is a statue of a *Triceratops* dinosaur near the Museum of Natural History. You can climb on him.

Have a wonderful trip!

SENDING FOR INFORMATION

1. Always include a self-addressed, stamped envelope (SASE).
2. Make sure you have written your whole name and address on the letter itself. Sometimes envelopes get lost.
3. Be exact about what you want.

STATE OFFICES OF TOURISM

Alabama
Alabama Bureau of Tourism
  & Travel
532 S. Perry St.
Montgomery, AL 36104-4614

Alaska
Alaska Division of Tourism
Pouch E
Juneau, AK 99811

Arizona
Arizona Office of Tourism
1480 E. Bethany Home Rd.,
  Suite 180
Phoenix, AZ 85014

Arkansas
Arkansas Department of Parks
  & Tourism
1 Capitol Mall
Little Rock, AR 72201

California
California Office of Tourism
1121 L St., Suite 103
Sacramento, CA 95814

Colorado
Colorado Tourism Board
5500 S. Syracuse Circle, #267
Englewood, CO 80111

Connecticut
Connecticut Department of
  Economic Development
Tourist Division
210 Washington St.
Hartford, CT 06106

Delaware
Delaware Tourism Office
99 Kings Highway
P.O. Box 1401
Dover, DE 19903

Florida
Florida Division of Tourism
126 W. Van Buren St.
Tallahassee, FL 32301

Georgia
Georgia Department of Industry
  & Trade
Tourist Division
P.O. Box 1776
Atlanta, GA 30301

Hawaii
Hawaii Visitors Bureau
2270 Kalakaua Ave., Suite 801
Honolulu, HI 96815

Idaho
Idaho Travel Council
Division of Economic &
  Community Affairs
Capitol Building, Room 108
Boise, ID 83720

Illinois
Illinois Office of Tourism
Department of Commerce &
  Community Affairs
310 S. Michigan Ave., Suite 108
Chicago, IL 60604

Indiana
Indiana Tourism Development
  Division
Indiana Commerce Center
1 N. Capitol Ave., #700
Indianapolis, IN 46204-2288

Iowa
Iowa Development Commission
Division of Tourism & Travel
Capitol Center
600 E. Court Ave., Suite A
Des Moines, IA 50309

Kansas
Kansas Department of Economic
  Development
Travel & Tourism Division
400 W. 8th, 5th Floor
Topeka, KS 66603

Kentucky
Kentucky Department of Travel
  Development
Capital Plaza Tower, 22nd Floor
Frankfort, KY 40601

Louisiana
Louisiana Department of
  Culture, Recreation,
  & Tourism
Office of Tourism
P.O. Box 74291
Baton Rouge, LA 70804-9291

Maine
The Maine Publicity Bureau Inc.
P.O. Box 2300
97 Winthrop St.
Hallowell, ME 04347-2300

Maryland
Maryland Office of Tourist
  Development
45 Calvert St.
Annapolis, MD 21401

Massachusetts
Massachusetts Department of
  Commerce & Development
Division of Tourism
100 Cambridge St., 13th Floor
Boston, MA 02202

Michigan
Michigan Department of
  Commerce
Travel Bureau
Town Center Building
333 S. Capitol Ave., Suite F
Lansing, MI 48933

Minnesota
Minnesota Department of
  Energy & Economic
  Development
Office of Tourism
240 Bremer Building
419 N. Robert St.
St. Paul, MN 55101

Mississippi
Mississippi Department of
  Economic Development
Division of Tourism
P.O. Box 22825
Jackson, MS 39205

Missouri
Missouri Division of Tourism
P.O. Box 1055
Jefferson City, MO 65102

Montana
Montana Travel Promotion
    Division
1424 Ninth Ave.
Helena, MT 59620-0411

Nebraska
Nebraska Department of
    Economic Development
Division of Travel & Tourism
301 Centennial Mall South
P.O. Box 94666
Lincoln, NE 68509

Nevada
Nevada Commission on
    Tourism
Capitol Complex
Carson City, NV 89710

New Hampshire
New Hampshire Office of
    Vacation Travel
P.O. Box 856
Concord, NH 03301

New Jersey
New Jersey Division of Travel
    & Tourism
CN 826
Trenton, NJ 08625

New Mexico
New Mexico Economic
    Development & Tourism
    Department
Montoya State Building
1100 St. Francis Dr.
Santa Fe, NM 87503

New York
New York State Department of
    Commerce
Division of Tourism
1 Commerce Plaza
Albany, NY 12245

North Carolina
North Carolina Department of
    Commerce
Division of Travel & Tourism
430 N. Salisbury St.
Raleigh, NC 27611

North Dakota
North Dakota Tourism
    Promotion
Capitol Grounds
Bismarck, ND 58505

Ohio
Office of Travel & Tourism
Department of Development
P.O. Box 1001
Columbus, OH 43216

Oklahoma
Oklahoma Tourism &
    Recreation Department
500 Will Rogers Building
Oklahoma City, OK 73105

Oregon
Oregon Economic Development
    Department
Tourism Division
595 Cottage St. N.E.
Salem, OR 97310

Pennsylvania
Pennsylvania Department of
    Commerce
Bureau of Travel Development
Forum Building, Room 416
Harrisburg, PA 17120

Rhode Island
Rhode Island Department of
    Economic Development
7 Jackson Walkway
Providence, RI 02903

South Carolina
South Carolina Department of
    Parks, Recreation, & Tourism
Division of Tourism
P.O. Box 71
Columbia, SC 29202

South Dakota
South Dakota Department of
    State Development
Division of Tourism
711 Wells Ave., P.O. Box 6000
Pierre, SD 57501

Tennessee
Tennessee Department of
    Tourist Development
P.O. Box 23170
Nashville, TN 37202

Texas
Texas Department of Highways
    & Public Transportation
11th and Brazos Streets
Austin, TX 78701

Utah
Utah Travel Council
Council Hall/Capitol Hill
Salt Lake City, UT 84114

Vermont
Vermont Travel Division
Agency of Development &
    Community Affairs
134 State St.
Montpelier, VT 05602

Virginia
Virginia Division of Tourism
202 N. Ninth St., Suite 500
Richmond, VA 23219

Washington
Washington Department of
    Trade & Economic
    Development
Tourism Development Division
101 General Administration
    Building
Olympia, WA 98504

West Virginia
West Virginia Department of
    Commerce
Tourism Division
Capitol Complex, Room B-564
Charleston, WV 25305

Wisconsin
Wisconsin Division of Tourism
Department of Development
123 W. Washington Ave.
Madison, WI 53702

Wyoming
Wyoming Travel Commission
I-25 at College Dr.
Cheyenne, WY 82002

District of Columbia
Washington, D.C, Convention
    and Visitors Association
1575 Eye St. NW
Washington, D.C. 20005

10
THE ARTS

ART BY KIDS

SCHOLASTIC INC. ART AWARDS PROGRAM

For more than 60 years, young people have entered the Scholastic Inc. Art Awards Program. Kids as young as 12 have won prizes. Each year there are about 150,000 entries. About 500 are accepted for the national show. You can enter work in these groups: 1. Oils; 2. Acrylics; 3. Watercolors; 4. Pencil Drawing; 5. Ink Drawing; 6. Pastels, Crayon, Charcoal; 7. Mixed Media; 8. Printmaking; 9. Graphic Design; 10. Textile Design; 11. Sculpture; 12. Pottery; 13. Jewelry; 14. Two- and Three-Dimensional Design; 15. Photography.

You must enter through your school. The contest is open only to kids in grades 7 through 12. Local shows supported by businesses, colleges, and other groups give gold keys and certificates of merit for prizes. Then local winners go to Scholastic Inc. for national judging. National prizes include about 100 scholarships, gold medals, certificates, and other awards. The best work is shown at the National High School Art Exhibition.

UNICEF CHILDREN'S ART COLLECTION

The Information Center on Children's Cultures is part of the U.S. Committee for UNICEF. UNICEF—the United Nations Children's Fund—is

Though Dana can't take the piano with her to parties, she can play many kinds of music on it—from jazz to classical. (John P. Edwards)

Klee Cat *by Dianne DeLair, age 13, Lincoln East Junior High School, Nebraska; medal for mixed media in 1986 (Scholastic Inc. Art Awards)*

Colorado poster design *by Kim Walker, age 13, Lamberton Middle School, Carlisle, Pennsylvania; medal for graphic design in 1986 (Scholastic Inc. Art Awards)*

Winter Breeze *by Stacey Guard, age 13, Knox Middle School, Salisbury, North Carolina; medal for printmaking in 1986 (Scholastic Inc. Art Awards)*

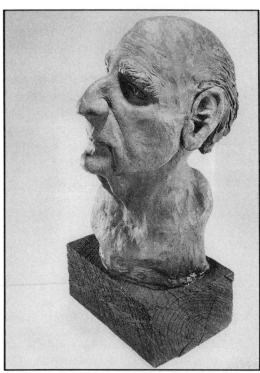

The Beginning of the End *by Shana Betz, age 13, Norton Middle School, Ohio; medal for sculpture in 1986 (Scholastic Inc. Art Awards)*

Children at Play *by Adrienne Richards, age 15, Australia (UNICEF International Children's Art Collection)*

A Disturbance of Bees *by Jiri Krutilek, age 12, Czechoslovakia (UNICEF International Children's Art Collection)*

Loy Krathong Festival *by Wattana Rajanawanich Kit, age 13, Thailand (UNICEF International Children's Art Collection)*

Cooking *by Tan Hui Lik, age 11, Malaysia (UNICEF International Children's Art Collection)*

that part of the United Nations helping children in need all over the world. The center has a collection of children's art from 160 countries and other places. The artists are five to 16 years of age. Thousands of pictures each show something about the place where the child artist lives. Some have been used in UNICEF wall calendars. Money made from the art goes to help the world's children.

Perhaps your local public library or children's museum would be inter-ested in displaying some of the art. Ask the adult in charge to write.

The Information Center on
Children's Cultures
U.S. Committee for UNICEF
331 East 38th Street
New York, NY 10016

If you are in New York, you might want to visit UNICEF House at 3 United Nations Plaza. You can see a multimedia exhibit.

PHOTOGRAPHY FACTS

FIRST CAMERA   Made over 500 years ago, the first camera was an entire dark room with a small hole in one wall to let in a beam of light. That beam carried the image of the scene outside and projected it on the wall across from the one with the hole. An artist could then trace the scene to make a picture. There was no film yet to make the picture of what the first camera "saw." This first camera was called the camera obscura. The pinhole camera of today works the same way, but it is small enough to carry, and it does have film inside to record what the camera "sees."

FIRST REAL PHOTOGRAPH   Over 150 years ago a Frenchman, Joseph Nicé-phore Niépce, took the first photo-graph with film that recorded what the camera "saw." In the photograph, you can see a roof of a barn, a tree, and a house.

CHILD PHOTOGRAPHER   At the turn of the century when Jacques-Henri Lar-tigue was five years old, someone gave him a camera. Almost right away, he was a good photographer. He took pic-tures of races, sports, and people doing ordinary things. The photographs were so good that they made him fa-mous. Many years later, in 1974, Lar-tigue made the official portrait of the president of his native country, France. He died in 1986 at age 92.

TAKING NATURE PICTURES

To take pictures of nature, stalk it like a hunter. Hide. Sit and wait. When you see what you have waited for, click the shutter fast or your prize will be gone.

GENERAL TIPS ON ANIMAL PICTURES
Try to catch a moving animal from the front—if it is not a mountain lion, that is! If the animal is moving *across* your view, use a slightly faster speed than if it is walking *toward* you. When taking pictures of small animals, get down on their level.

STALKING ANIMALS OUTDOORS Put black sticky tape on the shiny parts of your camera. That way the light won't reflect from there and startle your animal. Wear dull clothes or a camouflage suit, if you have one. Walk quietly in soft-soled shoes.

You will probably have more luck near water. Animals come there to drink. The best times are early morning and just before the sun goes down. Keep the sun behind you, but be careful that your shadow will be out of the picture. If you have to face into the sun, shade the lens with your hand. Face the wind so that your smell is behind you. Hide in the bushes or make a hiding place of leafy branches.

Set your camera for a fast shutter speed. If an animal is walking, a shutter speed of 1/250 is fast enough. If it is moving faster, you may need 1/500 to stop action—freeze movement. While you wait, think about framing your picture. Will you try for a picture of the animal and where it is going, or of the animal and where it has been, or of the animal and where it is?

Freeze when you see an animal. Point and focus the camera *ahead* of the animal—where it *will* be when you take the picture. Focus quickly. Take several pictures in a row if you can.

ANIMALS AT THE ZOO   Go at feeding time. Try to get as close as possible. If

Steve Delaney of the Environmental Protection Agency was able to get close enough to this egret to take its picture. (Steve Delaney, EPA)

the animals are in the shade, set the controls for a dark day. You can use a flash in the reptile house. Hold the camera at an angle to the glass in the aquarium.

BIRDS   Try taking pictures from inside the house. Hide behind the curtains at a window. Stay quiet. In parks, put out food to attract your subjects.

SEASHORE   To take pictures of waves, use a fast shutter speed if you want to stop action—freeze their movement. Use a slow shutter speed if you want to record their flow. Sand patterns show up best on a bright day, because with the bright light come dark shadows. Rock colors are clearer on a gray day when bright light and dark shadow don't get in the way of seeing the colors. To take pictures of tide pools, shade the camera and hold it at an angle to the water. Use a slow film because its fine grain will pick up more details.

CLOSE-UPS   You can take close-ups of leaves, stones, and little animals and flowers with a regular camera. With a close-up lens, you will be able to get even closer and still focus.

MAKING HOME VIDEOS
WHAT YOU NEED

1. camera with built-in microphone and deck
2. battery or AC adapter/battery charger
3. TV set to play back
4. connecting cables

Some cable TV companies will let you borrow a video camera. Call the company's program director and ask. Once you have a camera, study it. Learn the names of its parts from the manual that comes with it. You may need help setting up the camera, connecting the parts, and running it. An adult can come in handy for this.

Hand-held video cameras are easy to use. (Olympus Corporation)

WHAT CAN YOU VIDEOTAPE?

You don't want to tape things "just because." It's better to plan what you will do. Here are some ideas.

NEWS SHOWS What's happening in your neighborhood? Who's interesting? What problem is bothering people? Let's say what's bothering them is a plan to tear down an old building. You can make a show and include on-camera talks with people who are for or against the plan. Old people can tell what they remember of the building. Perhaps you can find still photographs to add to the sense of the building's history. You can videotape at different stages as the building is being torn down.

How about doing a family history? Talk with your grandparents on camera. Include things in the taping that tell something about your family—the family Bible, old pictures, things brought to the United States from the old country, for instance.

FAMILY HAPPENINGS Try videotaping family parties, holidays, and trips.

PLAYS Make up a play and videotape it.

ARTY VIDEO Try using the camera as an "eye." Tape the world as a cat sees it. Or do close-up videos of tree bark or patterns in the sand.

THE BASICS OF VIDEOTAPING

GENERAL TIPS A video shot is "framed" by its edges. The framed shot is what you see when you look in the camera. When framing the scene, don't cut off part of the subject's head. Don't put subjects exactly in the middle.

Use a tripod (a three-legged stand) to keep the camera steady. If you don't have one, use yourself as a tripod. Anchor your legs and brace your back against a wall or a tree. Sit at a table and brace yourself on it with your el-

bows. Sit or lie on the floor.

Don't shoot with the sun behind your subjects. Don't point the camera at direct sunlight.

Put dark things against light things. Put light things against dark things.

FOUR SHOTS There are four basic shots used in videotaping. They are used to show the viewer what to look at. Each one has a different purpose.

From left to right: long shot (LS); medium shot (MS); close-up shot (CU); extreme close-up shot (XCU)
(John Wanchik)

1. Long Shot (LS) The viewer sees the subject from fairly far away. This shot sets the scene. Use a wide-angle setting on a zoom lens.

2. Medium Shot (MS) The viewer sees the subject closer up. If the subject is a person, the viewer can tell what the person's face is like. This shot more nearly shows the viewer what to look at. Zoom to a middle setting on a zoom lens. (Use the ring on the camera for zooming.)

3. Close-up Shot (CU) All the viewer sees on the screen is the subject. If the subject is a person, the viewer sees him from the shoulders or neck up. With this shot, it's clear what is important. Zoom in almost to the highest telephoto setting on a zoom lens.

4. Extreme Close-up Shot (XCU) The subject is right before the camera. The viewer *has* to look at the subject. The detail of this shot shows feelings or the important parts of things. Zoom to maximum telephoto setting close to subject.

CAMERA ANGLES The camera angle shows what's going on between the viewer and the subject.

1. Normal Angle Shoot at eye level and in front of the subjects. At this angle, the subjects are speaking to the viewer.

2. Side Angle Shoot at eye level to one side or the other of the subjects. At this angle, the subjects seem to be speaking to each other. The viewer is looking in on the scene.

3. High Angle Shoot from above the

subjects. At this angle, the subjects seem smaller, less powerful, and less important than the viewer.

4. Low Angle Shoot from below the subjects. At this angle, the subjects seem larger, more powerful, and more important than the viewer.

TRANSITIONS—MOVING FROM ONE SHOT TO THE NEXT There are tricks for getting from one shot to the next. The best are those the viewer isn't aware of.

1. Zoom Zoom in with the camera's zoom lens from a long shot to a medium shot. You can also zoom out from a medium shot to a long shot. Try to be slow and steady.

2. Straight Cut At the end of a scene, pull the trigger of the camera to stop the tape. Put it on PAUSE while you set up the next scene. (Maybe going from scene to scene will take longer than a couple of minutes. If so, put the camera on STOP.) When ready, pull the camera trigger to start it again. There will be glitches. To avoid this, record a bit beyond the real end of the first scene before stopping the camera. Then, before starting the next scene, put the tape in REWIND. Play back to the real end of the first scene. Put the camera in PAUSE. Hit RECORD (or PLAY and RECORD). Then go to it. The unwanted extra beyond the end of the earlier scene will be erased.

3. Wipe At the end of a scene, slide a piece of black cardboard in front of the camera lens. When all you see is blackness when you look in the camera, put the camera in PAUSE, then RECORD/ STANDBY. Set up the next scene. Put the cardboard in front of the lens again. Then pull the camera trigger and slide the cardboard away. The wipe makes it seem that time has passed from one scene to the next.

CAMERA MOVES The way you move the camera is also important.

Dollying Move yourself and the camera in and out. Walk with it. You "dolly in" if you walk toward the subject. You "dolly out" if you walk away.

Trucking Move yourself and the camera to the left or the right. This way you can get a different angle on the subjects or you can follow them as they move.

Tilting Use your body to turn the camera lens up or down. Use this for angle shots and to follow action up or down.

Panning Use your body to turn the camera to the left or the right. You "pan left" or "pan right." You can show things in rows with this move.

SPECIAL CAMERA TRICKS Put a cone of rolled-up black paper in front of the lens. The scene will look as if it's at the end of a tunnel.

Cover the lens with an old stocking. The scene will soften and look hazy and dreamy.

MICROPHONES   Hold microphones between subjects about a foot below their mouths. With many people talking, put them in a half circle and place the mike in the middle. Always speak *over* the mike.

PLANNING THE VIDEO

Before you start, you need a scenario, a script, or a storyboard. A scenario is a kind of outline. A script is much more detailed. A storyboard is a board for arranging cards for each scene in different orders. For documentaries, a scenario is probably best. For a play, where the lines are set, you need a script.

ABBREVIATIONS   When you write shooting scenarios and scripts, you can use abbreviations.

C	camera
MIC	microphone
LS	long shot
MS	medium shot
CU	close-up

Celia, age 5, makes a videotape of her baby sister, Katie. (Olympus Corporation)

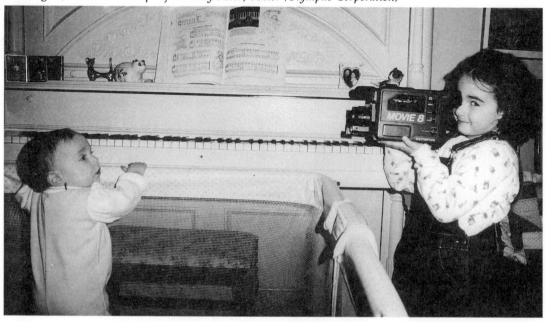

XCU	extreme close-up
PL	pan left
PR	pan right
TL	truck left
TR	truck right
DI	dolly in
DO	dolly out
TU	tilt up
TD	tilt down
ZI	zoom in
ZO	zoom out
take C	start camera
fade↑	fade up
fade↓	fade down
roll tape	start VTR recording
standby	get ready to begin

SHOOTING SCENARIO This is used for news shows and interviews. Since you don't know what people will say, you can't be exact. The scenario tells where and how to set up the camera. It lists the props. It shows the order of shots. Here's an example of part of a scenario.

Production title: "Making Hay"
Producer: Jack Smith
Location: hayfield at Finkel farm
Date: July 4
Time: 2:00 P.M.
Length of program: 4 minutes

Shot Number	Content of Shot	Time of Shot	Notes
1	a title card Run 60 sec of leader Open on card from wipe Close to wipe for 10 sec Artwork: Title Card 　Making Hay Produced by Jack Finkel Directed by Maria Ortiz	4 sec	Do in field
2	Jack Finkel interviews 　farmer Start with MS field, then 　zoom in to CU of 　farmer "Is it hot out here?" "How much hay have 　you made so far this 　year?" "What will you do if it 　rains?" "Will you have enough to 　last the year?" Close with ZO	2 min	interview questions

SCRIPT Use for plays and other projects where everything is decided ahead of time. A script is divided into three columns. The first column tells what the camera does. The middle one shows shooting time second by second. The last includes anything the viewer hears and who says it or what makes the sound. For example, here's a small piece of a script for a science fiction play. The play's name is *Slime City*.

Camera Shot	Time of Shot	Audio
CU slime.	5 sec	Zag: Yuck. George: We call that slime here on earth.
ZO slime. Alien Zag holding nose. Earthling George pointing to slime.	5 sec	Engine sounds. George: It comes from the garbage dump.

STORYBOARD With a storyboard, you have a card for each camera shot. You can arrange them in different ways. Here is a form for a storyboard card. You can fill it in for each scene.

Sequence no. _____ XCU CU MS LS (circle one) Camera angle Camera motion Special effects Time Transition to next sequence	Picture	Audio

CHECKLIST Your scenario, script, or storyboard is done. Now make a list of what you need to do before shooting. Here are some examples. Choose the players and crew. Set a time for videotaping. Write down what's needed—props, music, and artwork. Get someone to make artwork.

ARTWORK You can make artwork for titles and other written parts of your video. Use pieces of cardboard. Make them 6 x 8 inches, or slightly smaller than the screen. They should be light in color—gray is good—and stiff enough to stand alone. Use a dark color for lettering.

ON CAMERA

Here are hand signals the director uses
and what they mean.

1. Point at actor: Cue talent (Begin).
2. Lift up palms of hands: Speak up.
3. Push down palms of hands: Speak more softly.
4. Point to camera with arm over
   your head: Look at camera.
5. Pull fingers of your hands apart
   across the chest: Stretch it out (Go more slowly).
6. Roll one arm over the other: Wrap it up (Finish).
7. Draw index finger across throat: Cut (Stop filming).

INTERNATIONAL CHILDREN'S
FESTIVAL

Every year on Labor Day weekend, a three-day arts festival is held at Wolf Trap Farm Park, Virginia. Wolf Trap is a national park mainly for singing, dancing, and plays. Gifted people from all over the world come to perform.

A group called El Tayrona performs a Colombian folk dance. (Fairfax County Council of the Arts)

Some are children, like the Children's Folk Sports Troupe, who perform Chinese games and dances, a Symphonic Youth Band from Israel, and African folksingers. You might see *Little Red Riding Hood* in Spanish. There are singers, storytellers, puppeteers, dancers, mimes, rock and roll groups. Some are pros, and some put on their acts just for the love of it. In workshops at the festival, you can take part in arts and crafts: mask making, origami, face painting, Polish paper cutting, learning to write Hebrew or Chinese symbols. You can also learn to dance, mime, and act.

THE CHILDREN'S THEATRE COMPANY

One of the best children's theaters is in Minneapolis, Minnesota. Adults play the adult parts, but all of the children's parts are played by kids. Many kids have been acting with CTC for years. Rana Haugen, for instance, had been in more than 25 plays by the time she was 14. Once she played the lead in *The Little Match Girl*.

The actors rehearse 3 to 4 hours a day, five days a week. The children are excused from their schools to be in plays. They must make up all the schoolwork they miss, however.

The plays are wonderful. In *The Adventures of Babar* performed in 1981, actors made up to look like elephants drove cars and danced. For another play, an ocean liner was onstage. *The Marvelous Land of Oz, King Arthur and the Magic Sword, Little House on the Prairie, Beatrix Potter's Christmas, Hansel and Gretel*, and *Dracula* are among the plays that have been presented. In 1987, CTC took *Little Women* to 22 states and 80 cities.

CTC had its beginnings in 1961 when the Moppet Players put on eight plays for kids in the back room of an Italian restaurant. Their next theater was an old police station. At times the theater had to raise money to keep going. Kids went door-to-door collecting for the theater. "We Need a Miracle" was the

The Children's Theatre Company production of Pippi Longstocking, *1982–1983 season (George Heinrich)*

theme. They got it. Money rolled in. Now they have their own theater building.

At the close of the afternoon shows, kids can ask questions. A recent question, after *Peter Pan*, was, "How does Wendy fly?"

CHANGE YOUR FACE: STAGE MAKEUP

By using makeup you can change yourself into an old person, a monster, a clown, an alien. You can "write" a mood on your face—happy, sad, puzzled. When it's time to play a part, makeup can help.

THE KIT

You need a makeup kit. Good things to have are cork, matches, lipstick, eyebrow pencil, eyeliner, mirror, comb, cold cream, moisturizing cream, scissors, greasepaint sticks, crepe hair, spirit gum, spirit-gum remover, nose putty, stage powder, powder puff, eye shadow, artist's brushes. You also need a towel and tissues because makeup is messy.

Many of these things you already have. Others you can buy at a drugstore. You can find the stage powder, spirit gum, spirit-gum remover, nose putty, and greasepaint sticks at a theatrical supply store. The greasepaint sticks come in many colors. Start with the skin colors plus red, white, brown, carmine, bluish gray, and black. Add other colors as you need them.

You can also make greasepaint. Here's a recipe.

1 tablespoon cold cream
2 teaspoons cornstarch
1 teaspoon water
food coloring

Mix together the cold cream, cornstarch, and water. Then add food coloring to get the right color.

PUTTING ON MAKEUP AND TAKING IT OFF

First decide what kind of face you will put on. Then choose your greasepaint colors and other things. Fur makes a beard, for instance. You can use nose putty for a nose, of course, but nose putty can make warts and a long chin too.

Wear something to protect your clothes, and protect your hair as well. Wash your face and rinse it in cold water. Always apply makeup in light coming from overhead.

Now you are ready to begin. Put a thin layer of cold cream on your face. For the basic greasepaint color—the foundation—draw two lines across your forehead, one line down each cheek, one line across your chin, and two lines up and down your neck. Then spread the greasepaint evenly. When you redden your cheeks, blend

Another way to make up your face is to get it painted. (© 1985 Chicago Zoological Society)

that added color into the basic color on the edges. Put on powder. Do your eyebrows with a dark-colored eyebrow pencil, working out from your nose. Use eyeliner to outline your eyes. Apply lipstick.

To make a false nose, take a ball of nose putty and knead it in one hand. Make a fist with the other hand and stick the putty on a knuckle. Mold the putty to shape. Put it on your nose and smooth it out. If you are using a false nose, add it *first*, while your face is *clean*.

To take off makeup, first use cleansing cream. Then wash with soap and water.

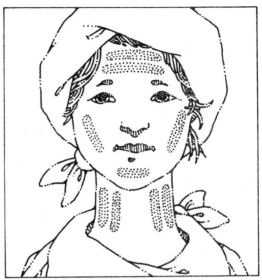

Where to place the lines of greasepaint

COSTUMES FOR ALMOST NOTHING

BIG BOX   Find a cardboard box—big but not taller than you are—that will fit loosely over your body. Cut a hole in the top of the box, big enough for your head to go through. You can be a house or a robot or . . . Paint the box to suit your idea.

PILLOWCASE   Take an old pillowcase. The open end will be the bottom of your costume. Cut a head hole in the other end of the case. Cut armholes on the sides. Cut a hole in the hem and run a string through. Put the pillowcase on. Stuff it with a pillow and pull the string tight. You are a giant marshmallow. Color the pillowcase with felt-tip pens to make other costumes. You can become a monster, for instance.

LEOTARD AND TIGHTS   These can be the start of a great costume. Add a cape, for example, to become a comic-strip hero. (You can also make costumes with one-piece pajamas or a sweat suit as the base.)

OLD CLOTHES   Wear old clothes to be a scarecrow, punker, or hobo.

SANDWICH BOARD   You need two pieces of cardboard, each about 24 ×

30 inches, and two strips of cloth 3 or 4 inches wide. Paint your message or design on the cardboard. Use the strips of cloth as shoulder straps to join the cardboard pieces. Slip the sandwich board over your head. It will hang from your shoulders.

HATS   Make a soldier hat from a piece of newspaper. Leave the paper folded. Leaving the paper lying flat, pull up the corners of the folded side. When the corners and the folded edges meet, crease the two new outside edges that are formed. This triangle is the top of the hat. To finish, turn up a single sheet straight across, flip, and turn up the other sheet the same way on the other side.

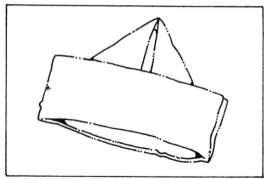
Soldier hat

You can also fold paper into cones for outer-space heads and into bonnets.

HAIR   Use ribbon or yarn for hair. Tape it around the bottom of a hat with masking tape.

UNBELIEVABLE (BUT REAL) SONG TITLES

"Come After Breakfast, Bring Your Lunch, and Leave Before Suppertime"
"Creaking Old Mill on the Creek"
"Five Salted Peanuts"
"Hoodle Addle"
"How Could You Believe Me When I Said I Love You When You Know I've Been a Liar All My Life?"
"I Faw Down and Go Boom"
"I Have Tears in My Ears from Lying on My Back Crying over You"
"I Scream, You Scream, We All Scream for Ice Cream"
"It's Like Getting a Donkey to Gallop"
"I've Got Those Wake Up Seven-Thirty, Wash Your Ears They're Dirty, Eat Your Eggs and Oatmeal, Rush to School Blues"

"Mairzy Doats"
"Make Believe (You're Glad When You're Sorry)"
"One Hour Ahead of the Posse"
"Powder Your Face with Sunshine"
"Rootie Tootie Tootie (The Kewtee Bear Song)"
"Six Lessons from Madame La Zonga"
"The Gal of a Pal of Mine"
"Walking the Floor over You"
"Where Did Robinson Crusoe Go with Friday on Saturday Night?"
"Yes, We Have No Bananas"

NATIONAL MUSIC CAMP

In summer over 2,000 girls and boys, ages eight to 18, beginning to advanced, come to study at Interlochen Center for the Arts in northwest Michigan. Kids in the Junior Division, for grades 3 to 6, try out musical instruments and take beginning music classes. Some play in the Junior String Orchestra and the Junior Wind and Percussion Ensemble. For those who like to sing there is the Junior Chorus. There are similar groups for older musicians, and the World Youth Symphony. That's not all. Kids can also learn arts like painting, ceramics, ballet, modern dance, and drama. To find out more, write:

National Music Camp
Interlochen Center for the Arts
Interlochen, MI 49643

You need a good ear to play bass violin—and a strong arm to carry it. Bass players are needed by both classical orchestras and rock and roll groups. (Wayne Brill, National Music Camp)

It takes a good ear to play the violin. (Wayne Brill, National Music Camp)

Players of many instruments are needed to form an orchestra. (Wayne Brill, National Music Camp)

INSTRUMENTS THE WIND PLAYS

AEOLIAN HARP   Find a board almost as long as your windowsill. Hammer six nails into the board, three at each end. Stretch three wire strings very tight from the nails at one end to the nails at the other end. Put wooden "bridges" under the strings. Place the harp on the windowsill. The wind will play it.

WIND CHIMES   You need nails or other objects that will sound when they strike one another. Tie them together at the end of a string or tie each to a string and let them cluster together. Hold the objects by the strings. Try them out to find a sound you like. Then fasten the loose end(s) of string to a stick or coat hanger. Hang the wind chimes outside or in your window, where the wind can reach them.

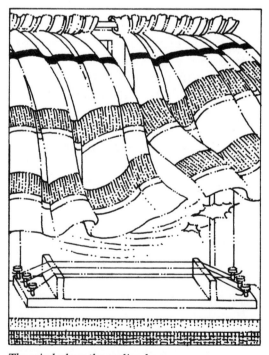

The wind plays the aeolian harp.

THE JUNK SYMPHONY

Music is everywhere. It grows out of noise, which you probably know a lot about. Why not organize your noise with a junk symphony? That way, you and your friends can play together, and the noise you make may just be a kind of music.

Things to play are everywhere. Some are for banging, and others are for tunes. Try to get a mix. Here are some ideas for instruments you can find or make.

1. Acorn hats, thimbles, and nutshells will fit on your fingers. Use all of one or some of each. Now tap out rhythms. You're making finger music.

2. For drums, use round cereal boxes, or stretch thin rubber over a big tin can with the ends out, or bang the bottom of a garbage can, or play the bottom of a cooking pot.

3. Strum a washboard.

4. Scrape a grater.

5. Make cymbals out of pot lids.

6. Use a baby rattle, or make one. Put little stones inside a metal box with a lid.

7. Make sand blocks. Glue sandpaper to blocks of wood and scrape the blocks together.

8. Make castanets. Tie buttons to your fingers and tap them together.

9. Here's another way to make castanets. Take two bottle caps the same size and place them on a surface you can't hurt. Hammer them flat. With a nail, hammer a hole in the middle of each. Now put a rubber band through each hole, to form loops either side of each cap. Use a loop to attach a cap to your thumb and adjust the fit by tying an overhand knot in the empty loop on the other side of the cap. Fit the other cap in the same way to your middle finger. To play the caps, clap them together.

10. Prepare more bottle caps, the same as in 9 through drilling the hole. Then use nails to attach the caps to a stick of wood, two caps on a nail. Shake the stick.

11. Peel off the top layer of a piece of corrugated cardboard (the kind with the ripply center). Strum the ripple side with a pencil.

These kids made their own instruments. (John P. Edwards)

12. Tie little bells on a string. Wear them around your wrist or your ankle and shake.

13. Make body noises: Click your tongue, snap your fingers, whistle a tune, and so on.

14. Put water in a pot, swirl it, and hit the side. Try using three or four pots of different sizes and with different amounts of water.

15. Make flowerpot bells. Find several flowerpots of different sizes. Tie big metal washers or big nails, each at one end of its own string. The washers or nails should be larger than the holes in the bottoms of the flowerpots. Drop a washer in each pot and pull the loose end of string through the hole. Tie the pots to a pole by the loose ends of string. Tie them in order, from biggest to smallest, and let them hang from the pole like bells. To play a tune, hit the flowerpot bells gently with a stick.

16. Take eight bottles, all the same size, with narrow necks. Line them up. Keep one empty. Fill the next with a little water. Tap it with a stick. Add or subtract water until you get a good tone. Now fill the next bottle with a bit more water, tap it, and fix the water level. Go down the row, filling each bottle a bit more full than the one before. Try a tune. Now tie the neck of each bottle with a piece of cord, wrapped twice. Then attach the bottles to a pole by the other ends of the cord. Hang the bottles in order, like the flowerpots in 15. Try another tune!

17. Blow across the top of an empty bottle until it makes a sound.

18. Bang two spoons together.

19. Swing corrugated plastic pipes around above your head.

Now that you have lots of instruments, give each of your friends one or two to play. Make up a symbol for each instrument and put the symbols on a checkerboard grid. When you point to the symbols, people play the instruments. You can point to more than one symbol at a time. Try different sound mixes. You could have the drums play a steady rhythm throughout the symphony. They would set the beat. You might plan a tune for the bells to play, a tune of three or four notes. It's your junk symphony!

YOUR OWN BAND?

Lots of kids have started their own bands. Even if a band doesn't last very long, it's good to start one. You learn to play with other people, and you learn to play better yourself.

There are things to decide at the start. What kind of group will you have? Will it play chamber music, rock, Latin, bluegrass, folk, jazz-rock, Top 40, church music? Will your band play for fun or for money? If you play for fun, you can make your own kind of music and create new musical ideas. If you play for money, you can learn about choosing music to please audiences. Either is good. Don't try to do both, though.

The Dazzling Dazzlers, an all-girl band (John P. Edwards)

GENERAL TIPS ON CHOOSING KIDS FOR YOUR BAND

1. They shouldn't be older than you are. If they are, they may take over.
2. They should be easy to get along with and willing to work hard. You should be able to count on them.
3. They should be able to read music. It helps if they can transpose music and figure out chord changes. In any case, they should be able to read their parts. Being able to play by ear helps too.
4. Good training in classical *and* popular music helps.
5. The drummer and bassist should be able to keep good time. They set the beat. If they show off, they can get the whole band off the beat.
6. Have auditions (tryouts). Ask possible band members over to play. Call it a jam session. Give them two or three numbers to practice. See how they get along.

INSTRUMENTS

Since you don't know how long your band will last, it's better if the players buy their own instruments. If the band buys the instruments, what will happen to them if the band breaks up? When buying instruments, try to get used ones. Ask a friend or a local music dealer. Put your name on your instrument. Learn how to take care of it. If you own a guitar, for example, learn to put on new strings.

PRACTICING

Decide what to practice in advance. At the end of each session, let the players know what songs you will practice at the next one. You might have practice sessions twice a week. Each session should last 1 or 2 hours. If 2 hours, have a 15-minute break in the middle.

Follow a plan for the practice session. Here is one many bands use.

1. Play a song the band knows well so they can get warmed up.
2. Work on a new song or the song you are having the most trouble with. Figure out what the trouble spots are and work on those. For example, if the band is playing off-key, work to play on key.
3. Take a break.
4. Work on other songs with problems. Do the song that needs the most work first.
5. End with a song the band likes to play and can play well.

During rehearsals, try to get the band members to listen to one another. They should be in tune and follow the beat.

Tape the practice. Listen at home, make changes, and practice weak parts.

If some players do not play as well as the others, work with them alone at another time.

Bands that play just for fun might want to have long jam sessions as part of rehearsal. Or you might decide to jam on only one number.

MUSICAL DECISIONS

Popular bands usually have their own sound. You can develop your band's sound too. It takes time. Decide what you want. Hard or soft? Down home or slick? Pairing instruments like piano and sax? Unusual instruments? Special beats? Vocals? Listen to songs on the radio and think about how they could be played differently. For instance, how would a song played fast sound if it were played slow?

How should you handle solos? Probably it is most fair to let all members have solos. The better players might have longer ones though.

GETTING GIGS

If you want to play for money, you should advertise. See page 372 for ideas. Ask a photographer friend to shoot a roll of film of your group. Don't look too weird, but don't look too straight either. Make a 5 × 7 inch glossy print from the best shot. Use the picture of your group to have a flier made. Include your group's name, phone number, and what kind of music you play. You might even add a list of songs.

Make a demo—short for demonstration—record. To do this, you will need a recording studio. Your record store should be able to give you a list of good ones. Recording studios usually charge by the hour. Practice enough ahead of time so that you will need the least amount of time in the studio. Plan on doing two or three songs. Each one should last less than 3 minutes. At the studio, play each number two or three times. Choose the best takes. The studio will make copies for you. Mail your demo to a disc jockey at your local radio station. Include your flier and a note. Perhaps you'll get your group on the air. Great advertising!

Think of who needs music. There are events: birthdays, graduations, picnics, dances, weddings, bar mitzvahs, and holidays. There are places: youth centers or YMCAs, old age homes, teen dance halls. There are programs: city recreation programs, park programs, day camps, summer camps, art or craft shows.

Find out who decides on the programs. Send that person a letter, your flier, and your demo. Then telephone and ask for an audition.

If someone offers you an audition, try to get that person to come to a practice. Play the numbers you know well. Keep them short.

WHAT TO CHARGE

Charge below the going rate, but not so low that people think you are no good. You might want to write up a price quote—one copy for you and the other for the group you may play for. Give the details: event, date, hours, music, price. The quote can become the agreement if you're hired and the bill once you've played.

COSTUMES

Keep costumes simple. They should not get in the way of playing. You might wear blue jeans and matching shirts. White is showy because it reflects stage lights. Wear shoes without heels.

BEFORE YOUR GIG

Double-check on what the group that hired you wants. That means date, time, length of performance, break lengths and times. Some people want announcements, fanfares, "Happy Birthday" or some other song for an occasion.

Make sure all the members of the band can come. Decide what songs you will play in the first set. Decide what to do if something goes wrong. You can call a break or present a solo. The drummer can carry on while you fix things. Taped music helps in a pinch. Plan to bring extra strings for the guitar and extra sticks for the drum—even extra instruments if you can find some.

Make a sign with your group's name on it. You can paint on a banner made of felt, for instance.

Check out the room. Live rooms have hard surfaces, like bare floors, that bounce back sound. Dead rooms have soft surfaces, like carpeted floors, that absorb sound. Listen to sound in the room. If the room is dead, plan to turn up the treble and turn down the bass. If the room is live, plan to turn up the bass and turn down the treble. If you are using a piano, have it tuned to the horns.

Mikes should pick up sound waves from the performers' side only. Public address speakers should be on the audience's side of the mikes.

Figure out the lighting.

THE GIG

Set up a couple of hours before the concert. Put your sign up onstage. Review what you will play in the first set. Start on time, even if not many people are there.

The usual set is 45 to 50 minutes long. If things are going well, you can play 5 or 10 minutes more. Breaks between songs should be short. Some songs should flow into the next ones to keep dancers going.

The flow of songs in the set depends on the kind of band you have. Rock bands often start and end big. If you play blues, you might begin with a lively song and end with a humorous one. Sing-alongs are good.

Don't show off with talk at the mike. Announce the name of the song and the soloist, if there is one. Give credit to songwriters.

At the end of the set, thank the audience, give the name of your group, and say you will be back after the break. At the end of the concert, thank the audience for coming. At social events like weddings, make no announcements—just play!

If someone makes a request, explain that you do your own material only.

POSSIBLE PROBLEMS AND SOLUTIONS

1. People want to sit in. Don't allow it. If you do, you'll have to let everyone sit in.
2. Players who are very good try to become stars and run everything. When things don't go their way, they say they will quit. Don't give in. It's not worth it to have people like this in your band.
3. Players can't decide on what kind of music to play. Ask them in the beginning what they want to play.
   Make a list and pick from it.
4. Players don't show up on time. Take them aside and tell them how unfair it is for them to keep other players waiting.
5. It's too much work to lead the band, choose the music, get the gigs, and so on. Have two managers. One is in charge of music—choosing songs, arrangements, solos. The other sets up rehearsals, sees about equipment, gets gigs.

ADVICE TO MANAGERS

1. Have good reasons for what you do, and be honest.
2. Ask—don't command.
3. Talk over problems at a special meeting before they get out of hand.
4. Keep a group notebook—a record of dates, expenses, notes from meetings.
5. Put the rules of the group in writing.

ADVERTISING

Many times in this book it is suggested that you advertise. Here are some ideas on how to go about it.

1. Make sure that important things, like your name, are placed so that the reader can easily find them.
2. Don't make posters *too* large. You will want to put them in store windows. Storekeepers don't want you to hog all the space they have. A good size is 12 × 18 inches. Writing on posters should be large enough to be read easily from a distance. Red shows up better than any other color. Keep posters simple.
3. Fliers are cheap pieces of advertising that you can send out or put up on bulletin boards. Keep them the standard size—8½ × 11 inches—of a piece of typing paper.
4. Put up fliers and posters on bulletin boards at schools and in other public buildings, in Laundromats, and in supermarkets. It's easier with two people to put up posters and fliers. Don't go alone.
5. Type news releases double-spaced. Tell all the important facts in the first paragraph. Include your phone number and the date of the event. Type FOR IMMEDIATE RELEASE at the top. Press releases get more notice if you send a letter along with them.
6. If you have a computer, think about using a desktop publishing program to make up your advertising pieces.
7. Try to get advertising on radio and TV. Call your local station and ask.
8. Sandwich signs work well for some events. They are easy to make. See pages 361–362 for directions. Parade around town. Be a piece of moving advertising. You can even do it on stilts. If you don't have any, take two big empty cans and punch a hole in the bottom of each with a nail. Thread the ends of a long piece of rope through the holes. Knot the ends inside the cans. Hold the rope, climb on the cans, and walk!
9. Don't forget word of mouth as a way of advertising. Call up people you know and ask them to spread the word.

This poster tells who, what, where, and when.

In the first days of TV, whole families gathered around their sets to watch the evening programs. (National Archives)

HOW HAS TV CHANGED YOU?

The only thing children do more than watch TV is sleep. In the United States, children watch about 24 hours of TV a week, on the average. That's 15,000 hours of watching by the time they finish high school. They spend less time in school!

People watching TV pick up bunches of information and put them together. They get a whole idea from a scene. Moods and images are important. Words are not so important. Kids who watch too much TV may not listen as carefully in real life either.

Is it true that TV turns kids into "couch potatoes"? Is a TV set a "boob tube," an "idiot box"? Does TV split families apart? Do kids learn anything from TV? These questions all have the same answer: "It depends. . . ."

PROBLEMS WITH TV

Life on TV is not real life. People drink and don't get drunk. Bad guys are always caught. Problems are solved in an hour or less. Things usually work out for the best. Not many people are poor or ugly. If you watch too much TV, you may mistake make-believe for real life.

Watching TV is not active. Kids learn just to sit back and watch. They don't learn to make things happen.

The more people watch TV, the less time they have to read. Kids don't get the practice they need to read easily and to learn from reading. TV even takes the place of talking!

WHAT'S GOOD ABOUT TV

TV can amuse people. What's wrong with having a good time? Nothing. TV can give kids a good time.

TV can be a magic window. Watching it, you can go places you have never been. You can meet interesting people. If you live in the city, you can see what living in the country is like.

If you live in the United States, you can see what living in China is like. You can learn how to do things. All through TV!

TV can relax people. Kids who are strung out can sometimes calm down and feel better by watching a bit of TV.

KNOW WHAT YOU ARE WATCHING

Know the tricks the camera plays. Pay attention to what the camera is doing and ask yourself why. Why are some scenes close-ups? Why does the camera zoom in sometimes? What use is a split screen? What does canned laughter do? What is the reason for a speaker you can't see who tells you what is going on? In short, try to get behind the scenes to see what makes TV work.

Watch good shows. That doesn't mean you have to watch documentaries only. But don't watch TV just because there seems to be nothing else to do. Decide ahead of time what TV shows you are going to watch. Ask yourself questions about them.

SITCOMS Are the characters interesting? Do they have real friendships with other characters? Is the show funny without being mean?

ACTION SHOWS Are they not too scary? Is there a reason for the action? If there is violence, is there a reason for it?

FAMILY SHOWS Are the families different and interesting? Do the characters help one another?

Your answers to these questions should be yes. Rate each program you watch with a number from 1 to 5. Give reasons for your rating.

Talk about the shows you watch. It's a good idea for your family to talk about the shows they watch together.

Watch many kinds of shows. Make a list of the shows you watch by kind:

When you gather around the set to watch TV, don't forget the popcorn—and your brain! (John Wanchik)

sitcoms, family shows, cartoons, sports, science fiction, news. Do you watch too much of one kind? Try to watch some other kinds too.

VIOLENCE ON TV

Do you think it is no big deal if somebody gets killed on TV? Is it funny to you if people on TV hit each other? If so, maybe you've been watching too much violence on TV.

Shows with violence should tell the truth, but often they do not. In real life, violence hurts. Flattened animals and people don't become round again and walk away. Bad guys are not always ugly so that you can tell right away who they are. Bad guys are not always caught. Bad guys do not always break down when police question them.

If you watch too many violent shows, you may start thinking that violence is more common and less serious than it is. It may seem to you that bad guys are on every corner and that you will have to use violence to defend yourself.

Violence *is* a part of life, but it is not a part of life to take lightly. Violence usually creates problems instead of solving them, and the problems it creates are very tough to solve. That is why, in real life, most people try hard to avoid ever using violence.

What TV puts in your brain is likely to stay there. Keep that in mind when you watch it.

DON'T BE FOOLED BY TV ADVERTISING

If you watch over 5 hours of advertising a week, you see 20,000 commercials a year. The most advertised items on TV for children? Cereals, snack foods, toys, candy, cookies. Sugar rules on TV!

Laws have been made about TV advertising, and here are some of them. Advertisers should keep the promises they make in ads. Things should look the same on TV as they really are. They should do what the advertiser says they do. Commercials should not advertise things that are unhealthy or dangerous for kids. It is against the law to advertise fireworks and vitamins directly to kids.

When you see a commercial on TV, notice how the camera works. It can show things at angles to make them look bigger. If a toy is shown alone, often you can't tell how big it is. Listen to the sound on the commercial. Is it part of the toy or just part of the ad?

Ask yourself some more questions. If the thing advertised is something to eat, will it make me healthier? If the thing is a toy, will it make me happy? How long will I really enjoy it? If my parents bought me all I asked for, where would I put it all? Do toys really get me friends, as TV sometimes makes me feel they will? Is the commercial nagging me to ask my parents to buy this for me? Is the toy as easy to put together as the commercial says it is?

Sometimes commercials tell you to buy something because you like a TV character. They may also tell you that you should want something because lots of kids own it. In these ways, advertisers use your feelings to make a sale. Remember that the people who write commercials want to sell you something. They really don't care if you are happy or popular.

KILLERS IN THE TOY BOX

Kids are buying more and more war toys. Companies that make war toys build TV shows around them. For instance, a company might make a war toy called LaserAlien, a human-looking monster that is really a ray gun. LaserAlien could be the hero of a violent cartoon show. The show would carry ads for the toy LaserAlien. The show sells the toy.

From 1982 to 1986 the number of hours of war cartoons on TV rose from

1½ to 43 per week. In 1986 the average child saw 250 war cartoons and 1,000 ads for war toys. War cartoons show 48 acts of violence in an hour.

People who study TV and children have found that war cartoons are not good for kids. The cartoons teach kids to hate. They also teach kids that violence solves problems. In real life, problems are not solved very well through violence. In real life, war is not a game.

There is a group working against war shows and war toys.

National Council on Television
Violence (NCTV)
P.O. Box 2157
Champaign, IL 61820

This group is asking for laws to stop companies from using cartoons to sell war toys. If you are against war toys too, write to NCTV. They can send you a list that rates shows for violence. Ask your family and friends not to buy war toys. Send your old war toys to NCTV. The NCTV has plans to make a statue for peace from them.

HOW TO GET BETTER TV

Find out the addresses of your local stations. You'll find them in the white pages of the telephone book under ABC, CBS, NBC, and PBS. Local TV stations east of the Mississippi River start with *W*. Those west of the Mississippi River start with *K*. Write a letter telling what changes you would like.

You can also write to your congress-man and to the editor of your local newspaper and to the Federal Communications Commission (FCC).

Federal Communications
Commission
Washington, DC 20554

Ask these people to look into bad TV programs and ads.

11
PROBLEMS

HENRY WINKLER TALKS TO KIDS

Henry Winkler is better known to kids as The Fonz. He starred in the popular TV series "Happy Days" and has made many other TV programs and movies. Mr. Winkler has always been very involved in groups and activities that help kids.

Henry Winkler was asked a couple of questions for this book. Here are his answers.

Question: What thing(s) do you know now that you wish you had known when you were a kid?

Henry Winkler: One of the hardest things in the world, and one of the easiest things in the world, and one of the most enjoyable things in the world, and one of the most complicated things in the world— is to be a kid. There are so many things that I wish I had known then that I know now. Like the simple fact: It'll be okay. A young

person going through a trauma— in school or with parents or in a social life—always thinks it's the

Henry Winkler, also known as The Fonz (Winkler/ Daniel Productions)

Being alone does not always mean being lonely. (John Wanchik)

end of the world. The pain of the trauma is always severe because it is magnified by a lack of experience. What I know now is just to hang in. What I know now is that it actually does get better. The wounds heal, relationships are mended if they're meant to be, or brand-new ones, stronger ones, are made.

Another thing I wish I had known then is that geometry is not all that crucial.

Question: People think that we kids are going to grow up and change the world—make it a better place in which to live. What changes do you think we should try to make?

Henry Winkler: It occurs to me that the most important change for kids to make, as kids, in order to make the world a better place, is somehow to understand that self-respect is strength. I find young people sometimes are so willing to follow, so willing to sell themselves short, not care about themselves, and, in turn, be so cruel to others who seem the slightest bit different.

I really believe that if you shake hands with yourself first, you can shake hands with anybody else in the world, at least at a respectful level. It then stands to reason that hostile conflict—in the home, at school, in the city, state, country, and the world—would be reduced.

PEGGY FLEMING TALKS TO KIDS

In the 1968 Winter Olympics in Grenoble, France, Peggy Fleming won the gold medal in women's figure skating. Since her retirement from competitive skating, she has been a special guest star with the Ice Follies, Holiday on Ice, and the Ice Capades. She has also starred in TV programs and was voted into the United States Figure Skating Association Hall of Fame.

When Peggy Fleming was asked some questions about growing up, here is what she had to say.

Question: What thing(s) do you know now that you wish you had known when you were a kid?

Peggy Fleming: I wish I had known how quiet and simple my life was when I was a kid. I would have appreciated, even more, having my parents take care of me, having lots of time and very little responsibility. I wish I had known to devote more attention to all my activities.

Childhood is a very special time that happens only once. How important it is to take advantage of school—to enjoy learning and to be a participant in various activities. Unfortunately many people don't realize all the terrific opportunities childhood presents until they become adults and those opportunities are gone. Enjoy being a kid!

Question: When you were growing up, was there a special person— teacher, parent, relative, friend— who helped you to become the person you are today? Who was that person, and what important things did you learn from that person?

Peggy Fleming: When I was growing up, my parents were very supportive. They encouraged me to do what I felt was right for me, and to think things through before making a decision. I don't recall any one person but, rather, many people who helped me to become the person I am today. I was always listening and watching. I would adapt what I liked in others to myself.

The most important thing I've learned is to have confidence in myself. We aren't all born with

Peggy Fleming, ice-skating champion (McCall's Patterns)

self-confidence. It takes a little work to learn to believe in yourself, but it is worth working at. Through self-confidence you can achieve many of the things in life that are important to you.

HOW TO USE THIS CHAPTER

This chapter is a serious one because it has facts about problems, and some of the problems are very serious. Of course, you can read the chapter from beginning to end. You can also flip through and read what catches your eye. However, this book has a Contents in the front and an Index in the back. If you want a quick idea of what's in this chapter, look in the Contents for a list of the sections and where you will find them. If you want to read about one special problem, look it up in the Index. For instance, if bullies are taking your lunch money, look up *b-u-l-l-i-e-s*. The Index tells you that help is on pages 392–393.

Some sections include facts on how the law comes into a problem. In Family Problems, for instance, you'll find facts on your rights if your parents divorce.

However, the law is different in every state, and it also changes. If you need to know about the law for kids, get an American Civil Liberties Union handbook by Martin Guggenheim and Alan Sussman, *The Rights of Young People* (New York: Bantam). Ask for the latest edition.

Remember, if you write to *any* group listed in this chapter, be sure to enclose a self-addressed, stamped envelope (See page 341).

Help is as close as your phone. (John Wanchik)

IMPORTANT TELEPHONE NUMBERS

Sometimes a telephone call will solve a problem fast. In an **emergency** call 911 or 0 for operator. With a telephone call to a **hotline**, you can get help with problems or the facts about them. *The call costs nothing.* Some good hotlines to know about are listed below. Don't give up if the line is busy. Keep calling back. For hotline numbers you need that aren't listed, call information, 1–800–555–1212.

| ABUSE | 1–800–333–4444 | National Rape Help Line |
| | 1–800–422–4453 | Child Help National Child Abuse Hotline |

Call if someone is abusing you or you know of a child who is being abused.

CANCER	1–800–638–6694	The National Cancer Institute
	1–800–492–6600 in Maryland	
CYSTIC FIBROSIS	1–800–344–4823	Cystic Fibrosis Foundation

DISABILITIES	1–800–221–6827	National Easter Seal Society
DRUGS AND	1–800–241–9746	National Drug Hotline
ALCOHOL	1–800–333–4444	National Drug and Alcohol Help Line
EPILEPSY	1–800–332–1000	Epilepsy Information Line
LEARNING DISABILITIES	1–800–345–8324	Association for Children with Learning Disabilities

Call the number above. When you hear the tone, press 112. Don't call between 1:00 P.M. and 6:00 P.M. eastern time.

| MISSING KIDS | 1–800–843–5678 | National Center for Missing & Exploited Children |

Call if you know where a missing child is. Call if you have been kidnapped.

PROBLEMS	1–800–333–4444	National Counseling Help Line
RUNAWAY	1–800–231–6946	The Runaway Hotline
	1–800–392–3352 in Texas	
	1–800–621–4000	The National Runaway Switchboard
	1–800–621–8000 in Illinois	The Illinois Youth Switchboard
	1–800–426–5678	Child Find of America, Inc.

Call if you have run away from home and want help getting a place to stay. Call if you would like to let your parents know where you are. Call if you need help getting back home.

STUTTERING	1–800–221–2483	National Center for Stuttering
SUICIDE	1–800–621–4000	The National Adolescent Suicide Hotline
	1–800–333–4444	Suicide Emergency Help Line
	1–800–448–8888	

FAMILY PROBLEMS

Many people think that families are made up of a mother, a father, and children; but families are not all the same. Some have either a mother or a father and one or more kids. Some have a father and a stepmother and one or

Some families are small. (National Archives)

Some families are big. (National Archives)

more kids. Some have a mother and a stepfather and one or more kids. Some include grandparents or aunts and uncles under the same roof. The kids in a family may not all have the same mother and father. None of these families is "broken." You don't have to live with your mother and your father to live in a family. It's very unlikely to happen, but what if both your parents die? Relatives or friends would be your family.

People in families sometimes fight. Some members can have serious problems that hurt the others. For example, a parent can be an alcoholic. In spite of what can go wrong in families, most are good to be a part of. Everywhere on earth, people are part of families.

DIVORCE

At least one kid of every four in the United States lived with only one parent in 1986. Half of the children born in the 1980s will spend at least part of their childhood living with only one parent. Why? Sometimes parents divorce.

ADVICE ABOUT YOUR FEELINGS   It's normal to be upset when your parents get a divorce. Grown-ups can do anything they want, you may think. You may feel that they have jerked you around. You may feel that you have no power over your life. Divorce is hard on everyone. Your parents don't feel good about it either.

If you are angry, that's normal and okay. You have a right to be angry. Don't let the anger work against you though. Don't play one parent against the other to get back at them. You probably can't choose where you live, but you can choose *how* you live. Divorce need not completely ruin your life.

SOME FACTS   You probably will not have a choice about which parent you will live with. You *can* tell the judge what you would like. That will help him or her decide. The parent who does not live with you usually has the right to visit with you. Your grandparents—both sets—still have the right to visit you.

ADVICE FROM KIDS   The *Kids' Book of Divorce* was written by kids for kids. Here are some facts and very good advice from it.

☐ Know what's happening with the divorce. Ask questions about what you want to know. It will affect how you live.

☐ You should know where you are going to live and how often you will see each parent.

☐ You have a right to know who's sleeping in your house.

☐ Life may be very hard before parents get all the terms settled between them.

☐ You should know why your parents are splitting up—unless the reason is very harsh, and is entirely between them, and has nothing to do with your life.

☐ Parents may stop loving each other, but they don't stop loving their kids.

BEING A STEPCHILD

Fairy tales often say bad things about stepmothers. Remember, fairy tales are make-believe. A real stepmother is just a woman your father has married. She can be good or bad. If you are lucky and work at it, she can turn into your best friend. The same holds true for stepfathers, stepbrothers, and stepsisters. In 1986 there were 35 million stepparents in the United States. By 1996, three of four United States families will have one stepparent or be headed by a single parent.

Being a stepchild may be hard in the beginning. You may be angry at your parents for getting a divorce. Who is the easiest person to take your anger out on? The stepparent. Why not risk losing the stepparent? Who wants the stepparent anyway? If you're angry with the stepparent, you don't risk losing your mother or father, you think.

After a divorce, you may feel that nothing is sure. You know that love can end. You can be afraid that your parents will stop loving you. And if *that's* true, then anyone can stop loving you.

It's hard to trust a stepparent. A stepparent didn't give birth to you. A stepparent can leave. The chances are, you think, that a stepparent is *more* likely than a parent to stop loving you. It's normal to think these things, but you should know, too, that they may not be true.

HINTS FOR BEING A STEPKID

Wait for love to grow between you and your stepparent.

When you visit your parent and stepparent, try to follow their rules. Don't compare the way you live at one parent's house with the way you live at the house of the other.

Don't carry tales from house to house.

As a stepchild, you may have a different kind of family history than your stepbrothers and stepsisters do. Leo Tolstoy, a Russian writer, said that all happy families are like one another and that all unhappy families are unhappy in their own way. Do you think this is true? If both families are happy, then try looking for how they are alike. What you find may comfort you. It may also give you a way to deal with living in two families.

Try to help solve the problem of how much power your stepparent should have. Should a stepparent act like a parent or like an older friend? Maybe you can take part in deciding. However, don't expect the stepparent to help you like a parent and not have the power to punish you like one. There should be rules about help with homework, bedtime, spanking.

Look at the bright side. You now have two houses to live in.

You can buy books about being in a stepfamily. Write the

Stepfamily Association of
America, Inc.
602 East Joppa Road
Baltimore, MD 21204

ADOPTION

If you are adopted, you probably know from your parents how happy they are to have you for a son or daughter. All the same, do you wonder who your "real" parents are? You might not want to meet them. Most adopted people don't. However, you might want to know important facts about them.

Medical histories can matter, for instance. Your parents probably learned anything important when they adopted you. Ask them to tell you what they know. Perhaps they already have. In most states, you can't look at your adoption records until you are a grown-up.

This group has books for children about adoption. You can write to them to find out more.

National Committee for Adoption
Suite 512, 2025 M Street, NW
Washington, DC 20036

WHICH CHILD IN THE FAMILY HAS IT BEST?

BEING AN ONLY CHILD   This may not be a *real* problem. In 1985, there were 13 million only children, about 50 percent more than there were 20 years before. Why? More and more people are having kids later in life, and raising children costs more and more money. By the time you finish high school, your parents will have spent somewhere between $80,000 and $200,000 on you.

Some only children wish they had brothers and sisters. If you are an only child and you feel this way, join clubs and get into sports.

On the good side, only children get more of their parents' time than they would if brothers and sisters shared it. Only children may be more outgoing—because they have to be. The grades and IQ test scores of only children average higher than those of children with brothers and sisters.

BEING OLDEST   Oldest kids say they get the blame for everything. Oldest kids say people are always telling them, "You're older. You should know better. You should set a good example." They have to fight all the battles with their parents, and the younger kids

gain by it. For instance, the oldest child may have to talk parents into letting her or him go on a date at 14. When the younger children want to go out on dates at that age, the parents give in more easily. On the bright side, oldest children had their parents all to themselves until the next child was born. They learn to take care of other people.

BEING IN THE MIDDLE   Middle children complain that they don't get babied, because they are not the babies of the family, and yet they don't get the privileges of the older children either. It seems no one pays attention to them. On the bright side, middle children are allowed to grow up. Parents don't expect too much too soon and don't spoil them either. They learn to get along with other people.

BEING THE YOUNGEST   Youngest children say their parents try to keep them as babies, they have no power with their brothers and sisters, and they have to wear hand-me-down clothes. On the bright side, youngest children get lots of attention, learn to value themselves, and have many people to learn from.

FAMILY FIGHTS

Most families have fights. Believe it or not, you can learn from fighting. Try not to argue, but to disagree. People who argue talk in raised voices. They get angry. Sometimes they say mean things to one another. When you disagree, you can be friendly. Listen. Don't jump in with your side before hearing what your parents have to say. When it's your turn, don't attack. Talk about how you feel.

Suppose you and your parents disagree about how late you can stay up at night. Don't scream at them. Don't yell, "But my friend Pete gets to stay up until midnight!" Try saying, "It makes me feel that I don't have enough time when I have to go to bed so early. By the time I finish my homework, I have to go off to bed." You may not win, but at least you won't feel bad about losing.

In lots of fights between parents and children, the kid says, "You're treating me like a baby! And you expect me to act like an adult." Why do parents keep kids from doing adult things? Usually it's *not* because they don't trust you. It's because they remember the awful chances they took as kids, and the memories scare them. They want to keep you safe. They know that sometimes you want to do things even when they are not safe. You are sure you can learn about yourself this way. You want the chance to grow up. You want to go against your parents' wishes and try out new things—life-styles, friends, values.

If you want to have adult privileges, try acting like an adult. Keep talking to your parents. Talk to them about changes you want. Be calm. Make sense. Be ready to give in on some points. Act grown-up, and you are more likely to get grown-up freedom.

FIGHTING WITH BROTHERS AND SISTERS

Why do you do it? It's easy to take out your anger about other problems on people you are close to. After all, your sister is your sister. She can't change that. She has to put up with you. Instead of fighting with her, talk to her about the problem you are really angry about. Or try to solve it yourself. You may think your parents like your brother more than they like you. If you think so, don't get angry with your brother and fight with him. Talk to your parents. Tell them how you feel.

If your fighting is just a habit, make the first move toward peace. Try to be as nice to your family as you are to your friends. Brothers and sisters can stay friends for life.

CHILD ABUSE

Some children are abused by their parents. That means that their parents beat them badly or give them bad touches. If a child is abused by a parent, he or she should tell someone, like a teacher, or call the hotline listed on page 382.

A child who has been abused will be protected. The parent will be helped to stop the abuse. Most often the abused child is not taken away from the family.

Not all spanking is child abuse. More than eight of ten American parents spank their children. Some adults think even this is wrong. Native Americans do not approve of grown-ups' hitting children. Spanking is against the law in Sweden.

ARE YOU A LATCHKEY KID?

If so, you are not alone. In the United States, at least two million children under the age of 13 are left alone part of the day. Usually they are left alone because their parents work. Latchkey children are *not* problem kids. They feel they can take care of themselves, and they can. However, if they need help it's there.

In some places there are hotlines for latchkey kids. They can call the hotline if they are afraid or lonely or bored. Some schools stay open late for after-school programs run by parents. The YMCA has programs too.

Here are some tips for latchkey kids.

1. Don't lose your house key. Put it on your belt loop. Wear it on a chain. Put it on a key ring and attach it to the zipper on your coat.
2. Know how to handle callers. Never tell a telephone caller you don't know that you are home alone. Never answer the door to strangers.
3. Know 911, the emergency number. Know the numbers of the police, fire department, paramedics, neighbors.

Kids play outdoors at the Salvation Army Settlement and Day Nursery in Providence, Rhode Island. (The Salvation Army Archives and Research Center)

IF YOUR PET IS LOST

It's a bad feeling to come home and find your pet gone. When pets leave home, usually it's not because they don't like you. They may be looking for a mate or a garbage can to raid or just plain adventure. On the Fourth of July, pets that are afraid of firecrackers can run away to escape the sound. Pets can also get lost when they wander, and sometimes they are stolen. If your pet gets lost, here are some steps you can take.

1. Don't panic.

How would you describe this dog if it were lost? (Ming Chen)

2. Search your neighborhood. Listen for animal noises. Make sure your pet was not locked up in a garage by accident.

3. Write down what your pet looks like. List breed, color, markings, sex, age, weight, size, tattoos, and scars. Then call the animal shelter, also known as the pound, to ask if your pet is there. Use your list to describe your pet, and have your animal's license number handy.

   When you call, the people at the shelter may have no record of your pet. Then it's a good idea to *visit* the shelter. Your pet may have lost its tags. It may not look the same to other people as it does to you. Bring your pet license with you and maybe a picture of you and your pet. You will also need money to bail out your pet if you find it there.

   Ask to look in the runs inside and outside. Fill out a card describing your animal. Then if it shows up at the shelter, the people there can call you. But don't count on them to do it. Keep checking. Animals are usually kept in shelters one week only, so you need to check often.

4. There may be more than one animal shelter in your area. Call every one that is listed in the telephone book. Ask at your local shelter about other shelters. Try the animal hospitals too. Ask your veterinarian where hurt animals with-

out ID are taken. Then call that animal hospital. Call all local vets and groomers to see if they have heard anything about your pet.

5. Make a lost animal poster. It should be big enough to be seen. Write LOST and REWARD at the top in big letters. Describe your pet, but don't tell everything on the poster. Be sure not to give your dog's name. If the animal is stolen, the thief wants to know its name to control it better. Do give your telephone number and the numbers of other people you know. That way the person who finds your pet can get in touch right away. Include a photograph of your pet too. For more about making posters, see page 372.

    Make several copies of your poster. Keep one so you can make more copies. Put up your poster in Laundromats and other public places. Pin it up at eye level. If you know where your pet was lost, put more posters in places right around there. Replace the posters if they are torn down. Send posters to humane societies and animal shelters.

6. Put an ad in the local paper. It should include the same facts as are on the poster.

7. Check FOUND notices every day.

8. Follow up every lead.

9. Don't go alone to meet a person who answers your poster.

10. When your pet is found, tell the animal shelters you have asked to watch for it.

Treating a dog well means giving it a lot of love. It also means keeping it safe from getting lost. (Mary Bloom)

Of course, it is better to make sure your pet doesn't get lost in the first place. Here are some ways you can do that.

1. Make sure your yard is fenced and the gate is kept shut.

2. Don't leave your pet alone outside.

3. License your animal. You can license your cat the same as a dog. Tell the licensing bureau if you change your address.

4. Get your pet an ID tag of heavy, colored plastic. Write your telephone number and the pet's license number inside the collar. A cat should have an ID on a collar that will come off if the cat gets hung up by it.

5. Make sure you have a picture of your pet.

6. Get your animal tattoed.

RUNNING AWAY

One of every seven kids leaves home at some point. Some who leave are as young as nine. Most go away *from* something rather than *to* something. Some are "runaways," kids who are away from home without their parents' approval. Some are "throwaways" or "pushouts," kids who have been thrown out of their homes. Some are "street kids," those who ran away a long time ago or are homeless. Some of these kids have been abused or come from violent homes.

Running away can be risky. You can end up with no place to stay. You can get killed. Some runaway kids live in bus stations, old buildings, motels, and cemeteries. It's not an easy life.

Runaways can call hotlines for help. Hotlines are free. They offer help with finding food and a safe place to stay. There are no traps or tricks. If kids don't want their parents to know where they are, hotline people will not tell. If kids want a way to get home or want to call home to let their parents know they are all right, then hotlines will give this help.

All a kid needs to use a hotline to call parents is their name and telephone number and a way of showing he or she is their kid—a birthmark, a secret joke, something just between the kid and the parents. The hotline will call the parents and ask the parents for a message for the kid. When the kid calls back, he or she will get the message.

The telephone numbers of runaway hotlines are given on page 383 of this book.

Trailways, the bus line, has Operation: Home Free. The company works with police and other officials. A runaway under 18 who wants to go home gets in touch with the police. The police call the parents. The kid is taken to the bus depot and sent home free, thanks to Trailways.

SCHOOL PROBLEMS

BULLIES   In 1986, fifth-grader Jason Reily and his mother filed a lawsuit. It was against his teacher, principal, and school district. He asked for $351,000 because they had not met his right to a safe, secure, peaceful school. He had been forced to change schools in 1985 because bullies were always attacking him.

Bullies in school are a big problem everywhere. There are bullies in big schools, small schools, city schools, country schools. Some kids are afraid to go to school because of them. They take kids' lunch money and push them around if they step out of line.

How can one bully have power over a whole group of kids? Here's how it works. The bully usually has two or three kids on his side. He beats up a kid with his gang cheering him on. Other kids are glad not to be the one he's picking on, so they say and do nothing. They want to help, but are afraid to.

The answer? A group of kids at a San Francisco school has one. They are called Conflict Managers. Three kids from each third- through fifth-grade classroom are voted in as Conflict Managers. Kids with problems can talk to them. They wear special T-shirts so that other kids know who they are. In fights, the Conflict Managers hold bargaining sessions. Here are the rules.

No breaking in when another
is talking
No name-calling
No lying

Other kids trust the Conflict Managers. Kids don't get slammed against walls anymore. The bullies are under control.

LEARNING DISABILITIES A ten-year-old kid once said, "I can think okay. What's wrong with me is just my words. I forget them and I can't manage them." He was a smart kid with learning problems. He had a different kind of mind.

Kids with learning problems have trouble reading. They may mix up *b* and *d, was* and *saw*. They can't listen, read, write, spell, or do math as well as they might want to. Each kid has a unique and special set of problems.

Experts still don't know the reasons why kids have learning problems. However, there is help if you have them. You *can* do something about them. You *can* learn. You *can* teach your mind to work better and better.

By law—P.L. 94–142—you are entitled to special education. See what your school has to offer. You can hire a tutor. These groups can also help if you write them.

Orton Dyslexia Society
724 York Road
Baltimore, MD 21204

Association for Children with
Learning Disabilities
4156 Library Road
Pittsburgh, PA 15234

The ACLD works to help children with learning disabilities and their parents. They sell easy-to-read books for older kids. You can also call their hotline. See page 383 for the number.

NEW SCHOOL Going to a new school can make you feel lost. You don't know anybody. You miss your old friends. To make new friends, join clubs that meet after school. Find people who are interested in the same things you are. Don't forget to write to your old friends.

SCHOOL AND THE LAW

Laws about you and school are based on the idea that school officials stand in place of your parents. However, you have certain rights.

IT IS AGAINST THE LAW
□ to hold religious services in public schools
□ to force a kid to go to a certain public school because of color, sex, or beliefs
□ for a teacher or principal to hit a student in these states: Hawaii, Maine, Massachusetts, New Hampshire, New Jersey, New York, Rhode Island, and Vermont. It is also against the law in the Los Angeles Unified School District. California may approve a bill to ban spanking in public schools.
□ for a kid to be expelled from school for something the parents did
□ to transfer a kid to another school as punishment, in most cases
□ not to go to school if you are under 16, in most states

Under the law, the principal and teacher can set dress codes and search your locker if they feel students are in danger.

Under the law, the school district or state can send you to any school and make you take certain classes.

HELP FOR SCHOOL PROBLEMS

ADULTS Usually there are several adults you can talk to at school—your teacher, the school psychologist or counselor, and the school nurse.

OTHER KIDS Many schools have a program called peer counseling. In this program, kids help other kids. Kids are more likely to talk with other kids than with adults. It's good for kids to know that somebody their age understands their problems and cares about them.

Schools with the program have courses where peer counselors learn to deal with problems like loneliness, drug abuse, suicide, and divorce. The counselors are taught how to listen. They learn not to offer advice. They learn to let the kid with the problem decide for himself what to do. The counselors try not to judge.

When a kid reports abuse or thoughts of suicide, the peer counselor tells an adult. Otherwise, secrets stay secrets. Peer counselors don't always work with kids with problems. Sometimes they help students new to the school.

FAT AND FASTING AND THROWING UP

Kids in the United States are surrounded by fat craziness. Thin is in. Our society is so afraid of fat that some children are afraid to eat—and don't.

But if thin is in, so is food. Just watch an hour or two of TV ads, if you don't believe it. People reward themselves with food. Mothers reward their kids with food. Kids are praised for eating and yelled at for not eating—until the kids get fat, that is. Some kids are unhappy because they are fat. Other people tease them, and the teasing hurts.

A 1986 study showed that girls care about their weight at a younger age than ever before. Half the nine-year-olds in the study had dieted. More than half thought they were fat. The truth? Only two of every ten really were overweight. Older girls were even more worried about their weight. Eight out of every ten girls ten and 11 years old had dieted.

Why do some kids think they are fat when they are not? They see very skinny models and other famous skinny people. Their parents are always talking about their own dieting, skipping meals, throwing out junk food sweets.

Why do some kids eat too much? Too much is asked of them, and they want an escape. They are sad or lonely or both. To feel better, they fill up on sweet stuff like cookies or candy. The food doesn't help much, especially since it adds to the worry about being fat, but they eat anyway.

There's a difference between adult dieting and kid dieting. Kids need more food energy than their parents do. Why? Kids are growing. Adults are not growing very much. After all, grown-up means grown *up*. Teenagers need food to ripen sexually. Teenage girls who diet too much and exercise too much can have backbone problems. Their bones can be brittle. It is dangerous to go on a strict diet. It could affect your growing.

However, it is not a bad idea to cut down on junk food. Junk food usually

About 200 years ago the French painter Jean-Honoré Fragonard painted these two sisters. In those days chubbiness was admired. (The Metropolitan Museum of Art)

contains too much fat and salt. Recent studies show that kids have too much cholesterol, a fatty stuff, in their blood. Too much is there from too much of certain kinds of fats in their diets and not enough exercise.

What is important? Eating healthy food and getting enough exercise. Everyone knows that, but doing it is easier for some kids than for others.

EAT RIGHT

Even if you want to get thinner, eat right. How? Dietician Linda Brown at Childrens Hospital of Los Angeles made up a sample healthy menu for one day. She made sure it included enough of all these basics.

1. 3 to 4 cups milk (or the equal in other dairy foods like yogurt, ice cream, cheese, pudding, or nondairy tofu)
2. two 1½- to 2-ounce servings of meat, poultry, fish, organ meat, or meat substitute

3. four servings or more of bread, cereal, and grain
4. four servings (⅓ cup each) of vegetables and fruit

Three of the four basic food groups: bread and cereal (below); vegetables and fruits (upper right); meat, poultry, fish, and beans (lower right) (USDA)

BREAKFAST

1 cup oatring cereal
½ cup whole or low-fat milk
1 slice whole-wheat toast
1 teaspoon margarine
1 cup apple juice

LUNCH

1 tuna sandwich
4 carrot sticks (½ raw carrot)
1 cup whole or low-fat milk
1 medium apple
1 oatmeal cookie

SNACK

1 cup fruit yogurt
1 cup grape juice
2 graham cracker squares

DINNER

2 baked chicken drumsticks (about 2
    ounces of meat)
½ cup rice
½ cup green beans
½ tomato, sliced, with 1 tablespoon
    Thousand Island dressing
1 whole-wheat dinner roll
1 teaspoon margarine
1 cup whole or low-fat milk
1 medium orange

SNACK

2 cups popcorn with 1 tablespoon
    margarine
1 cup lemonade

Children seven to ten years old and teenage girls need 1,650 to 3,300 calories a day. (A calorie is a measure of food energy.) If you exercise a lot, you may need the higher number of calories. Teenage boys and pregnant teenage girls need even more calories; they will need to eat more than is on the menu.

The fourth basic food group: dairy products (USDA)

TIPS ON HOW TO EAT AT FAST-FOOD PLACES

These tips are from Evelyn Tribole of Consulting Nutrition Services in Irvine, California.

☐ Drink orange juice instead of malts.

☐ Choose whole-grain buns when possible.
☐ Watch out for greasy buns, like biscuits and croissants, which have more fat than regular breads.

- Choose the salad bar. Eat vegetables like broccoli, cauliflower, celery, zucchini, tomatoes, spinach, beets, and carrots. Go lighter on lettuce. If you use lettuces, eat the dark green ones like romaine.
- Add beans to the salad to get some protein.
- Go light on bacon bits or skip them.
- Use vinegar or lemon juice and go lightly on oil.
- Avoid heavy, creamy dressings.
- Choose low-fat or nonfat milk over milkshakes.
- Go for broiled meats.
- Go for the smallest hamburger size.
- Avoid heavily battered fried chicken.
- Choose baked potatoes over french fries. Eat the baked potatoes plain without too much butter, cheese, or sour cream.

EXERCISE

Exercise is another part of growing up healthy. Studies show that most kids these days are not in good shape. They spend too many hours in front of the TV—watching those food ads! What does exercise have to do with fat? It burns calories. Here are some facts from a 1985 study.

1. Boys under ten should be able to do at least two pull-ups. Four of ten boys age six to 12 could do no more than one pull-up. One of four could not do any.

2. Girls under ten should be able to do at least one pull-up. More than half of the girls age six to 17 could not do any.

3. Kids should be able to hold their chins above a raised bar for 30 seconds. Nearly half of boys age six to 14 and more than half of girls age six to 17 could not do this for more than 10 seconds.

4. Kids should be able to run a mile in less than 10 minutes. One-third of boys age six to 12 and half of girls age six to 17 could not.

ANOREXIA AND BULIMIA

Some teenagers, usually girls, have a disease called anorexia nervosa. These kids starve themselves. They think of themselves as fat when they are really thin. They are "good" kids who do everything to please their parents and everyone else—except eat! Other teenagers have a disease like it called bulimia. They make themselves throw up after they have eaten, or they take laxatives. These problems are serious. *Most*, but not all, younger kids who worry about their weight are not thought of as anorexic or bulimic.

There are groups to help teenagers with these eating disorders.

ANRED (Anorexia Nervosa and Related Eating Disorders, Inc.)
P.O. Box 5102
Eugene, OR 97405

ANAD (National Association of Anorexia Nervosa and Associated Disorders)

Box 7
Highland Park, IL 60035

American Anorexia/Bulimia Association, Inc.
133 Cedar Lane
Teaneck, NJ 07666

Teenagers who are anorexic or bulimic need help from a doctor. These groups will send a list of doctors near you who deal in eating disorders.

GROUPS THAT HELP FAT KIDS

What if you are fat? There are several groups that help with this problem (if it really is a problem).

National Association to Aid Fat Americans, Inc.
P.O. Box 43
Bellerose, NY 11426

It's okay to be fat, says this group. It is not a diet club. Diet is between you and your doctor. Instead, the idea is fat pride. The group seeks to help you feel good about yourself. It helps with finding nice clothes in bigger sizes, making friends, having someone to back you up when you feel bad. If you write for their free pamphlet, it's your secret, unless you want to tell someone about it. The pamphlet talks about why you may eat too much. Are you doing it when unhappy or lonely? It asks if you eat too much or exercise too little. It gives advice on diet and dating. It includes a list to help with liking yourself, getting help, and becoming a doer.

Overeaters Anonymous
P.O. Box 92870
Los Angeles, CA 90009

This is not a diet club either. There are no weigh-ins. No one tells you what to eat. Instead, the club tells you that you are not alone. Members help one another make choices. You get a sponsor who will help you live one day at a time. When you are tempted to overeat or have a problem, there's someone to call. The purpose is to change yourself from inside. This club costs nothing. Write to find out more.

SEX

Sex is big business. Rock groups sing about it. Advertisers use it to sell things. People on TV seem to have sex all the time. And yet, another message is there too. That message is, Don't.

Sometimes it may seem that everyone else in the world is having sex. Don't believe it. Lots of kids brag about things they have not done. Half the kids who answered a May 1985 survey of teenagers by *Teen* had not yet dated. Half of teenagers do *not* have sex. Some doctors think it is not good for kids to have sex under the age of 17 or 18. Younger people are too unsure of themselves to be able to handle it. In fact, kids who feel good about themselves have sex later than kids who feel they are unloved or unwanted. Only one in every five kids 13 and 14 years

Love is everywhere. Alenushka, *or* Stories, *by Nicholas Nezhinsky, age 6, Ukrainian S.S.R. (UNICEF International Children's Art Collection)*

old has had sex. Sex can present problems: unwanted babies and diseases, for openers.

SEX QUESTIONNAIRE

Answer this questionnaire to see how much you know about sex.

1. You can't get pregnant if you do sex standing up.
2. You can't get pregnant if you have sex only once in a while.
3. You won't get pregnant the first time you have sex.
4. Plastic wrap folded around a boy's penis is as good as a condom.
5. Girls can prevent pregnancy by douching with soda pop.
6. Girls under 12 can't get pregnant.
7. Girls who have not yet had their first periods can't get pregnant.
8. Boys have stronger sex drives than girls.
9. The more often a boy has sex, the bigger his penis will be.
10. Masturbating will turn you queer.

11. Masturbating will make you blind or crazy.
12. Masturbating will make hair grow on your hands.
13. If a boy is turned on and can't complete a sex act, he will have physical problems that will hurt him.
14. When a girl says no, she means yes.
15. If a boy looks at another boy's penis, he is homosexual.
16. If you are attracted to a person of your own sex, you must be homosexual.
17. If you play around sexually with a person of your own sex when you are a child, you must be homosexual.

Every statement is false.

TEN BAD REASONS TO HAVE SEX NOW

1. Everyone is "doing it."
2. Your boyfriend or girlfriend is pushing you.
3. Your friends are pushing you.
4. To be grown-up
5. To find out what it is like
6. To hold on to a relationship
7. To make your parents mad
8. To stop feeling lonely
9. To be popular
10. To hurt or get back at someone.

TEN GOOD REASONS TO WAIT TO HAVE SEX

1. You don't want to.
2. You're not ready.
3. You don't want to be pregnant or get someone pregnant.
4. You don't want to get a sexually transmitted disease (STD).
5. Your religion says it's wrong.
6. You want to wait until you're in love or married.
7. It would upset your parents.
8. Your reputation might be hurt.
9. Your boyfriend or girlfriend isn't ready.
10. You're not using birth control.

The questionnaire and the lists of bad and good reasons come from a book called *Make a Life for Yourself*. It tells you how to make a life plan and to set goals. Here's where to write for it.

The Center for Population Options
1012 14th Street, NW, Suite 1200
Washington, DC 20005

GETTING HELP AND ANSWERS TO YOUR QUESTIONS

Ask your parents, the school nurse, your doctor, your health teacher, or someone at your church or synagogue. You can also call or visit the health department or a family planning clinic.

Planned Parenthood is a group that gives help. It has books, pamphlets, and video-tapes about sex, having your period, and how to say no to sex.

Planned Parenthood
810 Seventh Avenue
New York, NY 10019

DRUGS AND ALCOHOL

Nearly one of three fifth- and sixth-graders in the United States has tried cigarettes. More than half of seventh- and eighth-graders have. The National Council on Alcoholism reports that 100,000 ten- and 11-year-olds in 1985 said they got drunk at least once a week. That same year 4.6 million teenagers, ages 14 through 17, got into some kind of trouble using alcohol. Other drugs are a big problem for many kids. Drugs are harder on children than on adults because kids are still growing and adults are not.

Kids who do not use drugs want drugs kept out of the schools. They want drugs out of their lives and the lives of their friends.

If you want to stop drug abuse in your school or town, you can do something about it. If you already take drugs, you can stop. If your friend takes drugs, you can help him or her quit.

WHAT DRUGS DO TO PEOPLE

CLOVE AND OTHER TOBACCO-FREE CIGA-RETTES They are not harmless. They can hurt your lungs. You still inhale smoke.

SMOKELESS TOBACCO (CHEWING TO-BACCO AND SNUFF)   It has its own dangers. It can hurt your teeth and gums, and it can cause mouth cancer.

ALCOHOL   It's a drug, and a risky one. Depending on how much people drink and how fast, they may go through one, two, or three stages.

1. It is harder to make good choices and curb sudden wishes to do crazy things.
2. Memory, thinking, and speech become dull.
3. The drunk passes out, can even die.

Drinking can hurt your body. People who drink too much may throw up. Often they act like idiots and get into trouble.

A 12-ounce can of beer, a 6-ounce glass of wine, or 1 ounce of 100-proof hard liquor will each have the same effect on the body.

Cold showers and black coffee do not make you sober. They may wake you up, but it takes time for alcohol to wear off.

DOWNERS (TRANQUILIZERS AND SLEEP-ING PILLS)   They make people sleep. They slow down the brain. If you take too many, they can kill you. It is very risky to take them when drinking.

SNIFFING DRUGS   They fall into three groups: solvents (like glue, paint, and paint thinner), aerosols (things that come in spray cans), and nitrates and nitrous oxide. They all make people feel drunk and dizzy. They can poison your body. And people can overdose (OD) and die very fast with these drugs.

AMPHETAMINES (UPPERS)   They can make you dizzy, take away your desire to eat, hurt your heart, make you sweat, give you a fever.

COCAINE   It can give you ideas that are not true, cause you to act in a strange way, up your heart rate, make you sweat. It's addictive. Too much can kill you.

CRACK   A form of cocaine, it is very dangerous. It can make you act crazy and hurt your brain. Once you start using it, it's almost impossible to stop. It can kill you.

MARIJUANA (GRASS) AND HASHISH (HASH)   They warp your senses, cause you to be confused, are bad for your memory and thinking, and slow your energy. There are 421 chemicals in grass itself and over 2,000 in its smoke. Grass has more tar than cigarettes. Its smoke can cause cancer.

PCP   It can make you confused and violent. You don't act like yourself when you take PCP. Some people on PCP have drowned in shallow water because they couldn't tell which way was up. On PCP, people have trouble remembering, judging, and focusing their minds. They can become uneasy and depressed.

IF DRUGS ARE SO BAD, WHY DO SO MANY KIDS THINK THEY ARE SO GOOD?

Drugs are big business. People who sell drugs love to get kids hooked on them. Kids hooked on drugs mean money for them. Some kids take drugs because their friends do. Others think that drugs make them grown-up. The truth? Drugs actually stunt your growth. Still others take drugs because they are unhappy and troubled by problems at home or at school. For a while the drug taker may forget or feel powerful. These effects don't last for long. Drugs look like shortcut answers. They aren't. Drugs give the false sense that they can solve problems, but drugs *cause* problems.

WHAT TO DO FOR A FRIEND WHO HAS PROBLEMS WITH ALCOHOL OR DRUGS

Tell your friend, "I care too much about you to let you do this to yourself." Then get help for your friend. Send him or her to a local drug-abuse program. In an emergency, get help from a grown-up. Your friend then belongs at the hospital or drug crisis center.

Don't worry about being a tattletale. Drugs and alcohol can cause serious problems, especially for kids.

If your parent smokes, don't be too hard on him or her. How dangerous smoking is has not always been known. Many people started years ago when it was thought to be grown-up to smoke. Then it became a habit, and now it's hard to quit. Do tell your parent who smokes that it scares you.

GROUPS THAT HELP WITH DRUG AND ALCOHOL PROBLEMS

Alcohol Education for Youth and Community, Inc.
362 State Street
Albany, NY 12210

In workshops, kids 13 to 18 take charge of their own lives. They learn how to decide about alcohol and other drugs. Some are members of SADD, Students Against Driving Drunk. There is also a Teen Life Theatre of high school students who put on plays about drugs and alcohol. Kids in the audience get into the act during the plays. They even suggest scenes. You can get materials about drugs and alcohol from this group.

Alcoholics Anonymous
P.O. Box 459, Grand Central Station
New York, NY 10163

This is a group of people who have problems with alcohol. They see alcoholism as an illness that can hit anyone. They meet to try to solve their common problem and to help others do the same. If you want to stop drinking, you can join AA.

Alateen
Al-Anon Family Group
Headquarters, Inc.
P.O. Box 182, Madison Square
Station
New York, NY 10159-0182

Here is what one member has said about Alateen.

Only a child who has had to live with this problem can know what torture and heartbreak it is. I was 14 when I came to Alateen and finally leveled with myself about Mother's drinking. I felt a big iceberg melting inside me that night. I learned alcoholism is a disease, not a disgrace, and I met other teenagers whose parents suffered from the same illness.

What a difference this has made at home! Dad and I don't have to lie to each other

All kids want a happy family life. My Family *by Theresa Bruce, age 14, St. Vincent and the Grenadines (UNICEF International Children's Art Collection)*

about it anymore. The more we understand about Mother's illness, the more we understand that it has made us sick too. He and I have come to trust each other, and since we've started loving Mother again, we've quit making the situation worse for her.

If your life is affected by someone else's drinking and you are over 12, Alateen can help you. It was started by a teenage boy in 1957. His father, an alcoholic, had joined Alcoholics Anonymous (AA) and stopped drinking. His mother belonged to Al-Anon. Alateen is linked with AA and with Al-Anon, for relatives of alcoholics.

Alateen groups have an adult sponsor. Kids in Alateen get together to help one another. The idea is *not* to gripe about or try to change an alcoholic parent. Instead, Alateens learn to stop using a parent's alcoholism as an excuse for their own problems. They keep loving their alcoholic parent, but they learn to separate themselves from the parent's problems. Members can buy books, and there is a newsletter. If there is no group near you, you can be a Loner. Members of Alateen sponsor kids like you.

The Just Say No Foundation
1777 North California Boulevard
Walnut Creek, CA 94596

The Just Say No Clubs are groups of kids seven to 14 years of age who have promised not to use drugs or alcohol. In January 1985 in Oakland, California, First Lady Nancy Reagan gave a talk to kids against drug abuse. Those kids started the first Just Say No Club. Today there are about 10,000 clubs run by kids with grown-ups to help. Some call themselves Drugbusters.

Write to the above address for information on how to start a Just Say No Club. All you need are kids to join, an adult leader, and a safe place to meet like a school. Your Just Say No Club can be part of your school, church, neighborhood center, Scout troop, boys/girls club, or YMCA. Most clubs have 15 to 20 members and hold meetings at least two times a month. In the club you learn about drugs and how to avoid them. You also have fun playing games and sports, making things, taking field trips. You make up and act in skits against drug abuse. You do things to help others. Some clubs have Kid to Kid Education programs. May 15 is Walk Against Drugs Day. The foundation also sells buttons, T-shirts, and other items.

Just Say No Club Pledge
I pledge to lead a drug-free life. I want to be healthy and happy. I will say No to alcohol. I will say No to tobacco. I will say No to illegal drugs. I will help my friends say No. I pledge to stand up for what I know is right.

THREE STEPS TO SAY NO

The Just Say No Club has worked out these steps to use anytime someone tries to get you to do something you know is wrong: smoking, drugs, drinking, lying, cheating, picking on other kids, writing on walls—you name it.

1. Find out if what your friend suggests is okay. Sometimes you know right away that what a friend suggests is okay. For instance, "Let's study for our spelling test" is okay. Sometimes you know right away that it's wrong. "Let's go smoke this cigarette" is wrong. But sometimes you have to ask your friend—and

yourself—questions to find out if it's okay. "Is it safe?" "Is it legal?" "Could it hurt me?" "Would my parents allow it?"

2. If it's wrong, say no. As soon as you know that something your friend suggests is wrong, say, "No, thanks." Then tell him or her why. "That's against school rules." "I wouldn't feel right about doing that." Be prepared for a put-down in some instances.

3. Suggest other things to do. After you've said no and stated your reason, suggest other activities that are fun, healthy, safe, and legal. "Let's play ball instead." Let your friend know that you would like to be with him or her—but not if it means doing something that's wrong.

Do It Now Foundation
P.O. Box 21126
Phoenix, AZ 85036-1126

"Do it now," this group says. It's their message to people who say about drugs, "I'll quit tomorrow." Since 1967 the Do It Now Foundation has been helping kids say no to drugs. They also give information on other problems. Here's what this group says to do if you are the child of an alcoholic.

1. The first thing to do is to realize that you are not alone. Thousands of kids across the country have been through the same problem, have felt the same fears, and have dreamed the same dreams that you have for a happy family life where drinking is not a problem. These kids (and adults) have been where you are and know what you're feeling, and they're on your side.

2. The second thing to do about the problem is to tell someone about it. Maybe you have an interested teacher or a special friend or a favorite aunt or uncle. Talk with them about the problem and don't hold back. Even though it might seem easier and safer and less painful just to keep things a secret, the part that can really hurt you over the long term is keeping your pain and your problems all locked up inside you. Remember that other people understand and can help.

3. The last thing to do, if you think you're the child of an alcoholic, is to realize that it is not your fault. The best way you can help is to help yourself. Call one of the local Al-Anon or Alateen agencies listed in the phone book, or write this group.

Children of Alcoholics Foundation
540 Madison Avenue
New York, NY 10022

Do it now. Alcoholism may be your family's problem today, but it doesn't have to stay that way.

Teen-Age Assembly of America, Inc.
905 Umi Street, Suite 304
Honolulu, HI 96819

This group sponsors Youth Against

Drugs, a program to help kids say no to drugs. Kid-run councils and parent groups work to stop drug use in schools. If kids want to take part in their sports program, they must sign the pledge card. The pledge is simply ''I will not take drugs and I will not offer drugs to anyone else.

The NFY sponsors REACH America (Responsible, Educated Adolescents Can Help America). Through this project, high school kids teach younger kids about the bad effects of drugs.

National Federation of Drug-Free Youth
1423 North Jefferson
Springfield, MO 65802

FEELINGS

FRIENDS   Your best friend has stopped speaking to you, or your best friend has dropped you for another person. Maybe it's all in your mind. If it's not all in your mind, do something about it. Find out what's going on. Maybe you did something that hurt your friend, and you didn't realize it. Maybe your friend thinks you broke a promise, told something you promised not to tell, or said something catty to someone else. Don't fight back. If you want to get to be friends again, talk. Ask what happened. What if that doesn't work? Let go. Friends drift apart. Sometimes nothing can be done to stop it.

What if your friend is in trouble? What can you do if your friend wants to commit suicide? Or takes drugs? Or is abused? Get help. Tell someone. Don't think you're a tattletale. Being a friend, above all else, is caring about your friend's life and health.

SHYNESS   Remember that other people are shy too. Many fear not being liked. Many are afraid to speak up because of what people may say. Did you know that about one-third of grade school kids are shy? And *more* than one-third

A police-officer friend can listen to your problems and help you solve them. (National Association of Police Athletic Leagues)

of teenagers are shy. Shy kids find it harder to make friends. That makes them feel that they are not good enough to be anyone's friend. Listen to people. Ask questions. Tell people what it is you like about them. All these things are safe, good first steps in making friends because they make other people feel good.

LONELINESS Psychologist Nicholas Zill studied a group of children between seven and 11 years of age. Nine of every 100 of them had often felt "lonely and wished they had more friends." Ten of every 100 kids age 12 to 16 said they were lonely a lot. What kids are most likely to be lonely? Kids who push other kids around and try to be boss are likely to be lonely. Other kids don't like to be around them. Shy, withdrawn kids are also likely to be lonely.

If you are lonely, do something about it. Remember other kids are lonely too. Make the first move. Ask another kid about something he or she said in class. Pick up on old friendships. Join a club.

KID STRESS Long ago an Egyptian father told his son to study hard. If the son didn't, the father said, he might have to be a farmer whose "bed is the bare earth in the middle of his beasts." Now, in Japan, kids cram for national exams, sometimes 18 hours a day. It wouldn't be surprising if the Egyptian and Japanese boys both felt stress.

American kids feel stress too. They get headaches and stomachaches.

They grit their teeth without knowing it. They can't sleep. They get moody and touchy. It's hard for them to keep their minds on what they are doing, which adds to the problem of not doing as well in school as they should. While some kids under stress withdraw into themselves, others get mean and want to fight.

What causes stress? Things like divorce, not doing well in school, fear of nuclear war, violence. The most stress comes from hearing parents argue. Kids are afraid the argument means that parents will get a divorce. Older kids have the problems of growing up.

Leigh by Esther Porter, age 14, Stanton College Preparatory School, Jacksonville, Florida; prize for acrylics in 1986 (Scholastic Inc. Art Awards)

They have to deal with the need to be liked and to be like the other kids. And that's not all. Add sex and drugs and dating to the list.

If you are under stress, try to get help. Ask your school nurse or psychologist how to go about it. Or ask your doctor. Eating well and exercising help keep stress down.

DEPRESSION   It's normal to feel bad if you get a low grade in school or lose a friend or have problems with parents. Sometimes, though, kids can't get over feeling bad. Outgoing kids become withdrawn. Some kids eat too much to fill the empty place, while others try to starve themselves. They are tired all the time. Nothing interests them. They cry a lot. They think they will never feel better. There is no hope, they think, and they can't change anything. They are suffering from depression. They need help. If you think you are suffering from depression, talk to your school nurse or psychologist, your clergyman, or your doctor.

SUICIDE

In 1985, 12,000 American kids ages five to 14 were sent to the hospital for acting as if they were going to kill themselves. Most didn't really want to die. They wanted to make contact or to call attention to a problem, or they wanted to end their pain. Some felt trapped. One said, "I will die unhappy, but the unhappiness will be dead."

Kids who are thinking of killing themselves should get help. There are people to talk to—doctors, clergymen, teachers—and places to go—medical centers, suicide prevention centers. There are hotlines to call. See page 383 for numbers.

If you know a kid who talks of committing suicide, believe it. Stay with the kid. Get help. Tell someone. Don't think you're a tattletale.

SAFETY

KIDNAPPING   Most children who are kidnapped are kidnapped by parents. Their parents are divorced, one parent has custody, the other parent thinks the custody unfair and kidnaps the child.

Here are steps to take to keep from being kidnapped. They are from Child Find, Inc.'s *Color Me Safe.*

1. Always tell your parents or baby-sitter where you will be playing.
2. Never walk or play alone. Always walk or play with friends. It's safer.
3. Never play in an empty building or alley.
4. Never accept money, candy, or gifts from a stranger. Never talk to strangers.
5. Never go near a stranger's car, even to give directions.
6. When using public transportation, always sit close to the driver.
7. If you are scared or need help, tell a grown-up right away. Tell your parents, a teacher, or a police officer.
8. If you are approached by a stranger, yell loudly and run to the nearest house or store. Never be afraid to yell for help.
9. If you see a car in your neighborhood that seems strange, write down the license-plate number.
10. It is important to remember what a stranger looks like. Was the stranger a man or woman? Young or old? Tall or short? Heavy or thin? What color was the hair? What color were the clothes? If a man, did he have a beard?
11. Get to know the police officers in your neighborhood. They will always help you.
12. Learn how to lock and unlock your doors and windows. Keep them

These costumes are safe—no masks, light colors, and the right length. (Sylvia Zebrowski)

locked when you are home alone.
13. Never open your door to a stranger.
14. Learn to use the telephone to call for help.
15. Never stay alone in a car. Always go with your parents.
16. When you are shopping, always stay with your parents.
17. Never go into a public rest room alone. Always go with your parents or a grown-up you know.
18. Many children are fingerprinted in case they become lost. Your fingerprints are like those of no other kid.
19. Call the Child Find "get home" toll-free telephone number if you

think a parent is looking for you. See page 383 for the number.

20. Know your name, address, and phone number.

21. Don't tell a stranger who telephones that you are home alone. If the caller asks for your parents, say they are busy and will have to call back.

BEING SAFE AT HALLOWEEN Trick or treating? Don't go alone. If you are older, go in a group. Younger children should go with an older child or a grown-up.

Bring a flashlight or a "light stick" that glows. Remember that you are harder to see at night. Obey traffic laws. Cross the street at the corner and watch for cars. Don't run from house to house or walk between parked cars.

Don't eat anything before your parents take a look. The police department will check out strange candy. Hospitals will X-ray candy for you, but X rays don't show everything.

To avoid all the problems of trick or treating, go to a school or a shopping mall party.

In any case, wear a safe costume. Since a mask makes seeing difficult, use makeup instead. Make sure the colors in it are safe. If you must wear a mask, make sure the eyeholes are big enough. Your costume should be light in color so that people in cars can see you. Put some reflective tape on it too. Don't make your costume so long that you trip over it. If you buy a costume in a store, it should be labeled "flame resistant." That doesn't mean it *can't* catch fire. It does mean that it is not likely to catch fire. Don't wear high-heeled or oversize shoes. They can make you fall down.

Let a grown-up do the pumpkin carving so that you don't hurt yourself with the knife. Keep lighted pumpkins away from curtains and anything else that might catch fire.

BODY PROBLEMS

STUTTERING Winston Churchill, an Englishman, was prime minister of Great Britain in World War II. He was famous for his public speaking. Who would have guessed that when he was young he stuttered? When he was a teenager, he "cured" his stuttering by saying "mmmmmmmmmm" at the beginning of each sentence. He went on doing this all his life.

Kids who stutter are afraid of being called on in class. They have trouble talking on the telephone. No one really knows what causes stuttering. Stress may play a part. Many more boys than girls have the problem. Can you outgrow stuttering? Some experts say yes, and some say no. For little kids, it's normal to stumble over words. Some kids do stop stuttering when they get older. No one knows why. *It is not wrong to stutter.*

If you stutter, you can get help. See page 383 for the free hotline number to call.

DISABILITIES   Disabilities are problems people have with moving or with seeing or with hearing. A person with a disability may be in a wheelchair or may be blind or deaf.

Jamie Brazzell, the 1986 Easter Seal Child, cannot use his arms or legs. With a mouth pointer, he can use a computer. (National Easter Seal Society)

The National Easter Seal Society
for Crippled Children and Adults
2023 West Ogden Avenue
Chicago, IL 60612

The Easter Seal Society has a hotline. See page 383 for the number. The society wants to teach people the myths and the facts about those with disabilities. A myth is something people believe that is not true. Here are common myths, and the facts.

1. *Myth:* People who have disabilities are brave.
   Fact: Getting used to a disability means, not being brave, but learning how to change a way of living.

2. *Myth:* People who use wheelchairs are always sick.
   Fact: Not true. People who use wheelchairs often have a disability but are not sick. In hospitals, people who *are* sick use wheelchairs.

3. *Myth:* To use a wheelchair narrows a person's life.
   Fact: A wheelchair is like a car. It's something people use to get around.

4. *Myth:* People who can't hear well can read lips.
   Fact: Not all people who can't hear well can read lips. No one can always get every word.

5. *Myth:* People who are blind get a sixth sense.
   Fact: Blind people do learn to use their other senses better. They have no sixth sense, however.

6. *Myth:* People who have a disability like to be with "their own kind" (other people with disabilities).
   Fact: Not true. A person with a disability, for instance, might enjoy playing chess. Such a person would like to spend time with other people who play chess, whether or not they have disabilities.

7. *Myth:* People without disabilities must take care of those who have them.
   Fact: They can help when they want, but they don't have to.

Kids play hockey in wheelchairs at a Muscular Dystrophy Association summer camp. (Muscular Dystrophy Association, Inc.)

8. *Myth:* Children should not ask someone about his or her disability.
   Fact: Why not? There is nothing bad about having a disability.

9. *Myth:* The lives of people with disabilities are completely different from those of most other people.
   Fact: People with disabilities go to school, get married, work, have families, do laundry, shop for groceries, cry, pay taxes, get angry, plan, and dream like everyone else.

10. *Myth:* People with disabilities always need help.
    Fact: Many people with disabilities can take care of themselves and can *give* help.

11. *Myth:* There's nothing one person can do to help get rid of the barriers faced by persons with disabilities.
    Fact: You can help make changes by speaking up when people say bad things about people with disabilities, and by thinking of people with disabilities as human beings with many of the same feelings and needs you have.

If you have a disability, here are some myths you may have yourself.

1. *Myth:* People without disabilities don't want to meet or be around people who have disabilities.
   Fact: Maybe they just haven't met many people with disabilities before. Reach out, tell them your name, and help put them at ease.

2. *Myth:* When you have a disability, people offer help out of pity.
   Fact: They are probably just being polite. Accept their offer or turn it down politely.

3. *Myth:* People who offer help to people with a disability usually know how to give the help.
   Fact: Not always true. Tell them how to give the help you need, or you may get bounced around more than you would like.

4. *Myth:* People always offer to help when they see someone who might need it.
   Fact: People might not offer to help because they are lazy or afraid of what they don't know. Ask and you will probably get the help you need.

5. *Myth:* People without disabilities must give help to those with disabilities.
   Fact: Not true. People with disabilities can handle most daily problems.

6. *Myth:* Most people know little about how those with disabilities

live and really don't want to know more.

Fact: Not knowing something is not the same as not caring. Share yourself and talk to someone.

Here are some groups that help or give facts about people with disabilities.

Clearinghouse on the Handicapped
United States Department of Education
Room 3132 Switzer Building
Washington, DC 20202-2319

You can get a booklet from this group telling about the services offered by the United States Government for people with disabilities. These services include schools for the blind and deaf, libraries, health care. The booklet also tells how to get the facts about the rights of people with disabilities.

National Information Center for Handicapped Children and Youth (NICHCY)
Box 1492
Washington, DC 20013

This group has more facts about services for people with disabilities.

Muscular Dystrophy Association, Inc.
810 Seventh Avenue
New York, NY 10019

For people with muscular dystrophy, the MDA has clinics and other services. There are free MDA summer camps for kids with MD and other diseases. At these camps, kids can fish, swim, go horseback riding and boating, do arts and crafts, be in talent shows, go to cookouts, and camp out. The MDA also studies MD and works with schools. You can get a booklet written for children from the MDA.

CANCER For facts about cancer and ways kids with cancer can get help, here's where to write.

American Cancer Society
4 West 35th Street
New York, NY 10001

This boy is learning to play baseball at a Muscular Dystrophy Association summer camp. (Muscular Dystrophy Association, Inc.)

This group will send you a good booklet written for kids, some of it written by kids.

Candlelighters Childhood
Cancer Foundation
2025 Eye Street NW, Suite 1011
Washington, DC 20006

The Candlelighters is a group for parents of kids with cancer. It has some groups for teenagers with cancer or for kids who have brothers or sisters with cancer. There is a youth newsletter.

DIABETES   Here's where to write if you have diabetes.

Juvenile Diabetes Foundation
432 Park Avenue South
New York, NY 10016-8013

IF YOU ARE ARRESTED

ARREST   If you are arrested by the police, do give your name, your parents' names, and your address.

The police must, by law, read you your rights. These are your rights.

- *Not* to answer any other questions: The police must not force you to answer questions. Staying silent does not mean you are guilty.
- To stop answering questions at any time.
- To be told by the police that if you do answer any questions, anything you say can be used against you in court.
- To call your parents and a lawyer.
- To ask for and get a lawyer if you do not already have one.

Sometimes the police will hold you in a lockup until you go to court. If they do, you have certain rights.

- The place must be clean, with enough light, air, and room.
- You must have schooling.
- You must have a chance to exercise.
- If you are sick, you have the right to a doctor.
- You must have proper and clean clothes and bedding.
- You must be given things like soap so that you can keep yourself clean.
- You have the right to visitors.
- You must be able to get library books and other things to read.

COURT   If you are arrested, you may have to go to court. Parents or teachers also can try to bring you to court if they think you need certain kinds of care.

In many cases, kids do not end up in court. Instead, the court officials decide outside of court to send you back to your family or to help you in some other way. You are not likely to have to go to court if you fit this description.

□ You have never been in trouble with the law before.
□ What you did was not too serious.
□ You have a good school record.
□ You have no serious family problems.
□ You have a "good attitude."

If you do go to court, you are thought of as not guilty until you are *proven* guilty. Children go to special courts just for them. They do not have all the rights adults have. For example, usually they are not tried by a jury, a group of 12 people who decide your case. In many states you must be a certain age before you can be brought to court. In New York, for instance, a child under seven cannot be brought to court.

In court you do have some rights.

□ To face and question the person who said you did something wrong.
□ To have a lawyer.
□ Not to say things that will prove your guilt.

Children are never sentenced to die for a crime. You can be sentenced to go to a lockup without knowing how long you will have to stay there.

LOCKUPS Every year in the United States, between 300,000 and 500,000 children are locked up in adult jails and police lockups. About 400,000 more are put into juvenile lockups, and another 50,000 go to reformatories or state "training" schools. Most are charged with property crimes or "status offenses" like running away, truancy, or being "beyond the control" of their parents.

If you do go to a lockup, you have rights. For instance, you cannot be locked up alone—in solitary confinement—for too long.

WORK AND MONEY

Kids often think that their problems would be solved if only they had money. Sometimes they are right. To get money, you usually have to work for it, and it's not always easy for a kid to get a job. See page 372 for how to advertise, and—better yet—advertise with a résumé.

WRITE A RÉSUMÉ When you look for odd jobs, take along a résumé. In a short space, it tells your name, telephone number, age, what jobs you have done, your education, and so on. Even if you are applying for jobs just in the neighborhood, a résumé can help.

To begin working on your résumé, make a list of all the jobs you have done. You can include jobs not done for money. Then follow the sample to write them up.

RÉSUMÉ

Name: Bill Bernstein   Address: 24 Ridge Street, Smithson, New York
Telephone: 555-4321   Age: 12
Grade in School: 7th   Grade Average: B+

Experience

Job	For Whom	When
mowing lawns	the Urbanowskis	1987
baby-sitting	M. Marquez	1987
washing cars	the Smiths	1986
picking beans	J. Barnet	1986

References
Mrs. J. Barnet, 243 Alison Street, Smithson, New York 99987, 555-7856
Mr. L. Georgia, 88 Main Street, Smithson, New York 99987, 555-2233
Ms. Betty Florio, 4 L Street, Apt. 3, Smithson, New York 99987, 555-8765

Hourly Rates (I will bargain)
Mowing lawns--$5
Baby-sitting--$3
Dog walking--$4

SHOULD KIDS WORK?

The older you get, the more likely you are to work. It seems to be a sign of being a grown-up. Two out of three high school seniors work at part-time jobs. Younger kids find work here and there. They baby-sit or mow lawns or wash cars. Should young people work?

YES Some people think it's good for kids to work. They reason this way. Kids learn how important work is in life. They become good at skills they can put to use when they are grown-up. Work teaches kids to be on time, to plan, to dress for work. Working kids have to know how to be on a team and to deal with customers. It is good for kids to manage their time well. When they work, they have to fit in their schoolwork and time for fun. They don't have time to get in trouble. And they can save money for college or other important things—travel and special courses, for instance.

NO   Others say kids shouldn't work. They reason this way. Kids should give all they can to school. Working kids do less well in school, one study says. Because the work they do isn't very interesting, they decide they don't like working at anything. Kids who work may get into trouble more easily since they are away from home more. Because they have money, they can get into drinking alcohol and taking drugs and throwing their money away on useless things.

IF YOU DO WORK   Perhaps there is a smart way to work. Try following these rules.

1. Put school first.
2. Don't work after 9:00 P.M.
3. Don't work more than 10 hours a week.
4. Save "good" time for homework.
5. Keep some of your earnings for a long-term goal, like a car or college.

WORK AND THE LAW

Kids have the right to work. However, under the law, they are not allowed to have certain jobs, often because those jobs are unsafe.

Under the law, girls and boys should get the same pay for the same job.

If the job falls under the minimum wage law, kids should be paid minimum wage.

When you work, you might need to get a Social Security number. Call the United States Social Security Office to check. To get a Social Security number and card, you need your birth certificate and one other ID that includes age, such as a last report card or a library card.

You may have to pay income taxes if you work. Keep track of the money you make. Also keep track of the money you spend to make the money.

At the turn of the century boys and girls sold newspapers on the streets to make money. (Staten Island Historical Society)

Put the records in a book. Keep receipts.

In most states you need a permit to work if you are under 16. Ask at your school office about permits.

HELPING OTHERS WITH THEIR PROBLEMS

Why help others? You may have one reason or many, depending on your needs. You're bored. You want your life to have some point. It feels good to help someone. Someone helped you once, and you want to return the favor. You believe in a world in which people help each other.

CLUB PROGRAMS

Most kids' clubs have programs for helping other people.

Camp Fire, Inc.
4601 Madison Avenue
Kansas City, MO 64112

Programs include day-care centers, after-school programs, tutoring other kids with reading, camping for low-income kids and kids with disabilities.

The American Red Cross teaches several lifeguarding courses for kids. (American Red Cross)

4-H Youth Programs
United States Department of Agriculture
Extension Service
Washington, DC 20250

4-H gives kids ages nine to 19 ways of helping people in their town or city.

American Red Cross
National Headquarters
Washington, DC 20006

The Red Cross teaches first aid, lifesaving, and more.

FIRST AID AND CPR   You need to be 13 or to have finished grade 7. (Cardiopulmonary resuscitation, or CPR, can save the lives of people with heart attacks.)

BASIC RESCUE (LIFESAVING)   You need to be 11 and to have passed a swimming test and completed a course in basic water safety.

ADVANCED LIFESAVING   You have to be 15.

LIFEGUARD TRAINING   You have to be 16.

THE NAME OF THE GAME IS CARING

Those in grades 7 through 12 work as recreation leaders and learn how to plan and carry out an event.

I DO DECLARE, I'M AWARE This program helps grade school kids learn about themselves and their values. It suggests ways of helping out in school, at home, and in your town or city.

HUMANITY'S BRIDGE Those in grades 6 through 9 learn how to join together to build "human bridges" to solve problems, help people in pain, and give service to the community.

BABY-SITTING Kids age 11 or older learn how to prevent accidents, take care of an emergency, care for a child— and get the job!

BEING AN INSTRUCTOR AIDE There are programs by age group. The Name of the Game Is Caring is listed above. Basic Aid Training is for kids age 13

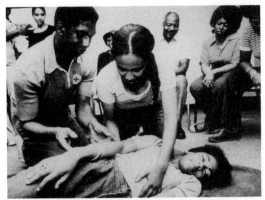

You can learn CPR through an American Red Cross program. (American Red Cross)

and up. Water Safety is for kids age 11 or older who have swimming skills and a Lifesaving or a Basic Rescue certificate. Boating Safety is for kids age 14 or older who have skill in boating and a Basic Rescue or an Advanced Lifesaving Certificate.

GROUPS THAT HELP THE WORLD'S CHILDREN

One of five children under 15 is poor. Many have to work at far too young an age. Many are sick. You can help. Alone or in a group, you can raise money to help the world's children.

UNICEF
The United States Committee for UNICEF
Group Programs Department
331 East 38th Street
New York, NY 10016

UNICEF's 1986 report "State of the World's Children" told the terrible facts. In 1985 more than three million children died because they did not get the proper shots. Thousands and thousands of kids go blind every year because they do not have enough vitamin A.

UNICEF could save the lives of millions of kids just by sending medical help. UNICEF does save the lives of about 800,000 kids a year. With more money, more kids could be saved. Here's what money can buy.

The price of a candy bar can feed a child for two days.

For 8¢ UNICEF can treat a child with malaria for a year.

20¢ buys enough vitamin A to save a child from going blind for a year.

$30 will provide a child with emergency food supplements for a year.

$68 will buy 20 blankets for a refugee center.

$150 will buy a pump to bring clean water to a village.

National UNICEF Day began October 31, 1950, when a Philadelphia Sunday school asked neighbors for spare change for needy children of other countries. The Sunday school collected $17. Now UNICEF has official ways you can help.

TRICK OR TREAT FOR UNICEF AT HALLOWEEN   You get ID tags, posters, safety tips, and orange cartons for collecting the money.

COIN$ FOR KIDS   Collect extra coins around the house and give them to UNICEF. You can get UNICEF cartons to hold them.

SKIP-A-SNACK OR JUNK AID FOR UNICEF   You, your school, or your community can skip snacks or junk food for a week and give the money to UNICEF.

Defense for Children
International–USA
P.O. Box 20475
Dag Hammarskjold Center
New York, NY 10017-9992

Many of the world's children are abused. Some are forced against their will to have sex or pose for sex pictures. Some must do work that is unsafe. Children are sometimes kidnapped. Children are sometimes put in adult jails. Some kids have had to leave their countries because of wars. Defense for Children International works to help kids. It fights for their rights and tries to change bad laws. It also works for kids to have enough to eat, a place to live, and health care.

OTHER WAYS TO HELP PEOPLE

1. Collect toys for kids who won't have much for Christmas. In most places the police and fire departments have boxes where you can leave toys.

2. Put on a play or sing or just visit in a home for senior citizens.

3. Help with a telethon.

4. Join the walk of a group that raises money by the mile.

Staging Events

If you are raising money for something, you'll probably stage some kind of event and sell tickets for it.

Pick a good day for the event. Make sure that nothing else is going on that day.

Give yourself plenty of time before the big day. Then add another week. Things nearly always go wrong.

Put one person in charge. That person should decide who does what. Rehearse!

To make more money at the show, sell lemonade or popcorn to the audience.

OTHER GROUPS THAT HELP CHILDREN

There are several groups helping poor kids all over the world. Through these groups you can sponsor a child. Being a sponsor usually costs quite a lot, so it is probably best to do through your school or club. Some groups helping children let you choose the age, sex, and country of the child you sponsor. You and the child can write letters to each other.

When you write, tell about yourself, where you live, what your school and town are like. Make your letters short. Ask about the child's school, favorite games, and home. Find out all you can about the country so that you can understand more about the child. Send pictures.

For more about being friends by letter, see pages 71–72.

These are two well-known groups.

Christian Children's Fund, Inc.
P.O. Box 26511
Richmond, VA 23261

Save the Children
54 Wilton Road, Dept PCA
Westport, CT 06880

This one is less well known.

Futures for Children
805 Tijeras NW
Albuquerque, NM 87102

Futures for Children was formed to help Native American children of the Southwest. Money given to this group is spent to keep Native American children in school and to help them in other ways. It buys braces and eyeglasses. It buys books. It is spent on tribal self-help projects like libraries, playgrounds, and pottery workshops. Your group could sponsor a child. You can choose a boy or a girl from one of several tribes—Navajo, Hopi, Zuni—or from one of six pueblos along the Rio Grande. Then you can write to the child. Futures for Children's slogan is "It's not a charity—it's a chance."

RAISING MONEY TO HELP PEOPLE

You or your group can get together to raise money. Don't forget to advertise! See page 372. Here are some money-raising ideas.

1. BIRTHDAY PARTY SERVICE Give birthday parties for kids, and charge. You'll need to plan ahead. Talk to the parents of the child. Find out the child's special interests and plan the party around them. Figure out what will go on every minute: games, food, present giving, and so on. You might make a paper-bag mask or hat for each child. Use crepe paper and balloons for decorations. To make balloons stick to the wall or ceiling, blow them up and then rub them against a wool sweater.

   Games are easy—Simon sez, potato race, blindman's buff. Here's one you can make up yourself. Take slips of paper and write down something to do on each—sing a song, pretend to be a robot or a cat, and so on. Make sure the things to do are safe and easy. Put the slips of paper in balloons, blow up the balloons, and put the name of each party guest on a balloon. The kids get the balloons, pop them, take out the paper slips, and do what the slips say. Each kid takes a turn. You can put fortunes in balloons instead and follow the same plan. Stick to good fortunes: You will be an astronaut when you grow up. You will get an A on your next test. Your summer vacation will lead to romance.

   If you have any talent in your group, put on a show with puppets, magic tricks, or clowns, perhaps. But make sure that the birthday kid is the star of his or her own party.

   A cake is a must. If you make it, you may need help. You can also make little fancy sandwiches with cookie cutters.

2. A DOG-WALKING SERVICE Be on time. Take only one dog at a time, and use a short leash. Plan interesting walks. Take along a Pooper-Scooper, and use it. Never leave the dogs alone.

3. A DOG-WASHING SERVICE For this you need leashes, a hose, tubs, dog shampoo, and old towels. If there is more than one of you, set up an assembly line. One kid washes, another dries, and so on. Give each dog a dog biscuit treat at the end of the wash.

4. WINDOW WASHING You need window cleaner, rags, sponge, squeegee, bucket, and newspapers. Do not wash windows you can't reach from the ground.

5. ERRAND SERVICE

6. LAWN MOWING, LEAF RAKING, AND SNOW SHOVELING

7. BASEMENT, ATTIC, AND GARAGE CLEANING Put trash into containers. Sort out stuff that's left. Then dust and sweep. Wash the shelves and the floor. Ask what the person wants to keep, and put it away. The rest is yours for a sale.

8. SALES Ask people to give you things to sell that they don't want. You might ask for just one item—books or records, for example—or you might have a yard or garage sale. Price the items low enough to sell but high enough to make some money. Let people bargain with you, especially later in the day. Make sure you have enough change.

Besides what people give you that's used, you can sell kid artwork. Or wild berries, flowers, or plants. Or lemonade and cookies. Or worms for fishing. Or vegetables and fruit from your garden.

9. BABY-SITTING—ONE KID OR SEVERAL Bring a bag or box of interesting stuff: books, balls, junk jewelry, crayons and paper, little jars, boxes, puppets, and so on. If you baby-sit more than one kid, make it like a nursery school. Plan it with a friend or two. You can have activities: a talent show, making paper-bag masks, drawing a mural together on a long piece of art paper or on newspapers taped to the wall. Include quiet time.

If you are too young to baby-sit, watch children while their mother does something else. (The "something else" might be studying or playing tennis.) The Red Cross has courses in baby-sitting. See page 421.

HELPING ANIMALS

If you love animals, you can work to help them. Animals need help. Wild animals are in danger of losing their homes in the United States and all over the world. Many a wild animal has watched its home ruined forever as a new house or parking lot was built. Some wild animals are hurt by traps. Others are hit by cars.

Pets need help too. Some have own-

If you love animals, maybe you can find a way to raise money to help them. (Mary Bloom)

ers that abuse or forsake them. Others get lost. Animal shelters in the United States take in 11.6 million unwanted dogs and cats every year. At least 7.6 million of these animals are killed. Below are names, addresses, and facts about groups that help animals.

The American Society for the Prevention of Cruelty to Animals
441 East 92nd Street
New York, NY 10128

This group has free fact sheets, including its 10 Most Unwanted List of animal abuses. It is more than 100 years old, and it is one of the biggest groups in the world. Its animal shelters are only in New York, but it gives facts about animals to anyone anywhere. It also protects endangered species everywhere.

American Humane Association
P.O. Box 1266
Denver, CO 80201-1266

"My Mother Said I Couldn't Have an Elephant" is the name of the AHA's guide for taking care of animals. This group sponsors Be Kind to Animals Week in early May. The AHA was started more than 100 years ago. Its purpose is to stop cruelty, neglect, abuse, and bad use of animals. The AHA works to change laws that are harmful to animals. It helps animals when they are lost. It checks to make sure animal actors are well cared for. The National Hearing Dog Project was started by the AHA.

Associated Humane Societies, Inc.
124 Evergreen Avenue
Newark, NJ 07114

Popcorn Park Wildlife Club
Booklet
c/o Associated Humane
Societies, Inc.
P.O. Box AF
Keyport, NJ 07735

Many hurt and lost animals have stayed alive, thanks to the Associated Humane Societies. You can belong to the Popcorn Park Wildlife Club, which gives money to the Popcorn Park Zoo. The zoo is for wild animals that have been found and can't be put back in the wild. Some have been hurt.

There are some colorful characters at the Popcorn Park Zoo.

Gidget, the blind monkey, who likes

peanut butter and jelly sandwiches

Pretty Boy, the deer, who eats Fig Newtons

Foxy Loxy, an ice-cream lover

Red and Star, ponies who were once in the circus

Heckel and Jeckel, watchdog geese

Dancer, the capuchin monkey who —you guessed it!—likes to dance

You can visit the zoo. It is open, free, in the afternoons. You can bring pet food, fruit, vegetables, seeds, hay, and nuts to help feed the animals. For $2 a month, you can help take care of an animal at the Popcorn Park Zoo. You get a card, a photograph of your animal, and a report. For more about zoo adoptions, see pages 212–215.

The Associated Humane Societies also back Animal Haven Farm. Here animals without homes live out their lives in peace. Animal Haven Farm has neighborhoods like Kitty City. The societies are also behind the Share-a-Pet program. If you join this program, you can send money to help take care of a homeless pet. The societies also have a Lost Pet Service.

Their magazine has a kids' section with a pen pal service. They also publish coloring books and storybooks. One of their books tells how to raise a baby squirrel that has been left by its mother, and how to let the squirrel loose in the wild when it is grown.

Humane Society of the United States
2100 L Street, NW
Washington, DC 20037

The society works to save the lives of wild animals and pets. It tries to change laws so that animals are helped. It tries, for instance, to protect sea animals, to stop the trapping of land animals, and to get better care for farm animals. *Kind News* is its newspaper for use in the classroom. The society also has pamphlets on animal care for children at low cost.

Here are some ways you can help animals, as suggested by the Associated Humane Societies. If you hold an event, be sure to advertise. See pages 423 and 372.

1. Form a club at school, or with your friends, to help animals at your local humane society. See Forming a Club, pages 145–146.

2. Ask your teacher if your class can visit the humane society or have someone from the humane society visit your class. Perhaps a veterinarian can visit. Take a class trip to the zoo. See a film on animal welfare.

3. Produce a play on animal welfare for your class or assembly.

4. Hold a carnival, pet show, cake sale, car wash, or play. Use what you make to help the humane society.

5. Have a pet-food drive for the humane society.

6. Start a letter-writing drive or get people to sign a petition for the protection of animals that are hunted, used in research, or endangered.

7. Save your money to have your pet spayed or neutered.

INDEX